MACROECONOMICS

MACROECONOMICS

Avi J. Cohen
York University
University of Toronto

Pearson Canada Inc., 26 Prince Andrew Place, North York, Ontario M3C 2H4.

9780134821290

1 17

Library and Archives Canada Cataloguing in Publication

Cohen, Avi J., author
    Macroeconomics / Avi J. Cohen.

ISBN 978-0-13-482129-0 (spiral bound)

    1. Macroeconomics—Textbooks. 2. Textbooks. I. Title.

HB172.5.C628 2018   339   C2017-907109-2

Contents

Pearson FlexText

Essential Employability Skills

Top skills employers seek:

Success in any sector is dependent upon more than core academic knowledge or technical and occupational skills. Employers need critical thinkers, problem solvers, and leaders to tackle the challenges of today's workplace. Employees with successful career paths learn to communicate effectively, engage appropriately with others, and be self-reliant. Effective career readiness and employability strategies develop the whole learner and incorporate personal and social capabilities; critical thinking and problem-solving skills; and academic and occupational knowledge.

That is what Pearson FlexText is all about.

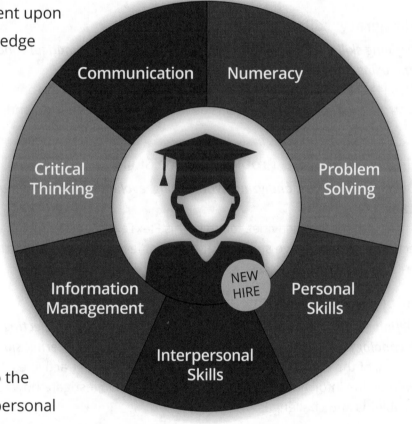

For more information on Pearson's commitment to employability, visit **pearsoned.com/employability**.

Pearson FlexText helps bridge the skills gap and helps students and instructors make the most of valuable face-to-face class time.

We created this resource to help students achieve academic success while also developing the key skills that hiring managers value in candidates.

Communication Skills

Defining skill areas: reading, writing, speaking, listening, presenting, and visual literacy
Students may not be developing their reading skills because they do not have access to course materials – either by choice or by circumstance. FlexTexts are affordable and accessible. FlexTexts include learning objectives and chapter summaries in combination with concise discussions of key topics to support reading comprehension, and provide individual and group activities that afford students the opportunity to practice their writing and communication skills.

Numeracy Skills

Defining skill areas: understanding and applying mathematical concepts and reasoning, analyzing and using mathematical data, and conceptualizing
This FlexText is designed to be an in-class activity workbook, one that allows faculty to provide instructional support to students as they apply mathematical and statistical analysis across a range of activities.

Critical Thinking & Problem-Solving Skills

Defining skill areas: analyzing, synthesizing, evaluating, decision making, creativity, and innovative thinking
The exercises and activities found in this FlexText are not simply factual, recall, or "skill and drill" activities. They engage students at different levels of Bloom's Taxonomy to help students develop critical thinking and problem-solving skills.

Information Management Skills

Defining skill areas: gathering and managing information, selecting and using appropriate tools and technology for a task or project, computer literacy, and internet skills
Not all of the exercises in a FlexText are pen-and-paper activities. Many require students to engage with online information and assets to help them investigate how to analyze and solve an array of problems and challenges.

Interpersonal Skills

Defining skill areas: teamwork, relationship management, conflict resolution, leadership, and networking
FlexText is designed to be brought into class. It can help to facilitate group work and collaborative problem solving, and activities can be implemented in ways that help students to develop their interpersonal skills.

Personal Skills

Defining skill areas: managing self, managing change, being flexible and adaptable, engaging in reflexive practice, and demonstrating personal responsibility
Making the decision to purchase course materials and actively engage with course content is one of the first steps toward demonstrating personal responsibility for success in school. The page layout of a FlexText also encourages note taking and promotes the development of strong study skills.

1 Scarcity, Opportunity Cost, Trade, and Models

LEARNING OBJECTIVES

L01 Explain scarcity and describe why you must make smart choices among your wants.

L02 Define and describe opportunity cost, the most important concept in economics.

L03 Describe how comparative advantage, specialization, and trade make us all better off.

L04 Explain how models like the circular flow model make smart choices easier.

L05 Differentiate microeconomic and macroeconomic choices, and explain the Three Keys model for smart choices.

LEARN ...

What do you want out of life? Riches? Love? Adventure? To make the world a better place? Happiness? Children? A long and healthy life? All of the above?

Many people believe economics is just about money and business, but economics can help you get what you want out of life. The Nobel Prize–winning author George Bernard Shaw said "Economy is the art of making the most of life." Economics is about getting the most for your money, but it is also about making smart choices generally. If you learn a little economics, it will help you make the most of your life, whatever you are after. That knowledge will help you better understand the world around you and the choices you face as a citizen.

You don't need to be trained as an economist to lead a productive and satisfying life. But if you can learn *to think like an economist*, you can get more out of whatever life you choose to lead, and the world will be better for it.

This chapter introduces the most important economic concepts — scarcity, opportunity cost, and comparative advantage. Because of scarcity, choices involve a trade-off, leading to the concept of opportunity cost — the single most important concept in all of economics. Incentives are also crucial for understanding choices. Opportunity cost and comparative advantage are key to understanding why specialization and voluntary trade make us all better off. The most basic choice is producing for yourself or specializing, trading in markets, and depending on others. We will use a simple example to explain the argument behind all cases for freer trade.

Thinking like an economist means building models. Your first model, the circular flow model, reduces the complexity of the economy to three sets of players — households, businesses, and governments — who interact in markets. Models are the mental equivalent of controlled experiments in a laboratory. The positive/normative distinction is also part of thinking like an economist, as is the difference between microeconomics and macroeconomics.

Scarcity and Choice

 L01 Explain scarcity and describe why you must make smart choices among your wants.

Can you afford to buy everything you want? If not, every dollar you spend involves a choice. If you buy the Nintendo Switch, you might not be able to afford your English textbook. If you treat your friends to a movie, you might have to work an extra shift at your job or give up your weekend camping trip.

It would be great to have enough money to buy everything you want, but it would not eliminate the need to make smart choices. Imagine winning the biggest lottery in the world. You can buy whatever you want for yourself, your family, and your friends. But you still have only 80-some years on this planet (if you are lucky and healthy), only 24 hours in a day, and a limited amount of energy. Do you want to spend the week boarding in Whistler or surfing in Australia? Do you want to spend time raising your kids or exploring the world? Will you go to that third party on New Year's Eve or give in to sleep? Do you want to spend money on yourself, or set up a charitable foundation to help others? Bill Gates, one of the richest people on Earth, has chosen to set up the Bill and Melinda Gates Foundation. With billions of dollars in assets, the Foundation still receives more requests for worthy causes than it has dollars. How does it choose which requests to fund?

Economists call this inability to satisfy all of our wants the problem of **scarcity**. Scarcity arises from our limited money, time, and energy. All mortals, even billionaires, face the problem of scarcity. We all have to make choices about what we will get and what we will give up. Businesses with limited capital must choose between spending more on research or on marketing. Governments must make similar choices in facing the problem of scarcity. Spending more on colleges and universities leaves less to spend on health care. Or if governments try to spend more on all social programs, the higher taxes to pay for them mean less take-home pay for all of us.

Because none of us — individuals, businesses, governments — can ever satisfy all of our wants, smart choices are essential to making the most of our lives. **Economics** is about how individuals, businesses, and governments make the best possible choices to get what they want, and how those choices interact in markets.

 # Practice...

1. Which statement about scarcity is *true*?
   a. Scarcity is only a problem for underdeveloped countries.
   b. Scarcity is only a problem for idealistic people.
   c. Every person faces scarcity.
   d. All of the above are true.

2. The problem of scarcity
   a. would disappear if we did not have to make choices.
   b. arises because of limited money, time, and energy.
   c. arises because limited human expectations cannot be satisfied with available knowledge.
   d. arises because of limited money, time, and memory.

Practice...

3. You can't get everything you want because you are limited by
   a. time.
   b. money.
   c. energy.
   d. all of the above.

4. The main implication of scarcity in economics is that people must
   a. make choices.
   b. be selfish.
   c. be unhappy.
   d. like money.

5. The problem of scarcity exists
   a. only when people are unemployed.
   b. only in economies with incentives.
   c. only in economies without incentives.
   d. in all economies.

Apply...

1. Olga chooses to live at home rather than move into residence during her first year of college.
   She often brags about the fact that she saves a lot of money by living at home.
   Provide some examples of what Olga may have given up by choosing to live at home.

   _____

   _____

   _____

   _____

2. Social activists argue that materialism is one of the biggest problems with society: If we all wanted less, instead of always wanting more, there would be plenty to go around for everyone. Do you agree with this statement? Why or why not?

   _____

   _____

   _____

   _____

Opportunity Cost

 Define and describe opportunity cost, the most important concept in economics.

Scarcity means you must choose. If you want the most out of what limited money and time you have, you need to make smart choices. A choice is a fork in the road. You have to compare the alternatives — where does each path take you — and then pick one. You make a smart choice by weighing benefits and costs.

Choices Are Trade-Offs

What are you going to do with the next hour? Since you are reading this, you are considering studying as one choice. If you were out far too late last night, or up taking care of a crying baby, sleep might be your alternative choice. If those are your top choices, let's compare benefits of the two paths from this fork. For studying, the benefits are higher marks on your next test, learning something, and perhaps enjoying reading this chapter. For sleep, the benefits are being more alert, more productive, less grumpy, and perhaps avoiding the pain of reading this chapter.

If you choose the studying path, what is the cost of your decision? It is the hour of sleep you give up (with the benefits of rest). And if you choose sleep, the cost is the studying you give up (leading to lower marks).

- A choice is a trade-off — you give up one thing to get something else.
- The **opportunity cost** of any choice is the cost of the best alternative given up.
- Opportunity cost is the most important concept for making smart choices.

Opportunity Cost Beats Money Cost

Opportunity cost is more important than money cost. Suppose you win a free trip to Bermuda that has to be taken the first week in December. What is the money cost of the trip? Zero — it's free. But imagine you have a business client who can meet to sign a million-dollar contract only during the first week in December. What is the opportunity cost of your "free" trip to Bermuda? $1 million. A smart decision to take or not take the trip depends on opportunity cost, not money cost.

All choices are forks in the road, and the cost of any path taken is the value of the best path you must give up. Because of scarcity, every choice involves a trade-off — to get something, you must give up something else. To make a smart choice, the value of what you get must be greater than the value of what you give up. The benefits of a smart choice must outweigh the opportunity costs.

Incentives Work   Since smart choices compare costs and benefits, your decisions will change with changes in costs or benefits. We all respond to **incentives** — rewards and penalties for choices. You are more likely to choose a path that leads to a reward, and avoid one with a penalty. A change in incentives causes a change in choices. If your business deal is worth only $100 instead of $1 million, you might take the trip to Bermuda. If you were up most of last night, you are more likely to sleep than to study. If you have a test tomorrow instead of next week, you are more likely to study than to sleep.

To make the most out of life and make smart decisions, you must always ask the questions, "What is the opportunity cost of my choice?" and "Do the additional benefits outweigh the opportunity costs?"

 # Practice...

6. In deciding whether to study or sleep for the next hour, you should consider all of the following *except*

   a. how much tuition you paid.

   b. how tired you are.

   c. how productive you will be in that hour.

   d. how much value you place on sleeping in that hour.

7. If business starts booming and companies compete to hire workers, the

   a. opportunity cost of upgrading to a college diploma increases.

   b. opportunity cost of upgrading to a college diploma decreases.

   c. incentive to drop out of college decreases.

   d. choice about going to college does not change as long as tuition does not change.

8. The opportunity cost of attending college

   a. is less than the money cost.

   b. depends only on what you could earn by working full-time.

   c. includes the income you could have earned working full-time.

   d. depends on the benefits of going to college.

9. In making a smart choice,

   a. the value of what you give up must be greater than the value of what you get.

   b. the value of what you get must be greater than the value of what you give up.

   c. if the value of what you give up is greater that the value of what you get, you should lower the value of what you give up.

   d. if the value of what you give up is greater that the value of what you get, you should raise the value of what you get.

10. Ayesha missed her shift at the restaurant to go to a soccer game. She paid $30 for the ticket, $20 for parking, and spent $10 on popcorn. If she had worked her shift, Ayesha would have earned $100. Her opportunity cost of attending the game is

    a. $60.

    b. $100.

    c. $150.

    d. $160.

 **Apply...**

3. Seat belts save lives. Suppose that a city doubles the penalty for being caught driving without a seat belt to try to increase seat belt use among drivers.

    a. Use the concepts of incentives and opportunity cost to explain how this policy will influence driver behaviour.

    _____

    _____

    _____

    b. Suppose the city evaluates the results of the policy and finds that the number of traffic deaths actually _increased_ after the policy was introduced. Can you think of a reason for this result?

    _____

    _____

    _____

4. Ashley, Doug, and Mei-Lin are planning to travel from Halifax to Sydney. The trip takes one hour by airplane and five hours by train. The air fare is $100 and train fare is $60. They all have to take time off from work while travelling. Ashley earns $5 per hour in her job, Doug $10 per hour, and Mei-Lin $12 per hour.

    Use the table below to calculate the opportunity cost of air and train travel for each person. Assuming they all make smart choices as economizers, how should each of them travel to Sydney?

Traveller	Train	Plane
Ashley		
a. Fare	$	$
b. Opportunity cost of travel time at $5/hr	$	$
Total Cost	$	$
Doug		
a. Fare	$	$
b. Opportunity cost of travel time at $10/hr	$	$
Total Cost	$	$
Mei-Lin		
a. Fare	$	$
b. Opportunity cost of travel time at $12/hr	$	$
Total Cost	$	$

 **Apply…**

5. Vladimir loves riding the bumper cars at the amusement park, but he loves the experience a little less with each additional ride. In estimating the benefit he receives from the rides, Vladimir would be willing to pay $10 for his first ride, $7 for his second ride, and $4 for his third ride. Rides actually cost $5 each for as many rides as Vladimir wants to take. This information is summarized in the table below.

Ride	1st	2nd	3rd
Additional benefit ($)	10	7	4
Additional cost ($)	5	5	5

   a. If Vladimir chooses by comparing total benefit and total cost, how many rides will he take?

   _____

   _____

   _____

   _____

   b. If Vladimir chooses by comparing additional benefits and additional costs for each ride, how many rides will he take?

   _____

   _____

   _____

   _____

   c. Is Vladimir better off by comparing total benefits and costs, or by comparing additional benefits and costs? Explain your answer behind Vladimir's smart choice.

   _____

   _____

   _____

   _____

   _____

   _____

Gains from Trade

L03 Describe how comparative advantage, specialization, and trade make us all better off.

Our standard of living is much higher than it was hundreds of years ago. Trade is the key to making all of us better off. Any time two people make a voluntary trade, each person feels that what they get is of greater value than what they give up. If there weren't mutual benefits, the trade wouldn't happen.

Opportunity cost is the key to the mutual benefits from trade. Here's a simple example. Jill and Marie are each self-sufficient pioneers producing food and shelter. Each grows her own wheat to make bread, and chops her own wood for fire and shelter. Figures 1 and 2 show the different possible combinations of bread and wood each can produce in a month.

Figure 1   Jill's Production Possibilities

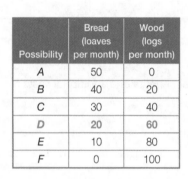

Possibility	Bread (loaves per month)	Wood (logs per month)
A	50	0
B	40	20
C	30	40
D	20	60
E	10	80
F	0	100

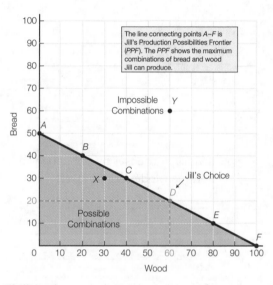

Figure 2   Marie's Production Possibilities

Possibility	Bread (loaves per month)	Wood (logs per month)
A	40	0
B	30	5
C	20	10
D	10	15
E	0	20

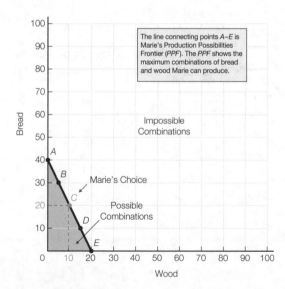

Because Jill and Marie are each self-sufficient, that means each can only consume what she produces herself. Jill chooses point *D* on her *PPF*, and Marie chooses point *C* on her *PPF*.

Production Possibilities Frontier

Each black line in the graphs is a **production possibilities frontier** —
PPF for short.

- A *PPF* shows the maximum combinations of products or services that
  can be produced with existing inputs.

- A *PPF* is the boundary between possible and impossible combinations
  of outputs.

- Points on the *PPF* are preferred to points inside the *PPF* because people
  prefer more to less.

Can Jill and Marie Make a Deal?

Can trade make both Jill and Marie better off? It doesn't look promising,
especially for Jill. Jill is a better bread maker than Marie and a better wood
chopper. Jill has an **absolute advantage** — the ability to produce at a lower
absolute cost than another producer — over Marie in both bread production
and wood production. Jill is more productive as a bread maker and as a wood
chopper.

If you are not keen on history, then in place of Jill and Marie, think of China
and Canada. If China can produce everything at lower cost than Canada, can
there be mutually beneficial gains from trade for both countries? What's the
benefit for China? Won't all Canadians end up unemployed?

Comparative Advantage

Mutually beneficial gains from trade do not depend on absolute advantage,
they depend on **comparative advantage** — the ability to produce a product or
service at a lower *opportunity cost* than another producer.

To calculate opportunity costs along any *PPF*, compare two adjacent possible
combinations, and use the formula

$$\text{Opportunity cost} = \frac{\text{Give Up}}{\text{Get}}$$

Figure 3 shows the opportunity cost calculations for Jill and Marie.
Opportunity cost is measured in term of what you must give up of the other
product.

Figure 3   Opportunity Costs for Jill and Marie

	Opportunity Cost of 1 Additional	
	Loaf of Bread	Log of Wood
Jill	Gives up 2 logs of wood	Gives up ½ loaf of bread
Marie	Gives up ½ log of wood	Gives up 2 loaves of bread
Comparative Advantage	Marie has comparative advantage (lower opportunity cost) in bread-making	Jill has comparative advantage (lower opportunity cost) in wood-chopping

Since comparative advantage is defined as lowest opportunity cost (not
lowest absolute cost), you can see that Marie has a comparative advantage in
bread-making, while Jill has a comparative advantage in wood-chopping.

HINT: Whenever you are trying to figure out comparative advantage, always
create a table like Figure 3, with the two traders in the rows, and the two
products in the columns.

Mutually Beneficial Gains from Trade

There are mutually beneficial gains from trade if people/countries specialize in producing the product in which they have a comparative advantage, and trade for the other product. According to comparative advantage, Jill should specialize in only chopping wood, and Marie should specialize in only making bread. Jill produces 100 logs of wood and no bread, and Marie produces 40 loaves of bread and no wood. They then trade 20 logs of wood for 20 loaves of bread along the blue Trade Lines below. Figure 4 tells the story of Jill and Marie's specialization and trade.

Figure 4   Mutually Beneficial Gains from Trade

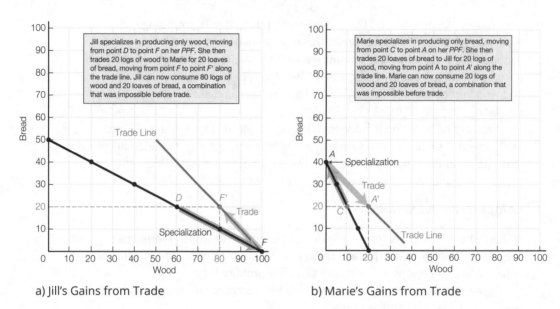

a) Jill's Gains from Trade

b) Marie's Gains from Trade

Achieving the Impossible

After trading, Jill and Marie are both better off than when they were each self-sufficient. Each can consume a combination of wood and bread — outside her *PPF* — that was impossible before trade. Voluntary trade is *not* a zero-sum game, where one person's gain is the other's loss. Both traders gain.

These gains from trade happen without anyone working harder, without any improvement in technology, and without new inputs.

There are gains for both Jill and Marie, even though Jill has an absolute advantage in producing everything at lower cost. Differences in opportunity costs — comparative advantage — are the key to mutually beneficial gains from trade. The trade can be between individuals, or between countries. That is why China trades with Canada, even though China can produce most things more cheaply than Canada can. There are still differences in comparative advantage based on opportunity costs.

All arguments you will ever hear in favour of freer trade are based on comparative advantage, which is based on the most important concept in economics — opportunity cost.

 **Practice...**

11. Mutually beneficial gains from trade come from

    a. absolute advantage.

    b. comparative advantage.

    c. self-sufficiency.

    d. China.

12. The simplest way to calculate opportunity cost is

    a. $\dfrac{\text{Give Up}}{\text{Get}}$

    b. $\dfrac{\text{Get}}{\text{Give Up}}$

    c. Give Up – Get

    d. Get – Give Up

13. In one hour, Chloe can bake 24 cookies or 12 muffins. Zabeen can bake 6 cookies or 2 muffins. For mutually beneficial trade, Chloe should bake

    a. cookies because she has a comparative advantage.

    b. cookies because she has an absolute advantage.

    c. muffins because she has a comparative advantage.

    d. muffins because she has an absolute advantage.

14. On a graph of a production possibilities frontier (*PPF*), impossible combinations of outputs are represented by

    a. the slope of the *PPF*.

    b. points inside the *PPF*.

    c. points on the *PPF*.

    d. points outside the *PPF*.

15. If Ying can increase production of houses without decreasing production of any other product, then Ying

    a. is producing inside his production possibilities frontier.

    b. is producing on his production possibilities frontier.

    c. is producing outside his production possibilities frontier.

    d. must prefer houses to any other product.

Apply...

6. Tova and Ron are the only two remaining inhabitants of the planet Melmac. They spend their 30-hour days producing widgets and woggles, the only two products needed for happiness on Melmac. It takes Tova 1 hour to produce a widget and 2 hours to produce a woggle, while Ron takes 3 hours to produce a widget and 3 hours to produce a woggle.

   a. For a 30-hour day, draw an individual *PPF* for Tova, then for Ron.

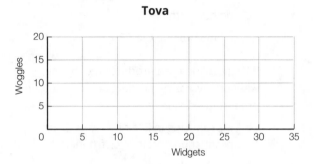

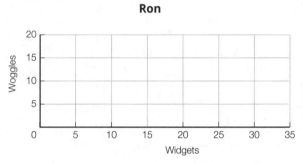

   b. To start, Tova and Ron are each self-sufficient. Define self-sufficiency. Explain what the individual *consumption possibilities* are for Tova, then for Ron.

   _____

   _____

   _____

   c. Who has an absolute advantage in the production of widgets? of woggles? Explain your answers.

   _____

   _____

   _____

   d. Who has a comparative advantage in the production of widgets? of woggles? Explain your answers.

   _____

   _____

   _____

   _____

   e. Tova and Ron each specialize in producing only the product in which she or he has a comparative advantage. One spends 30 hours producing widgets, the other spends 30 hours producing woggles. What will be the total production of widgets and woggles?

   _____

   _____

   _____

 **Apply...**

f. Tova and Ron exchange 7 widgets for 5 woggles. On your *PPF* diagrams in 6a, plot the new point of Tova's consumption, then of Ron's consumption. Explain how these points illustrate gains from trade.

_____

_____

_____

_____

7. The best auto mechanic in town (who charges $120/hour) is also a better typist than her office manager (who earns $20/hour). The mechanic decides to do her own typing. Is this a smart choice for her to make? Explain your answer. [*Hint:* Fill in the table. The best alternative employment for the office manager is another office job that also pays $20/hour.]

	O.C. of 1 Additonal Hour of	
	Mechanic Services	**Typing**
Mechanic		
Office Manager		
Comparative Advantage		

_____

_____

_____

_____

_____

8. Classroom Game — Is Trade Mutually Beneficial?

Before game starts, Instructor asks class, "Why do people trade?" Trade includes trading money for a product or service. Write answers on the board.

Every student should bring to class one or more small items they no longer want, or small candies.

Instructor gives students the opportunity to trade. No one is required to trade. Allow 5–10 minutes for trades. Students may trade more than once. At the end of trading, here are discussion questions for the Instructor to ask.

a. How many students made a trade?

b. For anyone who made at least one trade, "Why did you decide to trade?"

c. Of those who made trades, how many feel better off as a result of the trade(s)?

d. If anyone who trades says she or he is not better off, please explain why.

e. Why did some students decide not to trade?

f. Did the trading results support or disprove the reasons on the board about "Why do people trade?"

g. What conclusions can you draw from this game?

Thinking Like an Economist

L04 Explain how models like the circular flow model make smart choices easier.

Economists think like map-makers. To plan a trip across Canada, you could look at a satellite photo that captures every aspect of Canada that can be seen from space. But the photo doesn't show details that are important for your trip — roads, railways, or ferry services. A map is much more useful than the photo because it focuses your attention on the information that is most relevant for your task, and leaves all other information in the background.

Learning to think like an economist allows the key "roads" to making smart choices stand out. This kind of thinking makes it easier to make decisions and understand the complex world around you.

Let's apply this way of thinking to the definition of economics: Economics is about how individuals, businesses, and governments make the best possible choices to get what they want, and about how those choices interact in markets. Another famous definition of economics by Alfred Marshall, a legendary professor at the University of Cambridge, is "Economics is the study of mankind in the ordinary business of life."

Circular Flow Model

The maps that economists use are called economic models. A **model** is a simplified representation of the real world, focusing attention on what's important for understanding a specific idea or concept.

Figure 5   The Circular Flow of Economic Life

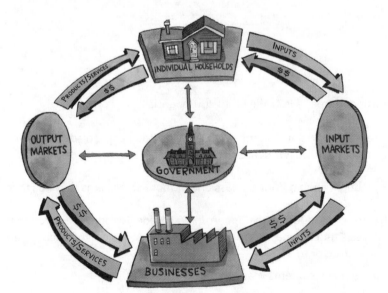

Figure 5 is an economic model called the *circular flow of economic life*. It shows the simplest big picture of how to think about economic choices. All the complexity of the Canadian economy is reduced to three sets of players: households, businesses, and governments. Individuals in households ultimately own all of the **inputs** of an economy — the productive resources used to produce products and services. The four types of inputs are labour (the ability to work), natural resources, capital equipment, and entrepreneurial ability. Even the assets of the largest corporations, such as Imperial Oil or Ford, are ultimately owned by individual shareholders.

Households and businesses interact in two sets of markets:

- In input markets, businesses buy the inputs they need to produce products and services; households are sellers.

- In output markets, businesses sell their products and services; households are buyers.

- Governments set the rules of the game and can choose to interact, or not, in any aspect of the economy.

- As part of the rules of the game, governments enforce **property rights** — legally enforceable guarantees of ownership of physical, financial, and intellectual property.

Models as the Economist's Laboratory

A good economic model helps you make smart choices, or helps you better understand or predict the facts of the world around you. To test models against the facts, economists do what natural scientists do. We assume that "other things are unchanged," to remove the influence of the factors left out of the simplified model. Here is a natural science example.

The law of gravity predicts that, all other factors unchanged, objects fall at the same rate regardless of their mass. If we drop a bowling ball and a feather from a tall building, and find the bowling ball hits the ground first, does that disprove the law of gravity? No, because we are not controlling for air resistance, which changes the path of the feather more than the bowling ball. To accurately test the law of gravity, we must perform the same experiment in a laboratory vacuum, so that we eliminate, or control for, the influence of air resistance as an "other factor." We need to keep all other factors unchanged.

Economists have it much tougher than scientists. We can't pause everything in the world while focusing only on the factors we are interested in. Instead, we have to use economic models to isolate the factors we think are important. Economic models focus attention on what is important by assuming that all other things not in the model are unchanged. Thinking like an economist and using economic models is the mental equivalent of the controlled experiments of the laboratory.

John Maynard Keynes once said, "Economics is a science of thinking in terms of models, joined to the art of choosing models which are relevant to the contemporary world."

Positive and Normative Statements

In trying to explain the facts of the world, economists, like other scientists, distinguish facts from opinions.

Positive statements are about what is; they can be evaluated as true or false by checking the facts.

Normative statements involve value judgments or opinions, and cannot be factually checked, tested, or shown to be true or false. A normative statement is based on personal values, which differ among individuals.

Practice...

16. All of the following are inputs *except*

   a. capital equipment.

   b. natural resources.

   c. governments.

   d. labour.

17. The players in the circular flow model include

   a. businesses, governments, inputs.

   b. households, businesses, governments.

   c. governments, input markets, output markets.

   d. governments, markets, countries.

18. In the circular flow model,

   a. businesses ultimately own all inputs of an economy.

   b. businesses are sellers and households are buyers in input markets.

   c. households are sellers and businesses are buyers in output markets.

   d. governments set the rules of the game.

19. A good economic model

   a. is easier to test than experiments in a laboratory.

   b. helps you understand or predict the economic world around you.

   c. includes as much information as possible.

   d. changes many factors at the same time.

20. Which statement is normative?

   a. You should call your mother every week.

   b. Drinking 14 beers in one hour will probably make you sick.

   c. Men live longer than women.

   d. Women live longer than men.

 # Apply...

9. If you are trying to decide whether to buy a car, what are the most important factors to focus on when making your decision? What are some of the factors that you ignore, or leave out of your decision? Explain how your thinking resembles an economic model.

_____

_____

_____

_____

_____

_____

Apply...

10. Answer these questions about the circular flow model.

    a. In input markets, who are the sellers and who are the buyers? Start at the top of the circular flow model and explain the process of selling and buying in input markets.

    _____

    _____

    _____

    _____

    _____

    b. In output markets, who are the sellers and who are the buyers? Start at the bottom and explain the process of selling and buying in output markets.

    _____

    _____

    _____

    _____

    _____

    c. When one "trip" around the circle has ended,
        i.   what have households received?
        ii. what do business end up with?
        iii. how do these end points set up the next "trip" around the circular flow?

    _____

    _____

    _____

    _____

    _____

    d. Governments enforce property rights as one of the "rules of the game." What happens to incentives to trade if there are no property rights? Illustrate your answer by picking any exchange/trade and describe what might happen without property rights.

    _____

    _____

    _____

    _____

    _____

    _____

to be continued

Apply...

continued

11. Identify each statement below as either positive or normative. If it is positive, rewrite it so that it becomes normative. If it is normative, rewrite it so that it becomes positive. For each positive statement, explain how you might test to see if it is true (matches the facts) or false.

a. A government tax on cigarettes will reduce sales of cigarettes.

b. The Government of Canada should raise taxes to reduce the deficit.

c. Imports from China are eliminating jobs in Canada.

d. Governments should impose rent controls to create more affordable housing.

Models for Microeconomics and Macroeconomics

L05 Differentiate microeconomic and macroeconomic choices, and explain the Three Keys model for smart choices.

The economic way of thinking, while always concerned with smart choices and their interactions in markets, can be applied on different scales to understand microeconomics and macroeconomics.

Microeconomics **Microeconomics** analyzes the choices made by individuals in households, individual businesses, and governments, and how those choices interact in markets. Microeconomic choices for individuals include whether to go to college or to get a job, whether to be self-sufficient or to specialize and trade, whether to take out a bank loan or to run up a credit card balance, and whether to get married or to stay single. Microeconomic choices for businesses include what product to produce, how much to spend on research and development of new products, which technology to use, which marketing strategy to use, and whether to outsource manufacturing to China or produce in Canada. Microeconomic choices for governments focus on individual industries. For example, should the government step in and regulate the mobile phone industry or let competition determine the winners and losers? How would a carbon tax affect car sales?

Macroeconomics   When we step back from individual details and look at the big picture, we are taking a "macro" view. **Macroeconomics** analyzes the performance of the whole Canadian (or any country's) economy and the global economy, the combined outcomes of all individual microeconomic choices. Macroeconomics focuses on overall outcomes of market interactions, including Canadian unemployment, inflation rates, government deficits and surpluses, interest rates set by the Bank of Canada, the value of the Canadian dollar, and international trade. Macroeconomics also examines the policy choices governments make that affect the whole economy — for example, whether to play an active economic role by spending and taxing (more likely for New Democrats or Liberals) or to leave the economy alone (more likely for Conservatives), whether to raise or lower taxes, whether to raise or lower interest rates, and whether to defend the value of the Canadian dollar or let it be determined by economic forces.

Microeconomics looks at the individual trees, while macroeconomics looks at the forest.

Three Keys Model for Smart Choices

Whether you are studying microeconomics or macroeconomics, all smart choices begin with microeconomic choices. Figure 6 shows a second economic model to guide smart microeconomic choices. This model doesn't look like a traditional map (no cities or roads), but it works like all maps and models do — focusing your attention on the information that is most useful for making a smart choice, and leaving other information in the background.

Figure 6   The Three Keys Model

- Key 1 is most important. Compare additional benefits and additional opportunity costs. This is the principle behind all microeconomic decisions.
- Keys 2 and 3 simply provide more of the details behind Key 1.

- Economists use the word "marginal" instead of "additional," so you can also read Key 2 as "Count only **marginal benefits** — additional benefits from your next choice — and **marginal opportunity costs** — additional opportunity costs from your next choice." Thinking like an economist means thinking at the margin.

- Key 3 details the costs to include, which people often miss.

- **Implicit costs** are the opportunity costs of investing your own money or time.

- **Negative externalities** are costs that affect others who are external to a choice or trade.

- **Positive externalities** are benefits that affect others who are external to a choice or trade.

If you are studying microeconomics, you will learn more about the details in The Three Keys model. The Three Keys, together with the circular flow model, will also guide your macroeconomic choices and understanding of the economy.

 **Practice…**

21. Microeconomics focuses on

   a. smart choices, while macroeconomics focuses on voluntary trade.

   b. the choices of individual economic players, while macroeconomics focuses on performance of the whole economy.

   c. performance of the whole economy, while macroeconomics focuses on the choices of individual economic players.

   d. opportunity costs, while macroeconomics focuses on negative and positive externalities.

22. Which headline is about macroeconomics?

   a. "Consumers switch from minivans to hybrids"

   b. "Amazon fights a tax on e-commerce"

   c. "Japan's economy is still in recession"

   d. "Farmers stop using pesticides"

23. Viki paid $12 to see the new *Star Trek* movie. Once inside, she must decide whether or not to buy popcorn for $4. Buying the popcorn is a smart choice if Vicki gets benefits of at least

   a. $4.

   b. $8.

   c. $12.

   d. $16.

24. Before starring in *Iron Man,* Robert Downey Jr. had acted in many movies with first-weekend box office revenues averaging $5 million. *Iron Man* earned $102 million in its first weekend. The success of *Iron Man* _____ the opportunity cost of hiring Robert Downey Jr. and _____ the marginal benefit to movie producers of hiring him.

   a. decreases; increases

   b. decreases; decreases

   c. increases; decreases

   d. increases; increases

25. To make a smart economic choice, consider all of the following *except*

   a. past costs and benefits.

   b. external costs and benefits.

   c. additional costs and additional benefits.

   d. implicit costs.

Apply...

12. List the Three Keys to smart choices, and highlight the most important words in each key.

_____

_____

_____

_____

_____

13. Highway 407 ETR in Toronto is a toll road that uses transponders to keep track of how many kilometres you drive on it, and then sends you a monthly bill. Highway 401 runs parallel to Highway 407 and is free. Why do drivers voluntarily pay the tolls? (Use opportunity cost in your answer.) Suppose the government could calculate the cost per kilometre of the pollution damage from your driving, and send you a similar monthly bill. How might that additional cost affect your decision to drive?

_____

_____

_____

_____

_____

_____

_____

14. The questions below are about differences between microeconomics and macroeconomics.

    a. Fill in the blanks.

    _____ analyzes the performance of the whole Canadian economy and the global economy, the combined outcomes of all individual microeconomic choices.

    _____ analyzes the choices made by individuals in households, individual businesses, and governments, and how those choices interact in markets.

    b. For each of the following media headlines, circle whether it is about microeconomics, macroeconomics, or if you are unsure which. Give a one-sentence explanation of your answer.

    i. "Will Mobile Phone Rates Fall as Shaw Buys Wind Mobile?"

    Micro / Macro / Unsure

    _____

    _____

    _____

to be continued

Apply...

continued

ii.   "Beyond Pricing Startup Helps AirBnB Homeowners Boost Revenues from Their Rentals"

Micro / Macro / Unsure

_____

_____

_____

iii.   "Loonie Takes Biggest Tumble in 3 Months after Bank of Canada Cuts Outlook for Growth"

Micro / Macro / Unsure

_____

_____

_____

iv.   "Why Pricing Traffic Congestion Is Critical to Beating It"

Micro / Macro / Unsure

_____

_____

_____

v.   "Government Deficit Fighting Not as Important as Investing in Infrastructure"

Micro / Macro / Unsure

_____

_____

_____

vi.   "Inflation Has Not Yet Followed Lower Unemployment in America"

Micro / Macro / Unsure

_____

_____

_____

vii. "Higher Alberta Minimum Wage Benefits Both Workers and Employers"

Micro / Macro / Unsure

_____

_____

KNOW...

Summary of Learning Objectives

1. Because of the problem of **scarcity,** you can never satisfy all of your wants. Making the most out of your life requires smart choices about what to go after, and what to give up.

2. Opportunity cost is the most important concept both in economics and for making smart choices in life. The **opportunity cost** of any choice is the cost of the best alternative given up.

3. Opportunity cost and comparative advantage are key to understanding why specializing and trading make us all better off. There are mutually beneficial gains from trade if each producer specializes in producing the product for which they have a **comparative advantage** — the ability to produce at a lower *opportunity cost* than another producer.

4. The circular flow **model,** like all economic models, focuses attention on what's important for understanding and shows how smart choices by households, businesses, and governments interact in input markets and output markets. Economists distinguish **positive statements** (about what is; can be evaluated as true or false by checking the facts) from **normative statements** (based on value judgments about what you believe should be; cannot be tested or evaluated as true or false by checking the facts).

5. The Three Keys model summarizes the core of microeconomics, providing the basis for smart choices in all areas of life. **Microeconomics** analyzes choices that individuals in households, individual businesses, and governments make, and how those choices interact in markets. **Macroeconomics** analyzes the performance of the whole Canadian (or any country's) economy and the global economy, the combined outcomes of all individual microeconomic choices.

Key Terms

absolute advantage: the ability to produce a product or service at a lower absolute cost than another producer

comparative advantage: the ability to produce a product or service at lower opportunity cost than another producer

economics: how individuals, businesses, and governments make the best possible choices to get what they want, and how those choices interact in markets

externalities: costs or benefits that affect others external to a choice or a trade

implicit costs: hidden opportunity costs of what a business owner could earn elsewhere with time and money invested

incentives: rewards and penalties for choices

inputs: the productive resources — labour, natural resources, capital equipment, and entrepreneurial ability — used to produce products and services

macroeconomics: analyzes performance of the whole Canadian (or any country's) economy and the global economy, the combined outcomes of all individual microeconomic choices

marginal benefits: the additional benefit from a choice, changing with circumstances

marginal opportunity cost: additional opportunity costs from the next choice

microeconomics: analyzes choices that individuals in households, individual businesses, and governments make, and how those choices interact in markets

model: a simplified representation of the real world, focusing attention on what's important for understanding

negative externalities: costs to society from your private choice that affect others, but that you do not pay

normative statements: based on value judgments about what you believe should be; cannot be tested or evaluated as true or false by checking the facts

opportunity cost: cost of best alternative given up

positive externalities: benefits to society from your private choice that affect others, but that others do not pay you for

positive statements: about what is; can be evaluated as true or false by checking the facts

production possibilities frontier (*PPF*): maximum combinations of products or services that can be produced with existing inputs

property rights: legally enforceable guarantees of ownership of physical, financial, and intellectual property

scarcity: the problem that arises because we all have limited money, time, and energy

Answers to Practice

1. **c** We all have limited money, time, and energy.
2. **b** Definition.
3. **d** All limited for all people.
4. **a** Because we can't have everything we want, we must choose.
5. **d** Scarcity is a universal problem.
6. **a** Paid tuition is the same for either choice.
7. **a** Going to college means giving up a good job with a higher wage.
8. **c** Opportunity cost includes income given up and money paid for tuition.
9. **b** Additional benefits of what you get must be greater than opportunity costs of what you give up.
10. **d** Money costs ($30+$20+$10) you could have spent on something else, plus income given up ($100).
11. **b** Differences in opportunity costs are key to gains from trade.
12. **a** See formula.
13. **c** Chloe's opportunity cost of muffins (2 cookies per muffin) is lower than Zabeen's (3 cookies per muffin).
14. **d** *PPF* represents maximum possible combinations.
15. **a** With unused inputs inside *PPF*, you can increase output without opportunity cost by using unemployed inputs.

16 **c** Governments set the rules of the game — are not inputs to production.

17. **b** These players interact in input and output markets.

18. **d** Other answers would be correct if switch businesses and households.

19. **b** Good models select information to include, change one factor at a time, and are hard to test because many factors change simultaneously in the real world.

20. **a** Notice the word *should*. Other statements can be shown to be true or false.

21. **b** Definition.

22. **c** About a country's economic performance.

23. **a** Compare only additional benefits from eating popcorn to additional cost of $4.

24. **d** Because moviegoers will pay more to see Downey, movie producers will pay more to hire him.

25. **a** All other costs and benefits are part of the Three Keys.

2 Demanders and Suppliers

LEARNING OBJECTIVES

L01 Explain why smart choices depend on marginal benefits, not total benefits, and on marginal costs, not total costs.

L02 Explain the law of demand, and describe the roles of substitutes and of willingness and ability to pay.

L03 Explain the difference between a change in quantity demanded and a change in demand, and list five factors that change demand.

L04 Explain the law of supply and describe the roles of higher profits and higher marginal opportunity costs of production.

L05 Explain the difference between a change in quantity supplied and a change in supply, and list six factors that can change supply.

LEARN...

In the circular flow model, governments set the rules of the game, but individuals (in households) and businesses make most of the choices. Individuals and businesses play roles both as demanders and as suppliers. In input markets, individuals are suppliers (of inputs labour, capital, land and entrepreneurship) and businesses are demanders. In output markets, businesses are suppliers (of products and services) and individuals, acting as consumers, are demanders.

In this chapter, you will learn what's behind our choices to demand or buy, and our choices to supply or sell. When things change — prices, incomes, technologies — you will also learn to analyze how choices change. What effect does advertising have on demand? Why are businesses using robots to replace human workers?

We choose among alternatives, or substitutes. Consumers choose between different phone plans, eating out or cooking at home, or getting to school by bike or transit. Businesses choose between producing different products, using different technologies, or deciding how many workers to hire.

All demand and supply decisions are based on Key 1 — choose (to demand or to supply) only when additional benefits are greater than additional opportunity costs. Smart demand and supply decisions are also made at the margin using Key 2 — count only additional benefits and additional costs.

You will learn all of the reasons behind consumers' willingness and ability to pay for products, and behind businesses' willingness to supply products to earn profits. The next chapter combines these reasons, putting together demand and supply to explain how prices and quantities are determined in markets.

Marginal Benefits and Marginal Opportunity Costs

L01 Explain why smart choices depend on marginal benefits, not total benefits, and on marginal costs, not total costs.

Marginal Benefits Change with Circumstances

As a consumer, the additional benefits or satisfaction you expect to get from a product or service depend on the circumstances.

Marginal Benefits Decrease with Quantity You just finished an intense workout at the gym and desperately want something to drink. Your buddy, who is always trying to make a buck, says, "I have a 6-pack of Gatorade. How much will you pay for a bottle?" The first Gatorade after a workout is very satisfying — it has a high marginal benefit, and you would be willing to pay a lot (while wondering if this guy is really a buddy). The second Gatorade is less satisfying, and a third might make you sick.

- Marginal benefit is key to how much you are willing to pay.
- Decreasing marginal benefit means decreasing willingness to pay for additional quantities of the same product or service.

The Diamond-Water Paradox A focus on marginal benefit helps make sense of the following paradox. What's more valuable in providing benefits or satisfaction — diamonds or water? Water is essential for survival, while diamonds are unnecessary. Why do diamonds cost far more than water? You solve the paradox by distinguishing marginal benefit from total benefit. You would die without water, so you are willing to pay everything you can for the first drink. But when water is abundant, what are you willing to pay, at the margin, for your next drink today? Not much. Marginal benefit is low, though the total benefit of all water consumed (including the first, life-saving drink) is high.

Diamonds won't keep you alive, but they are scarce, and desirable for that reason. What would you pay for your first diamond? A lot. Marginal benefit is high. Because diamonds are scarce, there aren't many out there, so total benefit is low.

- Willingness to pay depends on marginal benefit, not total benefit, so people are generally willing to pay more for a diamond (high marginal benefit) than for a glass of water (low marginal benefit).

Marginal Costs Change with Circumstances

For businesses, the additional cost of producing a product or service depends on the circumstances. Let's look at a business: Paola's Parlour for Piercing and Nails. With the labour and equipment in her shop, Paola can do piercings or paint fingernails. Her workers are equally skilled at piercing, but their fingernail skills differ from expert to beginner. Figure 1 shows the different combinations of fingernail sets and piercings that Paola's Parlour can produce in a day.

Figure 1   Paola's Parlour Production Possibilities Frontier (*PPF*)

Combination	Fingernails (full sets)	Piercings (full body)
A	15	0
B	14	1
C	12	2
D	9	3
E	5	4
F	0	5

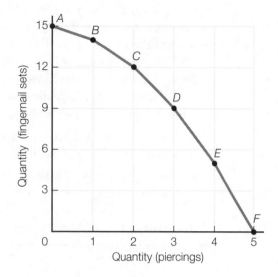

Marginal Costs Increase with Quantity   Look what happens if Paola wants to increase her production of piercings from 0 (combination *A*), to 1, to 2, . . . up to 5 (combination *F*). To get more piercings, Paola gives up doing nailsets. Remember,

$$\text{Opportunity cost} \; = \; \frac{\text{Give Up}}{\text{Get}}$$

Figure 2 shows, in the last column, the marginal opportunity costs to Paola of producing more piercings.

Figure 2   Paola's Parlour Marginal Opportunity Costs

Combination	Fingernails (full sets)	Piercings (full body)	Marginal Opportunity Cost of Producing More Piercings (fingernail sets given up)
A	15	0	$\dfrac{(15 - 14)}{1} = 1$
B	14	1	$\dfrac{(14 - 12)}{1} = 2$
C	12	2	$\dfrac{(12 - 9)}{1} = 3$
D	9	3	$\dfrac{(9 - 5)}{1} = 4$
E	5	4	$\dfrac{(5 - 0)}{1} = 5$
F	0	5	

As Paola increases her quantity supplied of piercings, her marginal opportunity costs increase, from 1 fingernail set given up for the first piercing to 5 fingernail sets given up for the fifth piercing. These increasing marginal opportunity costs (marginal costs for short) arise because Paola's staff are not equally good at painting. As Paola reduces fingernail output to produce the first piercing, which worker will she switch first? Remember all are equally good at piercing. She will switch the least productive fingernail painter. Her given-up, or forgone, fingernail production is small (1 set). To increase piercing production more, she has to switch more productive fingernail painters. Increasing marginal costs arise because inputs are not equally productive in all activities.

HINT: Why is the shape of Paola's *PPF* curved, while the *PPF*s for Jill and Marie in Chapter 1 are straight lines? As Jill (or Marie) switches between combinations of bread and wood, her marginal opportunity costs do not change because Jill's (or Marie's) skills do not change. She just changes the time spent on each task.

- When inputs are *not* equally productive in all activities, marginal opportunity costs increase with increases in quantity supplied.

- When inputs are equally productive in all activities, marginal opportunity costs are constant.

To be willing to supply more piercings, Paola's business needs a higher price to cover increasing marginal costs.

 # Practice...

1. All-you-can-eat buffet restaurants charge a fixed fee for eating. With each plate that Anna eats, she experiences

    a. decreasing marginal costs.

    b. increasing marginal costs.

    c. decreasing marginal benefits.

    d. increasing marginal benefits.

2. Thinking like economists, a dating couple should break up when

    a. total benefits of dating are greater than the total costs.

    b. total costs of dating are greater than the total benefits.

    c. marginal benefits of dating are greater than the marginal costs.

    d. marginal costs of dating are greater than the marginal benefits.

3. The price of diamonds is higher than the price of water because

    a. marginal benefits from diamonds are relatively high.

    b. marginal benefits from water are relatively high.

    c. total benefits from diamonds are relatively high.

    d. total benefits from water are relatively low.

4. If all inputs for a business are *not* equally productive in all activities, the opportunity cost of increasing output is

    a. decreasing.

    b. increasing.

    c. constant.

    d. high.

5. When all inputs for a business are equally productive in all activities, as the business increases output, marginal costs

    a. increase.

    b. decrease.

    c. are constant.

    d. are zero.

 # Apply...

1. You and your entrepreneurial buddy have a concession stand on the beach. It is a hot, sunny, crowded day, and you are selling a few $5 collapsible umbrellas as sun shades. The skies suddenly darken, rain begins to pour, and your buddy quickly switches the umbrella price sign to $10. Will you sell more or fewer umbrellas? Explain your thinking, and include the concept of marginal benefit in analyzing a customer's decision.

    _____

    _____

    _____

    _____

    _____

2. Employees do not like working long weekdays and on weekends, so employers offer higher wages for the extra time in the form of "overtime pay," which could be up to three times the regular wage. Use the concept of increasing opportunity cost to explain why it is important for businesses to offer overtime pay.

    _____

    _____

    _____

    _____

    _____

3. Suppose that an economy has the *PPF* in this table:

    a. Plot these possibilities on the graph, label the points, and draw the *PPF*.

Possibility	Production Possibilities	
	Maximum Units of Butter per Week	**Maximum Units of Guns per Week**
A	200	0
B	180	60
C	160	100
D	100	160
E	0	200

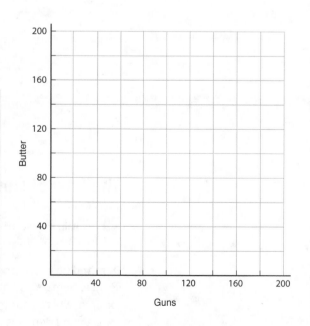

to be continued

Apply...

continued

b. If the economy moves from possibility *C* to possibility *D*, what is the opportunity cost, in units of butter, of one gun?

_____

_____

c. If the economy moves from possibility *D* to possibility *E*, what is the opportunity cost, in units of butter, of one gun?

_____

_____

d. In general, what happens to the opportunity cost of guns as the output of guns increases? In general, what happens to the opportunity cost of butter as the output of butter increases? What do these results imply about inputs to production?

_____

_____

_____

_____

e. Instead of the possibilities given, suppose the *PPF* is a straight line joining points *A* and *E*. What does that imply about opportunity costs and inputs?

_____

_____

_____

The Law of Demand

L02 Explain the law of demand, and describe the roles of substitutes and of willingness and ability to pay.

Demand describes consumers' willingness and ability to pay for a product or service. Demand is not just what consumers want. Your must put your money (or time) where your mouth is in order to demand a product or service.
Demand depends on

- how badly you want a product.
- how much you are willing and able to give up for it.

How Badly Do You Want It?

Economists describe all of your wants — and how intense each want is — as your **preferences**.

- The more intense your preference is for a product or service, the more you are willing to pay, because you expect a high benefit from satisfying that want.

- For all products or services, even those satisfying intense wants, there are decreasing marginal benefits for additional units consumed.

What Will You Give Up?

No matter how much you want something, your demand for it also depends on how much you are willing and able to give up for it. Notice I used the words *give up* instead of *pay* for it. For most products we want, we pay with money. But to satisfy many other wants, we have to give up our time or effort. Spending time studying means not seeing friends, not playing with your kids, or working less at your job. In comparing additional benefits and additional costs, cost always means *opportunity cost* — what you are willing to give up.

Substitutes   How much you are willing to give up depends on wants or preferences, but also on what your alternative choices are. **Substitutes** are products or services used in place of each other to satisfy the same want. The more substitutes there are, the less you are willing to pay for a product. If bottled water is available, how much will you pay for a Gatorade? The ability to listen to free music affects your willingness to pay for music.

Income   How much you are willing or able to give up also depends on what you can afford. Are you able to pay the price of the product you want? Can you afford to take the time to relax when you have a test tomorrow?

Demand is not just what consumers want. Your must put your money (or time) where your mouth is in order to demand a product or service.

Market Demand

For each individual, **quantity demanded** is the amount you actually plan to buy at a given price, taking into account everything that affects your willingness and ability to pay.

Market demand is the sum of the demands of all individuals willing and able to buy a particular product or service. In general, consumers buy a smaller quantity at higher prices because

- consumers switch to cheaper substitutes.

- fewer people can afford to buy.

This inverse relationship (when one goes up, the other goes down) between price and quantity demanded is so universal that economists call it the **law of demand**: If the price of a product or service rises, the quantity demanded of the product or service decreases. If the price falls, the quantity demanded increases. The law of demand works as long as other influences on demand besides price do not change.

Figure 3 on the next page illustrates the inverse relation between price and quantity demanded for the market demand for water.

Figure 3   Market Demand for Water

Row	Price ($ per m³)	Quantity Demanded (000's of m³ per month)
A	$1.00	5
B	$1.50	4
C	$2.00	3
D	$2.50	2
E	$3.00	1

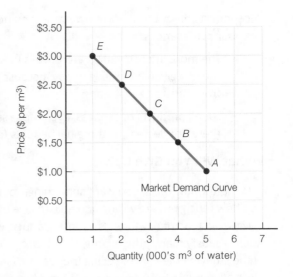

The **demand curve** shows the relationship between price and quantity demanded when all other influences on demand besides price do not change.

Two Ways to Read a Demand Curve

The demand curve is a simple yet powerful tool summarizing the two forces that determine quantity demanded — the switch to substitutes, and willingness and ability to pay. Because there are two forces, Figure 4 shows two ways to "read" a demand curve. Both readings are correct, but each highlights a different force.

Figure 4   Two Ways to Read a Demand Curve

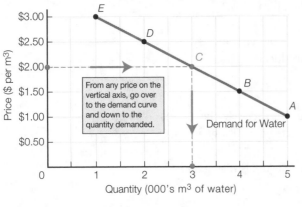

a) Reading the Demand Curve
   as a Demand Curve

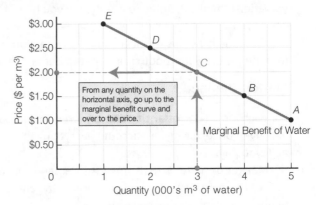

b) Reading the Demand Curve
   as a Marginal Benefit Curve

- To read as a demand curve — start at any price and go over and down to the quantity demanded. The demand curve shows, for any price, what will be the quantity demanded.

- To read as a marginal benefit curve — start at any quantity and go up and over to the price. The marginal benefit curve shows, for any quantity, the maximum price people are willing and able to pay for that last unit available. Increasing quantities have decreasing marginal benefits.

Both readings are movements along an unchanged demand curve. The law of demand works as long as other influences on demand besides price do not change.

Practice...

6. Your preferences measure
    a. the availability of substitutes.
    b. how limited your time is.
    c. the price of a product.
    d. how badly you want something.

7. Costs are
    a. the dollar price you pay.
    b. whatever you are willing to give up.
    c. the answer to the question "What do you want?"
    d. whatever you are willing to get.

8. When the price of a product rises,
    a. consumers look for more expensive substitutes.
    b. quantity demanded increases.
    c. consumers look for cheaper substitutes.
    d. consumers use more of the product.

9. A sociology class is a substitute for an economics class if
    a. attending the two classes has the same opportunity cost.
    b. the two classes satisfy the same want.
    c. both classes are at the same time.
    d. both classes are taught by the same instructor.

10. Which statement about demand is *true*?
    a. Demand describes a consumer's desire for a particular product or service.
    b. You have a demand for music when you download it for free.
    c. Your concerns about the environment affect your demand for cars.
    d. All of the above are true.

 # Apply...

4. What is the difference between wants and demands?

_____

_____

_____

_____

_____

to be continued

 **Apply...**

continued

5. You have tickets for a concert tonight that you have been looking forward to. Your mother, who is helping you pay your tuition, phones and says that it's very important to her that you come to Grandma's birthday party tonight. Using the law of demand, explain your decision — the concert or Grandma's party? [*HINT*: Think about opportunity cost.]

_____

_____

_____

_____

6. Classroom Game — Auction Demonstrating the Law of Demand
The best way to introduce the law of demand is to hold a real auction in class. The Instructor brings something students like (a Coke on a Pepsi-only campus, cookies, ...) and starts playing promoter, selling a wonderful (ice-cold Coke! Cookies made with real ginger!) product.

The rules of the game are:

- Instructor puts prices on the board, starting at $0, and asks students who are willing and able to pay that price to raise their hands. Instructor writes that quantity next to the price.
- Raise price in 50–cent increments, but jump to larger increments if that seems to work better.
- Students must pay with cash (no debit or VISA) and the highest bidder must buy the product.

Instructor questions after the auction ends:

a. What is the relation between price and quantity demanded on the board?

b. What factors went into your decisions, at each price, to raise your hand or not?

c. At what price did quantity demanded decrease the most?
What is it about that particular price that caused such a large decrease?

d. What conclusion can you draw about the important forces behind the law of demand?

Changes in Demand — Moving the Margins

L03 Explain the difference between a change in quantity demanded and a change in demand, and list five factors that change demand.

Quantity Demanded versus Demand

Demand summarizes all influences on a consumer's choice. Your demand for any product or service reflects your willingness and ability to pay. Willingness to pay depends on your preferences, what substitutes are available, and marginal benefit. Ability to pay depends on your income. As long as these factors (and a few more) do not change, the law of demand holds true: If the price of a product or service rises, the quantity demanded decreases.

But when change happens, economists distinguish between two kinds of change shown in Figure 5:

- If the price of a product or service changes, that affects *quantity demanded*.
  This is represented graphically by a movement along an unchanged demand curve.

- If anything else changes, that affects *demand*.
  This is represented graphically by a shift of the entire demand curve.

Figure 5   Change in Quantity Demanded versus a Change in Demand

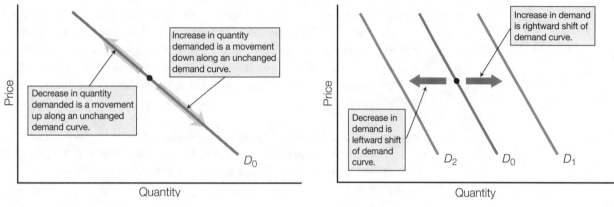

a) Change in Quantity Demanded

b) Change in Demand

Quantity demanded is a much more limited term than *demand.* Only a change in price changes *quantity demanded.* A change in any other influence on consumer choice changes *demand*.

Five Ways to Change Demand and Shift the Demand Curve

There are five important factors that can change market demand — the willingness and ability to pay for a product or service. They are

- Preferences
- Prices of related products
- Income
- Expected future prices
- Number of consumers

Preferences   Businesses advertise to try and get you to want their product, to persuade you that you need what they sell. An economist describes advertising as an attempt to increase your preferences for a product or service. Successful advertising increases your *willingness* to pay.

Any increase in consumers' willingness and ability to pay is called an **increase in demand** — a rightward shift of the demand curve. Any decrease in consumers' willingness and ability to pay is called a **decrease in demand** — a leftward shift of the demand curve.

Prices of Related Products   Many products (or services) you buy are related. Changes in the price of a different, related product affect your demand for the original product. There are two main types of related products — substitutes and complements.

Substitutes are products or services that can be used in place of each other to satisfy the same want. Headphones and earbuds are substitutes for listening to music. A rise in the price of a substitute (headphones) increases demand for the other product (earbuds).

Complements are products (or services) that are used together to satisfy the same want. Cars and gasoline are complements for driving. A fall in the price of a complement (cars) increases demand for the other product (gasoline).

Income   Having more money, or more income, increases your *ability* to pay. For most products and services, an increase in income increases demand (demand curve shifts rightward) and a decrease in income decreases demand. Economists call these products and services **normal goods**.

Not all products are normal goods. If you have been a poor student living on Kraft Dinner, you may never want to eat it again once you can afford real food. Economists call products and services for which an increase in income *decreases* demand **inferior goods** — products and services that you buy less of when your income increases. A decrease in income increases demand for inferior goods.

Expected Future Prices   A fall in the expected future price of a product (or service) decreases demand today — today's demand curve for that product shifts leftward. An expected future price rise increases demand today — today's demand curve shifts rightward.

Number of Consumers   An increase in the number of consumers increases demand — the market demand curve shifts rightward. A decrease in the number of consumers decreases demand — the market demand curve shifts leftward.

Figure 6 summarizes the differences between the law of demand (focusing on quantity demanded and movements along the demand curve) and the factors that change demand (and shift the demand curve).

Figure 6   Law of Demand and Changes in Demand

The Law of Demand *The quantity demanded of a product or service*	
Decreases if:	*Increases if:*
• price of the product or service rises	• price of the product or service falls

Changes in Demand *The demand for a product or service*	
Decreases if:	*Increases if:*
• preferences decrease	• preferences increase
• price of a substitute falls	• price of a substitute rises
• price of a complement rises	• price of a complement falls
• income decreases (normal good)	• income increases (normal good)
• income increases (inferior good)	• income decreases (inferior good)
• expected future price falls	• expected future price rises
• number of consumers decreases	• number of consumers increases

Why Bother Distinguishing between Quantity Demanded and Demand?

Between 2010 and 2012, gas prices in Canada rose from about $1 to $1.40 per litre. But the quantity of gasoline drivers bought actually *increased*. Does that disprove the "law of demand"? If nothing else changed during those years except the price of gasoline, the answer would be yes. The law of demand states that if the price of a product rises, the quantity demanded decreases, *as long as other factors besides price do not change*. But many things besides price also changed, including the number of drivers and cars. The increase in the number of drivers increased demand for gasoline. The effect of the increase in demand outweighed the price effect of the decrease in quantity demanded.

The distinction between quantity demanded and demand is the economist's equivalent of a controlled experiment. The law of demand holds constant all factors other than the price of the product to isolate the effect of a change in price on quantity demanded. When other factors change, we will use the shifts of the demand curve to analyze the effect of those factors.

 Practice...

11. Demand
    a. increases with a rise in price.
    b. is the same as quantity demanded.
    c. changes with income.
    d. decreases with a rise in price.

12. Some sales managers are talking about business. Which quotation refers to a change in *quantity demanded*?
    a. "Since our competitors raised their prices, our sales have tripled."
    b. "Because it's been such a warm winter, our sales of wool scarves are down from last year."
    c. "The Green movement has made our biodegradable products best-sellers."
    d. "We decided to cut our prices, and there was a big increase in our sales."

13. Which could cause a leftward shift of the demand curve for a product?
    a. increase in income
    b. decrease in income
    c. decrease in the price of a substitute
    d. all of the above

14. If the price of cars rises, the demand for tires
    a. increases.
    b. decreases.
    c. stays the same.
    d. depends on the price of tires.

15. If Kraft Dinner is an inferior good, a rise in the price of Kraft Dinner
    a. decreases the quantity demanded of Kraft Dinner.
    b. increases the quantity demanded of Kraft Dinner
    c. decreases demand for Kraft Dinner.
    d. increases demand for Kraft Dinner.

Apply...

7. The questions below are about the market for fidget spinners. The numbers in columns 1 and 2 of the table show the original market demand.

	Quantity Demanded	
Price	**Original D_0**	**New D_1**
$1	500	600
$2	400	500
$3	300	400
$4	200	300
$5	100	200

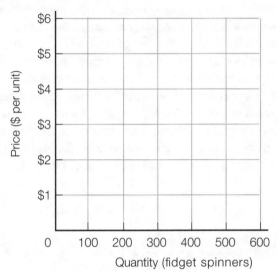

a. On the graph above, plot the points from the table and draw the original market demand curve. Label it D_0.

b. One year later, columns 1 and 3 show the new market demand. On the same graph, plot the new points and draw the new market demand curve. Label it D_1.

c. Describe this change by using some of the words — increase; decrease; demand; quantity demanded.

_____

_____

d. List changes in at least six factors that could explain the shift of the market demand curve from D_0 to D_1.

_____

_____

_____

_____

_____

_____

e. Reading D_0 and D_1 as marginal benefit curves, explain what changed for the 400th fidget spinner.

_____

_____

_____

_____

 **Apply...**

8. There are some "status goods," like Rolex watches, that people want to own because they are expensive. In contradiction to the law of demand, if Rolex watches were less expensive, fewer "status-seeking" consumers would demand them. Reconcile status products with the law of demand. How does the existence of cheap "knock-off" imitations of Rolex watches fit with the law of demand?

    _____

    _____

    _____

    _____

    _____

9. Roses sell for about $40 a bouquet most of the year, and at that price, worldwide sales are 6 million bouquets per month. Every February, the price of roses doubles to $80 a bouquet, but the quantity of roses demanded and sold also increases, to 24 million bouquets per month. The cost of producing roses doesn't change throughout the year. Does this violate the law of demand? Explain your answer.

    _____

    _____

    _____

    _____

    _____

The Law of Supply

LO4 Explain the law of supply and describe the roles of higher profits and higher marginal opportunity costs of production.

Demand is not just what you want. It is your willingness and ability to pay for a product or service. Similarly, supply is not just offering things for sale. **Supply** is the overall willingness of businesses (or individuals) to sell a particular product or service because the price covers all opportunity costs of production.

Market Supply

Quantity supplied is a more limited concept than supply. It is the amount you actually plan to supply at a given price, taking into account everything that affects your willingness to supply.

Market supply is the sum of the supplies of all businesses willing to produce a particular product or service. In general, businesses supply a larger quantity at higher prices. Rising prices create two incentives for increased quantity supplied:

- higher profits.
- the need to cover higher marginal opportunity costs of production.

This positive relationship between price and quantity supplied (both go up together) is so universal that economists call it the **law of supply**: If the price of a product or service rises, the quantity supplied increases. If the price falls, the quantity supplied decreases. The law of supply works as long as other factors besides price do not change.

Figure 7 illustrates the positive relation between price and quantity supplied for the market supply of piercings.

Figure 7   Market Supply of Piercings

Row	Price (marginal opportunity cost or minimum willing to accept per piercings)	Quantity Supplied (piercings)
A	$ 20	100
B	$ 40	200
C	$ 60	300
D	$ 80	400
E	$100	500

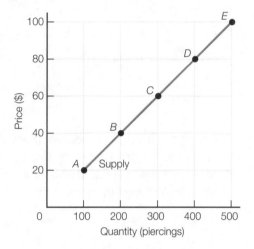

The **supply curve** shows the relationship between price and quantity supplied when all other influences on supply besides price do not change.

Two Ways to Read a Supply Curve

The supply curve is a simple yet powerful tool summarizing the two forces that determine quantity supplied — the desire for higher profits and the need to cover increasing marginal opportunity costs of production. Because there are two forces, Figure 8 shows two ways to "read" a supply curve. Both readings are correct, but each highlights a different force.

Figure 8   Two Ways to Read a Supply Curve

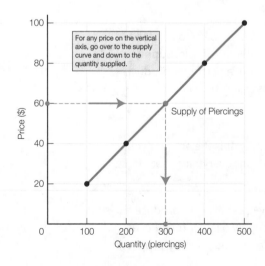

a)   Reading the Supply Curve
     as a Supply Curve

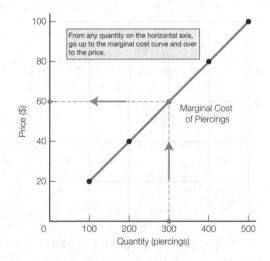

b)   Reading the Supply Curve
     as a Marginal Cost Curve

- To read as a supply curve — start at any price and go over and down to the quantity supplied. The supply curve shows, for any price, what will be the quantity supplied.

- To read as a marginal cost curve — start at any quantity and go up and over to the price. The marginal cost curve shows, for any quantity, the minimum price businesses will accept that covers all marginal opportunity costs of production.

Both readings are movements along an unchanged supply curve. The law of supply works as long as other influences on supply besides price do not change.

 # Practice...

16. When prices rise, individuals and businesses devote more of their time and resources to producing or supplying because

    a. of the desire for profits.

    b. higher profits usually mean higher costs.

    c. of the desire for higher prices.

    d. of higher demand.

17. As the price of a product or service *rises*,

    a. supply increases.

    b. quantity demanded increases.

    c. demand increases.

    d. quantity supplied increases.

18. Market supply is the

    a. sum of the minimum prices that each business is willing to accept for each quantity.

    b. sum of the quantities supplied by all businesses at each price.

    c. maximum amount each business is willing to accept for each quantity.

    d. maximum price each business will charge for each quantity.

19. A market has 10 identical businesses. When the price is $50, one business's quantity supplied is 70 units and market supply is

    a. 3500 units.

    b. 500 units.

    c. 700 units.

    d. 70 units.

20. When reading a supply curve as a marginal cost curve, each

    a. price tells you the quantity supplied at that price.

    b. price tells you the supply at that price.

    c. quantity tells you the maximum price business will charge for that unit.

    d. quantity tells you the minimum price business will accept to supply that unit.

Apply...

10. In the circular flow model, individuals in households are suppliers in input markets. The most common service we all supply is our labour — our ability to work. This question is about your labour supply choices.

a. Key 1— Choose only when additional benefits are greater than additional opportunity costs — also applies to choices about how many hours to work. What are the additional benefits of working more hours? What are the additional opportunity costs?

_____

_____

_____

_____

b. You normally work 10 hours a week at a part-time job paying $15 per hour, but your boss calls you in a panic and begs you to work as many hours next week as possible. The timing is terrible, as you have two tests, and your out-of-town best friend is coming soon for the only visit you will have in months. But the boss offers you double time of $30 per hour. What happens to the number of hours you choose to supply working? What non-work activities would you give up? [No right answers, just personal choices.]

_____

_____

_____

_____

_____

c. If the boss offers you triple time of $45 per hour, what happens to the number of hours you choose to supply working? What additional, different non-work activities would you give up?

_____

_____

_____

_____

d. Generally, as the price paid for your labour rises, what happens to the quantity of hours you are willing to supply? As you give up alternative uses of your time, do you give up the most valuable activities first, or the least valuable activities? Do your answers show the pattern of increasing marginal opportunity cost that Paola's Piercing and Fingernail Parlour (LO1 of this chapter) experiences in increasing the quantity of piercings supplied? Explain.

_____

_____

_____

_____

_____

_____

Apply...

11. This question is about supply.

a. State the Law of Supply. What are two reasons rising prices create incentives for increased quantity supplied?

_____

_____

_____

_____

b. There are two ways to read a supply curve. Explain how to read a supply curve as a supply curve. Which reason behind the law of supply is associated with the supply curve reading?

_____

_____

_____

_____

c. Explain how to read a supply curve as a marginal cost curve. Which reason behind the law of supply is associated with the marginal cost reading?

_____

_____

_____

_____

What Can Change Supply?

 Explain the difference between a change in quantity supplied and a change in supply, and list six factors that can change supply.

Quantity Supplied versus Supply

Supply summarizes all influences on business choices. Businesses' willingness to sell a particular product or service depends on profitability and marginal opportunity costs of production. But there are other factors that affect the willingness to produce a product or service. As long as those factors do not change, the law of supply holds true: If the price of a product or service rises, the quantity supplied increases.

But when change happens, economists distinguish between two kinds of change shown in Figure 9:

- If the price of a product or service changes, that affects *quantity supplied*. This is represented graphically by a movement along an unchanged supply curve.

- If anything else changes, that affects *supply*. This is represented graphically by a shift of the entire supply curve.

Figure 9 Changes in Quantity Supplied versus a Change in Supply

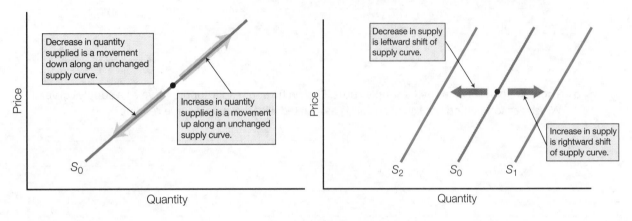

a) Change in Quantity Supplied

b) Change in Supply

Quantity supplied is a much more limited term than *supply*. Only a change in price changes *quantity supplied*. A change in any other influence on business choice changes *supply*.

Six Ways to Change Supply and Shift the Supply Curve

There are six important factors that can change market supply — business willingness to produce a product or service. They are

- Technology

- Environment

- Prices of inputs

- Prices of related products or services produced

- Expected future prices

- Number of businesses

Technology   A new technology increases productivity and decreases costs. At any price for a product, businesses supply a greater quantity because they make more profits. Or, for any quantity, marginal opportunity costs of production are lower, so businesses will accept a lower price for producing the same quantity.

Any increase in businesses' willingness to supply at any price is called an **increase in supply** — a rightward shift of the supply curve. Any decrease in businesses' willingness to supply is called a **decrease in supply** — a leftward shift of the supply curve.

Environment   Bad or good environmental changes — droughts, storms, earthquakes, global warming — can have an effect on supply. Droughts destroy crops, decreasing market supply and shifting the supply curve leftward. Good weather conditions produce bumper crops, increasing market supply and shifting the supply curve rightward.

Price of Inputs   If electricity prices fall, a business's energy costs fall. At any price for its products, a business earns higher profits and will supply more. Lower input prices increase market supply and shift the supply curve rightward.

Businesses must pay inputs a price that matches the best opportunity cost of the input owner. If wages are rising elsewhere, a business must raise wages to attract workers. Higher wages or other input prices means higher costs, and, at any price, lower profits. Market supply decreases. The supply curve shifts leftward.

Prices of Related Products and Services   Businesses can often use their inputs to produce more than one product or service. Paola's Parlour produces piercings and fingernail sets — those are related services because they use the same inputs. If the price of fingernail sets falls from $20 to $10 per set, Paola will shift inputs out of fingernails and into piercings, as relative profits are now higher in piercings. Lower prices for a related product or service increase the supply of the alternative product or service. The supply curve of the alternative (piercings) shifts rightward.

Expected Future Prices   A fall in the expected future price of a product or service increases supply today — today's supply curve for that product or service shifts rightward. An expected future price rise decreases supply today — today's supply curve shifts leftward.

Number of Businesses   An increase in the number of businesses increases market supply — the supply curve shifts rightward. A decrease in the number of businesses decreases market supply — the supply curve shifts leftward.

Figure 10 summarizes the differences between the law of supply (focusing on quantity supplied and movements along the supply curve) and the factors that change supply (and shift the supply curve).

Figure 10   Law of Supply and Changes in Supply

The Law of Supply *The quantity supplied of a product or service*	
Decreases if:	*Increases if:*
• price of the product or service falls	• price of the product or service rises

Changes in Supply *The supply for a product or service*	
Decreases if:	*Increases if:*
• _____	• technology improves
• environmental change harms production	• environment change helps production
• price of an input rises	• price of an input falls
• price of a related product or service rises	• price of a related product or service falls
• expected future price rises	• expected future price falls
• number of businesses decreases	• number of businesses increases

Why Bother Distinguishing between Quantity Supplied and Supply?

The average price of an ultrabook computer in Canada fell from around $2000 in 2010 to under $500 in 2016. But the quantity of ultrabook computers businesses sold increased. Does that disprove the "law of supply"? If nothing else changed during those years except the price of ultrabooks, the answer would be yes. The law of supply states that if the price of a product falls, the quantity supplied decreases, *as long as other factors besides price do not change.* But many things besides price also changed, including technological improvements in computer chips and falling input prices. Using the marginal cost reading of an increase in supply, at any quantity supplied, businesses were willing to accept a lower price because marginal opportunity costs of production were lower.

The effect of the increase in supply outweighed the price effect of the decrease in quantity supplied.

The distinction between quantity supplied and supply is the economist's equivalent of a controlled experiment. The law of supply holds constant all other factors than the price of the product to isolate the effect of a change in price on quantity supplied. When other factors change, we will use the shifts of the supply curve to analyze the effect of those factors.

 Practice...

21. Which factor does *not* change supply?

    a. prices of inputs

    b. expected future prices

    c. price of the supplied product or service

    d. number of businesses

22. The supply of a product or service increases with a(n)

    a. improvement in technology producing it.

    b. rise in the price of a related product or service produced.

    c. rise in the price of an input.

    d. rise in the expected future price of the product or service.

23. The furniture industry switches to using particleboard (glued wood chips) rather than real wood, reducing costs. This

    a. decreases supply.

    b. increases supply.

    c. does not change furniture supply.

    d. effect on supply depends on demand.

24. Which factor changes supply?

    a. income

    b. environmental change

    c. number of consumers

    d. price of a complement

25. Popeye's Parlour supplies both piercing and tattoo services. Higher prices for piercings cause Popeye's

    a. quantity supplied of tattoos to increase.

    b. quantity supplied of tattoos to decrease.

    c. supply of tattoos to increase.

    d. supply of tattoos to decrease.

 **Apply...**

12. Watch the video (http://tinyurl.com/flextext-robots) about an army of noodle-shaving robots invading restaurants in China. Here are questions for discussion:

    - What created the incentive for the invention of the robots?
    - How do you represent the invention of the robots using a supply curve?
    - Explain two ways to read the supply curve for meals with noodles, comparing supply before and after the invention.
    - Will robots cause unemployment for workers?

13. You have two part-time jobs, babysitting and pizza delivery. After younger babysitters start working for less, babysitting clients pay only $10 instead of $15 per hour. What happens to your supply of hours for delivering pizzas? Explain.

    _____

    _____

    _____

    _____

14. Your friend Pablo opens up a tattoo parlour because he thinks body art is a profitable industry. He is trying to forecast how different factors in the industry would affect supply in the market for tattoos. He knows you are taking a course in economics and asks you to verify whether his predictions are true or false. Explain any false prediction.

    a. The entry of new businesses into the industry will increase supply.
       True / False

    b. An increase in the minimum wage will increase supply.
       True / False

    c. A rise in the price of piercings (a related service) will reduce supply of tattoos.
       True / False

    d. An improvement in tattoo technology will increase supply.
       True / False

    e. A rise in the price of tattoos will increase supply.
       True / False

KNOW...

Summary of Learning Objectives

1. Consumers' willingness to pay depends on **marginal benefits**, not total benefits. Marginal benefits change with circumstances. The price at which businesses are willing to supply depends on **marginal costs**. Marginal costs are ultimately **opportunity costs**, and change with circumstances.

2. The **demand curve** combines two forces that determine quantity demanded — switch to substitutes, and willingness and ability to pay. The **law of demand** is that as price rises, quantity demanded decreases. The demand curve can be read as a demand curve and as a marginal benefit curve.

3. **Quantity demanded** changes only with a change in price — a movement along an unchanged demand curve. All other influences on consumer demand change **demand**. An **increase in demand** shifts the demand curve rightward, a **decrease in demand** shifts the demand curve leftward. Five factors that change demand are preferences, prices of related products, income, expected future prices, and number of consumers.

4. The **supply curve** combines two forces that determine quantity supplied — the desire for more profits, and the need to cover increasing marginal opportunity costs of production. The **law of supply** is that as price rises, quantity supplied increases. The supply curve can be read as a supply curve and as a marginal cost curve.

5. **Quantity supplied** changes only with a change in price — a movement along an unchanged supply curve. All other influences on business willingness to produce change **supply**. An **increase in supply** shifts the supply curve rightward, a **decrease in supply** shifts the supply curve leftward. Six factors that change supply are technology, environment, prices of inputs, prices of related products or services produced, expected future prices, and number of businesses.

Key Terms

complements: products or services used together to satisfy the same want

decrease in demand: decrease in consumers' willingness and ability to pay; leftward shift of demand curve

decrease in supply: decrease in businesses' willingness to produce; leftward shift of supply curve

demand: consumers' willingness and ability to pay for a particular product or service

demand curve: shows the relationship between price and quantity demanded, other things remaining the same

increase in demand: increase in consumers' willingness and ability to pay; rightward shift of demand curve

increase in supply: increase in businesses' willingness to produce; rightward shift of supply curve

inferior goods: products or services you buy less of when your income increases

law of demand: if the price of a product or services rises, quantity demanded decreases, other things remaining the same

law of supply: if the price of a product or services rises, quantity supplied increases, other things remaining the same

marginal benefit: additional benefit from a choice, changing with circumstances

marginal cost: additional opportunity cost of increasing quantity supplied, changing with circumstances

market demand: sum of demands of all individuals willing and able to buy a particular product or service

market supply: sum of supplies of all businesses willing to produce a particular product or service

normal goods: products or services you buy more of when your income increases

opportunity cost: cost of best alternative given up

preferences: your wants and their intensities

quantity demanded: amount you actually plan to buy at a given price

quantity supplied: amount you actually plan to supply at a given price

substitutes: products or services used in place of each other to satisfy the same want

supply: businesses' willingness to produce a particular product or service because price covers all opportunity costs

supply curve: shows the relationship between price and quantity supplied, other things remaining the same

Answers to Practice

1. **c**   After paying fixed fee, marginal cost of each additional plate is constant and equals zero.

2. **d**   Reverse of Key 1 — don't choose when marginal costs are greater than marginal benefits.

3. **a**   Price depends on marginal benefits, not total benefits.

4. **b**   If all inputs are equally productive, marginal cost is constant.

5. **c**   As inputs switch between tasks, no changes in opportunity costs.

6. **d**   Intensities of your wants.

7. **b**   *Give up* includes money, time, and effort.

8. **c**   With switch to cheaper substitutes, quantity demanded decreases.

9. **b**   Definition of substitutes.

10. **c**   Demand requires you to be willing *and able* to pay. Concern about the environment probably decreases your willingness to buy (pay for) a car.

11. **c**   Other answers are about *quantity demanded*.

12. **d**   Lowering prices moves along the demand curve. Other quotations are about changes in *demand* — shifts of the demand curve.

13. **d**   **a** true for inferior goods; **b** true for normal goods.

14. **b**   Cars and tires are complements.

15. **a** Price only affects quantity demanded. Change in income changes demand.

16. **a** Businesses want higher profits. High prices don't mean high profits if costs are also high.

17. **d** Rising prices increase quantity supplied, not supply, and decrease quantity demanded, not demand.

18. **b** Definition. Supply curve shows *minimum* prices businesses willing to accept.

19. **c** Adding 70 units for each of 10 businesses gives a quantity supplied of 700 units at the $50 price.

20. **d** Starting at a quantity, read a marginal cost curve up and over.

21. **c** Price changes quantity supplied.

22. **a** Only **a** shifts supply curve rightward. Other answers shift supply curve leftward.

23. **b** Rightward shift of supply curve.

24. **b** Other factors change demand.

25. **d** Piercings and tattoos are products related in production.

3

The Demand and Supply Model

LEARNING OBJECTIVES

L01 Describe what markets do and explain how shortages and surpluses affect market prices.

L02 Summarize how equilibrium prices match quantity demanded and quantity supplied and illustrate Adam Smith's concept of the invisible hand.

L03 Use the demand and supply model to predict how a change in demand or a change in supply affects equilibrium prices and quantities.

L04 Predict how combined changes in demand and supply affect equilibrium prices and quantities, and describe the modelling technique of comparative statics.

L05 Demonstrate the efficiency of markets using the concepts of consumer surplus and producer surplus.

LEARN...

Have you ever organized a milestone birthday party (20th, 50th, 80th?) and felt like it was a miracle everything worked out? There are so many details to coordinate — who's helping with the food, who's decorating the cake, who's tending bar, and what about toilet paper? Now imagine organizing one day in the life of Toronto. Think about the millions of consumers who each make hundreds of decisions about what to eat or which headphones to buy. Think about the thousands of businesses that decide what to produce, where to find inputs, who to hire. Somehow, businesses produce just about everything consumers want to buy — for a price. With no one in charge, it seems miraculous. How are all those billions of decisions coordinated so that you (and everyone else) can find the food you want for breakfast, the headphones you want at the electronics store, let alone water, jobs, gas, and places to live?

If all that doesn't seem enough of a miracle, consider that the coordination problem is a fast-moving target. Mexican food becomes fashionable, condos replace houses, new immigrants arrive with different tastes — and yet businesses adjust, and we all continue to find the changing items we look for.

Markets and prices are the keys to these apparent miracles. As consumers, we each make smart choices in our own interests. Businesses make smart choices in pursuit of profits. Markets, when they work well, create incentives that coordinate the right products and services being produced in the right quantities and at the right locations to satisfy our wants.

You will use the demand and supply model to understand how markets form prices. Those prices provide signals and incentives coordinating the choices of consumers and businesses. Whether you are trying to understand the decisions in a market economy, or just trying to get ahead in life, the demand and supply model is a powerful tool to help you make smart choices.

Price Signals from Combining Demand and Supply

L01 Describe what markets do and explain how shortages and surpluses affect market prices.

Markets Mix Competition and Cooperation

A **market** is not a place or a thing: It's a process — the interactions between buyers and sellers. Markets exist wherever there is a process of competing bids (from buyers or demanders) and offers (from sellers or suppliers). All markets contain a negotiation between a buyer and a seller that results in an exchange.

Markets are an unlikely mix of competition and cooperation. Buyers compete against each other trying to get the same product. Sellers compete with other sellers for customers by offering a lower price or higher quality.

When there is a voluntary exchange between a buyer and a seller, both sides cooperate and end up better off. A buyer only demands a product if the marginal benefit is at least as great as the price — the buyer's marginal opportunity cost. A seller only supplies a product if the price covers at least the marginal opportunity cost. "Better off" doesn't require the buyer to get the lowest price, or the seller to get the highest price. Any price for a product that is lower than the marginal benefit of the buyer and higher than the marginal opportunity cost of the seller benefits both buyers and sellers.

Where Do Prices Come From?

Prices are the outcome of a market process of competing bids and offers. But why do most stores sell Gatorade for $3 a bottle, or doughnuts for 99 cents? Where do these prices come from? Why do prices settle at particular numbers? The economist's answer to these questions is that prices come from the interaction of demand and supply in markets with appropriate property rights.

Paradoxically, the best way to understand why prices settle at particular numbers is to look at what happens in markets when prices have *not* settled. Figure 1 combines the market demand and supply curves for piercings.

Figure 1   Market Demand and Supply for Piercings

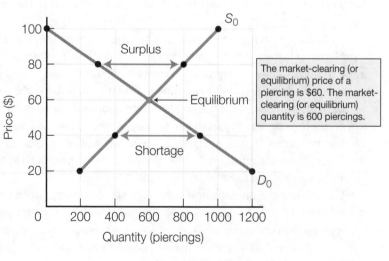

Price	Quantity Demanded	Quantity Supplied	Shortage (−) or Surplus (+)
$ 20	1200	200	−1000
$ 40	900	400	−500
$ 60	600	600	0
$ 80	300	800	+500
$100	0	1000	+1000

The market-clearing (or equilibrium) price of a piercing is $60. The market-clearing (or equilibrium) quantity is 600 piercings.

We know from the law of demand that consumers prefer lower prices, and we know from the law of supply that businesses prefer higher prices. How do prices get set in a way that combines these opposite goals?

Shortages and Frustrated Buyers   In Figure 1, what if the market price of piercings were $40? Consumers want to buy 900 piercings, but Paola and other piercing parlours are only willing to supply 400 piercings. There are 500 frustrated buyers (900 – 400 = 500) who are willing and able to pay $40 but can't get a parlour to do the piercing. This is a **shortage**, where quantity demanded exceeds quantity supplied. In markets with shortages, or **excess demand**, consumers experience long lineups and out-of-stock items at stores. Businesses experience products flying off the shelves. On the graph, the horizontal distance between the supply and demand curves at the price of $40 represents that shortage of 500 piercings. This is the red arrow labelled *shortage*.

Shortages encourage competition among buyers. The consumers who most want the piercing will be willing to pay a bit more than $40, rather than being left with nothing. Shortages create pressure for prices to rise. Rising prices then provide signals and incentives for businesses to increase quantity supplied, and for consumers to decrease quantity demanded, eliminating the shortage.

Surpluses and Frustrated Sellers   Instead of $40, what if the market price of piercings were $80 in Figure 1? Consumers want to buy only 300 piercings, but piercing parlours are eagerly willing to supply 800 piercings. There are 500 unsold piercings (800 – 300 = 500) and frustrated sellers. This is a **surplus**, where quantity supplied exceeds quantity demanded. In markets with surpluses, or **excess supply**, businesses experience underemployed inputs and unsold products. Those consumers willing and able to buy at the higher price experience their choice of where to buy and sellers who are eager to please. On the graph, the horizontal distance between the demand and supply curves at the price of $80 represents that surplus of 500 piercings. This is the blue arrow labelled *surplus*.

Surpluses encourage competition among sellers. The businesses that are most efficient or desperate for sales will cut their prices rather than be faced with idle workers and no revenues. Surpluses create pressure for prices to fall. Falling prices then provide signals and incentives for businesses to decrease quantity supplied, and for consumers to increase quantity demanded, eliminating the surplus.

Self-Interest at Work

What is remarkable about all of these price and quantity adjustments is that no consumer or business needs to know anything about anyone's personal wants or production capabilities. Prices serve as signals to buyers and sellers, and all anyone has to do is consider his or her own self-interest. As long as there is an imbalance between quantity demanded and quantity supplied, prices adjust and send signals for consumers and businesses to change their smart choices. As a byproduct of all these self-interested individual decisions made by complete strangers, markets provide the products and services we want.

Practice...

1. The place where buyers and sellers meet is called a(n)

    a. store.

    b. economy.

    c. market.

    d. party.

2. Voluntary exchange happens in a market when the

    a. price is less than the marginal opportunity cost of the seller.

    b. price equals or exceeds the marginal opportunity cost of the buyer.

    c. marginal benefit for the buyer is less than the price.

    d. marginal benefit for the buyer exceeds the price.

3. If a market is not at the market-clearing price,

    a. prices adjust.

    b. prices send signals for consumers and businesses to change their smart choices.

    c. quantities adjust.

    d. all of the above.

4. When the price is too high we see

    a. surpluses.

    b. frustrated buyers.

    c. excess demand.

    d. empty store shelves.

5. A shortage is the amount by which quantity

    a. supplied exceeds quantity demanded.

    b. demanded exceeds quantity supplied.

    c. supplied exceeds the equilibrium quantity.

    d. demanded exceeds the equilibrium quantity.

 Apply...

1. You are negotiating over the price of a new car with a car dealer. Explain how this process contains both cooperation and competition.

2. Apu wants to set the market-clearing equilibrium price, so he surveys all three families on his street to determine how many cappuccinos per day they are willing to buy at different prices. He gives them four price options. Their answers are summarized on the following table.

   a. What is the market quantity demanded for each price? Fill in the table.

Price per Iced Capuccino	Flanders Family Quantity Demanded	Van Houten Family Quantity Demanded	Simpson Family Quantity Demanded	Market Quantity Demanded
$1	2	5	5	
$2	1	3	4	
$3	0	1	3	
$4	0	0	2	

   Apu also estimates his costs and determines how many iced cappuccinos he is willing to sell. Apu's supply is summarized in the following table:

Price per Iced Capuccino	Apu's Quantity Supplied
$1	7
$2	8
$3	9
$4	10

   b. What is the market-clearing, or equilibrium, price? Explain.

   c. If Apu sets the price higher than the equilibrium price,
      i.   will there be a shortage or surplus in the market?
      ii. will there be pressure for the price to rise or fall? Explain.

to be continued

Apply...

continued

    d. If Apu sets the price lower than the equilibrium price,

        i. will there be a shortage or surplus in the market?

        ii. will there be pressure for the price to rise or fall? Explain.

3. Most provincial parks charge a fixed price for a camping permit, and allow you to reserve specific campsites in advance. By the time the summer holiday weekends arrive, all the permits are usually taken. There is excess demand but no price adjustment. Suggest a pricing system for provincial parks that allows them to take advantage of the higher demand for campsites on holiday weekends. Your system should explain who is competing and who is cooperating.

Equilibrium Prices and Adam Smith's Invisible Hand

 Summarize how equilibrium prices match quantity demanded and quantity supplied and illustrate Adam Smith's concept of the invisible hand.

The price that coordinates quantity demanded and quantity supplied is so important that economists have two names for it.

Market-Clearing Price

Market-clearing price is one name for the price that equalizes quantity demanded and quantity supplied. At the market-clearing price, there are no frustrated buyers or sellers. There is a match for every buyer and seller. All go home happy. Everyone who volunteers to exchange $60 for a piercing in Figure 1 (consumers buying and businesses selling) is better off, or they wouldn't have bought and sold.

Equilibrium Price

The second name is the **equilibrium price**. *Equilibrium* is a term from physics that means a balance of forces resulting in an unchanging outcome. The equilibrium price exactly balances forces of competition and cooperation to coordinate the smart choices of consumers and businesses. At the equilibrium price, there is no tendency for change, and no incentives for anyone — consumers or businesses — to change their own self-interested, smart decisions. Everyone has done the best they can in exchanging, given the wants and resources they started with.

The Invisible Hand

The fact that consumers find businesses have produced just about everything they want to buy, with no one in charge, and that billions of decisions get coordinated is due to the interaction of demand and supply in markets with appropriate property rights. The law of demand is shorthand for the smart choices of consumers. The law of supply is shorthand for the smart choices of businesses. Equilibrium prices and quantities result when smart choices are coordinated. The forces of competition are balanced with the forces of cooperation. Price signals in markets create incentives so that while each person acts only in her own self-interest, the unintended consequence is the coordinated production of all the products and services we want.

Perhaps the most famous phrase in economics that describes this outcome is Adam Smith's *invisible hand* in his 1776 book, *The Wealth of Nations*:

> When an individual makes choices, "he intends only his own gain, and he is in this . . . led by an invisible hand to promote an end which was no part of his intention. . . . By pursuing his own interest he frequently promotes that of the society more effectually than when he really intends to promote it."

The miracle is that markets channel self-interest as though "by an invisible hand" so that society produces the products and services we want, without the government doing anything beyond setting the rules of the game.

 ## Practice...

6. A price at which there are no shortages and no surpluses is a

    a. maximum price.

    b. minimum price.

    c. affordable price.

    d. market-clearing price.

7. Surpluses are eliminated by

    a. allowing prices to rise.

    b. allowing prices to fall.

    c. increasing quantity supplied.

    d. decreasing quantity demanded.

8. Market-clearing prices

    a. are set by the visible hand of government.

    b. scare away all consumers from the market.

    c. scare away all businesses from the market.

    d. balance the forces of competition and cooperation.

9. In equilibrium,

    a. the price consumers are wiling to pay equals the price suppliers are willing to accept.

    b. consumers would like to buy more at the current price.

    c. producers would like to sell more at the current price.

    d. the force of cooperation is stronger than the force of competition.

10. Price signals in markets

    a. require detailed information about preference and costs.

    b. coordinate the preferences of government officials.

    c. create incentives for producers to produce the products and services consumers want.

    d. lead consumers to favour the public interest rather than their private interests.

 **Apply…**

4. In an attempt to promote the social good of energy conservation, Toronto Hydro introduced the Peaksaver Program. Participating households received a $25 reward for allowing a "peaksaver" switch to be installed on their central air conditioners, which briefly turns off the air conditioner during peak demand times on hot summer days. Do you think the program would work without the $25 reward? Why or why not?

_____

_____

_____

_____

5. The table below shows the market for robotic rubber ducks.

Price	Quantity Demanded	Quantity Supplied
$40	500	300
$50	450	350
$60	400	400
$70	350	450
$80	300	500

a. If the price of a duck is $40, is there a shortage or a surplus? Of how many ducks? Explain who is frustrated, and how the forces of competition will change the smart choices of demanders and of suppliers.

_____

_____

_____

_____

b. If the price of a duck is $70, is there a shortage or a surplus? Of how many ducks? Explain who is frustrated, and how the forces of competition will change the smart choices of demander and of suppliers.

_____

_____

_____

_____

_____

Apply...

c. What is the equilibrium price? What is the equilibrium quantity?

_____

_____

_____

_____

6. Explain the idea of Adam Smith's *invisible hand*. Your explanation should illustrate the balance between the forces of competition and cooperation at equilibrium prices.

_____

_____

_____

_____

_____

What Happens to Equilibrium Prices and Quantities When Demand or Supply Change?

L03 Use the demand and supply model to predict how a change in demand or a change in supply affects equilibrium prices and quantities.

Even if markets settle at equilibrium prices and temporarily succeed in coordinating the plans of consumers and businesses, what happens when something changes? Will markets still be efficient?

Believe it or not, all stories so far about shortages, surpluses, mutually beneficial trades, and adjusting prices and quantities actually had very limited change. Yes, prices and quantities and smart decisions changed, but in the background I was holding constant the five major influences on demand and the six major influences on supply.

A demand curve isolates the relationship between price and quantity demanded by holding constant all other influences on consumers' choices — preferences, prices of related products, income, expected future prices, and number of consumers.

A supply curve isolates the relationship between price and quantity supplied by holding constant all other influences on businesses' choices — technology, environment, input prices, prices of related products produced, expected future prices, and number of businesses.

Instead of slogging through changes in each of the 11 influences, I have grouped them together — increases and decreases in demand, and increases and decreases in supply. Let's look at how these changes affect equilibrium prices and quantities. The starting point for each change is the equilibrium in the piercing market in Figure 1 on page 54.

Increases in Demand

Figure 2 shows an increase in demand.

Figure 2 Increase in Demand

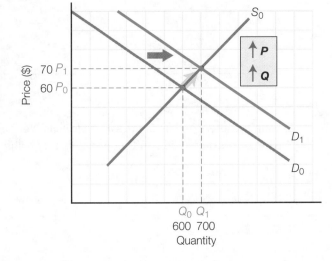

	Quantity Demanded		Quantity Supplied
Price	Original (D_0)	New (D_1)	(S_0)
$40	900 → 1150		400
$50	750 → 900		500
$60	600 → 850		600
$70	450 → 700		700
$80	300 → 550		800

The demand curve shifts rightward from D_0 to D_1. At every price, the new quantity demanded is 250 piercings *more* than the original quantity. At the original price of $60, there is now a shortage. Competition between consumers drives up the price, increasing the quantity supplied (a movement up along the unchanged supply curve). The equilibrium price rises ($\uparrow P$) from $60 to $70 and the equilibrium quantity increases ($\uparrow Q$) from 600 to 700. At the new equilibrium price, quantity demanded once again equals quantity supplied.

Decreases in Demand

Figure 3 shows a decrease in demand.

Figure 3 Decrease in Demand

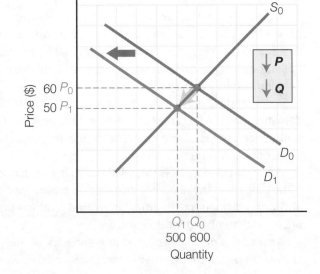

	Quantity Demanded		Quantity Supplied
Price	Original (D_0)	New (D_1)	(S_0)
$40	900 → 650		400
$50	750 → 500		500
$60	600 → 350		600
$70	450 → 200		700
$80	300 → 50		800

The demand curve shifts leftward from D_0 to D_1. At every price, the new quantity demanded is 250 piercings *less* than the original quantity. At the original price of $60, there is now a surplus. Competition between businesses for scarce customers drives down the price, decreasing the quantity supplied (a movement down along the unchanged supply curve). The equilibrium price falls ($\downarrow P$) from $60 to $50 and the equilibrium quantity decreases ($\downarrow Q$) from 600 to 500. At the new equilibrium price, quantity demanded once again equals quantity supplied.

Increases in Supply

Figure 4 shows an increase in supply.

Figure 4   Increase in Supply

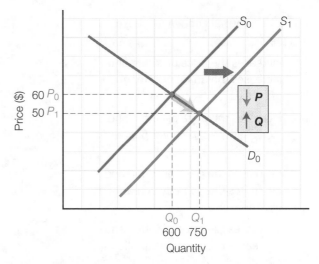

Price	Quantity Demanded (D_0)	Quantity Supplied		
		Original (S_0)		New (S_1)
$40	900	400	→	650
$50	750	500	→	750
$60	600	600	→	850
$70	450	700	→	950
$80	300	800	→	1050

The supply curve shifts rightward from S_0 to S_1. At every price, the new quantity supplied is 250 piercings *more* than the original quantity. At the original price of $60, there is now a surplus. Competition between businesses for scarce customers drives down the price, increasing the quantity demanded (a movement down along the unchanged demand curve). The equilibrium price falls ($\downarrow P$) from $60 to $50 and the equilibrium quantity increases ($\uparrow Q$) from 600 to 750. At the new equilibrium price, quantity demanded once again equals quantity supplied.

Decreases in Supply

Figure 5 shows a decrease in supply.

Figure 5   Decrease in Supply

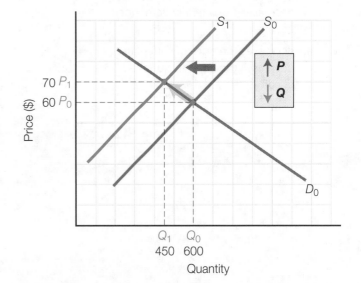

Price	Quantity Demanded (D_0)	Quantity Supplied		
		Original (S_0)		New (S_1)
$40	900	400	→	150
$50	750	500	→	250
$60	600	600	→	350
$70	450	700	→	450
$80	300	800	→	550

The supply curve shifts leftward from S_0 to S_1. At every price, the new quantity supplied is 250 piercings *less* than the original quantity. At the original price of $60, there is now a shortage. Competition between consumers drives up the price, decreasing the quantity demanded (a movement up along the unchanged demand curve). The equilibrium price rises ($\uparrow P$) from $60 to $70 and the equilibrium quantity decreases ($\downarrow Q$) from 600 to 450. At the new equilibrium price, quantity demanded once again equals quantity supplied.

 # Practice...

11. Coffee is a normal good. A decrease in income

   a. increases the price of coffee and increases the quantity demanded of coffee.

   b. increases the price of coffee and increases the quantity supplied of coffee.

   c. decreases the price of coffee and decreases the quantity demanded of coffee.

   d. decreases the price of coffee and decreases the quantity supplied of coffee.

12. An increase in the price of Pepsi (a substitute for coffee)

   a. increases the price of coffee and increases the quantity demanded of coffee.

   b. increases the price of coffee and increases the quantity supplied of coffee.

   c. decreases the price of coffee and decreases the quantity demanded of coffee.

   d. decreases the price of coffee and decreases the quantity supplied of coffee.

13. Farmland can be used to produce either cattle or corn. If demand for cattle increases,

   a. demand for corn increases.

   b. supply of corn increases.

   c. demand for corn decreases.

   d. supply of corn decreases.

14. The equilibrium price falls when supply

   a. increases or demand decreases.

   b. decreases or demand increases.

   c. increases or demand increases.

   d. decreases or demand decreases.

15. If bus fares fall but fewer people are riding the bus, it is likely that

   a. supply decreased.

   b. supply increased.

   c. demand decreased.

   d. demand increased.

 Apply...

7. Watch the SourceFed video (http://tinyurl.com/FlexText-bacon) containing two separate explanations for rising bacon prices. Here are questions for discussion:

    *   Draw a demand and supply diagram representing the initial equilibrium in the pork/bacon market.

    *   Using your diagram, how would you model the most important explanation for rising bacon prices? What is the most important factor that changes either the demand or supply curve?

    *   Draw another diagram, and model the other explanation [*HINT: Epic Mealtime*] for rising bacon prices. What is the most important factor that changes either the demand or supply curve?

        Instructor — you can do this exercise for the class as a whole, or break the students into small groups and have each group work out the analysis and report back.

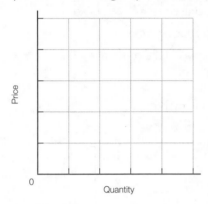 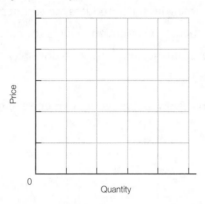

8. A tax on crude oil raises the cost of the most important input used to produce gasoline. A supporter of the tax claims that it will not raise the price of gasoline using the following argument. "While the price of gasoline may rise initially, that price increase will cause the demand for gasoline to decrease, which will push the price back down." What is wrong with this argument?

    _____

    _____

    _____

    _____

    _____

to be continued

Apply...

continued

9. The market for wine in Canada is initially in equilibrium. Beer is a close substitute for wine; cheese and wine are complements. Use demand and supply models to analyze the effect of each of the following (separate) events on the equilibrium price and quantity in the Canadian wine market. Assume that all other factors remain unchanged except for the event listed. For each of these five events, explain what happens to the equilibrium price (rises, falls, remains the same, or unable to predict) and the equilibrium quantity (increases, decreases, remains the same, or unable to predict).

    a. The income of consumers increases (wine is a normal good).

    b. Early frost destroys a large part of the world grape crop.

    c. A new churning invention reduces the cost of producing cheese.

    d. A new fermentation invention reduces the cost of producing wine.

    e. A new government study links wine drinking and increased heart disease.

    [Use the graphs below to draw your five models of the wine market.]

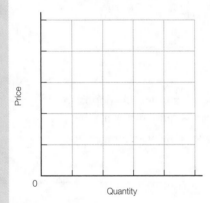
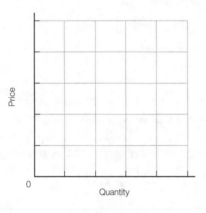
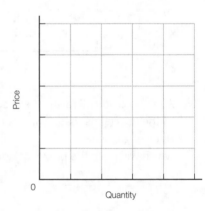

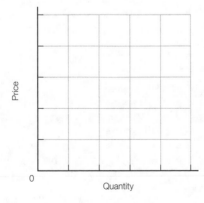
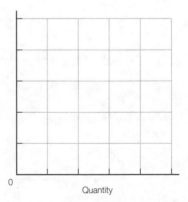

Predicting the Effects of Combined Changes in Demand and Supply

LO4 Predict how combined changes in demand and supply affect equilibrium prices and quantities, and describe the modelling technique of comparative statics.

Once you allow both demand and supply to change at the same time, the effects on the equilibrium price and quantity are a bit more complicated. Figure 6 shows those combined effects. P_0 and Q_0 are the original price and quantity before the changes. P_1 and Q_1 are the new equilibrium price and quantity after the changes in both demand and supply.

In all combinations of changes in both demand and supply, we can still predict the effect on *either* the equilibrium price or the equilibrium quantity. But there is not enough information to predict the effects on *both* price and quantity.

Figure 6   The Effects of Combined Changes in Demand and Supply

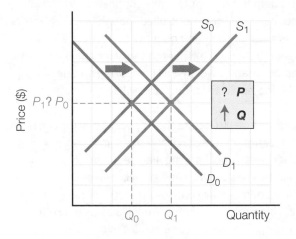

a) Increase in Both Demand and Supply

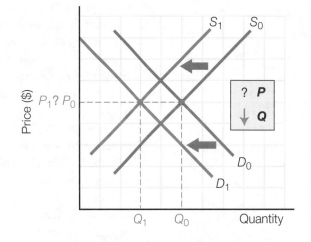

b) Decrease in Both Demand and Supply

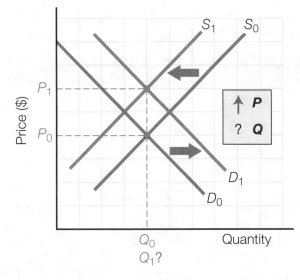

c) Increase in Demand and Decrease in Supply

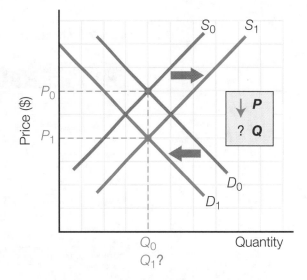

d) Decrease in Demand and Increase in Supply

Economists Do It with Models

All of these simple demand and supply graphs are models. They focus our attention on the reasons why mutually beneficial trades happen in a market, and select just enough information to predict where equilibrium prices and quantities will end up. As well, the models tell us when we do not have enough information to make predictions.

In the real world, all eleven factors that influence consumers' and businesses' choices are changing constantly. Demand and supply graphs are like controlled laboratory experiments. They hold all influences constant except one (or two), so we can see the effect of that influence alone.

Start in Equilibrium When I draw demand and supply curves that intersect at price P_0 and quantity Q_0, I am holding constant all eleven factors that can shift the demand or supply curves and influence consumers' and businesses' choices. At the original equilibrium outcome, there is no tendency for change. This is our starting point.

One Change at a Time In each "thought experiment" in Figures 2 – 5, I change one factor that affects demand or supply, while continuing to hold all other influences constant. The results of these controlled thought experiments are the new equilibrium outcomes of price P_1 and quantity Q_1. At the new equilibrium outcome, once again there is no further tendency for change. Even in Figure 6, when two factors change, we are still comparing an original equilibrium outcome with a second equilibrium outcome, while continuing to hold all other influences constant.

This simplified way of using a model to isolate the impact of one (or two) factors in the economy is called **comparative statics** — the comparison of two equilibrium outcomes. Static means unchanging. Each equilibrium is static — there is no tendency for change. We start with one equilibrium outcome, change a single factor that affects demand or supply, and then compare it to the new equilibrium outcome. This simplified comparison allows us to predict changes in price and quantity, despite all of the complexities in the real world.

My favourite saying for this way of thinking is "Economists do it with models." Figure 7 summarizes all possible effects of changes in demand and supply.

Figure 7 Effects of Changes in Demand or Supply

Change	Shifts of Curves	Effect on Equilibrium Price	Effect on Equilibrium Quantity
Increase in Demand	Demand shifts rightward	↑	↑
Decrease in Demand	Demand shifts leftward	↓	↓
Increase in Supply	Supply shifts rightward	↓	↑
Decrease in Supply	Supply shifts leftward	↑	↓
Increase in Demand and Increase in Supply	Demand shifts rightward; Supply shifts rightward	Need exact numbers to predict outcome	↑
Decrease in Demand and Decrease in Supply	Demand shifts leftward; Supply shifts leftward	Need exact numbers to predict outcome	↓
Increase in Demand and Decrease in Supply	Demand shifts rightward; Supply shifts leftward	↑	Need exact numbers to predict outcome
Decrease in Demand and Increase in Supply	Demand shifts leftward; Supply shifts rightward	↓	Need exact numbers to predict outcome

Practice...

16. Which will cause prices to fall?
    a. demand increases and supply decreases
    b. demand increases and supply increases
    c. demand decreases and supply decreases
    d. demand decreases and supply increases

17. If demand increases and supply decreases, this leads to
    a. higher prices.
    b. lower prices.
    c. chaos.
    d. a shortage in the market.

18. A technological improvement lowers the cost of producing coffee. At the same time, preferences for coffee decrease. The *equilibrium quantity* of coffee
    a. increases.
    b. decreases.
    c. remains the same.
    d. increases or decreases, depending on the relative shifts of demand and supply curves.

19. If both demand and supply increase, the equilibrium price
    a. rises and the equilibrium quantity increases.
    b. falls and the equilibrium quantity increases.
    c. could rise or fall, and the equilibrium quantity increases.
    d. could rise or fall, and the equilibrium quantity decreases.

20. If the equilibrium price of boots falls, either the demand for boots
    a. decreased or the supply of boots decreased, or both.
    b. increased or the supply of boots increased, or both.
    c. decreased or the supply of boots increased, or both.
    d. increased or the supply of boots decreased, or both.

Apply...

10. Predicting changes in equilibrium prices and quantities is harder when both demand and supply change at the same time. You run a halal butcher shop in Ottawa and expect an increase in the number of Muslims in Ottawa who prefer halal meat. Rents for retail space are also falling all over town. Predict what will happen to the equilibrium price for halal meat. Predict what will happen to the equilibrium quantity. Explain your predictions.

_____

_____

_____

_____

_____

_____

11. The market for coffee is originally in equilibrium with demand curve D_0, supply curve S_0, equilibrium price P_0 and equilibrium quantity Q_0. On the graph, draw and label the original equilibrium.

    Two events happen at the same time. There is a rise in wages of coffee pickers and a rise in the price of tea (a substitute for coffee).

    a. On the graph, draw any shift(s) in the demand and supply curves. Label any shifted demand curve as D_1 and any shifted supply curve as S_1. Label the new equilibrium price as P_1 and the new equilibrium quantity as Q_1.

    Based on your demand and supply model, predict what happens to the equilibrium price and to the equilibrium quantity.

Price

0

Quantity

_____

_____

_____

    b. What is the name of the modelling technique for making your predictions? Explain this technique in words.

_____

_____

_____

_____

 **Apply…**

12. Over the past year, the equilibrium price of beachballs fell from $8 to $4, but the equilibrium quantity of beachballs sold in the market increased from 100 to 150. This kind of observation seems to disprove the law of supply.

    a. State the law of supply.

    _____

    _____

    _____

    b. To save the law of supply for beachballs, give an example of a change in one factor behind either the supply or the demand curve that could explain how a price fall could be followed by an increase in the quantity sold. Identify both the factor and the direction of change.

    _____

    _____

    _____

    c. Draw a simple demand and supply graph that shows the original equilibrium price and quantity for beachballs, the change caused by your example in part b, and the new equilibrium price and quantity.

        Use the numbers above in the question to label the coordinates of the original equilibrium price and quantity, and the coordinates of the new equilibrium price and quantity.

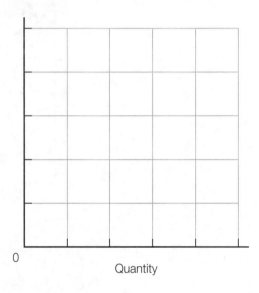

    d. Circle the correct answers. What happened in the beachball market was *caused by*

        a(n)   increase / decrease
        in   demand / quantity demanded / supply / quantity supplied

                    resulting in

        a(n)   increase / decrease
        in   demand / quantity demanded / supply / quantity supplied.

Consumer Surplus, Producer Surplus, and Efficiency

LO5 Demonstrate the efficiency of markets using the concepts of consumer surplus and producer surplus.

The demand and supply model allows us to predict changes in prices and quantities. We can also read demand and supply curves as marginal benefit and marginal cost curves. Focusing on marginal benefits and marginal costs allows us to measure the efficiency of market outcomes.

Consumer Surplus

Any market demand curve is also a marginal benefit curve. Figure 8 reproduces the demand curve from Figure 1 and labels it also as a marginal benefit (*MB*) curve.

Figure 8   Marginal Benefit and Consumer Surplus

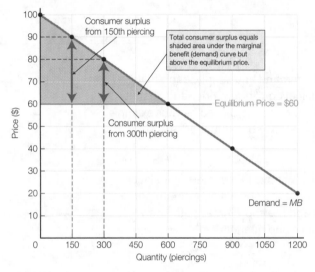

A *market* demand curve combines the willingness and ability to pay of *all* consumers in this market. Some consumers, with a high willingness and ability to pay, are located up at the top left of the demand curve. Others, with less willingness and ability to pay, are located further down along the demand curve.

To read the demand curve as a marginal benefit curve, start with a quantity and go up and over to see the maximum price someone is willing and able to pay. For the 150th piercing, someone is willing and able to pay $90. For the 300th piercing, someone is willing and able to pay $80.

At the equilibrium price in the market, everyone pays $60 for each piercing. But for each of the first 599 piercings, someone was willing and able to pay more. On the graph, that extra benefit is the vertical distance between the marginal benefit curve and the market price. Economists call this extra benefit **consumer surplus** — the difference between the amount a consumer is willing and able to pay, and the price actually paid. If we combine the consumer surplus for every piercing sold, the consumer surplus equals the green shaded area under the marginal benefit (demand) curve, but above the market price.

Producer Surplus

Any market supply curve is also a marginal cost curve. Figure 9 reproduces the supply curve from Figure 1 and labels it also as a marginal cost (*MC*) curve.

Figure 9   Marginal Cost and Producer Surplus

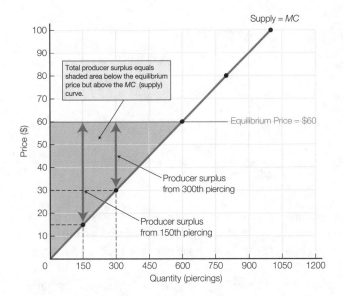

A *market* supply curve combines the supply decisions of *all* businesses in a market — the minimum prices businesses are willing to accept in order to supply piercings, covering all marginal opportunity costs of production. Businesses with low marginal opportunity costs are located down at the bottom of the supply curve. Others, with higher marginal opportunity costs, are located further up the supply curve.

To read the supply curve as a marginal cost curve, start with a quantity and go up and over to see the minimum price a business is willing to accept for producing that unit. For the 150th piercing, some business is willing to accept $15. For the 300th piercing, some business is willing to accept $30.

At the equilibrium price in the market, every business receives $60 for each piercing. But for each of the first 599 piercings, some business was willing to accept less. On the graph, that extra revenue above marginal cost is the vertical distance between the marginal cost curve and the market price. Economists call this extra benefit **producer surplus** — the difference between the amount a producer is willing to accept, and the price actually received. If we combine the producer surplus for every piercing sold, the producer surplus equals the blue shaded area below the market price but above the marginal cost (supply) curve.

Economic Efficiency

When Adam Smith's *invisible hand* works well, markets produce the products and services that consumers want, at competitive prices that are profitable for businesses, and everyone is happy. But happiness is relative. How do we know there isn't a better outcome out there? Consumer surplus and producer surplus are useful measures for comparing outcomes.

Figure 10, on the next page, combines the demand (marginal benefit) and the supply (marginal cost) curves from Figures 8 and 9.

Figure 10 Maximum Total Surplus

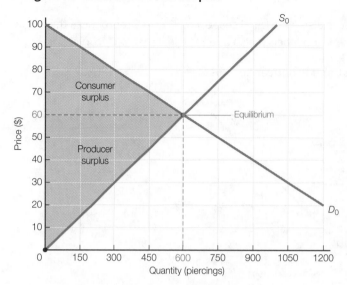

Combining the green area of consumer surplus with the blue area of producer surplus — the total shaded area — gives us the **total surplus**. The quantity that results in the "best" outcome is the quantity with the largest total surplus.

For every unit up to the 600th piercing, marginal benefit is greater than marginal cost. For each unit, there is some consumer willing and able to pay a price greater than the minimum price some producer needs to receive to be willing to supply it. At a price of $60, consumers and businesses both benefit from every unit produced. This is an **efficient market outcome**. Consumers buy only products and services where marginal benefit is greater than price. These products and services are produced at the lowest costs, and price just covers all opportunity costs of production. This is the outcome where the demand (marginal benefit) and supply (marginal cost) curves intersect.

Inefficient Outcomes

The only way to know if an efficient outcome is "best" is to compare it with other outcomes and to measure the total surplus. Figure 11 shows examples of inefficient outcomes that are not "best" and that have lower total surplus.

Figure 11 Inefficient Outcomes

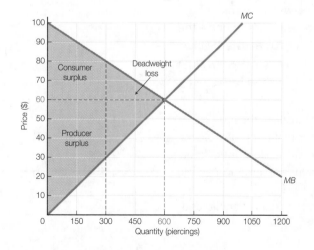

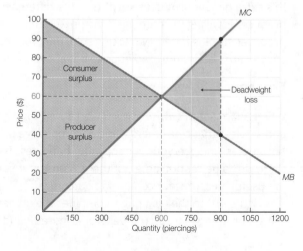

a) Inefficiency of Producing Too Little

b) Inefficiency of Producing Too Much

If output stopped at 300 units (graph a), the total area of consumer surplus (green) plus producer surplus (blue) is less than the total surplus for 600 units in Figure 10. The difference between the two areas of total surplus is the grey triangle labelled **deadweight loss**. The output of 300 units is inefficient because there are mutually beneficial trades that do not happen. Producing and selling all piercings between 300 and 600 would make consumers and producers better off because marginal benefits are greater than marginal costs.

If output continued beyond 600 to 900 units (graph b), there is a different deadweight loss from producing too much. For each unit beyond 600, marginal cost is greater than marginal benefit. This deadweight loss must be subtracted from the green consumer and blue producer surplus areas to calculate the total surplus for 900 units.

 Practice...

21. Consumer surplus is the

    a. difference between the amount a consumer is willing to accept and the price actually received.

    b. difference between the amount a consumer is willing and able to pay and the price actually paid.

    c. difference between the amount a consumer is willing and able to pay and the amount a producer is willing to accept.

    d. area under the marginal benefit curve.

22. Producer surplus is the area

    a. under the marginal benefit curve but above the marginal cost curve.

    b. under the marginal benefit curve but above the market price.

    c. below the market price but above the marginal cost curve.

    d. above the marginal cost curve.

23. For any quantity produced up to the efficient quantity, total surplus is the

    a. deadweight loss.

    b. area under the marginal benefit curve but above the market price.

    c. area above the marginal benefit curve but below the market price.

    d. area under the marginal benefit curve but above the marginal cost curve

24. If the quantity produced is more than the efficient market outcome,

    a. deadweight loss is eliminated.

    b. total surplus is greater than total surplus for the efficient market outcome.

    c. marginal cost is greater than marginal benefit.

    d. marginal benefit is greater than marginal cost.

25. In an efficient market outcome,

    a. products and services are produced at lowest cost.

    b. total surplus is the lowest.

    c. consumers buy only products and services where marginal benefit is less than price.

    d. deadweight loss is the highest.

Apply...

13. In the market for e-readers, at the prices of $40, $60, $80, $100, and $120, the following quantities are demanded: 2000, 1600, 1200, 800, and 600 units. The quantities supplied at those prices are: 400, 800, 1200, 1600, and 2000 units. Draw a graph of this market. For the 800th unit, what is the consumer surplus; what is the producer surplus?

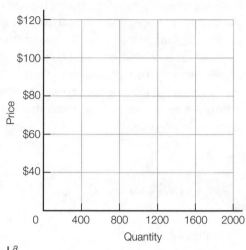

14. The figure shows the market for slugs. Note that the demand curve is also a marginal benefit curve, and the supply curve is also a marginal cost curve.

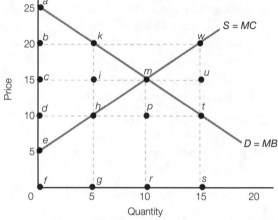

a. If the slugs market is efficient, describe the area of consumer surplus (use the labels of points around the edges of the area, e.g., area *abk*). Define consumer surplus without referring to an area.

_____

_____

_____

_____

b. If the slugs market is efficient, describe the area of producer surplus (use the labels of points around the edges of the area, e.g., area *abk*). Define producer surplus without referring to an area.

_____

_____

_____

c. If output is at *Q* = 5, describe the area of deadweight loss. Define deadweight loss.

_____

_____

_____

Apply...

d. If output stops at $Q = 5$, use the marginal benefit and marginal cost curves to describe the inefficiency that exists for a quantity like $Q = 6$.

_____

_____

_____

15. The figure shows the market for champagne. Note that the demand curve is also a marginal benefit curve, and the supply curve is also a marginal cost curve.

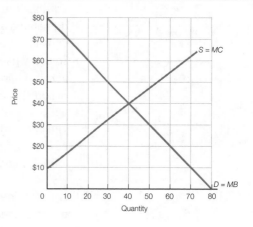

a. The champagne market is in equilibrium. Calculate the consumer surplus. Calculate the producer surplus. What is the total surplus?

_____

_____

_____

_____

b. What is the condition for an efficient market outcome?

_____

_____

_____

c. Suppose now that that there is overproduction in the champagne market and output is 60 bottles. Calculate the deadweight loss. What is the total surplus?

_____

_____

_____

_____

d.   How does total surplus compare to the answer in part a? Is the output of 60 bottles efficient?

_____

_____

_____

_____

KNOW...

Summary of Learning Objectives

1. **Markets** connect competition between buyers, competition between sellers, and cooperation between buyers and sellers. When there are **shortages**, competition between buyers drives prices up. When there are **surpluses**, competition between sellers drives prices down.

2. **Equilibrium prices** (or **market-clearing prices**) balance quantity demanded and quantity supplied, coordinating the smart choices of consumers and businesses. Price signals in markets create incentives, so that while each person acts only in her own self-interest, Adam Smith's invisible hand of competition produces the miracle of the ever-changing production of products and services we most want.

3. The demand and supply model allows us to predict the effects on equilibrium prices and quantities of a change in any of the five factors influencing demand or the six factors influencing supply.

4. For combined changes in demand and supply, we can predict the effect on *either* the equilibrium price or the equilibrium quantity. But there is not enough information to predict the effects on *both* price and quantity. All predictions of the demand and supply model use the technique of **comparative statics** to simulate a controlled laboratory experiment — comparing two equilibrium outcomes to isolate the effect of changing one (or two) factors at a time.

5. The concepts of **consumer surplus** and **producer surplus** are based on reading demand and supply curves as marginal benefit and marginal cost curves. An efficient market outcome has the largest **total surplus** — the sum of consumer surplus and producer surplus. Prices just cover all marginal opportunity costs of production, and consumers' marginal benefit equals businesses' marginal cost. An inefficient outcome has **deadweight loss**.

Key Terms

comparative statics: comparing two equilibrium outcomes to isolate the effect of changing one factor at a time

consumer surplus: the difference between the amount a consumer is willing and able to pay, and the price actually paid

deadweight loss: the decrease in total surplus compared to an economically efficient outcome

efficient market outcome: consumers buy only products and services where marginal benefit is greater than marginal cost; products and services produced at lowest cost, with price just covering all opportunity costs of production

equilibrium price: the price that equalizes quantity demanded and quantity supplied, balancing the forces of competition and cooperation, so that there is no tendency for change

excess demand (or shortage): quantity demanded exceeds quantity supplied

excess supply (or surplus): quantity supplied exceeds quantity demanded

market: the interaction between buyers and sellers

market-clearing price: the price that equalizes quantity demanded and quantity supplied

producer surplus: the difference between the amount a producer is willing to accept, and the price actually received

shortage (or excess demand): quantity demanded exceeds quantity supplied

surplus (or excess supply): quantity supplied exceeds quantity demanded

total surplus: consumer surplus plus producer surplus

Answers to Practice

1. **c** Definition.

2. **d** Price must cover marginal opportunity cost of seller and be less than marginal benefit for buyer.

3. **d** When prices change, so do smart choices and quantities.

4. **a** Excess supply and frustrated sellers.

5. **b** Horizontal distance between demand and supply curves at that price.

6. **d** Equilibrium price.

7. **b** Excess supply leads to price-cutting competition among sellers.

8. **d** Equilibrium is a balance of forces.

9. **a** No one wants to buy or sell more.

10. **c** Prices guide the *invisible hand*.

11. **d** Demand shifts leftward and fall in price moves down along unchanged supply curve.

12. **b** Demand shifts rightward and rise in price moves up along unchanged supply curve.

13. **d** Rise in cattle prices causes farmers to shift land from corn to cattle.

14. **a** Draw rightward shift of supply or leftward shift of demand.

15. **c** Leftward shift of demand causes fall in price and decrease in equilibrium quantity.

16. **d** Draw leftward shift of demand and rightward shift of supply.

17. **a** Draw rightward shift of demand and leftward shift of supply.

18. **d** Supply shifts rightward, demand shifts leftward, price definitely falls.

19. **c** See Figure 6a on page 67.

20. **c**   Leftward shift of demand or rightward shift of supply.

21. **b** Area under the marginal benefit curve and above the (market) price actually paid.

22. **c** Difference between the minimum price willing to accept and price actually received, for all units.

23. **d** Consumer surplus plus producer surplus.

24. **c** For any quantity greater than the equilibrium quantity, read up to the marginal cost and marginal benefit curves.

25. **a** Total surplus is highest, and consumers buy when *MB* > price.

4 From Microeconomics to Macroeconomics

LEARNING OBJECTIVES

L01 Explain how macroeconomics differs from microeconomics.

L02 Describe the fundamental macroeconomic question and the hands-off and hands-on positions on market failure, government failure, and government policy.

L03 Identify three key economic outcomes and five macroeconomic players whose choices produce those outcomes.

LEARN...

We are shifting our gaze from individual trees (microeconomics) to the whole forest (macroeconomics). Microeconomics looks at smart choices of individual consumers and businesses, while macroeconomics looks at the combined market outcomes of all of those individual choices.

According to Adam Smith's invisible hand, price signals in markets create incentives so that while each person (a focus on each tree) acts only in his self-interest, the unintended consequence is the production of all of the products and services we want (a healthy, growing forest). Macroeconomics questions how well Smith's invisible hand works in a wider context. When all the smart choices of individuals are combined, is the result the best outcome for the economy as a whole?

Consider this example. During tough economic times, many people are unemployed — they can't find jobs, aren't earning incomes, and cut back on their spending. Businesses aren't selling enough because consumers aren't buying — products sit on shelves and profits are down. But if only businesses would hire the people looking for work, those new employees would earn incomes and buy the unsold products. It seems everyone — workers and businesses — could be better off, yet those mutually beneficial exchanges don't happen. Why?

This is the core question for macroeconomics. Do smart choices by consumers and businesses imply that smart choices are being made for the economy as a whole? What are the implications of this question for government economic policy; for you as a consumer, a businessperson, and an investor; and for your choices as a voter?

Economists disagree far more about macroeconomics than microeconomics. This chapter simplifies those disagreement into two major camps, giving you a framework for understanding macroeconomics and for thinking about the appropriate role for government economic policy.

Macroeconomics Created Out of the Great Depression of the 1930s

(L01) Explain how macroeconomics differs from microeconomics.

Microeconomics analyzes the choices made by individuals, and how those choices interact in markets. According to the demand and supply model, markets react quickly to shortages, surpluses, or changes in demand or supply because prices adjust to smart choices. The result (coordinated through Adam Smith's invisible hand of competition) is the miracle of continuous, ever-changing production of the products and services we want.

This positive picture of markets working well often doesn't match history. Two of the most dramatic failures of markets over the last century — the Global Financial Crisis of 2008 and the Great Depression of the 1930s — included mass unemployment, falling living standards, bankruptcies, financial bubbles, and deflation or inflation.

2008 Global Financial Crisis

The Global Financial Crisis began with constantly rising housing prices in the U.S. (and Canada) between 1996 and 2006. This housing price bubble led homeowners, investors, mortgage lenders, and financial institutions to take bigger and bigger risks. Banks issued "sub-prime" mortgages with no down payments to borrowers who couldn't afford them, assuming that even if a borrower couldn't make his payments, the bank could sell the house at an ever-rising price to recover the loan. Banks and financial institutions bundled these mortgages together and sold them to others who received the mortgage payments. Selling these bundled mortgages provided more money for the financial institutions to provide even more mortgages, making it easier for house buyers to demand houses, which further inflated housing prices.

When housing prices began to fall, the bubble burst, and the value of all of those mortgages plunged. Investors and banks holding now almost worthless assets sold other assets to meet their obligations, and panicked selling led to the failure of banks and other financial institutions. Stock market values plunged 40 percent, housing prices kept falling, and in the U.S. borrowers walked away from houses that were worth less than what they owed on their mortgages. Businesses went bankrupt, the Canadian auto industry was in danger of collapse, and unemployment in Canada in 2009 peaked at 8.7%.

The Great Depression

People suffered worse hardships during the Great Depression. Triggered by a stock market bubble in 1929, economic activity collapsed. By 1933, 20 percent of the Canadian and U.S. workforce was unemployed, and output of products and services fell by more than 30 percent. The prices consumers paid for products and services fell by over 20 percent. Because of unemployment, wages were falling even faster. And falling prices for businesses are a disaster, as falling revenues make it harder to pay off existing debts, so there is less money to invest in expanding output or improving productivity. There were no government programs like employment insurance, welfare, health care, or the Canada Pension Plan to ease the suffering. Not until 1941, when the government began spending heavily on military production for World War II, did standards of living return to 1929 levels.

Keynes Creates Macroeconomics

The experience of the Great Depression led John Maynard Keynes to create macroeconomics with his famous 1936 book, *The General Theory of Employment, Interest, and Money*. If you studied economics before 1936, there were no macroeconomic textbooks. Most economists in 1929, at the start of the Great Depression, believed in the miracle of markets working well and adjusting to changes without any role for government besides enforcing the rules of the game.

Say's Law   The belief that market economies with flexible prices would always quickly self-adjust was based on work by Jean-Baptiste Say (1767–1832), a French economist and supporter of Adam Smith's views on free trade, the invisible hand, and markets. Say's Law claimed that "supply creates its own demand." We can illustrate Say's Law using the circular flow model in Figure 1.

Figure 1   The Circular Flow Model

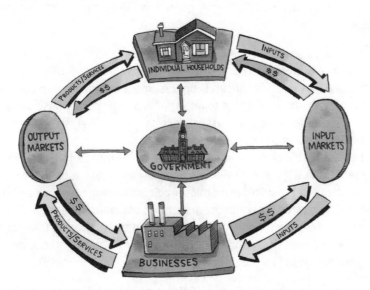

Starting at the top, households *supply* inputs to businesses in exchange for money. Households sell their inputs in input markets because they want the money to *demand* products and services in output markets. When households spend all of the money earned in input markets to buy products and services in output markets, supply does create its own demand. As the flow continues smoothly around the circle, markets adjust quickly to maintain steady growth in living standards, full employment, and stable prices. While there might be small, temporary ups and downs, in the long run, flexible prices quickly restore the balance between demand and supply, so that the economy produces good results and the miracle of markets.

In the middle of the Great Depression, economic events made people look for a better explanation of business cycles — the ups and downs of economic activity — especially the "downs" of decreasing spending, output, and living standards, combined with unemployment and deflation.

Keynesian Revolution   Keynes rejected Say's Law as a "special theory" that sometimes holds true but usually does not. Keynes's more "general theory" allowed both short-run and long-run answers to the question "How quickly do market economies adjust?"

What Was Different about Keynes's Macroeconomics?

Keynes explained the Great Depression and created macroeconomics by introducing five different ways of thinking. He focused on the

- short run (instead of the long run).
- effects of sticky prices that don't adjust quickly (instead of flexible prices).
- importance of saving and investment.
- role of money, banks, and expectations.
- connections between input and output markets.

Short Run versus Long Run   Given enough time, Keynes accepted that flexible prices and the self-adjusting mechanisms of demand and supply might bring market economies back to steady growth, full employment, and stable prices. But Keynes believed it could take decades, during which time there would be serious and needless human suffering. He believed proper government policy could correct the problems more quickly in the short run, which was his focus. He is famously quoted as saying, "In the long run, we are all dead."

Sticky versus Flexible Prices   Microeconomics teaches us that where there is an imbalance between demand and supply, prices adjust — prices are flexible. But the flexibility of prices depends on the amount of time that passes. In the short run, prices have less time to adjust — economists call these sticky prices. In the long run, as more time passes, prices are more likely to adjust and act like the flexible prices of microeconomic models.

The wage — the price of labour — is one of the most important prices for macroeconomics. If there is unemployment — an excess supply of workers in the labour market — microeconomics predicts that wages will fall and more workers will be hired (the quantity demanded of labour increases). But if wages are sticky — are slow to fall — then unemployment can persist for a long time.

Keynes believed that sticky prices, especially in labour markets, were more common than flexible prices.

Saving and Investment   Saving is important in a market economy because if creates a pool of funds that businesses can borrow to invest in building new factories and productive equipment that allow the economy to grow in the long run. But in the short run, saving means less spending.

If you save more from your income, your savings increase and your spending decreases. But if many people save more and spend less, businesses experience falling sales, cut back production, and lay off workers so that incomes fall. Paradoxically, the result may be *less* saving, because without employment income, people have to withdraw their savings from banks. Economists call this the **paradox of thrift**.

This is an example of the **fallacy of composition** — what is true for one (micro) is not necessarily true for all (macro). Here is another example. Suppose an individual farmer in Saskatchewan plants more wheat than usual and harvests a big bumper crop. The small farmer's increase in supply has little impact on the world price for wheat. The farmer's income goes up with a greater quantity sold and a constant price of wheat. But if *all* farmers plant more wheat and weather is good around the world, the great increase in supply drives down the world price of wheat so much that all farmers end up with less income than before.

Money, Banks, and Expectations   As the stories of the Global Financial Crisis and the Great Depression show, money, banks, and expectations play major roles in speculative bubbles that inflate, burst, and trigger downturns. Money and banks give people a way to save rather than spend their income

Expectations are particularly important for business investment decisions, which are central to explanations of business cycles and to increases in productivity that allow long-run growth in living standards. Keynes emphasized the roles of money, banks, and expectations as part of his macroeconomic focus on the whole economy. Microeconomics does not focus on these factors.

Connections between Input and Output Markets   Microeconomics focuses on the interaction of demand and supply in *input markets alone* or *in output markets alone*.

Suppose wages in the labour market — an input market — are higher than the equilibrium wage. Workers are eager to supply labour, but businesses are unwilling to hire workers at the higher wage. There is a surplus of labour. Microeconomics predicts that in the labour market alone, wages fall, restoring the balance between demand and supply, and coordinating the smart choices of households supplying labour with the smart choices of businesses demanding labour.

In output markets alone, price adjustments also coordinate the smart choices of consumers and businesses, balancing consumer demand with business supply of products and services.

Macroeconomics focuses on the *connections* between input and output markets. Even if wages are not sticky and fall, falling wages mean falling incomes. If you work 40 hours per week, and your wage falls from $20 per hour to $15 per hour, your weekly income falls from $800 to $600. Ouch! So your demand for products and services in output markets decreases. With decreased demand, businesses experience falling prices of outputs and, in turn, hire fewer workers.

The *connections* between input and output markets can block the coordination of smart choices. Income and spending depend on each other. Consumer spending is business income. Business spending is consumer income. If consumers and businesses both cut spending (as happened in the Global Financial Crisis), everyone's income falls and unemployment increases.

Figure 2 shows the possible breaks in connections between input markets and output markets that could come from any of the five macroeconomic ways of thinking Keynes introduced.

Figure 2   Broken Connections in the Circular Flow Model

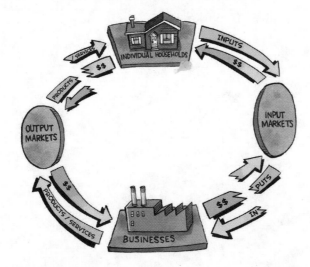

In the next section we will look at modern macroeconomic views on how quickly market economies self-adjust, and what that means for government macroeconomic policy.

 **Practice...**

1. The Great Depression of 1929 was worse than the Global Financial Crisis of 2008 because in 1929 there were no

   a. stock market crashes.

   b. government programs to help the unemployed.

   c. bank failures.

   d. falling prices.

2. During the Global Financial Crisis, all of these indicators fell *except*

   a. unemployment.

   b. housing prices.

   c. asset prices.

   d. stock market values.

3. Who said "In the long run, we are all dead?"

   a. D. Vader

   b. J. B. Say

   c. J. M. Keynes

   d. J. K. Rowling

4. When everyone saves money, total savings decrease. This is an example of

   a. the zero-sum scenario.

   b. the fallacy of combination.

   c. Say's Law.

   d. the paradox of thrift.

5. Before Keynes, J. B. Say and economists emphasized

   a. flexible prices.

   b. the short run.

   c. money, banks, and expectations.

   d. connections between input and output markets.

Apply...

1. Use the circular flow model to explain how supply can create its own demand. Who are the suppliers and the demanders in your explanation?

    _____
    _____
    _____
    _____

2. Keynes rejected Say's Law and helped create macroeconomics.

    a. List the five different ways of thinking that Keynes introduced with macroeconomics.

    _____
    _____
    _____
    _____
    _____
    _____
    _____
    _____
    _____

    b. Savings and investment are both important for economic growth.

        i. Explain the positive effect of saving. Does that effect happen in the short run or the long run?

    _____
    _____
    _____
    _____

        ii. Explain the negative effect of saving. Does that effect happen in the short run or the long run? What does Keynes call the negative effect of savings? Explain that general concept.

    _____
    _____
    _____
    _____
    _____

to be continued

Apply...

continued

3. The number of workers who are employed is determined by demand and supply in the labour market.

   a. On the graph, with the wage on the vertical axis and the quantity of labour hired on the horizontal axis, draw a demand and a supply curve for labour. Identify the equilibrium wage.

   b. Pick a wage that results in unemployment. Show on the graph what the quantity of unemployment will be at that wage.

   c. If wages (the price of labour) are flexible, what does microeconomics predict will happen in the labour market?

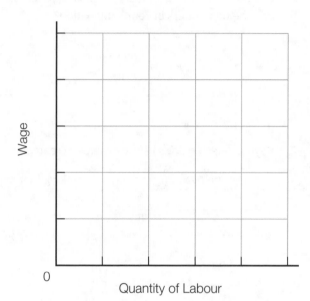

   d. If wages are sticky at the level you picked in part b, what happens in the labour market?

   e. Even if wages in the labour market fall to the equilibrium wage, what is Keynes's argument about the effect of this change on *output markets*?

_____

_____

_____

_____

_____

How Quickly Do Market Economies Self-Adjust?

L02 Describe the fundamental macroeconomic question and the hands-off and hands-on positions on market failure, government failure, and government policy.

Do markets coordinate smart individual choices to produce the miracle of the continuous, ever-changing production of the products and services we want (microeconomic focus), or do markets produce undesirable outcomes like unemployment, falling living standards, bankruptcies, financial bubbles, and deflation or inflation (macroeconomic focus)?

There is no single right answer to the question. Sometimes markets work well and quickly in coordinating individual choices, sometimes not. The following more precise rewording of the question will guide everything we discuss about macroeconomics.

The Fundamental Macroeconomic Question

If left alone by government,
how quickly do the price mechanisms of market economies adjust
to maintain steady growth in living standards, full employment, and stable prices?

More simply, if left alone, do markets quickly self-adjust?

The disagreements between Say and Keynes about the fundamental macroeconomic question continue today. Because there is no agreement among economists or politicians, you will have to decide which answers make most sense to you. The answers are important because they could make the difference between economic prosperity and recession. Your personal economic success will be affected by the macroeconomic performance of the economy, and that performance is affected by government policies that will be put in place by the politicians you elect.

Let me describe the differences between the two major camps in terms of "Yes — Markets Quickly Self-Adjust, So Government Hands-Off" and "No — Markets Fail Often, So Government Hands-On" answers to the fundamental macroeconomic question. The answers require an understanding of the concepts of market failure and government failure.

Market Failure and Government Failure

Since the Great Depression and Global Financial Crisis happened, is the only reasonable answer to the fundamental macroeconomic question, "No — Markets Fail Often, So Government Hands-On?" Despite these long-lasting business cycles, the answer "Yes — Markets Quickly Self-Adjust, So Government Hands-Off" is also possible because of the importance of the initial, qualifying phrase "if left alone by government." Markets can fail, but so can governments.

Market Failure   All economists agree that sometimes markets fail to produce outcomes in the public interest. This can happen because of externalities or economies of scale that allow large businesses to monopolize a market. In these instances, markets may produce outcomes that are inefficient or inequitable and not in society's best interests. When there is **market failure**, government policy that acts in the public interest can improve market outcomes.

Government Failure   It is also possible that government policy may *not* act in the public interest. Lobbying, campaign contributions, and political pressure can cause governments to act in the interests of businesses, labour organizations, or other special-interest groups. Even when aiming for the public interest, government policymakers often lack timely and accurate information for making smart policy decisions. The complexity of the economy, the banking system, changeable expectations, and connections to the global economy make it easy for government policymakers to make "honest mistakes" when trying to solve complex, interconnected macroeconomic problems. When government policy fails to serve the public interest, it is called **government failure.**

It is possible that the problems of business cycles or unemployment are caused by government failure — bad policy — rather than the market economy. Government failure certainly contributed to the severity of the Great Depression. So even when we see the ups and downs of economic activity, the answer to the question "If left alone by government, do markets quickly self-adjust?" may still be "Yes" if bad government policies *caused* the failure.

There is a joke that if you ask three economists a question, especially about macroeconomics, you will get five answers. So in sorting economists (and politicians) into only two camps — "Yes" and "No" answers to the fundamental macroeconomic question — I am simplifying their many differences. Let's look at the two camps and how their economics connect to politics.

Yes — Left Alone, Markets Quickly Self-Adjust, So Government Hands-Off

The "Yes — Markets Quickly Self-Adjust, So Government Hands-Off" camp of economists argue that, if left alone by government, the price mechanisms of market economies adjust quickly to maintain steady growth in living standards, full employment, and stable prices. They believe that business cycles, occasional unemployment, and inflation are caused by events outside the economy (like natural disasters or wars) or by bad government policies. The "Yes" camp argues that markets are the most flexible way for the economy to adjust to changes, even if those adjustments take some time. These economists believe that money, banks, and expectations don't significantly affect the exchanges of physical products and services around the circular flow, or block coordination between input and output markets.

Hands-Off   Believers that markets will self-adjust — usually quickly, always in the long run — see little role for government policy that interferes with markets. This camp believes that even when markets temporarily fail, government policy will likely make things worse, not better. Government failure is more likely than market failure. Therefore, the "Yes — Markets Quickly Self-Adjust, So Government Hands-Off" camp argues for a hands-off role for government. The first drawing in Figure 3 represents the hands-off approach of the "Yes" camp.

Figure 3   Government Hands-Off and Hands-On

Politicians on the right of the political spectrum — Conservatives and Libertarians in Canada, Republicans in the U.S. — fit into this camp, supporting a hands-off role for government. They believe that, if left alone by government, markets will eventually produce efficient outcomes and rising standards of living, full employment, and stable prices.

No — Left Alone, Markets Fail Often, So Government Hands-On

The "No — Markets Fail Often, So Government Hands-On" camp argues that, if left alone by government, the self-adjusting mechanisms of market economies can be slow and weak. As a result, business cycles happen often, with long periods of unemployment that reduce living standards, and with inflation or deflation. They believe that most economic problems are caused internally as unintended by-products of markets with sticky prices. This camp emphasizes that money, banks, and expectations can block the coordination between input and output markets. While they prefer the flexibility of market economies to any other economic system, these economists see self-interest and greed promoting speculative bubbles that inevitably cause cycles of boom and bust.

Hands-On   Believers that markets create economic problems and often fail, see an important role for government policy that serves the public interest. Market failure problems can be serious, and market failure is more likely than government failure. Therefore, the "No — Markets Fail Often, So Government Hands-On" camp argues for a hands-on role for government. The second drawing in Figure 3 represents the hands-on approach of the "No" camp. The hands are holding the broken connections between input and output markets that cause markets to fail.

Politicians on the left of the political spectrum — federal Liberals, New Democrats, and the Bloc Québécois in Canada, Democrats in the U.S. — fit into this camp, supporting a hands-on role for government. They believe that if left alone, markets will produce inequality in living standards, with much economic insecurity and hardship for those who do not possess skills that markets value. Government has a responsibility to maintain a social safety net to support the economic welfare of citizens left behind by markets, especially labour markets.

Macroeconomic Camps and Agreements

I have divided economists and politician into only two camps to give you a simplified framework to organize your study of macroeconomics. Your textbook or instructor may mention many more macroeconomic schools or models. Here is how they fit into the simplified camps.

Yes — Left Alone, Market Quickly Self Adjust, So Government Hands-Off
Keynes referred to economists before him who believed in Say's Law as Classical economists. That label continues. Modern economists in this camp include those labelled as Classical, Neoclassical, and New Classical. Rational Expectations, Monetarist, Supply-Side, and Real Business Cycle models also fit into this camp. These economists and models emphasize flexible prices, quickly self-adjusting markets, and a long-run focus on economic growth.

No — Left Alone, Market Fail Often, So Government Hands-On
Modern economists in this camp are all intellectual descendants of Keynes, and their schools and models contain his name — Keynesians, New Keynesians, Neo-Keynesians, and Post Keynesians. These economists and models emphasize sticky prices, slowly adjusting or failed markets, and a short-run focus on business cycles.

Agreements among Macroeconomists   Despite these differences, all macroeconomists agree that

- *there is some role for government in setting the rules of the game.* They differ on how small or large a role government policy to change the economy should play.

- *prices and markets adjust.* They differ on how long the adjustments take, and whether prices are flexible or sticky in adjusting.
- *savings and business investment are important in determining macroeconomic outcomes.* They differ on the whether interest rates or expectations are most important for investment decisions, and on how savings and investment interact in the loanable funds market.
- *business cycles happen in the short run.* They differ on whether the causes are external or internal to the economy, and on how markets respond after a boom or bust.
- *there is long-run economic growth.* They differ in focusing on the long-run successes of growth or the short-run problems of business cycles.

When you add the agreements to the disagreements, the differences between the camps are more subtle than a yes or no answer to the simple question, "If left alone, do markets quickly self-adjust?"

But thinking of the positions of only two camps — "Markets Quickly Self-Adjust, So Government Hands Off" and "Market Fail Often, So Government Hands-On" — will simplify your understanding of macroeconomics.

 **Practice...**

6. There is government failure when
   a. government policy serves the public interest.
   b. economists lie to politicians.
   c. policymakers are captured by special-interest groups.
   d. a minority government is defeated in the House of Commons.

7. If J. B. Say were alive today and voted in Canadian elections, he would probably support the
   a. Conservative Party of Canada.
   b. Green Party.
   c. federal Liberal Party.
   d. New Democratic Party.

8. The hands-on camp believes that
   a. demand creates its own supply.
   b. supply creates its own demand.
   c. market failure is worse than government failure.
   d. external events are a major cause of business cycles.

9. According to the "Yes — Markets Quickly Self-Adjust, So Government Hands-Off" camp,
   a. macroeconomic outcomes are different from microeconomic outcomes.
   b. Say's Law is true in the long run but not in the short run.
   c. prices are flexible.
   d. there are broken connections between input and output markets.

10. Macroeconomists agree
    a. that business cycles happen even without government failure.
    b. that prices and markets adjust, but disagree on how long it takes.
    c. that there is some role for government, but disagree on how big a role.
    d. on all of the above.

Apply...

4. What is the fundamental macroeconomic question?

    _____

    _____

    _____

5.   In your own words, list the key arguments for each side of the hands-off versus hands-on debate.

    _____

    _____

    _____

    _____

    _____

    _____

6. The "Yes — Markets Quickly Self-Adjust, So Government Hands-Off" and "No — Markets Fail Often, So Government Hands-On" camps have many disagreements. But macroeconomists also agree on many issues. Describe three issues about which they mostly agree.

    _____

    _____

    _____

    _____

    _____

    _____

    _____

    _____

Macroeconomic Outcomes and Players

L03 Identify three key economic outcomes and five macroeconomic players whose choices produce those outcomes.

Look again at the definition of macroeconomics, but notice the words now in italics — macroeconomics analyzes the *performance* of the whole Canadian economy and the global economy — the combined *outcomes* of all individual microeconomic choices.

Outcomes

We evaluate the performance of the Canadian economy by measuring the key outcomes: living standards (GDP), unemployment, and inflation.

Gross Domestic Product   The most important concept for understanding standards of living, and perhaps the most basic macroeconomic concept, is *gross domestic product* or GDP. GDP is the value of all final products and services produced annually in a country. Chapter 5 will define GDP and explain in detail how GDP is measured. In general, higher GDP means higher living standards.

Unemployment   In a market economy, to be able to buy products and services in output markets, you usually must earn income by selling something you own in input markets. For most households, that means finding a job — selling your labour to a business in input markets.

Money buys just about anything in a market economy. That is why being unemployed, and not earning money, is a serious problem. Chapter 6 will define unemployment and explain how unemployment is measured. In general, more unemployment is bad and less unemployment is good.

Inflation   In microeconomics, the price of any one product or service rises or falls with changes in demand and supply. In macroeconomics, *inflation* refers to a rise in the average level of all prices in an economy. *Deflation* is a fall in the average level of *all* prices. Chapter 6 will define inflation and deflation and explain how they are measured using the Consumer Price Index. In general, higher and unpredictable inflation is bad and lower and predictable inflation is good. Deflation has additional problems.

Once you can measure these outcomes of GDP, unemployment, and inflation, you will be better able to evaluate whether or not market economies maintain steady growth in living standards, full employment, and stable prices.

Macroeconomic Players

How do we connect macroeconomic outcomes such as GDP, unemployment, and inflation to smart individual microeconomic choices? One way to move from a microeconomic, single-tree focus to seeing the macroeconomic forest is to organize individuals into groups. There are already groups in the circular flow model — households, businesses, and government.

To explain macroeconomic outcomes, we must add two groups of players to the circular flow model: banks and other countries with whom we trade.

Here are all of the players whose combined choices produce macroeconomic outcomes.

Households as Consumers   Individuals in households supply labour and other inputs in input markets, and use the income they earn to buy products and services in output markets. We will focus on the choices households make about spending (or saving) the money they have earned. Because of this focus on spending, we will rename these players *consumers.*

You have two major choices as a consumer. You can spend or save your money, and you can buy products and services produced in Canada or imported from other countries. With our macroeconomic focus on the forest, we will not look at microeconomic individual choices like buying a Samsung or Apple phone.

Businesses   Businesses hire labour and other inputs from consumer households in input markets, and sell the products and services produced with those inputs in output markets. Businesses also make decisions about increasing output by building new factories and buying new machinery. Economists call business purchases of new factories and any new equipment **investment spending**.

Business input choices include hiring labour or not, and buying inputs domestically or importing from other countries. In selling outputs, businesses can choose to sell products and services domestically or to export them to other countries — wherever profits are highest. We will not look at microeconomic business choices such as whether Ford produces more cars or trucks.

Government   Besides setting the legal rules of the game for all economic activity, governments can choose to interact, or not, in any aspect of the economy. We will use *government* to represent all levels of government — federal, provincial, and municipal. But we focus largely on the federal government, the Government of Canada.

We focus on just two government choices: government purchases of products and services, and government taxes and transfer payments (such as Employment Insurance payments and Canada Pension Plan payments).

Government policy decisions to leave the economy alone or influence it — hands-off or hands-on — take two forms: fiscal policy and monetary policy.

Fiscal policy (discussed in Chapter 12) uses government purchases, taxes, and transfers to achieve steady growth, full employment, and stable prices.

Monetary policy is handled by the Bank of Canada and involves changing interest rates and the supply of money to achieve steady growth, full employment, and stable prices.

Bank of Canada and Banking System   The Bank of Canada, together with the banking system it oversees, is a new macroeconomic player to add to the circular flow model. The banking system takes deposits of money and makes loans to consumers and businesses. The key choice for banks is whether to make loans or not. The Bank of Canada is Canada's central bank, responsible for supervising the banking system, financial markets, and conducting monetary policy (discussed in Chapter 11).

Rest of the World (R.O.W.)   Our focus is on the Canadian economy. Canada is a relatively small player in the global economy and has trading relationships with many countries, especially the United States. What goes on in other countries has a large effect on macroeconomic outcomes in Canada.

Countries in the rest of the world can choose to buy Canadian products and services (exports from Canada) or not, and sell their products and services to us (imports to Canada) or to other countries. There are similar choices about where to invest money. Canadians can invest money in banks and financial assets in other countries, and the R.O.W. can invest money in Canadian banks and financial assets. Exchanges of exports, imports, and money all require exchanges between the Canadian dollar and other currencies. These choices affect the value of the Canadian dollar which has an impact on our economy (discussed in Chapter 10).

Practice...

11. Good outcomes for an economy include

 a. high GDP, low unemployment, and low inflation.

 b. high GDP, low unemployment, and high inflation.

 c. high GDP, high unemployment, and high inflation.

 d. low GDP, low unemployment, and low inflation.

12. Lower GDP per person generally means

 a. a decreasing population.

 b. an increasing population.

 c. lower unemployment rates.

 d. lower living standards.

13. Business purchases of new factories and equipment are called

 a. stock investments.

 b. investment spending.

 c. labour costs.

 d. exports.

14. Fiscal policy includes government changes in

 a. imports.

 b. interest rates.

 c. transfer payments.

 d. exports.

15. The group of macroeconomic players that makes most choices about investment spending is

 a. the Bank of Canada and the banking system.

 b. the rest of the world.

 c. businesses.

 d. government.

Apply...

7. In order to answer the fundamental macroeconomic question, we need to measure the performance of the market economy. Connect the performance criteria in the fundamental macroeconomic question to the three key macroeconomic outcomes.

8. List the five key macroeconomic players and the macro-related choices they make.

9. Which of the five key macroeconomic players are in the circular flow diagram (Figure 1 on page 83) and which players are missing (right now) from that diagram?

KNOW...

Summary of Learning Objectives

1. In moving from microeconomics to macroeconomics, what is true for individual choices may not be true for the economy as a whole — that is the **paradox of thrift**. Keynes created macroeconomics in the 1930s by rejecting **Say's Law** and focusing on the short run; the effects of sticky prices; the importance of saving and investment; the role of money, banks, and expectations; and connections between input and output markets.

2. The fundamental macroeconomic question is "If left alone by government, how quickly do the price mechanisms of market economies adjust to maintain steady growth in living standards, full employment, and stable prices?" The "Yes — Markets Quickly Self-Adjust, So Government Hands-Off" and "No — Markets Fail Often, So Government Hands-On" camps disagree on the **fallacy of composition**, the causes of business cycles, the flexibility of prices, the risk of **government failure** versus **market failure,** and the role for government **fiscal policy** and **monetary policy**. The camps have many areas of agreement, where the differences are in terms of emphasis.

3. Three key performance outcome of the Canadian economy are GDP, unemployment, and inflation. The outcomes are produced by the choices made by the five macroeconomic players: consumers, businesses, government, Bank of Canada and the banking system, and the rest of the world.

Key Terms

fallacy of composition: what is true for one is not true for all; the whole is greater than the sum of the parts

fiscal policy: government purchases and taxes/transfers to achieve steady growth, full employment, and stable prices

government failure: government policy fails to serve the public interest

investment spending: business purchases of new factories and equipment

market failure: market outcomes are inefficient or inequitable and fail to serve the public interest

monetary policy: the Bank of Canada changes interest rates and the supply of money to achieve steady growth, full employment, and stable prices

paradox of thrift: attempts to increase saving cause total savings to decrease because of falling employment and incomes

Say's Law: supply creates its own demand

Answers to Practice

1. **b** No social safety net programs.

2. **a** Unemployment increased.

3. **c** Justifying his short-run focus.

4. **d** Example of the fallacy of composition.

5. **a** Allow markets to quickly self-adjust and match demand with supply.

6. **c** So policy fails to serve the public interest.

7. **a** The belief that supply creates it own demand assumes markets quickly self-adjust.

8. **c** Markets fail to quickly self-adjust, so government should be hands-on.

9. **c** Flexible prices allow markets to quickly self-adjust.

10. **d** Also agree that savings and investment are important for long-run growth.

11. **a** High living standards, low unemployment, stable prices.

12. **d** Lower GDP per person often associated with economic downturns and higher unemployment.

13. **b** Definition.

14. **c** Government purchases, taxes, or transfers.

15. **c** Purchases of new factories and equipment.

5

GDP, Economic Growth, and Business Cycles

LEARNING OBJECTIVES

L01 Differentiate nominal GDP, real GDP, and real GDP per person, and demonstrate how each relates to living standards.

L02 Explain how to measure GDP by using value added and the equality of aggregate expenditure and aggregate income.

L03 Explain how economic growth occurs and how it is measured.

L04 Identify five limitations of real GDP per person as a measure of well-being.

L05 Describe business cycles in terms of real GDP and output gaps as a target for policymakers.

LEARN...

Why was my grandparents' standard of living so different from ours? My grandfather and grandmother were born in the 1890s, "courted" on horseback, and lived through the Great Depression. They took in boarders to make ends meet, and their apartment had few closets since, like many people, they had only a few changes of clothing. Although the prices they paid for products seem unimaginably low (10 cents for a silent movie, 15 cents for a pound of sausages), wages were also low. In 1935, the average wage for a Canadian factory worker, working 44 hours per week, was $870 a year. That's about 38 cents per hour!

What determined my grandparents' standard of living, and our much higher standard of living today? The answer has everything to do with GDP — gross domestic product. In this chapter, we will explore the challenges of measuring GDP and comparing Canadian GDP over different years. Changes in technology, productivity, quantities, and prices all affect GDP and our standard of living. Which changes increase living standards, and which cause ups and downs around a rising trend of living standards that allows us to enjoy walk-in closets, remote-controlled houses, and highly specialized products and services? And what changes in our living standards does GDP totally miss?

The term "GDP" is the stuff of the stories you may tell to your grandchildren about what life was like when you were young, when people used to drive cars with gasoline engines.

Nominal GDP and Real GDP

L01 Differentiate nominal GDP, real GDP, and real GDP per person, and demonstrate how each relates to living standards.

The dictionary definition of "gross" is "total, aggregate, overall, or combined." Those are macroeconomic words about the economy as a whole. Gross domestic product, or GDP, measures total output of the economy: the value of all final products and services produced annually in a country.

Many parts of GDP (products, quantities, prices) change over time, making it hard to compare GDP in different years. To sort out the influence of the changing parts, economists use more precise measures of GDP — nominal GDP, real GDP, and real GDP per person.

Nominal GDP

Nominal GDP is the value at *current* prices of all final products and services produced annually in a country. Let's examine the key words in this definition using the Canadian economy as an example.

Value   The worth, in Canadian dollars, of all the products and services produced.

Current Prices   To add together the value of all automobiles, piercings, movies, and every other final product and service, take the price of each and multiply by the quantity produced. Nominal GDP uses current prices, so to calculate nominal GDP for 1935, we use the prices and quantities current in 1935. To calculate nominal GDP for 2016, we use the prices and quantities current in 2016.

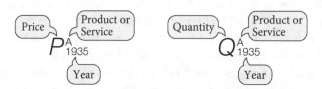

We can reduce this macro-size addition problem to a single line. The superscript letters *A, B, C, . . . Z* represent different products and services. For each product or service, *P* stands for its price, and *Q* stands for its quantity.

The nominal GDP calculation for 1935 is

$$\text{Nominal GDP}_{1935} = P^A_{1935}\, Q^A_{1935} + P^B_{1935}\, Q^B_{1935} + P^C_{1935}\, Q^C_{1935} + \ldots + P^Z_{1935}\, Q^Z_{1935}$$

The nominal GDP calculation for 2016 is

$$\text{Nominal GDP}_{2016} = P^A_{2016}\, Q^A_{2016} + P^B_{2016}\, Q^B_{2016} + P^C_{2016}\, Q^C_{2016} + \ldots + P^Z_{2016}\, Q^Z_{2016}$$

Nominal GDP for Canada for 2016 was over 400 times greater than 1935. But, before you conclude that we were over 400 times better off in 2016 than in 1935, look again at the two formulas. The increase from 1935 to 2016 could have been due to changes in prices or changes in quantities of products or service, or a combination of price and quantity changes.

The *source* of the increase in nominal GDP makes a big difference. If all of the increase were due to increased prices, then the higher nominal GDP in 2016 would have the same quantities of products and services as in 1935. We would be no better off. If all of the increase were due to increased quantities, then in 2016 we truly would have over 400 times as much "stuff" to satisfy our wants compared to 1935.

Final Products and Services A final product or service is consumed directly by consumers. A loaf of bread you buy at the bakery, or your new Honda Civic, are final products. The flour that the bakery buys as an input to make the bread or the steel Honda buys to make the car are called *intermediate products* and are not included in nominal GDP.

Produced Annually Nominal GDP for any year counts only the products and services produced in that year. Nominal GDP for 2016 includes only products and services actually produced in 2016. Used products, or products produced in previous years but resold later, are not counted.

Nominal GDP is measured as a **flow** — an amount per unit of time. Nominal GDP is usually calculated for a period of one year.

In a Country Nominal GDP for Canada includes all final products and services produced within the borders of Canada, no matter what the nationality of the business doing the producing. Honda Civics produced in Ontario are part of Canadian GDP even if the factory is owned and operated by the Japanese head office of Honda.

Real GDP

Real GDP is the value at *constant* prices of all final products and services produced annually in a country. The only word that is different from the nominal GDP definition is *constant* in place of *current*. By holding prices constant, any differences in real GDP between years must be due to differences in quantities of products and services.

If we calculate real GDP for 1935 and 2016, but keep prices constant at 2002 levels, we get

$$\text{Real GDP}_{1935} = P^A_{2002} Q^A_{1935} + P^B_{2002} Q^B_{1935} + P^C_{2002} Q^C_{1935} + \ldots + P^Z_{2002} Q^Z_{1935}$$

The real GDP calculation for 2016 is

$$\text{Real GDP}_{2016} = P^A_{2002} Q^A_{2016} + P^B_{2002} Q^B_{2016} + P^C_{2002} Q^C_{2016} + \ldots + P^Z_{2002} Q^Z_{2016}$$

By holding prices constant at the 2002 level, real GDP comparisons eliminate the effects of inflation (or deflation) and isolate changes in physical quantities of products and services only. Real GDP in 2016 was about 25 times greater than in 1935. We had about 25 times as much stuff in 2016 as in 1935, not 400 times!

For measuring the macroeconomic outcome of steady growth in living standards, real GDP provides much more useful information than nominal GDP.

Real GDP per Person

Real GDP is a better measure than nominal GDP for judging living standards, but there is an even more accurate measurement. **Real GDP per person** equals real GDP divided by the population of a country. Real GDP per person is the best measure of a country's ability to meet the material needs of its citizens.

Practice...

1. To calculate nominal GDP for 1935, we use the prices in

    a. 1935 and the quantities in 1935.

    b. 1935 and the quantities in 2002.

    c. 2002 and the quantities in 1935.

    d. 2002 and quantities in 2002.

2. You observe that nominal GDP increases between 2013 and 2016, and the population also increases. If the entire increase in nominal GDP is due to rising prices, then

    a. nominal GDP remains unchanged.

    b. real GDP remains unchanged.

    c. real GDP per person remains unchanged.

    d. living standards remain unchanged.

3. Real GDP per person is calculated as

    a. nominal GDP per person divided by real GDP.

    b. real GDP multiplied by the number of people in the country.

    c. real GDP divided by the number of people in the country.

    d. the number of people in the country divided by real GDP.

4. Which statement about nominal and real GDP is *incorrect*?

    a. Real GDP is measured as a flow.

    b. Real GDP per person is a better measure of standard of living than nominal GDP per person.

    c. Nominal GDP includes products and services produced within a country's borders, no matter what the nationality of the business doing the producing.

    d. If nominal GDP is greater this year than last year, there must be an increase in living standards.

5. In 2016, the country of Adanac produces 20 kilos of apples and 30 kilos of bananas. Both fruits were used only for final consumption and nothing else was produced. In 2016, a kilo of apples sold for $5 and a kilo of bananas sold for $10. Adanac's nominal GDP in 2016 was

    a. $50.

    b. $65.

    c. $350.

    d. $400.

Apply...

1. What is the definition of nominal GDP? What one word is different in the definition of real GDP? How does that word affect the accuracy of the measurement of living standards?

    _____

    _____

    _____

    _____

2. The base year for calculating real GDP is 2002.

    a. What is the relationship between nominal GDP and real GDP in 2002? Explain your answer.

    _____

    _____

    _____

    _____

    b. Prices rose every year between 1992 and 2002. What was the relationship between nominal GDP and real GDP for any year between 1992 and 2002?

    _____

    _____

    _____

3. Measured in constant 2002 U.S. dollars, India's real GDP in 2011 was $427 billion, while Israel's was $97 billion.

    a. Based on this information, can you decide which country had a higher standard of living? Explain.

    _____

    _____

    _____

    b. Which country had a higher standard of living in 2011? If necessary, find any additional information to answer the question.

    _____

    _____

    _____

    _____

Aggregate Expenditure, Income, and Value Added

L02 Explain how to measure GDP by using value added and the equality of aggregate expenditure and aggregate income.

Real GDP includes only *final* products and services — consumed directly by consumers — and excludes intermediate products and services to avoid double counting. The loaf of bread you buy at the bakery is a final product. When Subway buys that same loaf of bread to make sandwiches to sell, it is an intermediate product. Counting the value of the bread and the sandwiches is double counting. How do GDP statisticians decide which products and services are final, and which are intermediate, since the same product could be either?

Value Added without Double Counting

The solution to the double-counting problem comes from the business concept of value added. **Value added** is the value of a business's outputs minus the value of intermediate products and services bought from other businesses.

Here is a simple example with only one final product — bread. In Figure 1, a farmer grows wheat, which she sells to the miller, who grinds it into flour that he sells to the baker. The baker turns the flour into bread, and sells it to you, the consumer. Let's assume the farmer rents her land and pays herself wages, but uses her own seeds and doesn't buy any intermediate products or services from anyone else, so that the example doesn't have to go back in time forever.

Figure 1   Value Added Equals Value of Final Products and Services

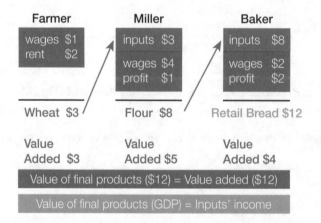

The farmer pays herself wages of $1 and pays rent of $2 to the landowner. She sells the wheat for $3 to the miller. The farmer's value added is

$3 = $3 (output) − $0 (intermediate products)

Because the farmer doesn't buy intermediate products or services, her value added (in red) equals the value of her wheat output.

The miller buys the wheat as an intermediate product (in blue), pays his workers wages of $4, earns a profit of $1, and sells the flour for $8. The miller's value added is

$5 = $8 (output) − $3 (intermediate products)

The baker buys the flour as an intermediate product (in blue), pays wages of $2, earns a profit of $2, and sells the organic, locally grown, artisanal bread to the final consumer for $12. The baker's value added is

$4 = $12 (output) − $8 (intermediate products)

Double Counting Here is the double-counting problem. If we add up the value of all intermediate products (wheat, flour) as well as the final product (bread) in Figure 1, we get $23 ($3 + $8 + $12). The $23 is not an accurate measure of what this simple economy produces because it includes the value of the wheat and flour multiple times. The accurate measure of GDP is the value of the only final product produced — one $12 loaf of bread.

Value Added Equals Value of Final Products and Services Look at the red value-added numbers in Figure 1. Summing the value added by each of the three businesses, $3 (farmer) + $5 (miller) + $4 (baker), we get $12. That number is the same as the value of the (only) final product or service produced. To calculate GDP, we don't have to sort out intermediate from final products or services. All we have to do is to sum the value added by each business.

Value Added Equals Inputs' Incomes Value added is the sum of all wages paid to workers, rent paid to landowners, and profits paid to business entrepreneurs. Value added not only equals the value of final outputs, it also equals the value of all incomes earned by owners of inputs ($12), shown at the bottom of Figure 1.

Aggregate Expenditure Equals Aggregate Income

Figure 2 is a simple circular flow of income and spending focusing on consumers and businesses. Government has been removed from the middle, and the diagram only shows money flows.

Figure 2   Simple GDP Circular Flow of Income and Spending

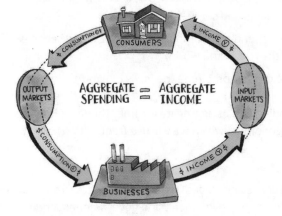

When Say's Law holds true, all income earned from supplying inputs is spent on demanding outputs. The two halves of the circular flow are equal in value. For GDP,

aggregate spending = aggregate income

spending on final products and services = payments to input owners

This is the same result as the bread example in Figure 1.

On the right side of Figure 2, economists use the letter *Y* for income. On the left side, the letter *C* represents consumption spending by consumers. Looking at Figure 3 we

- add business spending.
- move government out to the side.
- add the rest of the world.

Figure 3   Enlarged GDP Circular Flow of Income and Spending

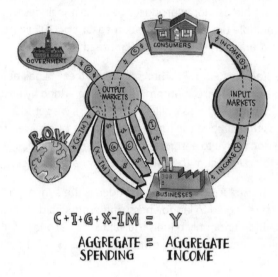

Flows of aggregate spending on the enlarged circular flow are

- *C* — consumption spending by consumers.
- *I* — business investment spending on factories and machines made by businesses.
- *G* — government spending on products and services.
- *X* — spending by the rest of the world (R.O.W.) on Canadian exports of products and services.
- *IM* — Canadian spending on imports of products and services produced by the rest of the world.
- *X – IM* — net exports, combining the flows of exports and imports.

Aggregate spending equals aggregate income. The most important equation in macroeconomics, which we will use frequently, is

$$C + I + G + X - IM = Y$$

Only products and services produced in Canada count toward Canadian GDP. Because some consumption, investment, and government spending is on imports, imports must be subtracted to accurately measure GDP.

Banks, Injections, and Leakages

The last player to add to the circular flow is the banking system. Figure 4 shows all money flows of all players.

Figure 4   Enlarged GDP Circular Flow of Income and Spending with Banking

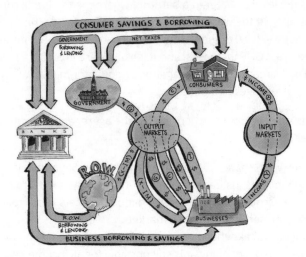

With the banking system, we can draw in two-way flows of savings (into banks) and borrowing (from banks). Consumers, businesses, R.O.W., and government all use the banking system.

There is also a two-way net taxes arrow between consumers and government. The income that consumers can spend or save is called **disposable income** — income after net taxes have been paid to government. **Net taxes**, represented by the letter *T*, equal taxes paid to government minus transfer payments (Employment Insurance, Old Age Security) consumers receive from government.

Injections and Leakages   There are two more concepts connected to the circular flow.

- An **injection** is spending in the circular flow that does not start with consumers. Government purchases (*G*), business investment spending (*I*), and exports (*X*) are injections.

- A **leakage** is spending that leaks out of (leaves) the circular flow through savings (*S*), net taxes (*T*), or imports (*IM*).

Injections and leakages are more than definitions. They allow us to explain when real GDP is unchanged, decreasing, or increasing. Start with the equation

$$C + I + G + X - IM = Y$$

All income (*Y*) is either spent (*C*), saved (*S*), or taxed away (*T*), so

$$Y = C + S + T$$

Combining the equations yields

$$C + I + G + X - IM = C + S + T$$

Rearranging terms yields

$$I + G + X = S + T + IM$$

Injections (*I* + *G* + *X*) equal leakages (*S* + *T* + *IM*).

When real GDP is unchanged, injections equal leakages. Think about real GDP as the level of water in a bathtub, where the tap is still running and the drain is open. If the water coming in (injections) equals the water going out (leakages), the level in the bathtub is unchanged. If injections are greater than leakages, real GDP increases, and if leakages are greater than injections, real GDP decreases. The unchanging, or equilibrium level of real GDP, is a balance of leakages and injections.

We will develop these concepts in the aggregate expenditure model in Chapter 8.

Say's Law with Banks   Leakages can threaten Say's Law. If consumers save their income instead of spending it, Say's Law seems to break down. All income earned by supply inputs in input markets is *not* spent demanding products and services in output markets.

But if banks take those savings and lend them to businesses that increase their investment spending, it is still possible for all income earned in input markets to create equal demand for products and services in output markets. The *loanable funds market* (discussed in Chapter 13) attempts to coordinate leakages like savings with injections like business investment.

 Practice...

6. The difference between the value of a business's output and the value of intermediate products and services bought from other businesses equals
   a. net exports.
   b. inputs' incomes.
   c. net taxes.
   d. injections.

7. Intermediate products and services are not counted in GDP because they
   a. reduce economic well-being.
   b. are only sold in input markets.
   c. are not consumed in the current year.
   d. would be double counted and overstate the value of GDP.

8. For the aggregate economy, income equals
   a. expenditure, but these are not generally equal to GDP.
   b. GDP, but expenditure is generally less than these.
   c. expenditure equals GDP.
   d. expenditure equals GDP only if we exclude government and rest of the world.

9. Leakages are spending that leaks out of the circular flow through
   a. taxes.
   b. savings.
   c. imports.
   d. all of the above.

10. Which statement is *false*?
    a. $C + I + G + IM - X = Y$
    b. $Y = C + S + T$
    c. $I + G + X = S + T + IM$
    d. $C + I + G + X - IM = Y$

 **Apply…**

4. The Beer Store gets beer from the brewery, and the brewery gets its barley from the barley farmer. Determine the value added at each stage using the following information:

    - The farmer pays herself $1, pays rent of $2 to the landowner, and sells the barley to the brewery for $3. She does not buy any intermediate products.
    - The brewer buys the farmer's barley for $3, pays his workers wages of $2, sells the beer to The Beer Store for $6, and earns a profit of $1.
    - The Beer Store buys the brewer's beer for $6, pays wages of $3, sells the beer to the final consumer for $10, and earns a profit of $1.

    a. If the economy consists only of the farmer, the brewer, and The Beer Store, calculate GDP using the value-added approach.

    b. Calculate GDP using expenditure on final products and services.

    c. Does Say's Law holds true in this example?
        [*HINT:* Calculate aggregate income (of wages, profits, and rent) and compare it to aggregate spending.]

5. The formula for calculating Canadian GDP is $C + I + G + X - IM = Y$. We don't want to count imports because GDP measures the value of all final products and services produced in Canada only. But why doesn't the formula simply ignore imports? Why are imports subtracted?

to be continued

 **Apply...**

continued

6. You are working with a classmate on a cross-country comparison of GDP and its components. He hands you his half of the work, and it is your responsibility to type it up. Unfortunately, his writing looks like chicken-scratch, and you can't contact him because his phone died.

a. Use your economic skills to complete the following table.

Spending (billions of $)	Paradise Island	Lost Island
Gross Domestic Product	100	7
Consumption	60	4
Investment	25	2
Government	?	2
Net Exports	5	?

b. What is the largest component of GDP on Paradise Island?

_____

_____

c. What is larger on Lost Island — exports or imports?

_____

_____

Potential GDP and Economic Growth

L03 Explain how economic growth occurs and how it is measured.

Steady growth in living standards requires an increase in the economy's potential for producing products and services. This is the subject of economic growth — how to increase potential GDP over time in a fast and sustainable way.

Potential GDP

Potential GDP, the outcome if Adam Smith's invisible hand works perfectly, is real GDP when all inputs — labour, capital, land (and other resources), and entrepreneurial ability — are fully employed. When real GDP equals potential GDP, the outcome for the economy as a whole is the same as when smart choices of households and of businesses are coordinated in each separate market.

Potential GDP per Person   Just as real GDP per person is a better measure of living standards than is real GDP, potential GDP per person is a better measure of maximum living standards than is potential GDP. Potential GDP per person equals potential GDP divided by the population. It is the highest material standard of living the economy is normally capable of producing if all existing inputs are fully employed.

Economic Growth

Economic growth is the expansion of the economy's capacity to produce products and services. Economic growth is caused by increases in the quantity or quality of a country's inputs — its labour, capital, land/resources, and entrepreneurship. These increases enhance the economy's capacity to produce more stuff, increasing potential GDP.

Economic Growth and Production Possibilities Frontier   A macro production possibilities frontier (*PPF* in Figure 5a) shows maximum combinations of products and services that a country can output when all inputs — labour, capital, land/resources, and entrepreneurship — are fully employed.

Figure 5   Macro Production Possibilities Frontier and Economic Growth

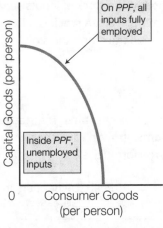

a) Macro Production Possibilities Frontier

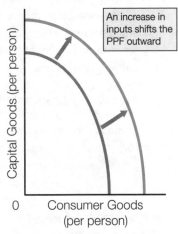

b) Economic Growth

- On the macro *PPF*, all inputs are fully employed; the economy is producing at potential GDP.

- Inside the macro *PPF*, some inputs are unemployed; the economy is producing below potential GDP.

When the quantity or quality of inputs increases, the macro *PPF* shifts outward (Figure 5b). Economic growth increases potential GDP (per person).

Sources of Economic Growth   Economic growth is caused by increases in the *quantity* or *quality* of a country's inputs, including technological change — labour, capital, land/resources, and entrepreneurship.

Increases in labour:

- *quantity* — from population growth; immigration; increase in labour force participation rate
- *quality* — from increases in **human capital** — increased earning potential from work experience, on-the-job training, and education

Increases in capital:

- *quantity* — from more factories and equipment
- *quality* — from technological change — improvements in quality of capital through innovation, research, and development

Increases in land and resources:

- *quantity* — by bringing land and resources not connected to markets into the circular flow
- *quality* — increases usually due to increases in capital used with land

Increases in entrepreneurship:

- *quantity* and *quality* interrelated; improvements from better management techniques, organization, and worker/management relations

When economic growth progresses smoothly, the stock of inputs serves as a basis for choices by all of the macroeconomic players. A **stock** is a fixed amount at a moment in time. Those choices then transform the stock of inputs, continuing in an ever-expanding circular flow.

Measuring Economic Growth Rates

There is economic growth when real GDP increases over time. The statistic for evaluating economic growth is the **economic growth rate,** the annual percentage change in real GDP per person. The formula is

$$\text{Real GDP per person growth rate (percent)} = \frac{\text{Real GDP per person this year} - \text{Real GDP per person last year}}{\text{Real GDP per person last year}} \times 100$$

Historical Growth Rates　The highest positive rates of annual economic growth occurred in the 1920s (7.4 percent in 1927), during World War II wartime production (17.1 percent in 1942), during the 1960s (4.6 percent from 1964 to 1966), and in the early 1970s (5.7 percent in 1973). Negative growth rates, where real GDP per person fell from the previous year, occurred in the Great Depression (–14.1 percent in 1931), in 1982 (– 4.0 percent), in 1991 (– 3.3 percent), and in the Global Financial Crisis of 2008/2009 (– 3.9 percent for 2009).

Between 1926 and 2016, the average annual rate of economic growth of real GDP per person in Canada was about 2.1 percent. Since we judge economic performance by growth rates, it is important to understand what the numbers mean. Is 2 percent a "good" number? How much better a number is the 7.4 percent of the Roaring '20s?

Compounding and the Rule of 70   Small differences in growth rates, like between 1 and 2 percent, make huge differences in living standards over time because of compounding.

If you put $100 in a savings account that pays 3 percent interest per year, at the end of the year you have $103. If you leave the money in the account, the second year you earn 3 percent, but this time on the original $100 plus the $3 in interest from the previous year. In year three, you earn 3 percent interest on $106.09, and the compounding continues as long as you leave your money in the account. How long does it take to double your money?

A simple rule answers the question and illustrates the compounded impact of small differences in growth rates. According to the **Rule of 70**, the number of years it takes for an initial amount to double is roughly 70 divided by the annual percentage growth rate of the amount. For our $100 at 3% example, 70 divided by 3 equals 23.3 years to double—to reach $200. Figure 6 shows the Rule of 70 for growth rates of 1 to 10 percent.

Figure 6   Rule of 70

Growth Rate (% per year)	1	2	3	4	5	6	7	8	9	10
Years to Double	70	35	23.3	17.5	14	11.7	10	8.8	7.8	7

With an average annual growth rate of 2 percent, real GDP per person doubles roughly every 35 years. If we go back 100 years, that means real GDP per person increases about 8 times. For a growth rate of 3 percent over the same time period, real GDP per person increases about 16 times. So a 1 percent difference in growth rates over 100 years means double the material standard of living. The huge effects of compounding comes from the long number of years the compounding is allowed to work.

Productivity, Growth, and Living Standards

Our standard of living improves over time because of increases in the quantity and quality of inputs, including technological change. Real GDP per person is the key measure of our standard of living, and productivity is the key *source* of our improving standard of living. **Productivity** is usually measured as the quantity of real GDP produced by an hour of labour. Increases in the quantity and quality of inputs increase labour productivity. Increased productivity allows an economy to produce more stuff, and allows us to work fewer hours to be able to afford the same stuff.

Without gains from trade, there are only two sustainable ways to increase real GDP per person. The first is to put a larger fraction of the population to work — increase the labour force participation rate. But labour force participation quickly reaches a limit once most people capable of working are working. The second is to increase productivity so that each worker produces more. Sustainable increases in real GDP per person are caused essentially by increases in productivity.

Paul Krugman, a Nobel Prize–winning economist who teaches at the City University of New York and writes for *The New York Times*, put it this way:

> Productivity isn't everything, but in the long run it is almost everything. A country's ability to improve its standard of living over time depends almost entirely on its ability to raise its output per worker.

Practice...

11. A macro production possibilities frontier shifts immediately from a change in

    a. unemployment.

    b. the quantity of inputs.

    c. the price of inputs.

    d. preferences for consumer goods and capital goods

12. Which is *not* a source of economic growth?

    a. more workers

    b. better-educated workers

    c. higher stock market prices

    d. increased quantities of capital equipment

13. Our long-run standard of living depends most on increases in

    a. population.

    b. employment.

    c. productivity.

    d. land and resources.

14. In 2016, nominal GDP was $250 and real GDP was $200. In 2017, nominal GDP was $360 and real GDP was $240. What is the growth rate of real GDP between 2016 and 2017?

    a. 20%

    b. 25%

    c. 40%

    d. 60%

15. Real GDP per person is growing at 3.5 percent per year in Canukistan. At this rate, how many years will it take for real GDP per person to double?

    a. 14

    b. 20

    c. 35

    d. 70

Apply...

7. Consider the sources of economic growth when answering these questions.

    a. In 2007, the Government of Ontario introduced Family Day, providing a new holiday from work and school in February. How does the additional public holiday affect the economy? What if the extra day off increased productivity in the rest of the year?

    _____

    _____

    _____

    b. Declining birth rates, increased life expectancy, and an aging population are leading to slower population and labour force growth. Explain why these demographic challenges will limit the future rate of economic growth.

    _____

    _____

Apply...

c. In 2008, labour productivity in the Canadian business sector decreased by 1.1 percent. It was the first annual decrease since 1996. The production of products and services by Canadian businesses decreased by 0.3 percent and hours worked increased. Explain why productivity decreases if output decreases and hours worked increase.

_____

_____

_____

d. While the entrepreneurial spirit exists in companies in Canada, the Competition Policy Review Panel concluded, in their study "Compete to Win," that Canada lacks sufficient entrepreneurial culture and ambition. Explain why entrepreneurship is a source of economic growth.

_____

_____

_____

8. Gagaland has a population of 500 in 2016 and 525 in 2017. Its real GDP is $5 500 000 in 2016 and $6 050 000 in 2017.

a. Calculate Gagaland's real GDP per capita in each year.

_____

_____

b. Calculate the growth rates of real GDP and real GDP per capita between 2016 and 2017.

_____

_____

_____

c. If Gagaland's economic growth rate of real GDP per capita continues at this rate, how many years will it take for real GDP per capita to double?

_____

_____

9. A country can increase labour force participation, which increases potential GDP, by allowing child labour and reducing vacation time. Do you think such choices should be allowed? Explain why or why not. What questions do such choices raise about the quest for profits and improved standards of living?

_____

_____

_____

_____

_____

_____

_____

Limitations of GDP as a Measure of Well-Being

L04 Identify five limitations of real GDP per person as a measure of well-being.

GDP, especially real GDP per person, is the single best measure of economic performance and of material standards of living. But that does not mean that the country with the highest real GDP per person has the highest quality of life or is the "best" country in which to live.

Real GDP per person is a limited measure of well-being, or quality of life, because it does *not* include:

- *non-market production* — Productive activities that are counted as part of GDP must be bought and sold in the input or output markets of an economy. Productive, non-paid household activities like cooking. cleaning, and childcare are not counted, yet improve the quality of life.

- *underground economy* — Activities purposefully hidden from government that are illegal, or legal but avoid taxes (cash payments for services, unreported tips), are not counted in real GDP. Economists estimate the size of the underground economy in Canada is between 5 and 15 percent of GDP.

- *environmental damage* — Real GDP does not subtract costs of environmental damage and resource depletion. When economic activity depletes non-renewable resources like oil, GDP goes up, but there is no subtraction for the fewer resources that are left for future generations.

- *leisure* — More leisure lowers real GDP, but leisure is desirable. Would you sacrifice some material standard of living in exchange for almost three more weeks of vacation a year that Europeans have over Canadians?

- *political freedoms and social justice* — Countries with high real GDP per person could have limited political freedoms and uneven distributions of income.

Higher real GDP per person does not always means a better quality of life. But if there are no significant changes over time in the extent of non-market production, the underground economy, environmental damage, leisure, political freedom, and social justice, the *growth rate of real GDP per person* is still the best measure of the *increase* in the standard of living and well-being for a country.

The United Nations Human Development Index (HDI) is a broader measure of quality of life that includes life expectancy, educational achievement, and income. See http://tinyurl.com/FlexText-HDI.

Practice...

16. The normal measurement of GDP *overestimates* economic well-being because it excludes

    a. non-market production.

    b. unreported home renovations.

    c. the effects of pollution.

    d. leisure time.

17. A country with an efficient and affordable system of government-financed health care probably has _____ real GDP and might have _____ well-being than other countries.

    a. lower; lower

    b. higher; higher

    c. lower; higher

    d. higher; lower

18. The United Nations Human Development Index is a measure of

    a. material standard of living.

    b. labour force participation.

    c. economic growth.

    d. well-being.

19. Which activities are part of the underground economy?

    a. ecstasy sales

    b. bartender tips

    c. cash payments for renovations

    d. all of the above

20. Justin goes from a stay-at-home father to a paid worker. He now earns $400 a week but pays $200 a week for day care and $200 a week for a housekeeper. Justin is better off by

    a. $0 and GDP increases by $0.

    b. $0 and GDP increases by $800.

    c. $400 and GDP increases by $0.

    d. $400 and GDP increases by $800.

Apply...

10. More and more people are eating their meals in restaurants instead of cooking at home. Explain how this social trend affects real GDP. How does it affect their quality of life?

_____

_____

_____

_____

11. Alberta is one of the wealthiest provinces in Canada. Alberta's real GDP grew at an annual rate of 2.2 percent between 1961 and 2003. Ecological economists used a broader measure of well-being to determine if Alberta's higher economic growth led to a better quality of life.

   a. Which of the following trends suggests that the well-being of Albertans decreased between 1961 and 2003: obesity rates increased, life expectancy increased, unemployment rates decreased, weekly wages increased, household debt increased, the gap between the rich and the poor increased, and greenhouse gas emissions increased.

_____

_____

_____

_____

   b. Based on the above trends, would you conclude that the overall well-being of Albertans increased or decreased over this period?

_____

_____

_____

_____

12. Of the five factors not included in real GDP as a measure of well-being, which makes the most difference to your personal quality of life? Explain why.

_____

_____

_____

_____

_____

The Language of Business Cycles

 Describe business cycles in terms of real GDP and output gaps as a target for policymakers.

When the economy lives up to its potential, real GDP equals potential GDP, and all inputs—labour, capital, land/resources, and entrepreneurship — are fully employed. Business cycles were described earlier as ups and downs of overall economic activity. More precisely, **business cycles** are fluctuations of real GDP around potential GDP.

To illustrate the language of business cycles, look at the last complete Canadian business cycle around the Global Financial Crisis in Figure 7.

Figure 7   Phases of a Business Cycle

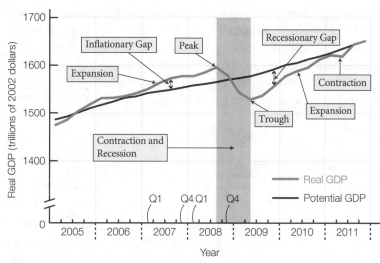

Based on Bank of Canada(2009). Rates and statistics: Indicators of capacity and inflation pressured of Canada.

Phases of a Business Cycle

The "boom and bust" of business cycles usually begins with the "boom." An **expansion** is any period (measured in quarters, or three-month blocks) during which real GDP increases. Real GDP expanded from 2005 to 2008. In the third quarter of 2008, the expansion reached a *peak* — the highest point of an expansion and a turning point when real GDP started decreasing. A **contraction** (the "bust") is any period during which real GDP decreases. In the second quarter of 2009 real GDP reached a *trough* — the lowest point of a contraction and a turning point when real GDP started increasing.

A **recession** is defined as two or more successive quarters of contraction of real GDP. The shaded orange area is a recession. A short one-quarter long contraction, like the one in the second quarter of 2011, is a contraction but not a recession.

There is no precise definition of a depression — it might be called "a really, really bad recession." Economists still have work to do on their language skills.

Output Gaps, Unemployment, and Inflation

The language of business cycles focuses on the ups and downs, highs and lows, of fluctuations in real GDP. There are two other important definitions that focus on fluctuations *around* potential GDP — the differences between real GDP and potential GDP.

Recessionary and Inflationary Gaps   Look again at Figure 7 on page 121. In a **recessionary gap**, real GDP is below potential GDP. For any time period, we can measure the size of the recessionary gap as the vertical distance between potential GDP and real GDP. Figure 7 labels the recessionary gap for the fourth quarter of 2009, but a recessionary gap exists for every quarter when real GDP is less than potential GDP. Labour, capital, land/resources, or entrepreneurship are not fully utilized, which is why actual GDP is less than potential GDP.

There is an **inflationary gap** when real GDP is above potential GDP. Figure 7 labels the inflationary gap for the third quarter of 2007. Not only are all inputs fully employed, the economy is working overtime. This overheated economic activity can cause inflation, hence the term *inflationary gap*. (You might be wondering, how can real GDP be above potential GDP when potential GDP is full employment? If so, good for you! The answer comes in the next chapter.)

Output Gaps   Both recessionary gaps and inflationary gaps measure the difference between actual output (real GDP) and the full employment output of an economy (potential GDP). Economists refer to both as **output gaps**, which are calculated as real GDP minus potential GDP. For recessionary gaps, the output gap is negative (real GDP less than potential GDP). For inflationary gaps, the output gap is positive (real GDP greater than potential GDP).

 # Practice...

21. A recession occurs when real GDP

    a. is negative.

    b. growth is negative.

    c. growth is negative for two quarters in a row.

    d. growth is negative for two years in a row.

22. An output gap is

    a. negative if real GDP is above potential GDP.

    b. negative for an inflationary gap.

    c. positive if real GDP equals potential GDP.

    d. positive for an inflationary gap.

23. The business cycle phase that occurs just after a peak is a(n)

    a. contraction.

    b. trough.

    c. expansion.

    d. deflation.

24. In Beyonceland, real GDP decreased continuously from $200 billion in 2016 to $160 billion in 2017. Potential GDP remained constant at $180 billion. Between 2016 and 2017 Beyonceland

    a. went from an inflationary gap to a deflationary gap.

    b. went from a peak to a trough.

    c. went from a negative output gap to a positive output gap.

    d. had a growth rate of – 25 percent.

25. In 2015, Adanac produced 20 kilos of apples and 30 kilos of bananas. Both fruits were used only for final consumption and nothing else was produced. In 2015, a kilo of apples sold for $5 and a kilo of bananas sold for $10. Using the same prices, economists estimate that potential GDP is $800. The output gap is

    a. + 400.

    b. – 400.

    c. +100.

    d. – 100.

 Apply…

13. Describe the sequence of a typical business cycle, beginning with an expansion and ending with an expansion.

_____

_____

_____

14. Look at the table below of data on real GDP and potential GDP for Dazedland.

DATA FOR DAZEDLAND		
Year	Actual Real GDP	Potential Real GDP
2007	200	200
2008	212	210
2009	211	220
2010	209	230
2011	240	240
2012	240	240
2013	248	248
2014	258	256
2015	254	264
2016	266	272

a. Identify the peaks and troughs of the business cycle for this economy.

_____

_____

_____

b. In which years is this economy in recession?

_____

_____

_____

c. In which years is there an inflationary gap? What is the output gap for these years (what is the number, and is it positive or negative)?

_____

_____

_____

d. What happened to productivity between 2011 and 2012?

_____

_____

_____

to be continued

Apply...

continued

15. The Statistics Canada data below show GDP and personal disposable income for the last two quarters of 2008 and the first quarter of 2009. Use this information to answer the following questions.

	3Q 2008	4Q 2008	1Q 2009
Change in real GDP (%) compared to previous quarter	0.1%	– 0.9%	– 1.4%
Consumption	$813 469	$807 018	$803 863
Government Spending	$264 462	$266 084	$266 884
Business Investment Spending	$318 616	$305 999	$288 780
Exports	$488 152	$464 964	$424 655
Imports	$584 824	$547 196	$485 937
Personal Disposable Income (millions $, current prices)	$955 512	$960 852	$955 260

a. When did the Canadian economy enter a recession?

b. What is the largest spending component of GDP?

c. Did any of the spending components of GDP increase since the third quarter of 2008?

d. What spending component of GDP decreased the most since the third quarter of 2008?

e. Did net exports increase or decrease between third quarter of 2008 and the first quarter of 2009?

f. Compare the fourth quarter of 2008 with the first quarter of 2009. Did disposable income increase over this period? Did real disposable income increase over this period?
[*HINT*: Prices fell over this period.]

KNOW...

Summary of Learning Objectives

1. GDP concepts measure the value of all final products and services produced annually in a country; **nominal GDP** combines changes in prices and quantities, **real GDP** measures only changes in quantities, and **real GDP per person** is the best measure of material standard of living.

2. **Value added** solves the problems of double counting and distinguishing final and intermediate products and services, and shows how aggregate spending equals aggregate income in circular flow diagrams. **Injections** into, and **leakages** out of, the circular flow help explain when real GDP is unchanged, decreasing, or increasing.

3. By increasing the quantity and quality of inputs, **economic growth** increases productivity and **potential GDP per person**, raising maximum possible living standards. In measuring economic growth rates, the **Rule of 70** shows how small differences in growth rates make huge differences in living standards over time because of the effects of compounding.

4. Real GDP per person is a limited measure of well-being because it excludes non-market production, the underground economy, environmental damage, leisure, and political freedoms and social justice.

5. Business cycles — fluctuations of real GDP around potential GDP — are periods of real GDP **expansion** and **contraction**. **Output gaps** — **recessonairy gaps** and **inflationary gaps** — measure the difference between real GDP and potential GDP, and "closing the gap" is an important target for policymakers.

Key Terms

business cycles: fluctuations of real GDP around potential GDP

contraction: period during which real GDP decreases

disposable income: aggregate income minus net taxes

economic growth: expansion of economy's capacity to produce products and services; increase in potential GDP per person

economic growth rate: annual percentage change in real GDP per person

expansion: period during which real GDP increases

flow: amount per unit of time

human capital: increased earning potential from work experience, on-the-job training, and education

inflationary gap: real GDP above potential GDP

injection: spending in the circular flow that does not start with consumers — government purchases (G), business investment spending (I), and exports (X) are injections

leakage: spending that leaves the circular flow through savings (S), net taxes (T), or imports (IM)

net taxes: taxes minus transfer payments

nominal GDP: the value at current prices of all final products and services produced annually in a country

output gap: real GDP minus potential GDP

potential GDP: real GDP when all inputs — labour, capital, land (and other resources), and entrepreneurial ability — are fully employed

potential GDP per person: real GDP per person when all inputs — labour, capital, land (and other resources), and entrepreneurial ability — are fully employed

productivity: measured as quantity of real GDP produced by an hour of labour

real GDP: the value at constant prices of all final products and services produced annually in a country

real GDP per person: real GDP divided by population

recession: two or more successive quarters of contraction of real GDP

recessionary gap: real GDP below potential GDP

Rule of 70: number of years it takes for the initial amount to double is roughly 70 divided by annual percentage growth rate

stock: fixed amount at a moment in time

technological change: improvements in quality of capital

value added: value of outputs minus the value of intermediate products and services bought from other businesses

Answers to Practice

1. **a** Current prices and current quantities.

2. **b** Real GDP is constant, but real GDP per person and living standards decrease.

3. **c** Definition.

4. **d** No increase in living standards if all of the increase due to rising prices, or if the population increases even if all of the increase due to increases in quantities.

5. **d** (20 kilos apples × $5 per kilo = $100) + (30 kilos bananas × $10 per kilo = $300) = $400.

6. **b** Value added = value of final products and services = inputs' incomes.

7. **d** The value of intermediate products are already included in the value of final products.

8. **c** Expenditure = revenues earned from sales of outputs, used to pay incomes of inputs.

9. **d** All are income not spent on Canadian GDP.

10. **a** $C + I + G + X - IM = Y$.

11. **b** Changes in the quantity or quality of inputs change potential GDP and shift the macro production possibilities frontier.

12. **c** Financial assets are not part of GDP or measures of growth.

13. **c** More output for less work.

14. **a** ($240 − $200) ÷ $200 = 0.2 = 20%.

15. **b** From Rule of 70. 70 divided by 3.5 = 20.

16 **c**   Other answers increase well-being.

17. **c**   Less health-care spending because efficient, but higher quality of life.

18. **d**   HDI is a broader measure of quality of life including life expectancy, educational achievement, as well as income.

19. **d**   Income that is illegal or unreported to tax authorities.

20. **b**   Market transactions are $800, but Justin earns and spends $400 per week.

21. **c**   Definition of recession.

22. **d**   Real GDP > potential GDP.

23. **a**   A peak is the highest point of an expansion and a turning point when real GDP starts decreasing or contracting.

24. **a**   Also went from positive to negative output gap, with growth rate of – 20 percent.

25. **b**   GDP is ($5 × 20) for apples + ($10 × 30) for bananas = $400.
Output gap = GDP − potential GDP = $400 − $800.

6 Unemployment and Inflation

LEARNING OBJECTIVES

L01 Explain what the unemployment rate measures and misses.

L02 Identify four types of unemployment, define the natural rate of unemployment, and connect unemployment to recessionary and inflationary output gaps.

L03 Explain how the inflation rate is calculated and what it misses.

L04 Use the distinction between nominal and real incomes and interest rates to identify losers and winners from the effects of inflation and deflation.

L05 Describe the Phillips Curve and its connections to demand-pull and cost-push inflation.

LEARN...

The fundamental macroeconomic question asks, "If left alone by government, how quickly do the price mechanisms of market economies adjust to maintain steady growth in living standards, full employment, and stable prices?"

GDP, unemployment, and inflation are the key outcomes for answering that question and judging the performance of the Canadian economy.

You constantly see headlines about unemployment rates, the job market, and inflation rates in the media. "Canada's unemployment rate falls to 6.3% — lowest in nearly nine years." "For young Canadians, a new reality: dealing with 'job churn.'" "Gas prices help slow annual inflation rate to 1.3% in May."

What do these headlines and numbers actually mean? In judging the performance of the economy, what are "good" numbers for unemployment and inflation, what are "bad" numbers, and why are the numbers different in different parts of the country? And what do these headlines mean for you personally? Your job prospects? Your standard of living? Your smart financial choices?

In this chapter you will learn how unemployment and inflation are measured, how they are connected to each other and to GDP, and how to find useful information to aid your job searches and saving and investment decisions.

Measuring Unemployment

L01 Explain what the unemployment rate measures and misses.

Unemployment is something everyone worries about. Not having a paying job, and not earning money in input markets, creates serious hardship — you can't afford to buy the necessities of life in output markets. Unemployment is not good for society either, because when people are not working, there are fewer products and services in output markets to meet everyone's needs.

Calculating the Unemployment Rate

Statistics Canada places everyone in the working-age population (age 15 and over) into one of three categories:

- employed — working full-time or part-time at a paid job.
- **unemployed** — not doing paid work and actively searching for a job, or on temporary layoff, or about to start a new job.
- not in the labour force — does not fit into employed or unemployed categories (full-time student, homemaker, retiree).

To count as unemployed, it is not enough to be without a job — you also must be actively searching for work.

To calculate the unemployment rate, Statistics Canada first calculates the **labour force** — the sum of the employed and the unemployed.

$$\text{Labour force} = \text{Employed} + \text{Unemployed}$$

The **unemployment rate** is the percentage of the people in the labour force who are unemployed — without work and actively seeking a job.

$$\text{Unemployment Rate} = \frac{\text{Unemployed}}{\text{Labour Force}} \times 100$$

The unemployment rate for July 2017 was 6.3 percent. Here are the numbers for that calculation.

$$\text{Unemployment Rate} = \frac{1\ 246\ 800}{19\ 668\ 700} \times 100 = 6.3\%$$

The size of the labour force is also used to calculate the **labour force participation rate** — the percentage of the working-age population who are in the labour force (employed or unemployed).

$$\text{Labour Force Participation Rate} = \frac{\text{Labour Force}}{\text{Working-Age Population}} \times 100$$

In July 2017, the working-age population was 29 919 200, so the labour force participation rate was

$$\text{Labour Force Participation Rate} = \frac{19\ 668\ 700}{29\ 919\ 200} \times 100 = 65.7\%$$

History of Unemployment Rates   Over the last 100 years in Canada, the highest unemployment rate was almost 20 percent during the Great Depression of the 1930s. The lowest was 1.2 percent during World War II. The highest post-war unemployment rate — 11.9 percent in 1983 — occurred during the recession of the early 1980s. The unemployment rate during the early 1990s recession reached 11.4 percent in 1993. And most recently, the 2009 unemployment rate reached 8.3 percent during the Global Financial Crisis.

What the Unemployment Rate Misses

Just as the measurements of GDP have limitations, so too do the measurements of unemployment. Each of the three categories — employed, unemployed, and not in the labour force — misses some part of the full unemployment story.

Involuntary Part-Time Workers   Some workers who are employed part time would rather have a full-time job, but can't find one. These *involuntary part-time workers* don't show up in the official unemployment rate — they are counted as employed.

Discouraged Workers   Most unemployed workers hope to find a job. But more than half of unemployed workers end up dropping out of the labour force. Workers drop out for many reasons, including returning to school or because they have given up on finding a job. **Discouraged workers** are those who want to work, but have given up actively searching for jobs. They do not show up in the unemployment rate.

Discouraged workers do change the labour force participation rate. During recessions, when it's harder to find jobs, more discouraged workers drop out of the labour force. Ironically, this causes the official unemployment rate to *fall* when more people are actually out of work.

For example, if 93 people are employed, and 7 people are not employed and seeking work, the official unemployment rate is 7 percent ($7 \div (93 + 7) \times 100$). But if one of those unemployed people gets discouraged and leaves the labour force, the official unemployment rate falls to 6 percent ($6 \div (93 + 6) \times 100$). The number of jobs has not increased but the unemployment rate goes down.

Regional Unemployment Differences   The national unemployment rate is calculated by aggregating (summing) the statistics for all provinces. That average hides regional differences in unemployment rates across Canada. Figure 1 shows the unemployment rates for July 2017 by province.

Figure 1   Provincial Unemployment Rates, July 2017

Province	Unemployment Rate
Newfoundland and Labrador	15.7
Prince Edward Island	10.0
Nova Scotia	7.9
New Brunswick	6.5
Quebec	5.8
Ontario	6.1
Manitoba	5.0
Saskatchewan	6.6
Alberta	7.8
British Columbia	5.3

Based on Labour force characteristics by province – Seasonally adjusted
http://www.statcan.gc.ca/daily-quotidien/170804/t003a-eng.htm

Practice...

1. Who is counted as unemployed?

   a. Sirena is a college student with no job.

   b. Miguel starts a new job in a week.

   c. Reetu stopped looking for work because she was unable to find a job.

   d. Rajinder is working part time but wishes he were working full time.

2. If Salma loses her job and starts looking for work, the

   a. labour force increases.

   b. labour force decreases.

   c. labour force participation rate remains unchanged.

   d. number of employed increases.

3. There are 19 million people employed, 1 million unemployed, and 25 million people 15 years of age or older. Which statement is *true*?

   a. The labour force is 19 million.

   b. The labour force participation rate is 80 percent.

   c. The unemployment rate is 4 percent.

   d. The unemployment rate is 1 percent.

4. The summer job market for post-secondary students starts in May. One year, 59 000 fewer students were employed compared to a year earlier. These students' labour force participation rate also fell over the year, from 75 percent to 69 percent. What is the correct interpretation of these numbers?

   a. More students are working.

   b. More students are in the labour force.

   c. Fewer students are looking for work.

   d. Fewer students are in the labour force.

5. Including discouraged workers in the official unemployment rate will

   a. raise the official unemployment rate.

   b. not change the official unemployment rate.

   c. lower the official unemployment rate.

   d. raise the full employment rate.

Apply...

1. State the formula for calculating the unemployment rate, and explain what each word in the formula means. Calculate the unemployment rate when there are 1000 people in the labour force and 50 of them are unemployed.

2. A labour force of 100 people has 8 unemployed persons.

   a. What is the unemployment rate?

   b. If one of the eight unemployed persons stops looking for work because he finds a new job, what is the new unemployment rate?

   c. If one of the eight unemployed persons does not find a job and stops looking for work because she becomes discouraged, what is the new unemployment rate?

3. How can your knowing the regional differences in unemployment rates help you in your job-search strategy?

The Natural Rate and Other Types of Unemployment

 L02 Identify four types of unemployment, define the natural rate of unemployment, and connect unemployment to recessionary and inflationary output gaps.

What do unemployment and cholesterol have in common?

Healthy and Unhealthy Unemployment

There are good and bad types of cholesterol. Good cholesterol — found in foods like olive oil — improves the health of your heart. Bad cholesterol — found in fried fast foods — is unhealthy and increases your risk of heart attacks. Similarly, there are healthy types of unemployment — those that help create a more dynamic economy — and unhealthy types of unemployment — those that hurt economic production.

Economists distinguish four main types of unemployment — frictional, structural, seasonal, and cyclical.

Frictional Unemployment   Market economies react quickly to change. When there are surpluses or shortages, prices change and create incentives for consumers and businesses to adjust their smart choices. Some businesses shrink and reduce employment, while others grow and hire additional workers. Jobs disappear and new jobs are created. Workers moving between jobs, or from school to a job, are part of the normal, healthy functioning of an ever-changing market economy.

This unemployment — workers between or searching for jobs — is called **frictional unemployment**. Frictional unemployment is "healthy" unemployment, and is not a problem that policymakers need to fix.

Structural Unemployment   Businesses and individuals in market economies not only react to change — they cause change. Competitive business innovations earn profits for the winners but destroy less productive or less desirable products and production methods. This competition can come from domestic or foreign businesses. Unemployment due to technological change or international competition that makes workers' skills obsolete is called **structural unemployment**.

Workers who are structurally unemployed need to retrain to find new and different jobs. There is a mismatch between the skills these workers have and the skills new jobs require. Like frictional unemployment, structural unemployment is "healthy" unemployment, part of the process of economic growth that yields rising living standards. But unlike frictional unemployment, structural unemployment is a problem that must be fixed through retraining.

Seasonal Unemployment   Jobs like fruit picking or snow shovelling only exist at certain times of the year. **Seasonal unemployment** is due to seasonal changes in the weather and is a healthy part of an economy that adapts to the seasons. It is not a problem needing a policy solution.

Cyclical Unemployment   Workers who lose their jobs because of contractions in economic activity suffer from cyclical unemployment. **Cyclical unemployment** is due to fluctuations over the business cycle — increasing during economic contractions and recessions and decreasing during economic expansions.

Cyclical unemployment is the one "unhealthy" unemployment — the bad, deep-fried type. Cyclical unemployment prevents the full employment part of the question: "If left alone by government how quickly do the price mechanisms of market economies adjust to maintain steady growth in living standards, *full employment*, and stable prices?" Cyclical unemployment is a problem that needs fixing, especially according to the hands-on view of market economies.

Figure 2 summarizes the different types of unemployment.

Figure 2   Types of Unemployment

Type of Unemployment	Healthy/ Unhealthy	Problem That Needs Fixing?	Cause
Frictional	Healthy	No	Normal, healthy market adjustments of demand and supply
Structural	Healthy	Yes (worker retraining)	Technological change, international competition, resource depletion
Seasonal	Healthy	No	Weather and seasons
Cyclical	Unhealthy	Yes (fiscal or monetary policy)	Business cycles

Natural Rate of Unemployment

What is "full employment?" Most people would say it means everyone is employed, that the unemployment rate is zero percent. Economists define it differently.

Full employment for economists is the unemployment rate when all markets, including labour input markets, are working well. There still will be frictional unemployment (people between jobs), structural unemployment (people needing retraining) and seasonal unemployment (people out of work because of nature). These unemployments are part of the healthy functioning of market economies. The term "full employment" that Statistics Canada uses includes frictional, structural, and seasonal unemployment.

The unemployment rate associated with full employment is called the **natural rate of unemployment.** It excludes the one "unhealthy" type of unemployment — cyclical unemployment from business cycles. Full employment is also defined as *zero percent cyclical unemployment*.

Natural Rate of Unemployment and Potential GDP

The natural rate of unemployment connects to the concepts of potential GDP and output gaps. At full employment — with no cyclical unemployment — real GDP equals potential GDP. The unemployment rate equals the natural rate and there is only frictional, structural, and seasonal unemployment.

Recessionary Gap   When the economy contracts and real GDP falls below potential GDP, there is a recessionary output gap. The additional unemployment caused by the contraction is cyclical unemployment. In a recessionary gap, the unemployment rate is above the natural rate due to cyclical unemployment.

Inflationary Gap   When the economy expands, real GDP can temporarily rise above potential GDP — there is an inflationary output gap. Not only are all inputs fully employed, the economy is working overtime. In the labour market, the unemployment rate decreases *below* the natural rate. More workers than normal are employed; frictional, structural, and seasonal unemployment drop below normal levels.

Real GDP can increase above potential GDP, at least for short periods of time, because the natural rate of unemployment at full employment is not zero percent, but *zero percent cyclical unemployment*. Full employment still has frictional, structural, and seasonal unemployment. These types of unemployment, especially frictional unemployment, can drop below normal full employment levels. This explains the Chapter 5 question of how real GDP can be above potential GDP.

Figure 3 summarizes the connections between output gaps and unemployment rates.

Figure 3   Output Gaps and Unemployment

Real GDP and Potential GDP	Output Gap	Unemployment Rate
Real GDP equals potential GDP	None	Natural rate of unemployment — full employment (only frictional, structural, seasonal unemployment)
Real GDP below potential GDP	Recessionary gap	Unemployment rate above natural rate (cyclical unemployment)
Real GDP above potential GDP	Inflationary gap	Unemployment rate below natural rate (less than normal frictional, structural, seasonal unemployment)

What Is the Natural Rate?   What is the natural rate of unemployment — the "target" rate that a hands-off believer in Say's Law could use to show that the economy is doing fine on its own without government policies? What rate would signal to a hands-on believer that government policy is needed to reduce unemployment?

Most economists say the natural rate is somewhere between 4 percent and 9 percent unemployment. Others argue that whatever unemployment exists is always the natural rate, so there is never a need for government involvement. Economists also disagree about whether the natural rate stays relatively constant over time, or changes frequently with changes in the economy that affect frictional and structural unemployment. We will explore these disagreements in later chapters.

 Practice...

6. Unemployment caused by a permanent collapse of the East Coast fishery is

    a. cyclical unemployment.

    b. discouraged unemployment.

    c. frictional unemployment.

    d. structural unemployment.

7. When Grade 13 was eliminated in Ontario, Grade 12 and Grade 13 students graduated in the same year, increasing the number of people leaving school to find jobs. What type of unemployment was unusually high that year?

    a. seasonal unemployment

    b. frictional unemployment

    c. structural unemployment

    d. cyclical unemployment

Practice...

8. When real GDP is above potential GDP,

    a. frictional unemployment is probably below normal levels.

    b. frictional unemployment is probably above normal levels.

    c. cyclical unemployment is probably above normal levels.

    d. structural unemployment is probably above normal levels.

9. At the natural rate of unemployment,

    a. frictional unemployment equals zero percent.

    b. unemployment equals zero percent.

    c. cyclical unemployment equals zero percent.

    d. frictional plus structural unemployment equals zero percent.

10. There is a recessionary gap when the unemployment rate is

    a. below the natural rate.

    b. at the natural rate.

    c. above the natural rate.

    d. at full employment.

Apply...

4. Explain the difference between cyclical and structural unemployment. How would you tell a cyclically unemployed person from a structurally unemployed person?

    _____

    _____

    _____

    _____

    _____

5. Suppose that the government asked your advice about reducing unemployment in Canada during the 2008–2009 recession brought on by the Global Financial Crisis.

    a. Which form(s) of unemployment should be reduced to zero?

    _____

    _____

    _____

to be continued

 **Apply...**

continued

b.   Are all forms of unemployment equally healthy (or equally unhealthy)? Explain.

_____

_____

_____

_____

_____

_____

_____

_____

_____

c.   Is frictional unemployment all that bad? Explain why waiting to find the right job in some ways is like waiting to find the right person to date in a relationship.

_____

_____

_____

_____

d.   Give an example of how you would reduce each form of unemployment.

_____

_____

_____

_____

_____

_____

_____

6.   Explain the connection between GDP output gaps and the unemployment rate.

_____

_____

_____

_____

Measuring Inflation

L03 Explain how the inflation rate is calculated and what it misses.

Inflation is a persistent rise in the average level of all prices. You will often see a headline, for example: "Statistics Canada today reported that consumer prices rose 1.2 percent in the 12 months to July 2017." The 1.2 percent is the annual inflation rate in Canada. It means that the same products and services that cost $100 in July 2016 cost $101.20 one year later.

The flip side of prices rising is the falling value of money. If products that used to cost $100 now cost $101.20, your hundred dollar bill no longer buys quite as much as it did last year. Your money's buying power has fallen in value.

Where does that number of 1.2 come from, and what does it mean? Is it a "good" number or a "bad" number in evaluating the performance of the economy? And why do policymakers worry about inflation?

Consumer Price Index

Every month Statistics Canada tracks the average prices urban consumers pay for a representative shopping basket of about 600 products and services. This shopping basket includes spending on housing, transportation, food, recreation, furniture, and clothing. Those prices are used to construct the **Consumer Price Index** (**CPI**), the most widely used measure of average prices.

The CPI calculates average prices for each of the 600 products and services and weights them by their relative importance in the basket. That weighted average of prices is the Consumer Price Index.

To make it easier to compare years, prices are measured against a base year. The base year is currently 2002, and the cost of the basket for that year is set at 100. The same products and services that cost $100 in 2002 cost $130.40 in July 2017. That's why the CPI is also called the cost of living index.

Calculating the Inflation Rate

The **inflation rate** is the annual percentage change in the Consumer Price Index (CPI). The general formula for the inflation rate between two years is

$$\text{Inflation Rate} = \frac{\text{CPI for current year} - \text{CPI for previous year}}{\text{CPI for previous year}} \times 100$$

The CPI in July 2017 was 125.9 and the CPI a year earlier in July 2016 was 123.0. Plugging those numbers into the inflation rate formula, we get

$$\text{Inflation Rate} = \frac{130.4 - 128.9}{128.9} \times 100 = 1.2\%$$

History of Inflation Rates   The inflation rate was under 2 percent during the early 1960s, but then increased during the Vietnam War. The highest rates occurred in 1975 (10.9 percent) and 1981 (12.4 percent), as a result of massive increases in the price of oil triggered by the Organization of Petroleum Exporting Countries (OPEC) and wars in the Middle East. Inflation rates fell during the recession of the early 1980s, due to deliberate actions by the Bank of Canada. They fell again during the recession of the early 1990s. Since then, the Bank of Canada, as part of its monetary policy (Chapter 11), has succeeded in keeping the inflation rate within its target range of 1 to 3 percent.

Core Inflation Rates   Because prices of energy and fresh foods go up and down so often, the inflation rate can change quickly from month to month. To get around large, brief fluctuations and identify long-term trends in inflation, the Bank of Canada calculates three core inflation rates — CPI-trim, CPI-median, and CPI-common. You can read about the details on the Bank of Canada website (bankofcanada.ca). These core inflation rates remove different short-run price fluctuations, with the shared goal of identifying long-run, underlying trends in inflation.

Deflation   Prices can rise *and* fall. **Deflation** is the opposite of inflation — a persistent *fall* in average prices and a rise in the value of money. During a deflation, the CPI falls over time, and the calculated rate of change is negative. The "inflation rate" during a period when prices fell by 2 percent would be – 2 percent. Canada, unlike Japan, has not experienced deflation, but we will discuss the serious risks of deflation shortly.

What the Inflation Rate Misses

There are challenges in using the Consumer Price Index to measure inflation (or deflation), just as there are challenges in measuring GDP or the unemployment rate. To isolate price changes, the Consumer Price Index keeps quantities constant. But in the real world, as prices change, consumers change the quantities of products and services they buy. Also, consumers eagerly buy new and improved versions of products and services. The inflation rate misses these two important trends.

Switch to Cheaper Substitutes   When the price of gasoline rises, people drive less and switch to public transit. That is the law of demand — when the price of a product rises, we tend to buy less of it. We all save money, and reduce our cost of living, by switching to cheaper substitutes. The unchanged quantities of products and services in the basket of the Consumer Price Index do not include the switch to cheaper substitutes, so the CPI *overstates* increases in the cost of living.

New and Better Products   The unchanged basket of the Consumer Price Index also misses the introduction of new products and changes in quality of existing products. There is no easy way to compare the cost of living in a year when new products or services like the iPhone or tablet computers are introduced, to an earlier year when they didn't exist. Because the CPI doesn't capture these improvements in product quality, it again *overstates* increases in the cost of living.

Statistics Canada is aware of these unavoidable limitations of all price indexes, and updates the contents of the CPI shopping basket from time to time to reflect changes in consumer spending habits and in products. The Bank of Canada estimates that the official inflation rate, based on the Consumer Price Index, *overstates* increases in the cost of living by about 0.5 percent. So an official inflation rate, for example, of 3 percent, translates into an actual increase in cost of living of 2.5 percent.

Practice...

11. If the CPI was 120 in 2015 and 126 in 2016, the inflation rate was

   a. 5 percent, above the Bank of Canada's target range for inflation.

   b. 5 percent, within the Bank of Canada's target range for inflation.

   c. 20 percent, above the Bank of Canada's target range for inflation.

   d. 20 percent, within the Bank of Canada's target range for inflation.

12. A basket of products and services cost $200 in the base year. If the Consumer Price Index (CPI) in the current year is 250, then the cost of the basket in the current year is

   a. $125.

   b. $250.

   c. $450.

   d. $500.

13. Inflation is a fall in the

   a. number of people looking for work.

   b. value of money.

   c. average price level.

   d. value of all final products and services produced.

14. A negative inflation rate means that average prices in the economy are

   a. positive.

   b. constant.

   c. rising.

   d. falling.

15. What does the inflation rate miss?

   a. new products

   b. better products

   c. switch to cheaper substitutes

   d. all of the above

 **Apply…**

7. If the CPI last year was 115.0 and it's 116.5 this year, what is the annual inflation rate?

_____

_____

8. Anya lives on campus and goes to Loblaws to get groceries. In her first year of school her grocery bill was $1000. In her second year her grocery bill for the same food climbed to $1100.

    a. What grocery inflation rate does Anya face? Will this be the inflation rate for the economy as a whole? Explain your answer.

_____

_____

_____

_____

    b. If some of the products on Anya's grocery list in her second year are new and better products, would your answer in part a be an underestimate or overestimate of her cost of living in the second year?

_____

_____

_____

_____

    c. If Anya's income increases by 5 percent over this period, what happens to her grocery purchasing power?

_____

_____

_____

_____

9. The table below gives data for Tropicanaland, where there are three consumption goods: bananas, coconuts, and grapes.

    a. Complete the table by calculating the cost of buying the base-year quantities, and the cost for buying the same quantities of each product in the current year.

DATA FOR TROPICANALAND					
		Base Year		Current Year	
Goods	Quantity in Base-Period Basket	Price ($)	Spending ($)	Price ($)	Spending ($)
Bananas	120	6		8	
Coconuts	60	8		10	
Grapes	40	10		9	

 # Apply...

b. What is the spending on the basket of goods in the base year? in the current year?

_____

_____

_____

_____

c. If the cost of buying the base-year basket is set to 100, what is the Consumer Price Index for the current year?

_____

_____

_____

d. Based on these numbers, would you predict consumers would make any substitutions between goods between the base year and the current year? If so, what kind of problems would this create for your measurement of the CPI?

_____

_____

_____

_____

Effects of Inflation and Deflation

L04 Use the distinction between nominal and real incomes and interest rates to identify losers and winners from the effects of inflation and deflation.

Why do we worry about inflation? If, *on average*, all prices rise by the same percentage, including input prices that determine incomes as well as output prices, then people can afford to buy the same products and services before and after the inflation. What's the problem?

Problems arise because inflation has uneven effects. *On average* hides differences between losers and winners.

Nominal versus Real

The distinction between *nominal* and *real* exposes the differential effects of inflation and deflation. **Nominal income** is the value at *current* prices of what you earn (from wages, rent, interest, and profits). If you earn $30 000 a year before taxes and deductions, your nominal income is $30 000. **Real income** is the value at *constant* prices of what you earn. Real income adjusts for the effects of inflation to measure purchasing power — quantities of products and services your nominal income can buy.

The simplest description of the relationship between nominal income and real income is

$$\begin{array}{l}\text{Percentage change} \\ \text{in Real Income}\end{array} = \begin{array}{l}\text{Percentage change} \\ \text{in Nominal Income}\end{array} - \text{Inflation Rate}$$

If, *on average*, nominal income goes up by 5 percent and the inflation rate is 5 percent, there is no change in real income. Purchasing power, the quantities of products and services you can buy, remains the same.

Let's look at the effects of inflation, before turning to deflation.

Losers and Winners from Inflation

Who loses and who wins from inflation can also depend on whether the inflation is unexpected — an unanticipated surprise — or expected — you saw it coming and adjusted your smart choices accordingly. The examples below are for unexpected inflation.

Inflation Losers The most obvious losers from inflation are people living on fixed incomes, like anyone with a pension that pays a fixed, nominal dollar amount each month. Inflation reduces the purchasing power of their unchanged dollar incomes. If the inflation rate is 5 percent, but their nominal income is unchanged (0 percent change), the formula above shows that real income decreases by 5 percent. They can buy 5 percent fewer products and services than before the inflation.

Savers lose from unanticipated inflation. Savings account dollars do not change with the inflation rate. As prices rise, those savings account dollars buy less than before. Inflation reduces the purchasing power of savings.

Lenders also lose. When there is unanticipated inflation, borrowers are paying back dollars that are worth less than the dollars they borrowed. If someone borrows $1000 for a year and there is inflation, the $1000 the lender gets back won't buy the same quantity of products and services as the $1000 loaned out.

Inflation Winners What lenders lose, borrowers win. With unanticipated inflation, borrowers are paying back dollars that have less purchasing power than the dollars they borrowed.

Nominal and Real Interest Rates

Inflation affects more than the value of the dollars loaned and borrowed. Inflation has an important effect on the interest rates charged (or earned) on loans, or paid on savings accounts. To understand these effects, let's return to the distinctions between nominal and real, and between anticipated and unanticipated inflation.

The **nominal interest rate** is the interest rate observed in the markets, paid on mortgages or loans, or earned on savings accounts. If your savings account pays 5 percent interest per year, that is a nominal interest rate. If you kept $1000 in the account for a year, at the end of the year you would earn $50 in interest (0.05 × $1000 = $50) added to the $1000, for a total of $1050.

But what can you buy with those $1050? If the inflation rate over the year has been zero, then the extra $50 on your original $1000 increases your purchasing power by 5 percent. But if average prices rose over the year by 3 percent — an unanticipated inflation rate of 3 percent — that $50 now buys 3 percent fewer products and services than before. Your purchasing power from the earned interest has only increased by 2 percent.

The realized **real interest rate** adjusts the nominal interest rate to remove the effects of inflation.

Real Interest Rate = Nominal Interest Rate − Inflation Rate

If the inflation rate over the year was 3 percent, then the real interest rate you received, or realized, on your savings account was

Real Interest Rate = 5% − 3% = 2%

The nominal interest rate calculates how many extra dollars you receive or pay at the end of a year. The realized real interest rate calculates the purchasing power you have gained or lost at the end of a year. If the unexpected inflation rate is greater than the nominal interest rate, the real interest rate is negative! Even with interest payments, you would lose purchasing power on your savings or investment. It would have been smarter to spend the money on products or services at the beginning of the year rather than saving or lending.

Real interest rates are more important than nominal interest rates for making smart saving and investing decisions.

Worries about Expected Inflation

Even expected inflation can cause problems for the economy. Imagine this scenario: You have been working on a one-year contract that pays $3000 a month. While the inflation rate this year has been zero, you expect energy prices to rise next year. Because of that, you fear the inflation rate — the cost of living — will rise by 4 percent. In negotiating a new contract, what monthly pay rate will you ask for?

If you are like most people, you will think, "The cost of living next year will be 4 percent higher. Unless I get at least a 4 percent raise, my income won't keep pace with the rising cost of living. My standard of living will go down. I'd better ask for at least $3120 a month (4 percent of $3000 is $120)."

Once expectations of inflation begin, many people think the same way. Businesses, expecting higher prices for inputs, set output prices higher to protect their profits. Banks, expecting inflation, use the formula for real interest rates to increase nominal interest rates on loans to protect the real rate of interest they will receive. When workers, businesses, and banks expect inflation, they reasonably try and protect themselves by pushing up wages, prices of output, and interest rates. This creates self-fulfilling expectations — by reacting to the expectation of inflation we may cause inflation.

Once inflation starts, expectations of higher inflation rates can keep rising, creating a vicious cycle that, if not broken, runs the risk of spiralling out of control. Self-fulfilling expectations of inflation helped cause the last sharp rise in inflation rates and nominal interest rates in the early 1980s.

Worries about Unpredictable Inflation

Whether inflation is unexpected or expected, its unpredictability causes a different problem for businesses. Producing for output markets takes time. Businesses must make commitments today for production that will only come to market in the future. If your business is not sure of a steady supply of inputs at predictable prices, your costs become unpredictable, and profits unstable. Unpredictability creates risk, and risk discourages business investment in future production. Business planning works best when prices are stable, or when inflation is running at a steady, predictable rate.

Worries about Deflation

Deflation is the opposite of inflation — a persistent fall in average prices and a rise in the value of money. At first, deflation sounds attractive. As consumers, we all like lower prices, and even those on fixed incomes would seem to benefit. But a persistent fall in average prices sets up a dangerous downward spiral.

Once average prices begin falling, new attitudes begin. Consumers, believing that prices will go even lower, hold off on buying products and services, since they will get a lower price by waiting. Sales drop and businesses cut back production and employment. Wages, which also fall with falling average prices, will fall further as the economy contracts and unemployment increases. This deflationary spiral becomes the reverse image of the inflationary spiral.

Savers, Lenders, and Borrowers   A rise in the value of money sounds attractive. Deflation increases the purchasing power of any money you have in the bank. Deflation benefits savers and lenders — the opposite effect of inflation, which hurts them.

But deflation hurts borrowers. When consumers or businesses pay back loans, they are paying back more valuable dollars — in purchasing power — than the dollars they borrowed. Deflation also means consumers' incomes and businesses' revenues are falling. Consumers and businesses have less ability to pay back loans, whose dollar amounts do not change.

Falling Asset Prices   During persistent deflation, the value of assets — like houses and equities — also falls. Imagine you bought a house for $300 000 with a $200 000 mortgage. Deflation sets in, and every month the value of your house falls, but your mortgage payments stay the same. Soon, your mortgage could be higher than your house's value — you actually owe more on your house than it is currently worth. During the Global Financial Crisis, many homeowners in the United States faced that unfortunate reality. Average U.S. home prices kept falling until 2012.

The Lesson of Japanese Deflation   Japan suffered from a decade of deflation after its real estate bubble burst in 1991. Partly as a result of the destructive downward spiral of deflation, the Japanese economy suffered *two decades* of economic stagnation, almost no growth, and significant unemployment.

Lessons learned from the Japanese experience is one reason policymakers took strong action to try to avoid deflation during the Global Financial Crisis.

Practice...

16. Inflation can harm those who

   a. keep money under their beds.

   b. save money in the bank.

   c. live on fixed incomes.

   d. do all of the above.

17. If Samarah gets a 10 percent raise in salary but her real income increases by 7 percent, the inflation rate is

   a. 17 percent.

   b. 3 percent.

   c. – 3 percent.

   d. 13 percent.

18. Gina lends George $1000. George agrees to pay her $1100 next year. They both expect an inflation rate of 4 percent. At the end of the year, the inflation rates turns out to be only 3 percent. This unexpected change is

   a. bad for both Gina and George.

   b. good for George but bad for Gina.

   c. good for Gina but bad for George.

   d. irrelevant, a deal is a deal.

19. Business investment is

   a. discouraged by unpredictable inflation but encouraged by deflation.

   b. discouraged by unpredictable inflation or by deflation.

   c. encouraged by unpredictable inflation or by deflation.

   d. encouraged by unpredictable inflation but discouraged by deflation.

20. During deflation, the

   a. value of housing falls.

   b. value of housing rises.

   c. value of money falls.

   d. borrowers are better off than the lenders.

 Apply...

10. Alvero runs his own computer business. Between 2002 and 2007, inflation was running at a steady, predictable rate. When the Global Financial Crisis hit in 2008, the inflation rate became less predictable.

   a. In an environment of stable inflation, will Alvero be more likely to raise wages and maintain his workforce without frequent strikes?

   _____

   _____

   _____

   b. Explain how wage changes in input markets contribute to inflation in output markets, and the role of self-fulfilling expectations.

   _____

   _____

   _____

   c. Explain why business planning and investment are more difficult in an environment of price uncertainty.

   _____

   _____

   _____

   _____

   d. The falling value of money also affects wage rates. The nominal wage is the wage in your contract and recorded on your pay stub. If you agree to a wage that increases by 5 percent per year, then 5 percent is the increase in your nominal wage rate. If Alvero needs to reduce the rate of increase in the wages paid to his workers, is it easier to do this when there is inflation or deflation? Explain.

   _____

   _____

   _____

11. If you are expecting deflation to begin soon, what actions would you take to try and make yourself better off in the future? If other consumers had the same expectation, and took similar actions, what would be the effect on the economy?

   _____

   _____

   _____

   _____

   _____

Apply...

12. You own a house in Toronto (lucky you) and want to sell. Everyone is expecting real estate prices to start falling. What would be a smart choice for timing your sale? What effect might your smart choice have on the real estate market?

_____

_____

_____

_____

Unemployment and Inflation Trade-Offs

L05 Describe the Phillips Curve and its connections to demand-pull and cost-push inflation.

Before 2010, Alberta had among the lowest unemployment rates in Canada and the highest inflation rates. During the peak of the oil-driven boom in 2006, unemployment dipped as low as 3 percent, below Alberta's natural rate of unemployment (or equivalently, employment above full employment levels). The Alberta economy was growing quickly, and demand for labour was far greater than the supply. Businesses faced labour shortages. Even entry-level positions at Tim Hortons offered $18 an hour to attract scarce workers.

Demand was so great, and wages so high, that workers from as far away as the Maritimes moved to Alberta to take the higher-paying jobs. But there was a trade-off. While unemployment was low, prices were rising. The Consumer Price Index (CPI) showed an inflation rate for Alberta in 2006 of 3.9 percent, almost twice the national inflation rate of 2 percent.

The Alberta experience is not unique. There is often a trade-off between unemployment and inflation. In countries around the world, situations with low unemployment often trigger high inflation, and situations with high unemployment are often associated with low inflation.

The Phillips Curve

The trade-off between unemployment and inflation was made famous by a New Zealand–born economist named A.W. Phillips. He collected data for the United Kingdom showing an inverse relation between unemployment and inflation. In years when the unemployment rate was lower, the inflation rate was higher. In years when the unemployment rate was higher, the inflation rate was lower. The visual representation of that data took the form of a curve, which became known as the **Phillips Curve**. Most countries, including Canada, showed the same inverse relation. The Canadian numbers for 1946 – 1969 are shown in the Phillips Curve in Figure 4 on the next page.

Figure 4   Phillips Curve in Canada, 1946–1969

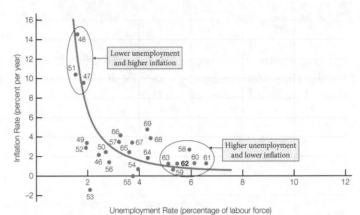

Source: Based on Leacy, F.H., ed. 1983. *Historical Statistics of Canada.* 2nd ed. Series D135-145. Ottawa: Statistics Canada; Statistics Canada CANSIM Table 326-0021, http://cansim2.statcan.gc.ca. Accessed on September 2, 2009; p. 111

Each red point on the graph represents a year between 1946 and 1969. The blue curve drawn through the points is like the one Phillips sketched to "fit" the data points. Notice that at the top left of the Phillips Curve, there are points with lower unemployment and higher inflation. At the bottom right of the curve are points with higher unemployment and lower inflation.

Demand-Pull Inflation

The story behind the Phillips Curve's inverse relation between unemployment and inflation is basically the Alberta story. For years corresponding to points on the top left of the Phillips Curve, the economy was booming, with rapid growth and low unemployment. During expansion years, the economy often produces output near potential real GDP, or even slightly above potential GDP. All inputs, including labour, are fully employed. There is no cyclical unemployment, and frictional, structural, and seasonal unemployment rates may fall below normal. Demand is greater than supply in input markets — there are shortages — putting upward pressure on business costs, including wages. Since incomes are also increasing with higher wages, demand for output is strong — people have more money and are buying more things — making it easier for businesses to raise output prices to match rising costs.

Downward Demand-Pull Deflation   For years corresponding to points on the bottom right of the Phillips Curve, the demand-pull story works in reverse — decreases in demand pull prices down. During contractions, if demand for output decreases relative to supply, businesses have unsold products and services. Businesses may cut their prices to try to sell the inventory that is piling up in warehouses. Businesses will also cut back production, laying off workers. Real GDP falls, and unemployment increases. There is a recessionary gap.

It is hard to get a raise when people all around you are out of work and eager to find a job or take yours. Increased unemployment puts downward pressure on wages, allowing businesses to cut output prices or have smaller price increases. High unemployment means consumers have less income to spend, putting more downward pressure on output prices. Decreased demand causes surpluses of unsold products and services, leading businesses to cut prices, or at least not raise them as quickly. There is a bust instead of a boom, with higher unemployment and lower inflation.

The demand-pull inflation story explains the Phillips Curve's trade-off between unemployment and inflation. Economists were confident about this trade-off between unemployment and inflation. Then the 1970s happened.

Supply Shocks and Cost Push-Inflation

In 1973, the Organization of Petroleum Exporting Countries, OPEC, restricted oil outputs. The world price of oil skyrocketed from US$3 per barrel to $12 per barrel — a 400 percent increase! Because energy costs are a large part of the cost of most products and services, businesses around the world faced dramatically higher costs.

    While businesses raised prices to try and cover rising energy costs, consumers had far less income to spend after paying dramatically higher fuel bills for driving and home heating. Prices were rising, but output decreased. While the Canadian economy didn't technically fall into a recession, the rate of economic growth slowed and unemployment increased. These events repeated with a second oil price rise in 1979. Figure 5 extends Figure 4 to include the years 1970 to 2013, years with rising oil prices.

Figure 5   Phillips Curve in Canada, 1946–2013

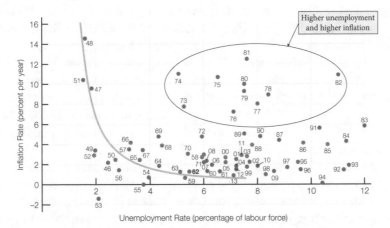

Source: Based on *Historical Statistics of Canada* (2nd ed.) Series D124-145; Statistics Canada Table 282-0002, series v2461224, Table 282-0087, series v2062815; Statistics Canada Table 3260021.

    The original, obvious trade-offs between inflation and unemployment — the blue Phillips Curve — disappear. There are now points on the figure, like those for 1973, 1974, and 1982, that have combinations of both higher unemployment and higher inflation. The demand-pull story of inflation failed to explain the combination of higher unemployment and higher inflation.

    Supply shocks are events that directly affect businesses' costs, prices, and supply — they are not caused by changes in demand. Energy price rises, droughts that reduce the supply of food, and natural disasters that destroy inputs are all examples of negative supply shocks.

Cost-Push Inflation   Supply shocks like the oil price rises do not fit the demand-pull inflation story behind the Phillips Curve's trade-off between unemployment and inflation. A new story emerged called **cost-push inflation**. Supply, not demand, plays the leading role in this story. A decrease in supply caused by increasing costs is the key force pushing up output prices.

    While average prices are rising, sales of products and services are decreasing — real GDP decreases. Since businesses are decreasing production, unemployment increases. The economy experiences a double dose of bad news — higher inflation and higher unemployment — also called **stagflation**. The word *stagflation* is a combination of *stagnation* — the economy is standing still or falling into recession with higher unemployment — and the rising prices of *inflation*.

Figure 6 summarizes the differences between demand-pull and cost-push inflation.

Figure 6   Types of Inflation

Type of Inflation	Demand–Pull	Cost–Push
Phase of business cycle	Expansion	Contraction
Unemployment	↓ unemployment	↑ unemployment
Inflation	↑ inflation	↑ inflation
Relation between Unemployment and Inflation	Trade-off (Phillips Curve)	Combination (Stagflation) Shifting Phillips Curve

Beyond the Phillips Curve

There are immediate trade-offs between inflation and unemployment as the original Phillips Curve suggests. But over longer periods of time, the trade-offs and explanations become more complicated due to changes in the natural rate of unemployment and changes in inflation expectations.

The original Phillips Curve of Figure 4 is a short-run relationship assuming that inflation expectations and the natural rate of unemployment do not change over time. If the expected rate of inflation or the natural rate of unemployment change, the short-run Phillips Curve can shift. The resulting long-run Phillips Curve (not discussed here) helps explain the data points that do not fit on the original, unchanged Phillips Curve.

Another challenge to our understanding of the relationship between unemployment and inflation is the combination of low inflation and low unemployment in recent years. This is the opposite of the stagflation combination of high inflation and high unemployment. We will have to wait and see what new explanations economists come up with.

 Practice...

21. Economists believed there was a clear trade-off between unemployment and inflation until the

    a. 1950s.

    b. 1970s.

    c. 1990s.

    d. Global Financial Crisis.

22. If the Phillips Curve is true, which could never happen?

    a. invention of the Phillips screwdriver

    b. inflation

    c. stagnation

    d. stagflation

Practice...

23. The Phillips Curve is consistent with the story of _____ inflation.

    a. demand-pull
    b. demand-push
    c. cost-pull
    d. cost-push

24. Cost-push inflation is caused by

    a. negative demand shocks.
    b. positive demand shocks.
    c. negative supply shocks.
    d. positive supply shocks.

25. Which is *not* part of the story of downward demand-pull deflation?

    a. Workers have difficulty getting raises.
    b. Consumers have less income to spend.
    c. Businesses face shortages of inputs.
    d. Businesses have unsold products and services.

Apply...

13. Describe the differences between demand-pull inflation and cost-push inflation.

    _____

    _____

    _____

    _____

14. These questions are about the Phillips curve.

    a. Why did OPEC actions end the original Phillips curve?

    _____

    _____

    _____

    _____

    b. Does the OPEC example demonstrate demand-pull inflation or cost-push inflation? Why?

    _____

    _____

    _____

    _____

to be continued

Apply...

continued

c. Between 2002 and 2007 there were strong gains in employment and large reductions in the unemployment rate. Labour force participation rates in Canada were at record highs in 2007 and Canada's unemployment rate sank to a 33-year low of 5.8 percent in 2007. Are the 2002 to 2007 trends in the inflation rate and unemployment rate consistent with the Phillips curve?

_____

_____

_____

15. Go to the Statistics Canada website (statcan.gc.ca) and find data on Canadian unemployment and inflation rates since 2014. If necessary, ask your instructor for advice about where to look. If you were to plot the combinations of unemployment rates and inflations rates on a graph like the one for the Phillips Curve, where would most of the points be located? How would you describe the combination of unemployment and inflation rates?

_____

_____

_____

_____

KNOW...

Summary of Learning Objectives

1. The **unemployment rate** measures the percentage of the **labour force** who are out of work and actively searching for jobs, but misses involuntary part-time workers, discouraged workers, and regional differences.

2. There are four types of **unemployment** — **frictional, structural, seasonal,** and **cyclical** — but only cyclical unemployment is both unhealthy and a problem. The **natural rate of unemployment** occurs at **full employment**, when there is only healthy frictional, structural, and seasonal unemployment. Relative to the natural rate, the unemployment rate is higher in a recessionary gap and lower in an inflationary gap.

3. **Inflation** is measured by changes in the **Consumer Price Index**. The inflation rate overstates increases in the cost of living by missing switches to cheaper substitutes and new/improved products and services. **Core inflation rates** remove short-run price fluctuations to identify long-run, underlying trends in inflation.

4. Distinguishing **nominal** versus **real incomes** and **interest rates** exposes the effects of inflation/deflation on standards of living and savings/investment decisions. Losers from inflation include those on fixed incomes, savers, and lenders. Borrowers are winners. Expectation of inflation can cause inflation. **Deflation** is worse than inflation.

5. The **Phillips Curve** shows a short-run trade-off between unemployment and inflation consistent with **demand-pull inflation**. **Stagflation** (simultaneous unemployment and inflation) caused by negative **supply shocks** and **cost-push inflation** complicate the original Phillips Curve.

Key Terms

Consumer Price Index (CPI): measure of the average prices of a fixed shopping basket of products and services

core inflation rates: remove volatile, short-run price fluctuations to identify long-run, underlying trends in inflation

cost-push inflation: rising average prices caused by decreases in supply

cyclical unemployment: due to fluctuations over the business cycle

deflation: a persistent fall in average prices and a rise in the value of money

discouraged workers: want to work but have given up actively searching for jobs

frictional unemployment: due to normal labour turnover and job search; healthy part of a changing economy

full employment: there is only frictional, structural, and seasonal unemployment

inflation: a persistent rise in the average price level and a fall in the value of money

inflation rate: annual percentage change in the Consumer Price Index

labour force: employed plus unemployed

labour force participation rate: percentage of working-age population in the labour force (employed or unemployed)

natural rate of unemployment (full employment): unemployment rate at full employment, when there is only frictional, structural, and seasonal unemployment

nominal income: value at current prices of what you earn

nominal interest rate: observed interest rate; equal to the number of dollars received per year in interest as a percentage of the number of dollars saved/loaned/invested

Phillips Curve: graph showing an inverse relation between unemployment and inflation

real income: value at constant prices of what you earn; adjusts for inflation to measure purchasing power

real interest rate: nominal interest rate adjusted for effects of inflation

seasonal unemployment: due to seasonal changes in weather

stagflation: combination of recession (higher unemployment) and inflation (higher average prices)

structural unemployment: due to technological change or international competition that makes workers' skills obsolete; there is a mismatch between the skills workers have and the skills new jobs require

supply shocks: events directly affecting businesses' costs, prices, and supply

unemployed: not employed and actively seeking work

unemployment rate: percentage of the people in the labour force who are unemployed — without work and actively seeking a job

Answers to Practice

1. **b** Unemployed means not doing paid work and actively searching for, or about to start, a new job.

2. **c** Working or searching for work, Salma is part of the labour force.

3. **b** (20 million ÷ 25 million) × 100 = 80 percent.

4. **d** Lower labour force participation and fewer students working.

5. **a** Discouraged workers are officially not counted as unemployed.

6. **d** Workers' fishing skills now obsolete, so need to retrain to find new and different jobs.

7. **b** Part of normal labour turnover and job search for that year.

8. **a** More workers than normal employed, so frictional, structural, or seasonal unemployment drop below normal levels.

9. **c** Definition of natural rate. Still has frictional, structural, and seasonal unemployment.

10. **c** Unemployment above the natural rate means cyclical unemployment.

11. **a** (126 − 120) ÷ 120 × 100 = 5 percent, above the Bank of Canada's target range for inflation of 1 to 3 percent.

12. **d** A CPI of 250 is 2.5 times as big as the base year CPI value of 100. 2.5 × $200 = $500.

13. **b** Inflation is a rise in average prices and a fall in the value of money.

14. **d** Falling prices and a rise in the value of money.

15. **d** All not measured in the official calculation.

16. **d** Inflation reduces the purchasing power of money.

17. **b** Percentage change in real income (7%) = 10% increase nominal income − 3% inflation rate.

18. **c** Both expect a 6 percent real rate of interest (10% − 4%), but the realized rate of interest is 7 percent, good for the lender but bad for the borrower.

19. **b** Deflation causes falling sales and makes it harder to pay back business loans.

20. **a** Asset prices fall, value of money rises, lender are better off than borrowers.

21. **b** OPEC oil price shocks in the 1970s.

22. **d** Stagflation combines high unemployment and high inflation.

23. **a** During an expansion, unemployment decreases and shortages in markets as the economy approaches potential GDP cause rising prices.

24. **c** Events that directly increase business input costs or decrease inputs.

25. **c** Surplus of unemployed inputs puts downward pressure on input prices.

7 The Aggregate Supply and Aggregate Demand Model

LEARNING OBJECTIVES

L01 Explain long-run aggregate supply and its relation to potential GDP and macroeconomic performance outcomes.

L02 Explain the difference between a change in aggregate quantity supplied and a change in aggregate supply, and differentiate long-run from short-run effects of supply shocks.

L03 Explain the difference between a change in aggregate quantity demanded and a change in aggregate demand, and list five shocks that change aggregate demand.

L04 Use the aggregate supply and aggregate demand model to explain long-run macroeconomic equilibrium and steady growth in living standards, full employment, and stable prices over time.

L05 Use the aggregate supply and aggregate demand model to predict changes in real GDP, unemployment, and inflation from aggregate supply and demand shocks.

LEARN...

What made Wayne Gretzky the highest-scoring hockey player of all time? Talent, discipline, and hard work, of course. Some say his greatness came from following this father's advice: "Skate to where the puck is going, not to where it is." By anticipating the play, Gretzky was able to be in the right place at the right time to score goals. Similarly, success in business depends on anticipating the market. You can get rich if you supply products or services that consumers want, when they want them, or if you correctly anticipate where stock prices or real estate values are going.

This chapter examines the choices behind the key macroeconomic performance outcomes of real GDP, unemployment, and inflation. Macroeconomic outcomes begin with supply choices made by consumers, businesses, and governments. You will see the choices that macroeconomic players make, and how the players' separate smart choices add up to aggregate supply and aggregate demand.

The aggregate supply and aggregate demand model provides a playbook for thinking about macroeconomics. This will help you understand the action in the economy — when and why it hits the targets of steady growth in living standards, full employment, and stable prices, and when it misses with business cycles, unemployment, and inflation. You may not achieve Gretzky's greatness, but understanding his father's advice will help you make smarter choices on the economic field of play and evaluate economic policies that politicians will ask you to vote for.

Potential GDP and Long-Run Aggregate Supply

 Explain long-run aggregate supply and its relation to potential GDP and macroeconomic performance outcomes.

The aggregate supply and aggregate demand model — a simplified representation of the real word — provides a framework that allows us to understand the macro economy's performance.

Production Possibilities Frontier and Long-Run Aggregate Supply

To build this model, we return to the macro production possibilities frontier (*PPF*) from Chapter 5, reproduced in Figure 1a.

Figure 1   Production Possibilities Frontier and Long-Run Aggregate Supply

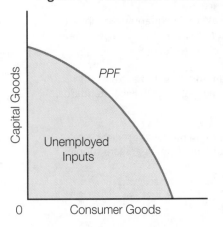

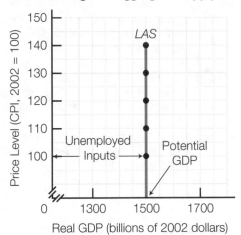

a) Macro Production
    Possibilities Frontier (*PPF*)

b) Long-Run Aggregate Supply

Production Possibilities Frontier   The macro *PPF* shows the maximum combinations of consumer goods and capital goods that the economy can produce. At any point on the *PPF*, inputs are fully employed and the economy is producing at potential GDP. Points inside the *PPF* represent unemployed inputs — workers without jobs, factories not operating, farmland not producing crops. Inputs do not appear on the graph. The *PPF* takes the quantity and quality of inputs as given to focus attention on potential GDP — the outputs that those inputs can produce. There are also no prices on the graph, only quantities of outputs.

Long-Run Aggregate Supply   Figure 1b transfers the potential GDP of the *PPF* to a new graph with the economy's real GDP on the horizontal axis and price level on the vertical axis. Real GDP is measured in constant 2002 dollars. The price level is measured by the Consumer Price Index (CPI), where the price level in 2002 equals 100. Again, inputs do not directly appear on the graph.

   Long-run aggregate supply is the economy's potential GDP — the quantity of real GDP supplied when all inputs are fully employed. The long-run aggregate supply curve (*LAS*) is a vertical line at potential GDP. No matter what the price level is at potential GDP, the quantity of real GDP does not change. If the price level rises from 100 to 140, the quantity of real GDP remains at $1500 billion.

Just as all points inside the *PPF* in Figure 1a represent unemployed inputs, all quantities of real GDP less than potential GDP in Figure 1b represent unemployed inputs, including unemployed workers.

Long-run aggregate supply represents two of the macroeconomic performance targets — potential GDP and full employment. The macroeconomic targets of economic growth and stable prices will appear as we develop the rest of the model.

Long Run versus Short Run

The aggregate supply choices of macroeconomic players depend on the time period. That is why the words "long run" are in the definition of long-run aggregate supply.

In macroeconomics, long run and short run are *not* defined in calendar time as a number of months or years. The **long run** is a period of time long enough for all prices and wages to adjust so that Adam Smith's invisible hand works well. In the long run, prices adjust to equilibrium prices that coordinate smart choices, and the economy is producing at potential GDP. The **short run** is a period of time when some input prices do not change — they do not adjust to clear all markets and some choices are not coordinated.

Long-run aggregate supply is the full-employment outcome of coordinated smart choices, while short-run aggregate supply, coming next, looks at the choices that consumers, businesses, and governments make first.

 Practice...

1. Points inside the macroeconomic *PPF* represent

   a. unemployed inputs.

   b. quantities of real GDP less than potential GDP.

   c. short-run choices.

   d. all of the above.

2. The long run is a period of time

   a. greater than 1 year.

   b. greater than 10 years.

   c. when the economy is at potential GDP.

   d. when some input prices do not change.

3. Long-run aggregate supply represents the macroeconomic performance targets of

   a. stable prices and potential GDP.

   b. full employment and potential GDP.

   c. economic growth and stable prices.

   d. economic growth and full employment.

4. Unemployment is represented by points

   1. inside the macro *PPF*.

   2. outside the macro *PPF*.

   3. to the left of *LAS*.

   4. to the right of *LAS*.

   a. 1 and 3

   b. 1 and 4

   c. 2 and 3

   d. 2 and 4

5. On the graph of the macro production possibilities frontier (*PPF*), inputs

   a. increase as you move down along the *PPF*.

   b. decrease as you move down along the *PPF*.

   c. are on the horizontal axis and outputs are on the vertical axis.

   d. do not appear.

Apply...

1. Are points inside the production possibilities frontier (*PPF*) short-run or long-run points? What about points on the *PPF*? Explain.

   _____

   _____

   _____

   _____

2. All economic models are a simplified representation of the real word, focusing attention on what's important for understanding a specific idea or concept. To focus, models must simplify and leave out less important factors.

   a. What does the macro production possibilities frontier model focus attention on? What economic factors does it leave out?

   _____

   _____

   _____

   b. What does the long-run aggregate supply curve focus attention on? What economic factors does it leave out?

   _____

   _____

   _____

3. For the *LAS* curve, why does an increase in the price level not cause business suppliers to increase their quantity supplied, as would happen for a microeconomic market supply curve?

   _____

   _____

   _____

   _____

   _____

Short-Run Aggregate Supply

 LO2 Explain the difference between a change in aggregate quantity supplied and a change in aggregate supply, and differentiate long-run from short-run effects of supply shocks.

Macroeconomic supply plans with existing inputs are similar to microeconomic choices about quantity supplied. Microeconomics' law of supply states that as the price of a product or service rises, the quantity supplied increases. Macroeconomic supply plans connecting price and quantity supplied are added together for all of the macroeconomic players. Businesses are the most important players. For prices, we use the average price level in the economy, as measured by the Consumer Price Index. For quantities, we use real GDP, which adds together the quantities of all final products and services produced in an economy, valued at constant prices.

Short-Run Aggregate Supply Curve

Short-run aggregate supply is the quantity of real GDP that macroeconomic players plan to supply at different price levels. Figure 2 adds a short-run aggregate supply curve (*SAS*) to the long-run aggregate supply curve of Figure 1b. The short-run aggregate supply curve is upward-sloping because *input prices are fixed in the short run*. When the price level rises, higher output prices with fixed input prices mean more profits, so businesses plan to increase the quantity supplied of real GDP. A fall in the price level has the opposite effect, decreasing the quantity supplied of real GDP.

Figure 2   Short-Run and Long-Run Aggregate Supply

	Price Level (CPI)	Short-Run Real GDP Supplied (billions of 2002 dollars)
A	100	1300
B	110	1400
C	120	1500
D	130	1600
E	140	1700

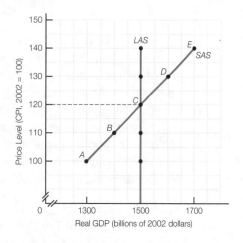

The *LAS* curve and *SAS* curve intersect at point *C*, with a price level of 120 and real GDP of $1500 billion. Only at this intersection will short-run supply plans hit the target of potential GDP. The supply plans at points *A* and *B* are less than potential GDP and the supply plans at points *D* and *E* are greater than potential GDP. All of these combinations of price levels and quantities of real GDP are just plans — we will see whether or not the plans work out after adding aggregate demand.

The Law of Short-Run Aggregate Supply   The **law of short-run aggregate supply** states that as the price level rises, the aggregate quantity supplied of real GDP increases. With fixed input prices, higher output prices create incentives for increased production through higher profits and by covering higher marginal opportunity costs of production.

Increase in Potential GDP and Aggregate Supply

Any decision that increases the quantity or quality of inputs increases an economy's potential GDP. In the language of the aggregate demand and aggregate supply model, supply plans that increase input quantity or quality **increase aggregate supply**.

An increase in aggregate supply is economic growth — the expansion of the economy's capacity to produce products and services. Figure 3 shows the effects of an increase in the quantity or quality of inputs.

Figure 3   Increase in Potential GDP

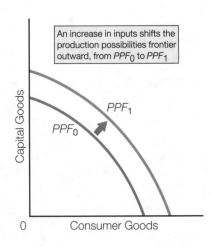

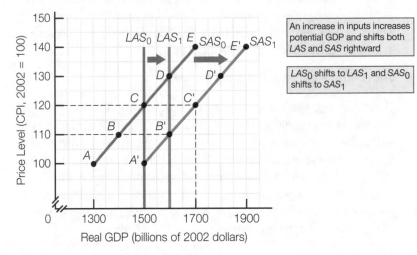

a) Outward Shift *PPF*

b) Rightward Shift *LAS* and *SAS*

In Figure 3a, the increase in inputs shifts the production possibilities frontier out, from PPF_0 to PPF_1. It is now possible to produce greater combined quantities of consumer goods and capital goods. In Figure 3b, the increase in inputs shifts both the long-run aggregate supply curve (LAS_0) and the short-run aggregate supply curve (SAS_0) together rightward to LAS_1 and SAS_1.

Changes in the quantity or quality of inputs, including technological change, shift both *LAS* and *SAS* in the same direction. An increase in inputs shifts both *LAS* and *SAS* rightward. A decrease in inputs (for example, from a natural disaster) shifts both *LAS* and *SAS* leftward.

Input Prices and Aggregate Supply   What happens to aggregate supply if input prices change? The short-run aggregate supply curve (*SAS*) assumes input prices are fixed. So if input prices change, only the *SAS* curve shifts. Figure 4 shows the effect of a rise in input prices.

Figure 4 Input Prices and Aggregate Supply

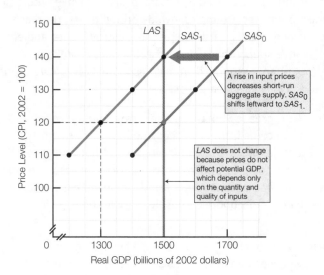

A rise in input prices decreases short-run aggregate supply. SAS_0 shifts leftward to SAS_1.

LAS does not change because prices do not affect potential GDP, which depends only on the quantity and quality of inputs

A rise in input prices — for example, a rise in wage rates — decreases short-run aggregate supply and shifts the short-run aggregate supply curve leftward from SAS_0 to SAS_1. At any price level, rising input prices reduce profits so businesses decrease their real GDP supplied. Falling input prices increase short-run aggregate supply and shift SAS rightward.

But rising (or falling) input prices do not affect potential GDP, so long-run aggregate supply and the LAS curve do not shift. When input prices change, short-run aggregate supply changes but long-run aggregate supply does not.

Supply Shocks and Short-Run Aggregate Supply

Short-run aggregate supply is largely determined by the plans and choices that macroeconomic players — Canadian businesses, consumers, and government — make. But events beyond the players' control also affect aggregate supply.

These **supply shocks** are events that directly affect business costs, prices, and supply. Negative and positive supply shocks can shift the aggregate supply curves. Supply shocks can affect long-run aggregate supply and short-run aggregate supply, but we will focus on the effect on short-run aggregate supply and the SAS curve.

Figure 5 Supply Shocks and Short-Run Aggregate Supply

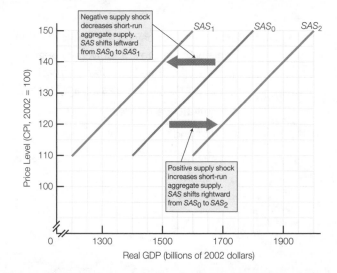

Negative supply shock decreases short-run aggregate supply. SAS shifts leftward from SAS_0 to SAS_1

Positive supply shock increases short-run aggregate supply. SAS shifts rightward from SAS_0 to SAS_2

Negative Supply Shocks Decrease Short-Run Aggregate Supply

Some negative supply shocks are caused by natural disasters, while others are created by rising input prices. Examples include droughts that decrease the supply of agricultural products, earthquakes that destroy inputs, and energy price increases. A negative supply shock in macroeconomics is similar to a decrease in supply (not quantity supplied) in microeconomics. Negative supply shocks shift *SAS* leftward in Figure 5 on the previous page.

Positive Supply Shocks Increase Short-Run Aggregate Supply

Positive supply shocks can come from new ideas and new resources or falling input prices. Examples include scientific discoveries that lead to more productive, lower-cost technologies, and lower world prices for resource inputs. A positive supply shock in macroeconomics is similar to an increase in supply (not quantity supplied) in microeconomics. Positive supply shocks shift *SAS* rightward in Figure 5.

Figure 6 summarizes the differences between the law of short-run aggregate supply (moving along an unchanged *SAS* curve) and the factors that change short-run aggregate supply — negative and positive supply shocks (shifting the *SAS* curve).

Figure 6   Law of Short-Run Aggregate Supply and Changes in Short-Run Aggregate Supply

The Law of Short-Run Aggregate Supply *In the short run, the aggregate quantity supplied of real GDP*	
Decreases if:	*Increases if:*
• price level falls	• price level rises

Changes in Short-Run Aggregate Supply *The short-run aggregate supply of real GDP*	
Decreases if:	*Increases if:*
• businesses do not replace depreciating equipment and inputs	• businesses plan to increase quantity or quality inputs
• negative supply shock raises price for resource inputs	• positive supply shock lowers price for resource inputs
• negative supply shock destroys inputs	• positive supply shock improves technologies

 ## Practice...

6. Aggregate quantity supplied increases if

    a. the price level rises.

    b. the price level falls.

    c. prices for inputs rise.

    d. prices for inputs fall.

7. Aggregate supply of real GDP increases if

    a. input prices increase.

    b. output prices increase.

    c. productivity increases.

    d. all of the above.

8. Businesses start paying high wages only to people with college and university degrees. If people plan ahead and start increasing their education, this increases aggregate

    a. quantity demanded.

    b. demand.

    c. quantity supplied.

    d. supply.

Practice...

9. Government investments to improve the quality of public infrastructure like roads, sewers, and transit

   a. shift only *LAS* rightward.

   b. shift both *LAS* and *SAS* rightward.

   c. increase aggregate quantity supplied.

   d. do not shift *LAS* or *SAS*.

10. Which media headline describes a shift of the *SAS* curve only?

    a. "Increased consumer spending is expected to lead to inflation, with no change in real GDP."

    b. "Decreased consumer spending may lead to recession."

    c. "Higher wage settlements may lead to inflation."

    d. "Faster growth from more women entering the labour force."

Apply...

4. What happens to the long-run aggregate supply curve (*LAS*) if the population increases? Can you predict what that will do to living standards? Explain your thinking.

   _____

   _____

   _____

   _____

5. Explain the difference between a change in aggregate quantity supplied and a change in aggregate supply.

   _____

   _____

   _____

   _____

6. You own a pickle business and currently supply (sell) 1000 jars a month at a price of $5 per jar. Pick a specific supply shock (negative or positive) and explain your willingness — or not — to supply pickles at that same $5 price after the shock.

   _____

   _____

   _____

   _____

Aggregate Demand

 Explain the difference between a change in aggregate quantity demanded and a change in aggregate demand, and list five shocks that change aggregate demand.

Once short-run aggregate supply decisions are made, workers earn incomes in input markets, and products and services are available in output markets. Demand plans are mostly about buying products and services in output markets. Consumers are the most important players, but businesses, government, and the rest of the world (R.O.W.) also demand Canadian-produced products and services.

All macroeconomic players make their supply plans and demand plans in the short run. For aggregate demand, there is no distinction between the long run and the short run. You will be happy to know that there is only one concept of aggregate demand to learn — in the short run.

Long-run aggregate supply (*LAS*) is a performance target — potential GDP — where we want the economy to end up. That target is the same for short-run aggregate supply or aggregate demand choices.

Aggregate Demand Curve

Macroeconomic demand plans for spending are similar to microeconomic choices about quantity demanded. The microeconomic law of demand states that as the price of a product or service rises, the quantity demanded decreases. For macroeconomics we must add together the demand plans connecting price and quantity demanded for all of the macroeconomic players. As in aggregate supply, for price we use the economy's price level as measured by the Consumer Price Index. For quantities we use real GDP.

Aggregate demand (*AD*) is the quantity of Canadian real GDP that macroeconomic players plan to demand at different price levels.

$$AD = planned\ C + I + G + X - IM$$

In Figure 7, each point on the aggregate demand curve (*AD*) corresponds to a row on the table of numbers. Each quantity of real GDP demanded in the last column comes from adding up all *planned* consumption, *planned* investment, *planned* government spending, and *planned* net exports.

Figure 7   Aggregate Demand

	Price Level (CPI)	Real GDP Demanded (billions of 2002 dollars)
A'	100	1700
B'	110	1600
C'	120	1500
D'	130	1400
E'	140	1300

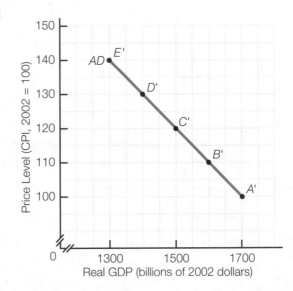

The Law of Aggregate Demand   The **law of aggregate demand** states that as the price level rises, aggregate quantity demanded of real GDP decreases. While the macroeconomic law of aggregate demand looks just like the microeconomic law of demand, there is a surprising difference in the explanations behind them.

Microeconomics looks at the demand for one particular product. For example, when the price of Beats headphones rises, you switch to cheaper substitutes like other headphones, or the not-so-great earbuds that came with your phone. Macroeconomics looks at the aggregate demand for *all* products and services. When the price level rises for *all* products and services produced in Canada, there are no cheaper Canadian substitutes to switch to.

Foreign Trade Effect   You can still use microeconomics' inverse relation between price and quantity demanded. But the macroeconomic law of demand works for different reasons especially, Canada's connection to the rest of the world. When average prices of all Canadian products and services rise, *imported* products and services produced in other countries become relatively cheaper for Canadian consumers. And as prices of Canadian *exports* rise, the rest of the world buys less of them, switching to cheaper substitutes from other countries. When Canadians buy more imports and R.O.W. buys fewer Canadian exports, the aggregate quantity demanded of Canadian products and services decreases. This is called the **foreign trade effect.**

This difference in the explanations behind the microeconomic law of demand and the macroeconomic law of aggregate demand is an example of the **fallacy of composition** — what is true for one is not necessarily true for all.

Real Balances and Interest Rate Effects   There are two other reasons behind the downward-sloping aggregate demand curve that reinforce the foreign trade effect. The **real balances effect** suggests that a rise in the price level — inflation — reduces the real purchasing power of your savings or other assets. With less valuable real assets, people often decrease their consumption spending, so aggregate quantity demanded decreases. According to the **interest rate effect**, a rise in the price level increases nominal interest rates, decreasing the investment spending component of aggregate quantity demanded.

Demand Shocks and Aggregate Demand

Holding other factors constant, a change in the price level changes the aggregate quantity demanded of Canadian products and services, moving along an unchanged aggregate demand curve. **Demand shocks** are changes in any factor other than the price level that change aggregate demand and shift the aggregate demand curve.

Figure 8 on the next page illustrates how demand shocks shift the aggregate demand curve (*AD*). Negative demand shocks are factors that decrease aggregate demand and shift the aggregate demand curve leftward, from AD_0 to AD_1. Positive demand shocks are factors that increase aggregate demand and shift the aggregate demand curve rightward, from AD_0 to AD_2.

The five most important factors that cause demand shocks and change aggregate demand are expectations, interest rates, changes in government policy, GDP in R.O.W., and exchange rates between the Canadian dollar and other currencies.

Figure 8   Demand Shocks and Aggregate Demand

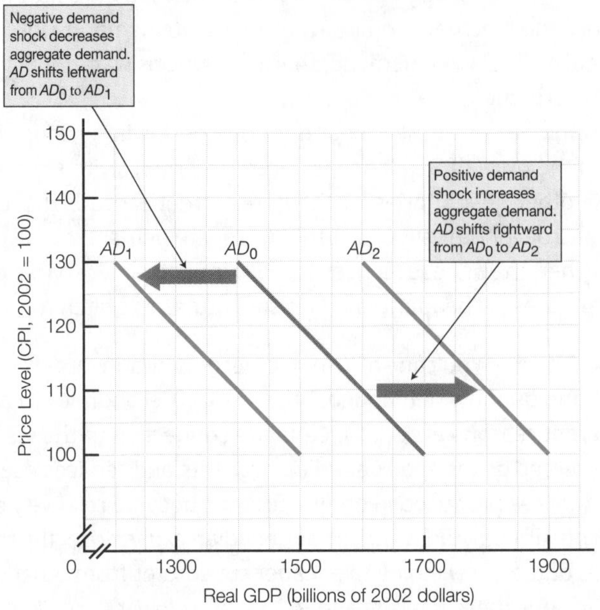

Expectations   Investment plans are based on expectations about an uncertain future. When an entrepreneur decides about the profitability of investing in a factory that will produce output and revenues lasting for 10 years, she must estimate costs and prices 10 years into the future. Even if she hires the best accountant in the world, those estimates are ultimately guesses based on expectations.

More pessimistic expectations about future economic conditions are a negative demand shock — investment spending decreases and aggregate demand decreases. More optimistic expectations are a positive demand shock — investment spending increases and so does aggregate demand. Expectations can similarly affect consumer spending.

Interest Rates   Interest rates affect aggregate demand largely through their impact on business investment spending. Factories and machinery must be paid for before they produce revenues for a business. Most businesses borrow the money to finance long-term investments, just as most consumers borrow to finance buying a house.

Rising interest rates are a negative demand shock. Borrowing to finance investment projects becomes more expensive and fewer investment projects are profitable. Aggregate demand decreases. Falling interest rates are a positive demand shock. Borrowing becomes cheaper and more investment projects become profitable. Aggregate demand increases.

Government Policy   Government policy changes affect aggregate demand. Fiscal policies involve tax and spending changes. Higher taxes are a negative demand shock. Consumers and businesses have less money to spend, decreasing aggregate demand. Decreases in government spending on products and services are also a negative demand shock. Tax cuts and increases in government spending are positive demand shocks, increasing aggregate demand.

Monetary policy by the Bank of Canada (coming in Chapter 10) affects interest rates and exchange rates, which in turn affect aggregate demand.

GDP in R.O.W. R.O.W. plans to demand Canadian exports change with changes in real GDP in other countries. Decreases in GDP in R.O.W. are a negative demand shock, decreasing the demand for Canadian exports and decreasing Canadian aggregate demand. Increases in GDP in R.O.W. are a positive demand shock.

Exchange Rates Exchange rates among currencies (more in Chapter 9) change R.O.W. planned demand for Canadian exports and Canadians' spending on imports. When the Canadian dollar rises in value relative to the U.S. dollar or other currencies, Canadian exports become more expensive, so Americans and R.O.W. will buy fewer of them. Imports become cheaper, so Canadians buy more of them. When the Canadian dollar falls in value relative to other currencies, our exports become cheaper and R.O.W. will demand more of them. Imports become more expensive and we buy fewer of them.

A rise in the exchange rate is a negative demand shock, decreasing exports and increasing imports, decreasing Canadian aggregate demand. A fall in the exchange rate is a positive demand shock, increasing exports and decreasing imports, increasing Canadian aggregate demand.

Figure 9 summarizes the difference between the law of aggregate demand (moving along an unchanged *AD* curve) and the factors that change aggregate demand — negative and positive demand shocks (shifting the *AD* curve).

Figure 9   Law of Aggregate Demand and Changes in Aggregate Demand

The Law of Aggregate Demand *The aggregate quantity demanded of real GDP*	
Decreases if:	*Increases if:*
• price level rises	• price level falls

Changes in Aggregate Demand *The aggregate demand for real GDP*	
Decreases if negative demand shock:	*Increases if positive demand shock:*
• expectations more pessimistic	• expectations more optimistic
• interest rates rise	• interest rates fall
• government spending on products and services decreases or taxes increase	• government spending on products and services increases or taxes decrease
• GDP in R.O.W. decreases	• GDP in R.O.W. increases
• value of Canadian dollar rises	• value of Canadian dollar falls

Nothing

Practice...

11. A rising price level

    a. decreases aggregate demand.

    b. increases aggregate demand.

    c. decreases aggregate quantity demanded.

    d. increases aggregate quantity demanded.

12. Which is *not* an explanation for the downward-sloping aggregate demand curve?

    a. real balances effect

    b. interest rate effect

    c. foreign trade effect

    d. expectations effect

13. Which is a negative demand shock?

    a. lower value of the Canadian dollar

    b. higher income taxes

    c. rising input prices

    d. rising price level

14. Aggregate demand in Canada increases if

    a. China buys more Canadian oil.

    b. GDP in India decreases.

    c. Canada buys more Porsches from Germany.

    d. the value of the Canadian dollar rises.

15. A new government fiscal policy to build more public infrastructure like roads, sewers, and transit

    a. increases aggregate demand.

    b. increases aggregate quantity demanded.

    c. decreases aggregate quantity demanded.

    d. decreases short-run aggregate supply.

Apply...

7. Use the fallacy of composition to explain the difference between the microeconomic law of demand and the macroeconomic law of aggregate demand.

8. What is the difference between the equation of $Y = C + I + G + X - IM$ for calculating actual GDP, and the equation for aggregate demand?

9. Abigail sells shoes. She makes her supply decisions based on the level of consumer expectations and confidence in the economy.

   a. Consumer confidence in Canada declined toward the end of 2008, but then started to improve in the spring of 2009. How do these trends in consumer confidence impact aggregate demand in general?

   b. Suppose that Canadian business leaders have optimistic expectations about the economic recovery. How does this affect aggregate demand?

   c. If Abigail anticipates strong demand conditions in the economy, describe her supply plans.

Long-Run Macroeconomic Equilibrium

 Use the aggregate supply and aggregate demand model to explain long-run macroeconomic equilibrium and steady growth in living standards, full employment, and stable prices over time.

The model of aggregate supply and aggregate demand enables you to explain real-world macroeconomic events. If there is a recession in the United States, what happens to GDP in Canada, to our unemployment, or to inflation? The aggregate supply and aggregate demand model gives you a framework for analyzing economic news and making smarter choices for your personal success.

Let's start using the model to explain the best possible macroeconomic outcome — when the smart choices of all players are coordinated and the economy hits the performance targets for real GDP, unemployment, and inflation.

Economists describe the outcome of *macroeconomic equilibrium* as aggregate demand matching the aggregate supply. Equilibrium means balance — there is no tendency for change. My favourite definition of equilibrium is by University of Cambridge economist, Joan Robinson: "In equilibrium, no one is kicking himself." Figure 10 shows an example that is both a short-run macroeconomic equilibrium and a long-run macroeconomic equilibrium.

Figure 10 Short-Run and Long-Run Macroeconomic Equilibrium

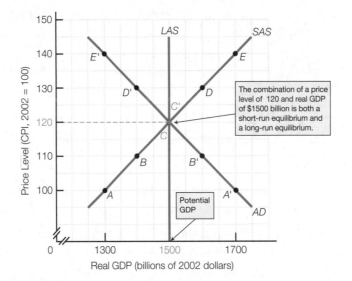

Short-Run Equilibrium with Existing Inputs

Short-run macroeconomic equilibrium is the point where short-run aggregate supply (*SAS*) and aggregate demand (*AD*) intersect. In Figure 10 it is at real GDP of $1500 billion and a price level of 120.

To see why this is an equilibrium — with no tendency to change — look at what happens if the price level is different. At higher price levels, short-run aggregate quantity supplied is greater than aggregate quantity demanded. There is a surplus of products and services that creates pressure for output prices to fall. Competition between suppliers to get rid of unsold output drives down the price level, increasing aggregate quantity demanded and decreasing aggregate quantity supplied.

At lower price levels, aggregate quantity demanded is greater than short-run aggregate quantity supplied. There is a shortage of products and services that creates pressure for output prices to rise. Competition among consumers for scarce products and services drives up the price level, decreasing aggregate quantity demanded and increasing aggregate quantity supplied.

There is no tendency for change only at the equilibrium combination of real GDP of $1500 billion and price level of 120.

Long-Run Equilibrium with Existing Inputs

In **long-run macroeconomic equilibrium**, the intersection of short-run aggregate supply (*SAS*) and aggregate demand (*AD*) also intersects long-run aggregate supply (*LAS*). In long-run equilibrium, the aggregate quantity supplied and aggregate quantity demanded of real GDP both equal potential GDP.

The price level (120) and aggregate demand ($1500 billion) turn out to be exactly what suppliers expected when they made their production plans. Suppliers are happy because their products and services get sold at expected prices, and demanders are happy because their spending plans are realized. Consumers earned enough income in input markets to buy the products and services they planned for in output markets. Input prices, especially the wage rate, have adjusted so that all inputs — labour, capital, land/resources, and entrepreneurial ability — are fully employed. The price level is stable — there are no pressures for output prices or input prices to change. This long-run equilibrium with existing inputs is the world of Say's Law — supply creates its own demand — and Adam Smith's invisible hand works perfectly.

Equilibrium over Time with Increasing Inputs

To fully explain the hands-off answer to the fundamental macroeconomic question — if left alone by government, the price mechanisms of market economies *do quickly adjust* to maintain steady growth in living standards, full employment, and stable prices — we also must look at changes over time in this macroeconomic equilibrium.

Business investment spending is the key to steady growth in living standards and continued full employment and stable prices over time. As business investment increases the quantity and quality of inputs, potential GDP increases.

Figure 11   Economics Growth, Rising Living Standards, Full Employment, and Stable Prices

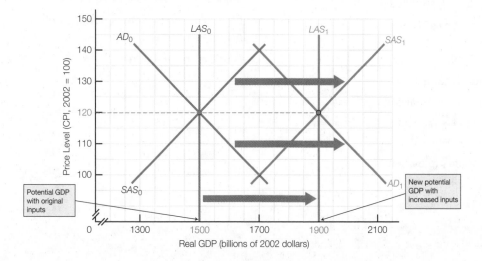

The story of rising living standards in Figure 11 on the previous page begins with long-run and short-run equilibrium at the point where SAS_0, AD_0, and LAS_0 all intersect. Real GDP is originally $1500 billion and the price level is 120. Business investment that increases the quantity and quality of inputs shifts SAS_0 and LAS_0 together rightward, to SAS_1 and LAS_1. Potential real GDP increases to $1900 billion. But will that increased aggregate supply create its own increased aggregate demand? It can. Increased employment in new and improved factories increases incomes in input markets, so aggregate demand shifts rightward, from AD_0 to AD_1. The new long-run (and short-run) equilibrium is at real GDP of $1900 billion. The quantity supplied of real GDP equals the quantity demanded. There is no excess demand pulling up average prices; no excess supply pulling down average prices. The price level stays constant at 120.

As long as the increase in real GDP is greater than any increase in population, real GDP per person grows. Since the economy is once again at potential GDP (on the LAS_1 curve), unemployment remains at the natural rate of (full) employment and the price level is stable. When Say's Law remains true, the circular flow of real GDP increases smoothly from year to year, producing economic growth, rising living standards, full employment, and stable prices.

 Practice...

16. In short-run macroeconomic equilibrium

    a. the price level is stable.

    b. short-run aggregate supply (*SAS*) equals aggregate demand (*AD*).

    c. real GDP equals potential GDP.

    d. all of the above are true.

17. Short-run macroeconomic equilibrium *always* occurs when the

    a. economy is at full employment.

    b. economy is below full employment.

    c. quantity of real GDP demanded equals the quantity of real GDP supplied.

    d. *AD* curve intersects the *LAS* curve.

18. In long-run macroeconomic equilibrium

    a. nominal GDP equals real GDP.

    b. nominal GDP equals potential GDP.

    c. short-run aggregate supply (*SAS*) equals aggregate demand (*AD*).

    d. the natural rate of unemployment equals zero.

19. New business investment that increases inputs causes all of the following *except* a(n)

    a. rise in the price level.

    b. increase in *LAS*.

    c. increase in *SAS*.

    d. increase in *AD*.

20. When there is economic growth with rising living standards,

    a. business investment increases both *LAS* and *SAS*.

    b. potential GDP is greater in the new long-run macroeconomic equilibrium.

    c. increased employment in new factories increases income, so *AD* increases.

    d. all of the above are true.

Apply...

10. These questions combine micro and macro definitions of equilibrium.

    a. What are the microeconomic definitions of short-run equilibrium and long-run equilibrium?

    _____

    _____

    _____

    _____

    b. What are the macroeconomic definitions of the short run and of the long run?

    _____

    _____

    _____

    _____

    c. What is the connection between the long-run equilibrium definition of micro and the long run in macro?

    _____

    _____

    _____

    _____

    _____

11. Explain the difference between a short-run and a long-run macroeconomic equilibrium.

    _____

    _____

    _____

    _____

    _____

12. The table below describes price levels and real GDP numbers for the economy of Macroville.

Price Level	Aggregate Demand	Short-Run Aggregate Supply	Long-Run Aggregate Supply
100	800	300	600
110	700	400	600
120	600	500	600
130	500	600	600
140	400	700	600

to be continued

Apply...

continued

a. What is potential GDP in Macroville?

_____

_____

b. What is the short-run equilibrium price level and real GDP in Macroville?

_____

_____

c. Is Macroville in long-run equilbrium? Explain.

_____

_____

_____

Aggregate Demand and Aggregate Supply Shocks

L05 Use the aggregate supply and aggregate demand model to predict changes in real GDP, unemployment, and inflation from aggregate supply and demand shocks.

Business suppliers will be kicking themselves if aggregate demand does not match short-run aggregate supply at the potential GDP target (*LAS*). Maybe they produced too many products and services that are sitting unsold on shelves, or they did not produce enough to satisfy unexpected consumer demand. Consumer household demanders will also be kicking themselves if the economy is not in long-run macroeconomic equilibrium. Either businesses begin laying off workers and reducing consumer households' incomes, or consumers will be disappointed at not finding enough of the products and services they planned to buy. There is disappointment all around.

When expectations are not realized, macroeconomic outcomes do not work out as planned. What the macroeconomic players expected to be smart choices turn out to be not-smart choices. Adjustments are necessary to get back to smart choices, and these adjustments are the stuff business cycles are made of. Recessions and expansions are the result of mismatches between aggregate demand and aggregate supply.

There are four mismatch cases that move an economy away from the long-run equilibrium targets: a negative demand shock, a positive demand shock, a negative supply shock, and a positive supply shock.

Negative Demand Shocks

What happens if, after macroeconomic players make short-run aggregate supply decisions in input markets, there is a negative aggregate demand shock — a decrease in aggregate demand?

In Figure 12, start at the long-run equilibrium intersection of LAS_0, SAS_0, and AD_0. Aggregate demand decreases to AD_1.

Figure 12   Negative Demand Shock

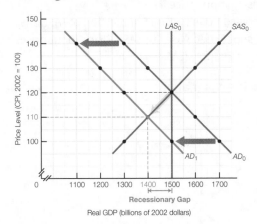

Look at the new short-run equilibrium where AD_1 intersects SAS_0. As a result of the negative demand shock, the price level falls, real GDP decreases, and unemployment increases. Since real GDP is below potential GDP, there is a recessionary gap.

This was the scenario of the Global Financial Crisis. When the U.S. housing price bubble burst, business investment spending fell dramatically and consumers cut back spending and increased savings. This caused a negative demand shock, decreasing aggregate demand, which put downward pressure on average prices. Real GDP decreased, businesses laid off workers, and the economy fell into a recessionary gap.

Positive Demand Shocks

What happens if, after macroeconomic players make short-run aggregate supply decisions, there is a positive aggregate demand shock — an increase in aggregate demand?

In Figure 13, start at the long-run equilibrium intersection of LAS_0, SAS_0, and AD_0. Aggregate demand increases to AD_2.

Figure 13   Positive Demand Shock

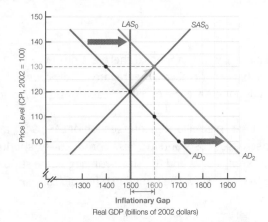

Look at the new short-run equilibrium where AD_2 intersects SAS_0. As a result of the positive demand shock, the price level rises, real GDP increases, and the unemployment rate decreases temporarily below the natural rate. Since real GDP is above potential GDP, there is an inflationary gap.

Negative Supply Shocks

What happens if, after macroeconomic players make short-run aggregate supply decisions, there is a negative aggregate supply shock — such as a decrease in aggregate supply caused by rising input prices?

In Figure 14, start at the long-run equilibrium intersection of LAS_0, SAS_0, and AD_0. Short-run aggregate supply decreases to SAS_1. Rising input prices do not change long-run aggregate supply (LAS_0).

Figure 14   Negative Supply Shock — Stagflation

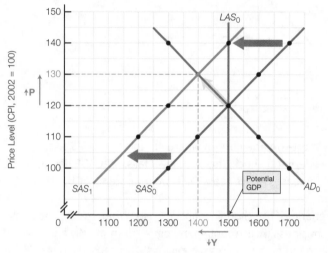

Look at the new short-run equilibrium where SAS_1 intersects AD_0. As a result of the negative supply shock, the average price level rises, real GDP decreases, and unemployment increases. Real GDP falls below potential GDP. This combination of higher inflation and increased unemployment creates stagflation — inflation and recession together.

The oil price shocks of the 1970s were a negative supply shock. In response to rising oil prices, businesses raised prices to cover rising energy costs. But consumers couldn't buy the same quantities of products and services as before, since they were using more of their income to pay dramatically higher gasoline and home energy bills. Inflation stayed high, output decreased, and unemployment increased. Stagflation!

Positive Supply Shocks

Starting from long-run equilibrium, what happens if there is a positive aggregate supply shock — such as an increase in aggregate supply caused by technological improvements that increase the quality of capital and dramatically lower costs?

In Figure 15, start at the long-run equilibrium intersection of LAS_0, SAS_0, and AD_0. Technological change decreases costs and increases productivity, shifting both the long-run aggregate supply curve and the short-run aggregate supply curve together rightward to LAS_1 and SAS_1. The rightward shift of LAS is an increase in potential GDP.

Figure 15   Positive Supply Shock — Increase in Potential GDP

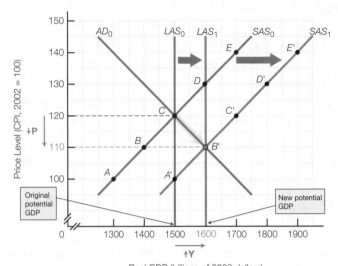

Real GDP (billions of 2002 dollars)

Look at point *B'*, where the new *LAS₁*, *SAS₁*, and unchanged *AD₀* all intersect. As a result of the positive supply shock, the price level falls, real GDP increases, and the economy remains at full employment at the increased potential GDP.

Instead of stagflation's combination of three undesirable outcomes (decreased real GDP, unemployment, and inflation), the outcome of a positive supply shock is three desirable outcomes: increased real GDP, full employment, and lower inflation.

Using the *AS/AD* Model to Think Like an Economist

With so many shocks and outcomes to keep track of, the aggregate supply and aggregate demand model can feel overwhelming. Here are some tips to make it easier to master.

Demand Shocks   Demand shocks, whether negative or positive, move unemployment and inflation in opposite directions, as the Phillips Curve suggests. In a recessionary gap, higher unemployment is associated with lower inflation. In an inflationary gap, lower unemployment is associated with higher inflation.

Supply Shocks   The language of output gaps — recessionary gaps versus inflationary gaps — does *not* apply to the outcomes of supply shocks. Unemployment and inflation move in the same direction. After a negative supply shock, higher unemployment is associated with higher inflation (stagflation). After a positive supply shock, lower unemployment is associated with lower or stable inflation.

Simple Rules for Using the *AS/AD* Model   Here's how to use the aggregate supply and aggregate demand model.

- Remember that *LAS* is different from *SAS* and *AD*.
  LAS is a performance target for the economy.
  SAS and *AD* are short-run plans and choices made by macroeconomic players.

- When analyzing any economic situation, always start the story in long-run macroeconomic equilibrium, where *LAS*, *SAS*, and *AD* all intersect.

- Model a macroeconomic event as one of the four possible shocks — positive/negative aggregate supply/demand shocks.

- At the new equilibrium, examine the results of the shock on real GDP, unemployment, and inflation.

Using the *AS/AD* model this way is another exercise in **comparative statics** — the comparison of two equilibrium outcomes. Each equilibrium is static — there is no tendency for change. We start with one equilibrium outcome, change a single factor that affects aggregate supply or aggregate demand, and then compare it to the new equilibrium outcome. This simplified comparison allows us to predict changes in real GDP, unemployment, and inflation, despite all of the complexities in the real world.

The *AS/AD* model is powerful. You can use it to analyze the effects of any of the three factors changing aggregate supply, the six factors changing aggregate demand, and the positive or negative direction of each factor. That's eighteen different scenarios you can predict from one model, focusing attention on the key performance outcomes of real GDP, unemployment, and inflation.

How to Return to Long-Run Macroeconomic Equilibrium   In using the macroeconomic *AS/AD* model, the new equilibrium is usually a short-run, but not a long-run, equilibrium. Until the economy reaches long-run equilibrium, there are still forces at work that continue to change the outcome. For example, after a negative demand shock, the economy is in a recession — real GDP is below potential GDP, unemployment is above the natural rate, and there is downward pressure on prices.

What adjustments will markets make to return to the long-run equilibrium of steady growth in living standards (at potential GDP), full employment, and stable prices? How quickly will those adjustments happen? And will markets make the adjustments on their own, or is there a role for hands-on government policy? Hands-off and hands-on economists disagree about the answer to these questions. We will return to those differences in chapter 13, Controversies in Macroeconomics.

Practice...

21. Which shock causes stagflation?

    a. positive supply shock

    b. negative supply shock

    c. positive demand shock

    d. negative demand shock

22. Rising average prices and decreased unemployment most likely come from a

    a. positive supply shock.

    b. negative supply shock.

    c. positive demand shock.

    d. negative demand shock.

23. A positive supply shock causes

    a. falling average prices.

    b. decreased real GDP.

    c. increased unemployment.

    d. stagflation.

24. in the Global Financial Crisis, changes in unemployment and inflation moved in opposite directions — unemployment went up and inflation went down. This outcome is the result of a

    a. positive supply shock.

    b. negative supply shock.

    c. positive demand shock.

    d. negative demand shock.

25. The language of output gaps — recessionary gaps and inflationary gaps —

    a. applies only to outcomes of demand shocks.

    b. applies only to outcomes of supply shocks.

    c. applies to outcomes of both demand shocks and supply shocks.

    d. does not apply to outcomes of demand shocks or supply shocks.

Apply...

13. The economy is originally in long-run macroeconomic equilibrium. Graphically illustrate the short-run effects of an increase in the wage rate. What happens to the price level, real GDP, and unemployment?

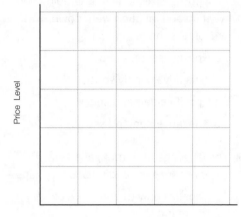

_____

_____

_____

_____

_____

_____

_____

14. When the H1N1 flu virus appeared in 2009, the World Health Organization declared it a pandemic. A Canadian study estimated that an extreme flu pandemic would reduce annual GDP growth by up to 1 percentage point in the pandemic year.

   a. Fewer workers are available during a pandemic because people get sick, die, need to care for others who are ill, or avoid work in fear of getting the illness. If fewer people work, what kind of shock is this?

   _____

   _____

   _____

   b. Consumers may reduce face-to-face transactions in fear of getting the illness. What kind of shock is this?

   _____

   _____

   _____

 **Apply...**

15. The table below shows data for aggregate demand and short-run aggregate supply for an economy. Long-run aggregate supply is 1.1 trillion 2002 dollars.

Price Level	Aggregate Demand (trillions of 2002 dollars)	Short-Run Aggregate Supply (trillions of 2002 dollars)
100	1.3	0.9
105	1.2	1.0
110	1.1	1.1
115	1.0	1.2
120	0.9	1.3

a. Graph this economy's AD_0, SAS_0, and LAS_0 curves, and show the original macroeconomic equilibrium. What kind of equilibrium is this — short run or long run? If there is an inflationary or recessionary gap, identify how large it is.

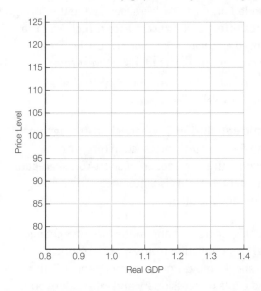

b. At every price level, the quantity of real GDP demanded decreases by $0.2 trillion. Plot the new aggregate demand curve on your graph, and show the new equilibrium. What kind of equilibrium is this — short-run or long-run? If there is an inflationary or recessionary gap, identify how large it is.

c. When there is a short-run equilibrium but not a long-run equilibrium, there are still forces at work that continue to change the outcome. Given what you know about the new equilibrium, what forces are at work, and what variables might change? How would those changes affect the AD, SAS, or LAS curves?

KNOW...

Summary of Learning Objectives

1. **Long-run aggregate supply** models the macroeconomic target outcomes of potential GDP and full employment with existing inputs. The **long run** is a period of time long enough for all prices and wages to adjust to equilibrium and the economy is producing at potential GDP. The **short run** is a period of time when some input prices do not change.

2. According to the **law of short-run aggregate supply** (*SAS*), as the price level rises, aggregate quantity supplied of real GDP increases. This is a movement along an unchanged *SAS* curve. Increases in the quantity or quality of inputs, together with **supply shocks**, change aggregate supply and shift the *SAS* and *LAS* curves. Changes in input prices shift only *SAS*.

3. According to the **law of aggregate demand**, as the price level rises, aggregate quantity demanded of real GDP decreases due to the **foreign trade effect**, **real balances effect** and **interest rate effect**. This is a movement along an unchanged *AD* curve. $AD = planned\ C + I + G + X - IM$. **Demand shocks** — from changes in expectations, interest rates, government policy, GDP in R.O.W., and exchange rates — change aggregate demand and shift the *AD* curve.

4. **Short-run macroeconomic equilibrium** is where short-run aggregate supply (*SAS*) and aggregate demand (*AD*) intersect. In **long-run macroeconomic equilibrium**, the intersection of short-run aggregate supply (*SAS*) and aggregate demand (*AD*) also intersects long-run aggregate supply (*LAS*) at potential GDP.

5. The aggregate supply and aggregate demand model predicts changes in real GDP, unemployment, and inflation from aggregate supply and demand shocks. Demand shocks move unemployment and inflation in opposite directions, and explain recessionary and inflationary output gaps. Supply shocks move unemployment and inflation move in the same directions. The language of recessionary and inflationary gaps does *not* apply to supply shocks.

Key Terms

aggregate demand: quantity of real GDP macroeconomic players plan to demand at different price levels

comparative statics: comparing two equilibrium outcomes to isolate the effect of changing one factor at a time

demand shocks: changes in factors other than the price level that change aggregate demand and shift the aggregate demand curve

fallacy of composition: what is true for one is not true for all; the whole is greater than the sum of the parts.

foreign trade effect: inverse relation between a higher price level and decreased aggregate quantity demanded due to decreased exports and increased imports

increase in aggregate supply: increase in economy's capacity to produce real GDP caused by increases in quantity or quality of inputs

interest rate effect: inverse relation between a higher price level and decreased aggregate quantity demanded due to higher nominal interest rates and decreased investment spending

law of aggregate demand: as the price level rises, aggregate quantity demanded of real GDP decreases

law of short-run aggregate supply: as the price level rises, aggregate quantity supplied of real GDP increases

long run: period of time long enough for all prices and wages to adjust to equilibrium; the economy is at potential GDP

long-run aggregate supply: potential GDP; the quantity of real GDP supplied when all inputs are fully employed

long-run macroeconomic equilibrium: where short-run aggregate supply (*SAS*), aggregate demand (*AD*), and long-run aggregate supply (*LAS*) all intersect

real balances effect: inverse relation between a higher price level and decreased aggregate quantity demanded due to a decrease in the purchasing power of assets

short run: period of time when some input prices do not change; all prices have not adjusted to clear all markets

short-run aggregate supply: quantity of real GDP that macroeconomic players plan to supply at different price levels

short-run macroeconomic equilibrium: where short-run aggregate supply (*SAS*) and aggregate demand (*AD*) intersect

supply shocks: events directly affecting businesses' costs, prices, and supply

Answers to Practice

1. **d** Real GDP = potential GDP at points on macro *PPF* in the long run.

2. **c** Definition. Long and short run not measured in calendar time.

3. **b** Any price level can be associated with potential GDP; growth requires shift of *LAS*.

4. **a** See Figure 1 on page 158.

5. **d** No inputs or prices on the *PPF* graph.

6. **a** Movement up along an unchanged *SAS*.

7. **c** Increases in quality of inputs (including technological change) increase productivity and shift both *SAS* and *LAS* rightward.

8. **d** Increases the quality of inputs, increasing aggregate supply.

9. **b** Increases in inputs increase both short- and long-run aggregate supply.

10. **c** Rise in input prices decreases short-run aggregate supply.

11. **c** Movement up along an unchanged aggregate demand curve.

12. **d** Change in expectations changes business investment spending and shifts the aggregate demand curve.

13. **b** **a** negative demand shock, **c** negative supply shock, **d** decreases aggregate quantity demanded.

14. **a** Increased exports.

15. **a** Tax cuts and increased government spending are positive demand shocks.

16. **b** Other answers true for long-run equilibrium.

17. **c** Equilibrium may occur at other answers, but doesn't *always* occur there.

18. **c** In long-run equilibrium, real GDP = potential GDP and cyclical unemployment = 0.

19. **a** See Figure 11 on page 173. If new business investment causes rightward shifts of *SAS* and *LAS* (but not *AD*), the price levels fall.

20. **d** See Figure 11 on page 173.

21. **b** Leftward shift of *SAS* decreases GDP and increases unemployment and inflation.

22. **c** Rightward shift of *AD* increases GDP, decreases unemployment, and causes rising prices.

23. **a** Falling prices, increased real GDP, and decreased unemployment.

24. **d** Demand shocks cause unemployment and inflation to move in opposite directions.

25. **a** Does not apply to supply shocks, where unemployment and inflation move in the same directions.

8 The Aggregate Expenditure Model and Multipliers

LEARNING OBJECTIVES

L01 Use the circular flow model to explain the aggregate expenditure model, and the roles of plans, injections, and leakages.

L02 Use the aggregate expenditure model to calculate equilibrium expenditure, and explain how Keynes's equilibrium model differs from Say's Law.

L03 Describe the concept of the multiplier, and show how to calculate it graphically, mathematically, and in terms of injections and leakages.

L04 Connect the aggregate expenditure model to the concept of aggregate demand in the aggregate supply and aggregate demand model.

LEARN...

Modern macroeconomics uses the aggregate supply and aggregate demand model (*AS/AD*) to explain all three macroeconomic performance outcomes — real GDP, unemployment, and changes in the price level (inflation and deflation).

John Maynard Keynes, in his 1936 book, *The General Theory of Employment, Interest, and Money*, created a simpler model that *assumed the price level was unchanged*. This simplification allowed Keynes to focus on what determines real GDP, unemployment, and business cycles. Writing during the Great Depression, when inflation was not a problem, Keynes focused on the pressing problems of unemployment and lack of spending in economic downturns. His model, called the aggregate expenditure model, focuses on the demand, or spending, side of the economy. Aggregate expenditure and aggregate demand are very similar concepts — the main difference is that aggregate expenditure ignores prices.

If you were studying economics before the 1970s, the Keynesian aggregate expenditure model was the only model you would have learned — there was no aggregate supply and aggregate demand model. Today, most of Keynes's insights are incorporated into *AS/AD* model, which also includes the price level. But there are some benefits to learning the aggregate expenditure model, which gives a more graphically intuitive illustration of injections, leakages, and the multiplier.

Expenditure Plans and the Circular Flow

L01 Use the circular flow model to explain the aggregate expenditure model, and the roles of plans, injections, and leakages.

You can see the origins of the Keynesian aggregate expenditure model in the familiar enlarged circular flow in Figure 1. Expenditure and spending mean the same thing. **Aggregate planned expenditure** (*AE*) = planned consumption spending (*C*) + planned business investment spending (*I*) + planned government purchases (*G*) + planned exports (*X*) – planned imports (*IM*).

Figure 1   Enlarged GDP Circular Flow of Income & Spending with Banking

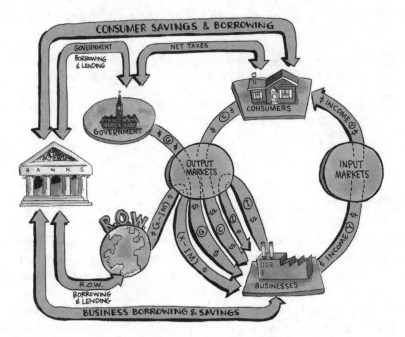

Overview of the Aggregate Expenditure Model

In the circular flow, and in equilibrium in the aggregate expenditure (*AE*) model, aggregate expenditure equals aggregate income equals real GDP (*Y*), or

$$AE = \text{planned } (C + I + G + X - IM) = Y$$

To develop the model, look more closely at the parts of the circular flow. The income that consumers can spend or save is called **disposable income** (*YD*) — aggregate income after net taxes have been paid to government. **Net taxes**, represented by the letter *T*, equal taxes paid to government minus transfer payments received from government.

Injections and Leakages   There are two more concepts connected to the circular flow.

- An **injection** is spending in the circular flow that does not start with consumers. Government purchases (*G*), business investment spending (*I*), and exports (*X*) are injections.

- A **leakage** is spending that leaks out of (leaves) the circular flow through savings (*S*), net taxes (*T*), or imports (*IM*).

Injections and leakages are more than definitions. They allow us to explain when real GDP is at an equilibrium level (with no tendency for change), is decreasing, or is increasing. Start with the equation

$$C + I + G + X - IM = Y$$

All income (Y) is either spent (C), saved (S), or taxed away (T), so

$$Y = C + S + T$$

Combining the equations yields

$$C + I + G + X - IM = C + S + T$$

Rearranging terms yields

$$I + G + X = S + T + IM$$

Injections ($I + G + X$) equal leakages ($S + T + IM$).

Adjusting to Equilibrium Real GDP   Injections and leakages are the key to understanding how the *AE* model determines the equilibrium level of real GDP. When real GDP is at the equilibrium level (with no tendency for change), injections equal leakages. Think about real GDP as the level of water in a bathtub, where the tap is still running and the drain is open. If the water coming in (injections) equals the water going out (leakages), the level in the bathtub is unchanged.

If injections are greater than leakages, real GDP increases, and if leakages are greater than injections, real GDP decreases. When the economy is not in equilibrium, the quantity of output adjusts. These quantity adjustments differ from the adjustments in a micro demand and supply model or in a macro aggregate supply and aggregate demand model. In those models, when a market or the economy are not in equilibrium, there are shortages or surpluses. *Prices adjust* to return to equilibrium.

In the *AE* model, prices are assumed not to change — prices are fixed. Therefore, all adjustments to equilibrium are changes in the *quantity of real GDP*. If macroeconomic players plan to spend more on real GDP than the economy has produced, businesses can't keep up with sales, and increase the quantity of output. If spending plans are less than the output produced, businesses have inventory piling up on shelves and decrease output. This focus on quantity adjustment instead of price adjustment is the fundamental difference between the Keynesian *AE* model and the macro *AS/AD* model.

We will spend the rest of this chapter developing simple numerical and graphical illustrations of the *AE* model.

Consumption and Saving Plans

Aggregate Planned Expenditure (AE) = planned ($C + I + G + X - IM$)

Let look at the parts of planned spending, starting with planned consumption (C). The consumption function is the relation between planned consumption (C) and disposable income (YD), other things unchanged

- Disposable income equals income minus net taxes, or
- $YD = Y - T$

Here is a numerical example of a consumption function we will use in our aggregate expenditure model. Taxes are a lump sum of 100. For simplicity, there are *no* proportional taxes that might take a percentage of your income.

$$C = 0.8YD$$

$$T = 100$$

Since $YD = Y - T$

$$C = 0.8(Y - T)$$

$$C = 0.8(Y - 100)$$

$$C = 0.8Y - 80$$

In this example, the number 0.8 is the **marginal propensity to consume** (*MPC*), the fraction of a change in disposable income that is spent on consumption. For every additional dollar of disposable income, consumers plan to spend 80 cents.

What will consumers do with the other 20 cents of additional disposable income? They will save it. Associated with the consumption function is a saving function — the relation between planned saving (*S*) and disposable income (*YD*), other things unchanged.

All disposable income (after taxes) is either spent on consumption or saved. So

$$C + S = YD$$

$$S = YD - C$$

In our simple example, $C = 0.8YD$, so

$$S = YD - 0.8YD$$

$$S = 0.2YD$$

The number 0.2 is the **marginal propensity to save** (*MPS*), the fraction of a change in disposable income that Is saved. For every additional dollar of disposable income, consumers plan to save 20 cents.

Since every additional dollar of disposable income is either spent on consumption or saved, the marginal propensity to consume plus the marginal propensity to save always equals 1.

$$MPC + MPS = 1$$

Other Spending Plans

In building our simple aggregate expenditure model, we assume that business investment spending (*I*), government spending on products and services (*G*), and spending on exports by the rest of the world (*X*) are each fixed. These parts of aggregate planned expenditure that are independent of real GDP (income) are called **autonomous spending** (*A*). The specific numbers we use are

$$I = 250$$

$$G = 150$$

$$X = 180$$

The last part of aggregate expenditure is planned spending on imports (*IM*). Import spending *does depend* on real GDP — as real GDP and incomes increase, so does spending on imports. The import function for our model is

$$IM = 0.3Y$$

For every additional dollar of income, planned spending on imports increases by 30 cents. The number 0.3 is the **marginal propensity to import** (*MPIM*), the fraction of a change in income that Is spent on imports.

Both planned consumption spending (*C*) and import spending (*IM*), which depend on real GDP (income), are called **induced spending**.

The next section combines all of the spending plans into the complete aggregate expenditure model.

 Practice...

1. The fraction of the last dollar of disposable income saved is the

    a. saving function.

    b. marginal propensity to consume.

    c. marginal propensity to save.

    d. marginal propensity to dispose.

2. Which statement is *false*?

    a. $Y = C + S + T$

    b. $MPC + MPS = 1$

    c. $YD = Y - T$

    d. $YD = C - S$

3. If the savings function is $S = 0.3YD - 50$, then the consumption function out of disposable income (*YD*) is

    a. $C = 50 + 0.3YD$.

    b. $C = 50 + 0.7YD$.

    c. $C = -50 + 0.7YD$.

    d. $C = 0 + 1.3YD$

The table below shows the relationship between disposable income (*YD*) and planned consumption expenditure (*C*). Use the table to answer questions 4 and 5.

YD	100	200	300	400	500
C	225	300	375	450	525

4. The marginal propensity to consume (*MPC*) is

    a. decreasing as *YD* increases.

    b. increasing as *YD* increases.

    c. constant at 0.75.

    d. constant at 0.25.

5. The marginal propensity to save (*MPS*) is

    a. decreasing as *YD* increases.

    b. increasing as *YD* increases.

    c. constant at 0.75.

    d. constant at 0.25.

Apply...

1. Injections and leakages are important parts of the circular flow diagram.

    a. Define injections. List three types of injections.

    _____

    _____

    _____

    _____

    b. Define leakages. List three types of leakages.

    _____

    _____

    _____

    _____

2. In the aggregate expenditure model, explain why the level of equilibrium expenditure is where injections equal leakages. In your explanation, define equilibrium and use the bathtub analogy.

    _____

    _____

    _____

    _____

    _____

    _____

    _____

    _____

3. Explain the difference between *autonomous spending* and *induced spending,* and give examples of each.

    _____

    _____

    _____

    _____

    _____

    _____

    _____

The Aggregate Expenditure Model

L02 Use the aggregate expenditure model to calculate equilibrium expenditure, and explain how Keynes's equilibrium model differs from Say's Law.

Here are all of the parts of the simple aggregate expenditure model.

$$C = 0.8Y - 80 \text{ (from } C = 0.8YD \text{ and } T = 100)$$

$$I = 250$$

$$G = 150$$

$$X = 180$$

$$IM = 0.3Y$$

$$AE = \text{planned } (C + I + G + X - IM) \text{ so}$$

$$AE = 0.8Y - 80 + 250 + 150 + 180 - 0.3Y$$

$$\mathbf{AE = 500 + 0.5Y}$$

Based on this aggregate expenditure function, Figure 2 shows each part of aggregate expenditure for different levels of real GDP (Y).

Figure 2   Aggregate Planned Expenditure for Different Levels of Income

Row	Real GDP (Y)	Consumption (C)	Investment (I)	Government Purchases (G)	Exports (X)	Imports (IM)	Aggregate Planned Expenditure $AE = C+I+G+X-IM$
		Planned Expenditure					
A	600	400	250	150	180	180	800
B	800	560	250	150	180	240	900
C	**1000**	**720**	**250**	**150**	**180**	**300**	**1000**
D	1200	880	250	150	180	360	1100
E	1400	1040	250	150	180	420	1200

For any level of real GDP, read across the row of the table to see the value of each part of aggregate planned expenditure. Notice that for any level of real GDP (600, 800, 1000, 1200, 1400), the numbers for investment ($I = 250$), government purchases ($G = 150$) and exports ($X = 180$) are always the same. They are also all *injections* into the circular flow.

The numbers for consumption (C) and imports (IM) change with different levels of real GDP. These numbers are part of the calculation of leakages out of the circular flow. Leakages are savings (S), net taxes (T), and imports (IM). Savings equal disposable income minus consumption spending, or

$$S = YD - C$$

Since net taxes always equal 100, disposable income (YD) equals income (Y) minus 100, so

$$S = Y - 100 - C$$

Reading down the rows of Figure 2, when $Y = 600$, $S = 100$; $Y = 800$, $S = 140$; $Y = 1000$, $S = 180$; $Y = 1200$, $S = 220$; $Y = 1400$, $S = 260$.

In Figure 2 on the previous page, notice that for some levels of real GDP (600, 800), aggregate planned expenditure is *greater than* real GDP. For other levels of real GDP (1200, 1400), aggregate planned expenditure is *less than* real GDP. For real GDP = 1000, aggregate planned expenditure *equals* real GDP. The level of real GDP where aggregate planned expenditure equals real GDP is called **equilibrium expenditure**. Only at the equilibrium expenditure level of real GDP are spending plans exactly equal to the quantity of real GDP produced (and equal to income).

The determination of equilibrium expenditure is so important in the Keynesian model that we are going to look at it three ways — graphically, mathematically, and using injections and leakages. The graphical illustration is easiest to see.

Equilibrium Expenditure and the 45° Line Graph

Figure 3, based on the table of numbers in Figure 2, is often called "the 45° Line Graph."

Figure 3   Aggregate Expenditure Equilibrium

Row	Real GDP (Y)	Aggregate Planned Expenditure (AE)	Unplanned Inventory Changes (Y−AE)
A	600	800	−200
B	800	900	−100
C	**1000**	**1000**	**0**
D	1200	1100	+100
E	1400	1200	+200

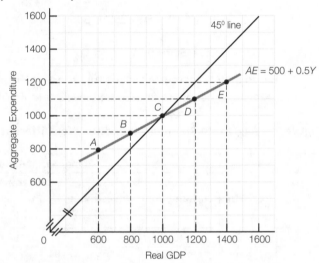

The horizontal axis measures real GDP, and the vertical axis measures aggregate planned expenditure. The 45° line extending from the origin of the graph shows all points where aggregate planned expenditure equal real GDP. If there is an equilibrium expenditure, it must be somewhere on the 45° line.

The AE curve is based on the aggregate expenditure function, $AE = 500 + 0.5Y$. Points on the AE curve correspond to rows in the table.

The equilibrium level of real GDP is at point C on the graph, where the AE curve crosses the 45° line. In equilibrium, aggregate planned expenditure equals real GDP (1000). In equilibrium, there is no tendency for change.

To understand why the equilibrium is at real GDP = 1000, look at the last column of the table — unplanned inventory changes. At points like A or B, aggregate expenditure is greater than real GDP. Businesses sell everything they produce, and more. The only way to meet demand is to sell from inventories sitting in warehouses.

This is an unplanned decrease in inventories. Seeing that demand is greater than current production, businesses increase output, increasing real GDP. As long as planned expenditures are greater than real GDP, businesses have an incentive to increase output and real GDP.

At points like D or E, aggregate expenditure is less than real GDP. Businesses cannot sell everything they produce, so inventories are piling up in warehouses.

This is an unplanned increase in inventories. Seeing that demand is less than current production, businesses decrease output, decreasing real GDP. As long as planned expenditures are less than real GDP, businesses have an incentive to decrease output and real GDP.

Only at the equilibrium level of real GDP, where aggregate expenditure exactly equals output, is there no tendency for change.

The Mathematics of Equilibrium Expenditure

Only in equilibrium does planned expenditure equal output. This is where the aggregate expenditure curve crosses the 45° line on the graph. Mathematically, this is the same as

$$AE = Y$$

In our simple model, the aggregate expenditure function is

$$AE = 500 + 0.5Y$$

Since $AE = Y$ in equilibrium, we can substitute Y for AE.

$$Y = 500 + 0.5Y$$

Subtracting 0.5Y from both sides of the equation gives

$$0.5Y = 500$$

Dividing both sides of the equation by 0.5 gives

$$Y = 1000$$

Injections and Leakages in Equilibrium Expenditure

Injections — spending in the circular flow that does not start with consumers — and leakages — spending that leaks out of (leaves) the circular flow — give the final illustration of equilibrium expenditure.

The injections in our simple model are all independent of GDP. Investment ($I = 250$), government purchases ($G = 150$) and exports ($X = 180$) add up to 580.

Leakages are savings (S), net taxes (T), and imports (IM). Net taxes equal 100. Saving and import spending depend on the level of real GDP.

For any level of real GDP (on the horizontal axis), Figure 4 shows the corresponding injections and leakages.

Figure 4   Injections and Leakages and Equilibrium Expenditure

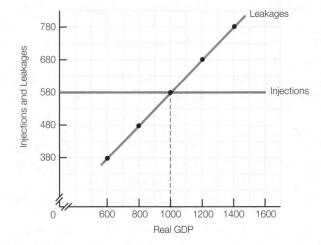

On the previous page, the horizontal line for injections of 580 does not change, no matter what happens to the quantity of real GDP. The upward-sloping leakages line plots the sum of savings (S), net taxes (T), and imports (IM) for each quantity of real GDP. As real GDP increases, so do levels of saving and import spending.

At the equilibrium level of real GDP (Y = 1000), injections equal leakages equal 580. At levels of real GDP below equilibrium, injections are greater than leakages. Returning to the bathtub metaphor, if the water coming in (injections) is greater than the water going out (leakages), the level of water in the bathtub (real GDP) rises. At levels of real GDP above equilibrium, leakages are greater than injections. If the water going out of the bathtub (leakages) is greater than the water coming in (injections), the level of water in the bathtub (real GDP) falls.

Only at the equilibrium level of real GDP, where injections equal leakages, is there no tendency for change. That is the equilibrium expenditure.

Say's Law, Potential GDP, and Equilibrium Expenditure

Let's step back from all of the graphical and mathematical details of the Keynesian aggregate expenditure model and reflect on what it means.

In most economic models, equilibrium is both a situation where there is no tendency for change, *and a desirable outcome*. In the simplest demand and supply model, equilibrium is where quantity demanded equals quantity supplied, and there are no shortages and surpluses. The equilibrium outcome clears the market and is efficient in best satisfying the demands of consumers, at the lowest prices businesses are willing to accept.

As in most economic models, Keynes's aggregate expenditure equilibrium is a situation where there is no tendency for change. But unlike most models, *aggregate expenditure equilibrium is not necessarily a desirable outcome*.

Before Keynes, most economists believed that market economies with flexible prices would always quickly self-adjust to produce socially desirable outcomes. This belief was based on work by Jean-Baptiste Say (1767–1832), a French economist and supporter of Adam Smith's views on free trade, the invisible hand, and markets. **Say's Law** claims that "supply creates its own demand." In the circular flow diagram of Figure 1 on page 188, households *supply* inputs to businesses in exchange for money. Households want the money to *demand* products and services in output markets. When households spend all of the money earned in input markets to buy products and services in output markets, supply does create its own demand. Say's Law suggests, using modern economic terms, that when demand (aggregate expenditure in Keynes's model) equals supply (real GDP), the economy will be at full employment and potential GDP.

In the middle of the Great Depression, Say's Law could not explain the terrible social hardships of idle factories and mass unemployment. Keynes rejected Say's Law as a "special theory" that sometimes holds true but usually does not. Keynes's more "general theory" allowed both socially desirable and undesirable outcomes.

In Keynes's model, *aggregate expenditure equilibrium is not necessarily at full employment or potential GDP*. And if the aggregate expenditure equilibrium is at a level of GDP below potential GDP, there is no tendency for change. The economy remains stuck in a recession (or depression), unless the government steps in with fiscal or monetary policy to return to potential GPD and full employment.

Unlike the aggregate supply and aggregate demand model in Chapter 7, Keynes's model does *not* focus on the supply side, and does *not* have a long-run aggregate supply curve representing potential GDP and full employment. Translating Keyne's model into the terms of the aggregate supply and aggregate demand model, Keynes's aggregate expenditure equilibrium is a **short-run macroeconomic equilibrium**, where the short-run aggregate supply curve (*SAS*) intersects the aggregate demand curve (*AD*).

Review Figure 12 in Chapter 7, where AD_1 intersects SAS_0. That short-run equilibrium real GDP is less than potential GDP. Short-run equilibrium GDP may also equal potential GDP, or be greater than potential GDP. Say's Law is only true for the special case of **long-run macroeconomic equilbrium** at potential GDP.

Keynes is famously quoted as saying that "In the long run, we are all dead." What he meant was that market economies, if left alone by government, would take too long to adjust to long-run macroeconomic equilibrium. With appropriate fiscal or monetary policy, the government could move the economy more quickly to long-run macroeconomic equilibrium and avoid needless suffering.

 # Practice...

6. The aggregate expenditure function shows the relationship between aggregate planned expenditure and

    a. disposable income.

    b. real GDP.

    c. consumption spending.

    d. the price level.

7. If there is an unplanned increase in inventories, aggregate planned expenditure is

    a. greater than real GDP, and businesses will increase output.

    b. greater than real GDP, and businesses will decrease output.

    c. less than real GDP, and businesses will increase output.

    d. less than real GDP, and businesses will decrease output.

8. If $AE = 50 + 0.6Y$ and $Y = 200$, unplanned inventory

    a. increases are 30.

    b. increases are 75.

    c. decreases are 30.

    d. decreases are 75.

9. If $AE = 180 + 0.8Y$, then autonomous spending is _____ and equilibrium expenditure is _____ .

    a. 180; 100

    b. 100; 180

    c. 180; 900

    d. 900; 180

10. On the 45° line graph, the aggregate planned expenditure function

    a. is above the 45° line when real GDP is above equilibrium real GDP.

    b. is below the 45° line when real GDP is below equilibrium real GDP.

    c. intersects the 45° line at the equilibrium level of real GDP.

    d. intersects the 45° line at the level of autonomous spending.

 **Apply...**

4. An economy has the following components of aggregate expenditure:

    $C = 130 + 0.9Y$

    $I = 70$

    $G = 30$

    $X = 20$

    $IM = 0.15Y$

    where C, I, G, X, and IM stand for, respectively, planned consumption, investment spending, government purchases, exports, and imports. Y is real GDP. There are no taxes, so $YD = Y$.

    a. What is the equation of the aggregate expenditure function?

    b. What is the equilibrium expenditure?

5. An economy has the following components of aggregate expenditure:

    $C = 220 + 0.8Y$

    $T = 100$

    $I = 60$

    $Y = 70$

    $G = 20$

    $X = 30$

    $IM = 0.05Y$

    where C, T, I, G, X, and IM stand for, respectively, planned consumption, net taxes, investment spending, government purchases, exports, and imports. Y is real GDP. YD is disposable income.

Apply...

What is the equation of the aggregate expenditure function?

_____

_____

_____

_____

_____

_____

_____

_____

6. In most economic models, equilibrium is both a situation where there is no tendency for change and a desirable outcome. How is Keynes's aggregate expenditure model different from most economic models?

_____

_____

_____

_____

_____

_____

_____

_____

_____

The Multiplier

L03 Describe the concept of the multiplier, and show how to calculate it graphically, mathematically, and in terms of injections and leakages.

Keynes's aggregate expenditure model also introduced a concept called "the multiplier" that is still an important part of modern macroeconomic theory. For any change in autonomous spending (A) — investment spending (I), government purchases (G) or exports (X) — the **multiplier** predicts the effect on equilibrium expenditure and real GDP (Y).

Let's again review Figure 1, the circular flow diagram on page 188. Injections and leakages, money flowing into and out of the circular flow, are key to understanding the story behind the multiplier. Let's start with government purchases — an injection — and look at what happens in Figure 1.

Suppose the government spends $100 million to buy a new bridge: *G* goes up by $100 million. That means aggregate expenditure (*C* + *I* + *G* + *X* − *IM*) goes up by the $100 million injection in this first round of spending. Here is a surprise — the full effect on equilibrium expenditure is *more than* $100 million. To see how, let's follow the circle.

Initially, bridge-building businesses (at the bottom of the circle) get $100 million. Following the circle up to the right, that means incomes of everyone working for the businesses — workers, owners, suppliers — goes up by $100 million. What do people do with that additional income? The government takes some of the income as taxes — a leakage out of the circular flow (the net taxes from consumers to government at the top). People save some — another leakage out of the circular flow (consumer saving and borrowing flow at the very top). Some of that new spending is on imports — the final leakage (the net export flow between businesses and R.O.W.). But even after all of those leakages, everyone will use their remaining additional income on new spending in output markets on Canadian products and services.

Suppose leakages are 50 percent of additional income. In our simple aggregate expenditure model, where *AE* = 500 + 0.5Y, the coefficient of 0.5 on *Y* means that for every additional dollar of income, spending on Canadian products and services goes up by 50 cents, and the other 50 cents goes to leakages (taxes, saving, imports). The 50 percent rate of leakages comes from adding the marginal propensity to save (*MPS* = 0.2) and the marginal propensity to import (*MPIM* = 0.3). Because taxes in our simple model are a fixed amount (100), additional income does not create any additional taxes.

After the $50 million in leakages, businesses in Canada still receive $50 million in a second round of spending. The story, and the flow around the circle, repeats. There will again be leakages from this $50 million, but 50 percent of the income will again turn into new spending on Canadian products and services. In the third round of spending, businesses in Canada will receive $25 million. The circles of spending and income continue getting smaller and smaller, and eventually fade away. Figure 5 shows the cumulative effect of all of the rounds of spending. In this example, the $100 million injection of government spending increases equilibrium expenditure by $200 million after all of the rounds of spending are finished.

Figure 5   The Multiplier

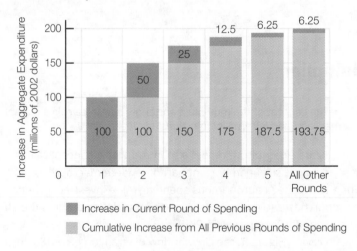

Increase in Aggregate Expenditure (millions of 2002 dollars)

■ Increase in Current Round of Spending
■ Cumulative Increase from All Previous Rounds of Spending

Equilibrium Expenditure and the Multiplier

The multiplier is easiest to see in the graph of the aggregate expenditure function. Figure 6 reproduces our simple aggregate expenditure function of $AE = 500 + 0.5Y$ as AE_0.

Figure 6   Equilibrium Expenditure and the Multiplier

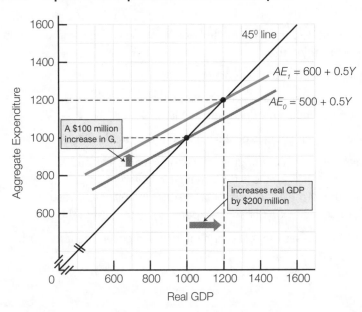

When government purchases increase by $100 million, all other things unchanged, the new aggregate expenditure function ($AE = C + I + G + X - IM$) is $AE_1 = 600 + 0.5Y$. There is a parallel, upward shift of the aggregate expenditure function by a distance of $100 million. But the new equilibrium expenditure increases by $200 million, from $1000 million to $1200 million. The $100 million increase in injections has a multiplied impact on real GDP. In this example, the multiplier is 2.

The Multiplier Formula

There are three formulas for calculating the exact number for the multiplier. All of the formulas give the same number, but use different methods.

In our model, a change in autonomous spending (A) of $100 million caused a $200 million change in real GDP (Y). For this first formula,

$$\text{Multiplier} = \frac{\text{Change in } Y}{\text{Change in } A} = \frac{\$200 \text{ million}}{\$100 \text{ million}} = 2$$

The second formula for the multiplier come from the aggregate expenditure function. In our model, $AE = 500 + 0.5Y$

$$\text{Multiplier} = \frac{1}{1 - \text{slope } AE \text{ function}} = \frac{1}{(1 - 0.5)} = 2$$

The third formula is also related to the aggregate expenditure (AE) function. The slope of the AE function tells us the fraction of every additional dollar of income (Y) that is spent on Canadian products and services. In our model, that fraction is 50% (0.5). That means (1 − slope AE function) tells us the fraction of every additional dollar of income that is *not spent* — that leaks out of the circular flow through savings, taxes, or spending on imports.

$$\text{Multiplier} = \frac{1}{\% \text{ of leakages from additional income}} = \frac{1}{0.5} = 2$$

In our model, the leakages from additional income come from the marginal propensity to save (MPS = 0.2) and the marginal propensity to import ($MPIM$ = 0.3). So the percentage of leakages from additional income equals 0.5 (0.2 + 0.3).

The Size of the Multiplier No matter what formula you use, the size of the multiplier will be larger, the

- larger the slope of the AE function.
- larger the percentage of every additional dollar of income spent on Canadian products and services.
- smaller the percentages of leakages from the circular flow.

The multiplier formulas work for any change in autonomous expenditures (A). Our example is for a change in government purchases (G = 100), but the formulas also work for changes in business investment spending (I) or spending on Canadian exports (X) by the rest of the world.

Chapter 11 discusses the role of the multiplier in government fiscal policy.

 # Practice...

11. If the multiplier is 3 and exports increase by $5 million, equilibrium real GDP

   a. increases by $2 million.

   b. increases by $8 million

   c. increases by $15 million.

   d. decreases by $15 million.

12. If a $200 decrease in business investment spending causes equilibrium real GDP to decrease by $600, the multiplier is

   a. – 3.

   b. 3

   c. – 1/3.

   d. 1/3

13. If leakages out of the circular flow are 40 percent of additional income, what is the size of the multiplier effect?

   a. 5

   b. 4

   c. 3

   d. 2.5

14. If the slope of the AE function is 0.75, what is the value of the multiplier?

   a. 4

   b. 2.5

   c. 0.75

   d. 0.25

15. Which decreases the value of the multiplier?

   a. decrease in the marginal propensity to import

   b. increase in the marginal propensity to consume

   c. decrease in the marginal propensity to save

   d. increase in the marginal propensity to save

Apply...

7. The aggregate expenditure function is $AE_0 = 400 + 0.5Y$.

   a. What is the equilibrium level of real GDP (Y)?

   _____

   _____

   _____

   _____

   b. Business investment spending decreases, leading to a new aggregate expenditure function of $AE_1 = 200 + 0.5Y$. What is the amount of the decrease in business investment spending (I)?

   _____

   _____

   _____

   c. Calculate the multiplier using two different methods.

   _____

   _____

   _____

   _____

   _____

   _____

   _____

   _____

8. The aggregate expenditure function is $AE_0 = 250 + 0.75Y$. Then the government increases spending by 100.

   a. What is the initial effect of this increase of 100 in the first "round" of spending?

   _____

   _____

   _____

   _____

   b. What is the effect on the second "round" of spending?

   _____

   _____

   _____

   _____

to be continued

Apply...

continued

c.   What is the total effect on real GDP after all rounds of spending?

_____

_____

_____

_____

_____

9.   What are the three formulas for the multiplier?

_____

_____

_____

_____

_____

From Aggregate Expenditure to Aggregate Demand

L04   Connect the aggregate expenditure model to the concept of aggregate demand in the aggregate supply and aggregate demand model.

Keynes's aggregate expenditure model focuses on the demand or spending side of the economy, while mostly leaving aside the supply side. Aggregate expenditure and aggregate demand are very similar concepts — the main difference is that aggregate expenditure ignores prices.

With one last set of graphs, we can connect the aggregate expenditure model to the concepts of aggregate demand in the aggregate supply and aggregate demand model (*AS/AD*) of Chapter 7. We will use the *AS/AD* model for all future discussion of macroeconomic events and policies.

Introducing Price Level Changes to the Aggregate Expenditure Model

The aggregate expenditure function — AE = planned ($C + I + G + X - IM$) — assumes that that the price level in the economy is unchanged. Let's now look at what happens to aggregate planned expenditure when we allow prices to change. There are three main effects on aggregate expenditure.

Foreign Trade Effect   When average prices of all Canadian products and services rise, imported products and services produced in other countries become relatively cheaper for Canadian consumers. As prices of Canadian exports rise, the rest of the world buys less of them, switching to cheaper substitutes from other countries. When Canadians buy more imports (*IM*) and R.O.W. buys fewer Canadian exports (*X*), aggregate planned expenditure on Canadian products and services decreases. This **foreign trade effect** causes a downward shift of the aggregate expenditure function.

Real Balances Effect   The **real balances effect** suggests that a rise in the price level — inflation — reduces the real purchasing power of savings and other assets. With less valuable real assets, people decrease their consumption spending (*C*), so aggregate planned expenditure decreases, causing a downward shift of the aggregate expenditure function.

Interest Rate Effect   According to the **interest rate effect**, a rise in the price level increases nominal interest rates, decreasing the business investment spending (*I*) component of aggregate expenditure, causing a downward shift of the aggregate expenditure function.

All three effects reinforce each other. A rise in the price level causes a downward shift of the aggregate expenditure function (to AE_1). A fall in the price level works in reverse, causing an upward shift of the aggregate expenditure function (to AE_2). Figure 7a shows the effects of changes in the price level on aggregate planned expenditure.

Figure 7   Equilibrium Expenditure and Aggregate Demand

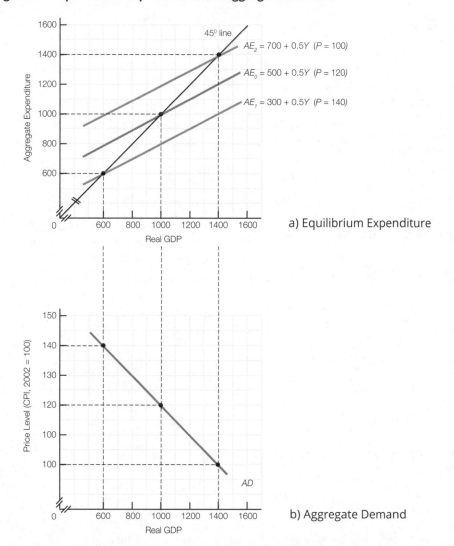

a) Equilibrium Expenditure

b) Aggregate Demand

On the previous page, AE_0 is the aggregate expenditure function for an initial price level , arbitrarily set at $P = 120$. If the price level rises to $P = 140$, the aggregate expenditure function shifts down to AE_1. If instead, the price level falls from $P = 120$ to $P = 100$, the aggregate expenditure function shifts up to AE_2.

For each of the three aggregate expenditure functions in Figure 7a, Figure 7b combines the equilibrium expenditure with the price level. The horizontal axis measures real GDP, the same as in Figure 7a. The vertical axis is different. The price level is on the vertical axis, measured by the consumer price index (*CPI*), where the price level in 2002 equals 100.

Aggregate demand is the quantity of real GDP macroeconomic players plan to demand at different price levels. The price level changes in part a that shift the *AE* function and equilibrium expenditure correspond to movements along the aggregate demand curve (*AD*) in part b. In general, as the price level rises (from $P = 100$ to 120 to 140), the aggregate quantity demanded of real GDP decreases (from $Y = 1400$ to 1000 to 600). Aggregate quantity demanded decreases with rising prices for the same reasons aggregate planned expenditure decreases — the foreign trade effect, the real balances effect, and the interest rate effect. This is the **law of aggregate demand**, explained in detail in Chapter 7.

 ## Practice...

16. A rise in the price level
    a. decreases aggregate expenditure and is a movement along the aggregate demand curve.
    b. decreases aggregate expenditure and shifts the aggregate demand curve.
    c. increases aggregate expenditure and is a movement along the aggregate demand curve.
    d. increases aggregate expenditure and shifts the aggregate demand curve.

17. Which effect does *not* shift the aggregate expenditure function?
    a. foreign trade effect
    b. consumption effect
    c. real balances effect
    d. interest rate effect

18. When the price level falls,
    a. the foreign trade effect decreases net exports.
    b. the interest rate effect decreases consumer spending.
    c. equilibrium real GDP increases.
    d. equilibrium real GDP does not change.

19. The aggregate demand curve is a relation between real GDP and
    a. aggregate planned expenditure.
    b. actual expenditure.
    c. the inflation rate.
    d. the price level.

20. A fall in the price level is a
    a. movement down along the aggregate expenditure curve and a shift of the aggregate demand curve.
    b. movement up along the aggregate expenditure curve and a shift of the aggregate demand curve.
    c. shift of the aggregate expenditure curve and a movement down along the aggregate demand curve.
    d. shift of the aggregate expenditure curve and a movement up along the aggregate demand curve.

👪 Apply...

10. Initially, the price level is 75, and the aggregate expenditure function is

    $$AE_0 = 200 + 0.5Y \qquad (P_0 = 75)$$

    When the price level falls to 50, the new aggregate expenditure function is

    $$AE_1 = 300 + 0.5Y \qquad (P_1 = 50)$$

    a. Use this information to calculate the coordinates of two points on the corresponding aggregate demand curve (*AD*). [*HINT*: Your answer must pair an equilibrium level of real GDP (*Y*) with a price level (*P*).]

    _____

    _____

    _____

    _____

    _____

    _____

    b. Roughly plot the points on the graph below. It is not necessary to draw them accurately, but clearly identify the coordinates (value of *Y*, value of *P*) for each point. Connect the points to draw the aggregate demand curve.

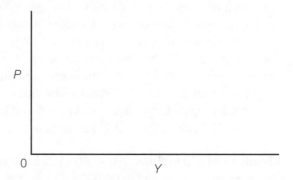

11. Continuing from Apply question 10, suppose with the price level held constant at 75, an increase of 100 in exports shifts the AE_0 function to

    $$AE_2 = 300 + 0.5Y \qquad (P_2 = 75)$$

    Calculate a third point for the graph above. Is it on the same aggregate demand (*AD*) curve? Explain what you think happened.

    _____

    _____

    _____

to be continued

Apply...

continued

12. Explain in words how the effects of price-level changes on the *AE* curve generate an *AD* curve.

_____

_____

_____

_____

_____

_____

KNOW...

Summary of Learning Objectives

1. For any level of real GDP and income, the aggregate expenditure model shows aggregate planned expenditure (*AE*) of consumer spending (*C*), business investment spending (*I*), government purchases (*G*), exports (*X*), and imports (*IM*). **Autonomous spending** plans are independent of real GDP and include *I*, *G*, and *X*. **Induced spending**, which changes with changes in real GDP, include *C* and *IM*. The model comes from the circular flow model and highlights **injections** (*I*, *G*, *X*) and **leakages** [savings (*S*), net taxes (*T*), imports (*IM*)], while keeping the price level unchanged.

2. **Equilibrium expenditure** in the aggregate expenditure model is where planned expenditure equals real GDP. Graphically, this equilibrium is where the aggregate expenditure curve crosses the 45° line. Only in equilibrium are injections and leakages equal. In aggregate expenditure equilibrium, there is no tendency for change, but the **short-run macroeconomic equilibrium** may be below potential GDP and full employment, and is not necessarily a desirable **long-run macroeconomic equilibrium**.

3. For any change in **autonomous spending**, the **multiplier** predicts the effect on equilibrium expenditure and real GDP. The multiplier works through rounds of spending in the circular flow. There are three equivalent formulas for calculating the multiplier. The multiplier is larger, the larger the slope of the *AE* function, the larger the percentage of additional income spent on Canadian products and services, and the smaller the percentage of leakages from the circular flow.

4. The aggregate expenditure function shifts upward or downward with changes in the price level, due to the **foreign trade effect**, the **real balances effect**, and the **interest rate effect**. Price level changes that shift the *AE* function and change equilibrium expenditure correspond to movements along the **aggregate demand** curve (*AD*).

Key Terms

aggregate demand: quantity of real GDP macroeconomic players plan to demand at different price levels

aggregate planned expenditure (*AE*): = planned consumption spending (C) + planned business investment spending (*I*) + planned government purchases (*G*) + planned exports (*X*) – planned imports (*IM*)

autonomous spending: parts of aggregate planned expenditure that are independent of real GDP

consumption function: relation between planned consumption (*C*) and disposable income (*YD*), other things unchanged

disposable income: aggregate income minus net taxes

equilibrium expenditure: level of real GDP where aggregate planned expenditure equals real GDP

foreign trade effect: inverse relation between a higher price level and decreased aggregate expenditure due to decreased exports and increased imports

induced spending: parts of aggregate planned expenditure that depend on real GDP

injection: spending in the circular flow that does not start with consumers: *G* (government spending), *I* (business investment spending), *X* (exports)

interest rate effect: inverse relation between a higher price level and decreased aggregate expenditure due to higher nominal interest rates and decreased investment spending

law of aggregate demand: as the price level rises, aggregate quantity demanded of real GDP decreases

leakage: spending that leaks out of the circular flow through taxes, savings, and imports

long-run macroeconomic equilibrium: where short-run aggregate supply (*SAS*), aggregate demand (*AD*), and long-run aggregate supply (*LAS*) all intersect

marginal propensity to consume: fraction of a change in disposable income that is spent on consumption

marginal propensity to import: fraction of a change in income that is spent on imports

marginal propensity to save: fraction of a change in disposable income that is saved

multiplier: predicts the effect on equilibrium expenditure and real GDP of a change in autonomous spending

net taxes: taxes minus transfer payments

real balances effect: inverse relation between a higher price level and decreased aggregate expenditure due to a decrease in the purchasing power of assets

Say's Law: supply creates its own demand

short-run macroeconomic equilibrium: where short-run aggregate supply (*SAS*) and aggregate demand (*AD*) intersect

Answers to Practice

1. **c** *MPS* is fraction of a change in disposable income that is saved.

2. **d** $YD = C + S$

3. **b** $C = YD - S = 1YD - 0.3YD + 50$

4. **c**   As *YD* increases by 100, *C* increases by 75. So *MPC* = 0.75.

5. **d** As *YD* increases by 100, *C* increases by 75. So *MPC* = 0.75.
Since *MPC* + *MPS* = 1, *MPS* = 1 – 0.75.

6. **b** Real GDP, which is also equal to income.

7. **d** Businesses are not selling everything they produce,
so they decrease production.

8. **a** $Y = 200$ implies $AE = 50 + 0.6(200) = 170$.
Unplanned inventories = $Y - AE$ = +30

9. **c** In equilibrium $Y = 180 + 0.8Y$, so $0.2Y = 180$, $Y = 900$.
Autonomous spending is the part of the *AE* function
that does not depend on Y.

10. **c** *AE* is above the 45° line when real GDP is below
equilibrium real GDP, and below the 45° line
when real GDP is above equilibrium real GDP.

11. **c** Exports are autonomous (positive) spending,
so $5 million × 3 = $15 million.

12. **b** Multiplier = change in real GDP (*Y*) divided by change
in autonomous investment (*A*) = –$600 ÷ –$200 = +3.

13. **d** 1 ÷ 0.4 = 2.5.

14. **a** Multiplier = 1 ÷ (1 – slope of *AE* function) = 1 ÷ (1 – 0.75) = 1 ÷ 0.25 = 4.

15. **d** Increase in leakages from the circular flow.

16. **a** Increase in price level decreases aggregate expenditure
due to three effects, leading to movement up along *AD* curve.

17. **b** See discussion in chapter.

18. **c** *AE* shifts upward. Foreign trade effect increases net exports,
and interest rate effect increases consumer spending and
business investment spending.

19. **d** Aggregate demand is the quantity of real GDP macroeconomic players
plan to demand at different price levels.

20. **c**   *AE* shifts upward, so a lower price level (*P*) is associated with
an increased level of equilibrium GDP (*Y*).

9 Exchange Rates and the Balance of Payments

LEARNING OBJECTIVES

L01 Explain how demand and supply in the foreign exchange market determine the value of the Canadian dollar.

L02 Identify five forces causing exchange rate fluctuations.

L03 Trace how exchange rates cause aggregate demand shocks that affect real GDP, unemployment, and inflation.

L04 Describe how purchasing power parity and rate of return parity provide standards for exchange rates.

L05 Distinguish the two main parts of the balance of payments accounts, and explain why they must add up to zero.

LEARN...

With a population 10 times larger than Canada's, the United States has more products to choose from and often lower prices, at least in U.S. dollars. In 2012, when one Canadian dollar traded for one U.S. dollar, Canadians crossed the border to shop in record numbers. It felt like everything in the United States was on sale.

What determines the value of the Canadian dollar? Why is it sometimes worth as little as 60 cents U.S. or as much as US$1.10? What determines exchange rates, the price of one country's money in terms of another country's money? Who do people trade Canadian dollars for U.S. dollars, euros, or Japanese yen?

Interest rates help determine the value of the Canadian dollar. When interest rates in Canada rise, the value of the Canadian dollar usually increases, which affects how much we pay for products imported from elsewhere and how expensive our exports are for the rest of the world to buy. By affecting the prices and quantities of net exports, the value of the Canadian dollar influences the key macroeconomic outcomes of real GDP, unemployment, and inflation. The Canadian dollar's value and net exports also affect the flows of moneys of different countries across international borders.

A "high" value for the Canadian dollar is better for cross-border Canadian shoppers, but is it better for the economy as a whole than a "low" dollar? And how do we know what counts as "high" or "low?" We will look at the deeper forces beyond demand and supply that determine the value of the Canadian dollar.

Demand and Supply of Canadian Dollars

 Explain how demand and supply in the foreign exchange market determine the value of the Canadian dollar.

"How much does that dollar cost?" That question is not as silly as it sounds. It's asking, "What's the exchange rate?" An **exchange rate** is the price at which one currency exchanges for another. If the Canadian dollar is worth 95 cents U.S., the exchange rate of the Canadian dollar for the U.S. dollar is US$0.95. You need 95 cents U.S. to buy one Canadian dollar. The exchange rate is the price for buying Canadian dollars with another country's currency.

Exchange rates for all currencies are determined in the **foreign exchange market**, a worldwide market for buying and selling currencies. Exchange rates fluctuate constantly. A fall in the exchange rate — if the price of a Canadian dollar falls from US$0.95 to US$0.80 — is a **currency depreciation**. A rise in the exchange rate is a **currency appreciation**. The foreign exchange market has buyers (demanders) and sellers (suppliers), like all other markets. Identifying demanders and suppliers helps explain exchange rates and why they fluctuate so much.

Non-Canadians Demanding Canadian Dollars

If you live and work in Canada, you are paid in Canadian dollars. You don't need to go to the foreign exchange market to buy Canadian dollars. The demanders of Canadian dollars on the foreign exchange market are largely non-Canadians from the rest of the world.

The main reasons non-Canadians demand Canadian dollars are to

- buy Canadian exports.
- buy Canadian assets (bonds, businesses, real estate).
- speculate on the future value of the Canadian dollar.

Law of Demand for Canadian Dollars   The law of demand applies to Canadian dollars, just as it applies to any product or service — as the price rises, the quantity demanded decreases. The exchange rate is the price of a Canadian dollar. The **law of demand for Canadian dollars** states that as the exchange rate rises, the quantity demanded of Canadian dollars decreases.

When the exchange rate rises, the U.S. dollar prices that non-Canadians pay for Canadian exports and assets rise. Look at Figure 1. Suppose a month's supply of Tim Hortons coffee costs C$100. Canadian consumers pay this price no matter what happens to the exchange rate. When the exchange rate is US$0.60 per Canadian dollar, a U.S. consumer pays US$60 for the coffee. If the exchange rate rises to US$1.00 per Canadian dollar, the same C$100 coffee rises in price to US$100. As the exchange rate rises, non-Canadians will not buy as many exports and assets. With fewer purchases by non-Canadians, the quantity demanded of Canadian dollars on the foreign exchange market decreases.

Figure 1   Price of Tim Hortons Coffee in Canada and United States

Price of 1 Canadian Dollar (US$ per C$)	Price of Month's Supply of Tim Hortons Coffee in Canada (in C$)	Price of Month's Supply of Tim Hortons Coffee in U.S. (in US$)
US$ 0.60	C$ 100	US$ 60
US$ 1.00	C$ 100	US$ 100

Canadians Supplying Canadian Dollars to Non-Canadians

Who supplies Canadian dollars to the worldwide foreign exchange market? Any Canadian going cross-border shopping in the U.S. wants U.S. dollars. You must supply Canadian dollars in exchange. Your demand for U.S. dollars is also a supply of Canadian dollars.

In the unique world of the foreign exchange market, the demand for one currency is the supply of another.

The main reasons Canadians supply Canadian dollars on the foreign exchange market are to

- buy imports from the rest of the world.

- buy assets (bonds, businesses, real estate) from the rest of the world.

- speculate on the future value of the Canadian dollar.

Law of Supply for Canadian Dollars   The law of supply applies to Canadian dollars — as the price rises, the quantity supplied increases. The exchange rate is the price of a Canadian dollar. The **law of supply for Canadian dollars** states that as the exchange rate rises, the quantity supplied of Canadian dollars increases.

When the exchange rate rises (appreciates), U.S. products, services, and assets become less expensive for Canadians, so Canadians buy more of them. But to buy more from the U.S., Canadians must increase the quantity supplied of Canadian dollars to get more U.S. dollars. A rise in the exchange rate increases the quantity supplied of Canadian dollars in the foreign exchange market.

Determining the Exchange Rate

The exchange rate of the Canadian dollar is determined by the interaction of demand and supply in the foreign exchange market. Figure 2 combines numbers for quantity demanded and quantity supplied of Canadian dollars.

Figure 2   Foreign Exchange Market for Canadian Dollars

Price of 1 Canadian Dollar (US$ per C$)	Quantity Demanded (billions of Canadian dollars per month)	Quantity Supplied (billions of Canadian dollars per month)
US$ 0.60	90	30
US$ 0.70	80	40
US$ 0.80	70	50
US$ 0.90	**60**	**60**
US$ 1.00	50	70
US$ 1.10	40	80

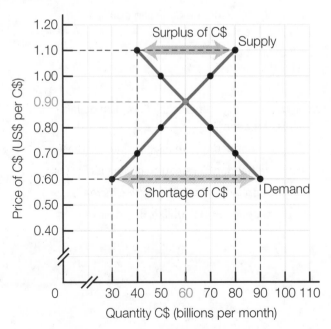

The equilibrium, or market-clearing, exchange rate — US$0.90 — is at the intersection of the demand and supply curves.

At any lower exchange rate (like US$0.60), there is excess demand. As in any market with a shortage, competition among buyers (demanders) for the scarce Canadian dollars causes the price of a Canadian dollar to rise. At any exchange rate above equilibrium (like US$1.10), there is excess supply. There is a surplus, so competition among sellers (suppliers) to find customers for the Canadian dollars they can't get rid of causes the price of a Canadian dollar to fall.

Reciprocal Exchange Rates   In the foreign exchange market, the demand for one currency is the supply of another. The demand and supply for Canadian dollars is the same as the supply and demand for U.S. dollars. The same principle applies to exchanges between all currencies.

We have described the price of one Canadian dollar in terms of the number of U.S. dollars it takes to buy it. We can also describe the price of one U.S. dollar in terms of the number of Canadian dollars it takes to buy it. These two exchange rates are mirror images of each other and are called *reciprocal exchange rates*. When the price of one Canadian dollar is US$0.90, then the price of one U.S. dollar is 1 ÷ 0.90 = 1.11. It takes C$1.11 to buy one U.S. dollar. US$0.90 and C$1.11 are reciprocal exchange rates.

Because of these connections, when the Canadian dollar appreciates against the U.S. dollar, the U.S. dollar depreciates against the Canadian dollar. Just as the demand for one currency is the supply of another currency, the appreciation of one currency is the depreciation of another.

 # Practice...

1. An exchange rate of C$1.00 = US$0.90 means

    a. 1 Canadian dollar is worth 90 cents U.S.

    b. 1 U.S. dollar is worth 1.11 cents Canadian.

    c. the price of one Canadian dollar is 90 cents U.S.

    d. all of the above.

2. If the exchange rate for the Canadian dollar falls, the quantity

    a. demanded of Canadian dollars decreases.

    b. demanded of Canadian dollars increases.

    c. supplied of Canadian dollars increases.

    d. supplied of U.S. dollars decreases.

3. All of the following create a demand for Canadian dollars in the foreign exchange market *except*

    a. Alejandro from Mexico pays tuition to Seneca College in Ontario.

    b. Richard from New York buys a Government of Canada bond.

    c. Alexa from Ohio goes on a shopping trip in Toronto.

    d. Siri from Manitoba goes shopping in New York.

Practice...

4. Which statements are *true*? A higher value of the Canadian dollar makes

1   R.O.W. imports and assets more expensive for Canadians.

2   R.O.W. imports and assets less expensive for Canadians.

3   Canadian exports and assets more expensive for non-Canadians.

4   Canadian exports and assets less expensive for non-Canadians.

a. 1 and 3

b. 1 and 4

c. 2 and 3

d. 2 and 4

5. When there is a surplus of Canadian dollars in the foreign exchange market, competition among

a. sellers raises the exchange rate.

b. sellers lowers the exchange rate.

c. buyers raises the exchange rate.

d. buyers lowers the exchange rate.

Apply...

1. When you cross the border to shop in the United States, explain how you are participating in the foreign exchange market.

_____

_____

_____

_____

_____

2. You are making travel plans for winter break. You find an all-inclusive vacation package in Cancun, Mexico, for a reasonable price (in Canadian dollars), so you message your friends about it. Days later, when your friends finally agree, the price (in Canadian dollars) has jumped by over C$100. You complain to the Mexican company selling the vacation package, but they tell you that their price (in Mexican pesos) hasn't changed. Describe what happened.

_____

_____

_____

to be continued

Apply...

continued

3. In your own words, explain what a reciprocal exchange rate is. Use an exchange rate between U.S. and Canadian dollars to demonstrate your answer.

Fluctuating Exchange Rates

L02 Identify five forces causing exchange rate fluctuations.

Exchange rates are like dance partners who move quickly and effortlessly *together*. When one dance partner glides forward, the other glides backward. When demand for Canadian dollars increases, the supply of Canadian dollars decreases. Changes in demand usually move with changes in supply. The demand for one currency is the supply of the other.

Five economic forces change demand and supply and explain why exchange rates fluctuate:

- interest rate differentials.
- inflation rate differentials.
- changes in Canadian real GDP.
- changes in R.O.W. demands for Canadian exports and R.O.W. prices.
- changes in expectations.

Interest Rate Differentials

In the foreign exchange market, money flows almost instantly to where the rate of return — the interest rate on an investment — is highest. When investors buy bonds, stocks, businesses, or real estate, they search worldwide for the highest rate of return. If they can earn a 5 percent return in Canada, they will not accept a 3 percent return in the United States. The difference between the two interest rates is called the **interest rate differential**.

Increase in Canadian Interest Rate Differential   An increase in the Canadian interest rate differential makes Canadian assets more attractive to investors. Investors outside of Canada need Canadian dollars to buy those assets, increasing the demand for Canadian dollars. Canadian investors also want to invest more in Canada and less in the United States, decreasing their demand for U.S. dollars, which decreases the supply of Canadian dollars.

The increase in demand and decrease in supply of Canadian dollars *both* raise the price of the Canadian dollar. An increase in the Canadian interest rate differential raises the exchange rate.

Figure 3 shows the effect of an increase in demand and decrease in supply of Canadian dollars. The exchange rate rises quickly because the shifts of both curves cause the Canadian dollar to appreciate, from US$0.90 to US$1.00.

Figure 3   Increase in Demand and Decrease in Supply of Canadian Dollars in Foreign Exchange Market

Price of 1 Canadian Dollar (US$ per C$)	Quantity Demanded (billions of C$ per month)		Quantity Supplied (billions of C$ per month)	
	Original (D_0)	New (D_1)	Original (S_0)	New (S_1)
US$ 0.60	90 → 100		30 → 20	
US$ 0.70	80 → 90		40 → 30	
US$ 0.80	70 → 80		50 → 40	
US$ 0.90	60 → 70		60 → 50	
US$ 1.00	50 → 60		70 → 60	
US$ 1.10	40 → 50		80 → 70	

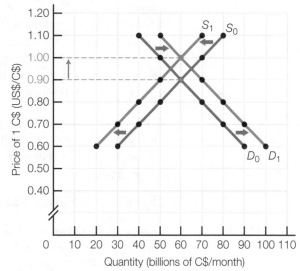

Decrease in Canadian Interest Rate Differential   A decrease in the Canadian interest rate differential decreases the demand for Canadian dollars and increases the supply of Canadian dollars. As Figure 4 shows, a decrease in the Canadian interest rate differential lowers the exchange rate — the Canadian dollar depreciates.

Figure 4   Decrease in Demand and Increase in Supply of Canadian Dollars in Foreign Exchange Market

Price of 1 Canadian Dollar (US$ per C$)	Quantity Demanded (billions of C$ per month)		Quantity Supplied (billions of C$ per month)	
	Original (D_0)	New (D_2)	Original (S_0)	New (S_2)
US$ 0.60	90 → 80		30 → 40	
US$ 0.70	80 → 70		40 → 50	
US$ 0.80	70 → 60		50 → 60	
US$ 0.90	60 → 50		60 → 70	
US$ 1.00	50 → 40		70 → 80	
US$ 1.10	40 → 30		80 → 90	

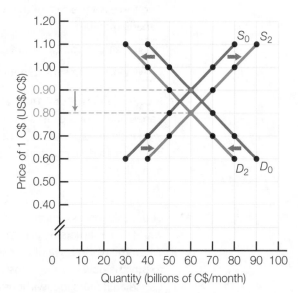

Inflation Rate Differentials

The inflation rate differential is the difference in inflation rates between countries. Changing prices of products and services affect exchange rates through imports and exports.

Increase in Canadian Inflation Rate Differential   When the inflation rate in Canada is higher than inflation rates in other countries, Canadian products and services, including exports, become relatively more expensive. The R.O.W. buys fewer Canadian exports and therefore demands fewer Canadian dollars. Imports from R.O.W. become relatively less expensive for Canadians, who buy more imports and need more U.S. dollars. The increased Canadian demand for U.S. dollars is also an increased supply of Canadian dollars.

An increase in the Canadian inflation rate differential decreases demand and increases the supply of Canadian dollars, so the Canadian dollar depreciates, as in Figure 4 on the previous page.

Decrease in Canadian Inflation Rate Differential   A decrease in the Canadian inflation rate differential increases demand and decreases supply of Canadian dollars, as in Figure 3 on the previous page. The Canadian dollar appreciates.

Changes in Canadian Real GDP

Changes in Canadian real GDP affect imports and investors, but with opposing effects on exchange rates.

With increasing Canadian real GDP,

- increased imports cause a slight depreciation from increased supply of Canadian dollars (increased demand for U.S. dollars to buy imports), but no change in demand for Canadian dollars.

- increased investor confidence in a growing economy causes strong appreciation, like an increase in the interest rate differential.

- the net effect is the Canadian dollar appreciates.

Decreasing Canadian real GDP has the opposite effects.

R.O.W. and Canadian Exports

Two forces in the rest of the world have important effects on the value of the Canadian dollar:

- demand for Canadian exports.

- world prices for Canadian resource exports.

R.O.W. Demand for Canadian Exports   Increased R.O.W. demand for Canadian exports causes the Canadian dollar to appreciate slightly. There is an increased demand for Canadian dollars, but no change in the supply of Canadian dollars. Decreased R.O.W. demand for Canadian exports has opposite effects.

World Prices for Canadian Resource Exports   Canada is a major exporter of oil, gold, potash, nickel, and other resources. Resource prices are set in worldwide markets. There are no separate Canadian prices for these resources. When the world price of oil rises, non-Canadians require more Canadian dollars to buy the now more expensive Canadian oil. This increases the demand for Canadian dollars, but without any change in the supply of Canadian dollars. Rising world prices for Canadian resource exports cause the Canadian dollar to appreciate relative to non-resource producing currencies. Falling world prices have opposite effects, causing the Canadian dollar to depreciate.

Watch the news for a day when there is a large increase in world oil prices. Chances are, the exchange rate for the Canadian dollar also rises.

Speculators and Changing Expectations

Currency speculators are the most important players determining fluctuations in exchange rate. About 99 percent of currency trading is done by speculators hoping to make money by buying a currency at a low exchange rate and selling it later at a higher exchange rate.

If most speculators expect a rise in the future value of the Canadian dollar, they buy now, increasing the demand for Canadian dollars and raising the exchange rate. Expectations of a rise in the exchange rate can cause a self-fulfilling appreciation of the Canadian dollar. Expectations of a fall in the exchange rate can have the opposite effects of a self-fulfilling depreciation.

Speculators also reinforce and speed up the effects of the other forces on exchange rates. Changes in interest rate differentials, inflation rate differentials, Canadian real GDP, R.O.W. demand for Canadian exports, and worldwide resource prices normally take months to affect exchange rates. But speculators learned the same economics lessons you are learning about exchange rates.

For example, as soon as the Canadian interest rate differential increases, speculators immediately increase their demand for Canadian dollars, confident that the relative rise in Canadian interest rates will eventually raise the price of the Canadian dollar. If enough speculators act in the same way at the same time, their increased demand makes the expectation of a higher Canadian dollar come true instantly.

Think of Figure 5 as a checklist that speculators use to predict the future price of the Canadian dollar. It's also a good study device for reviewing the forces causing fluctuating exchange rates.

Figure 5   Forces Changing the Price of the Canadian Dollar

Canadian Dollar Appreciates (exchange rate rises)	Canadian Dollar Depreciates (exchange rate falls)
Canadian interest rates rise relative to other countries	Canadian interest rates fall relative to other countries
Canadian inflation rate falls relative to inflation rates in other countries	Canadian inflation rate rises relative to inflation rates in other countries
Real GDP in Canada increases	Real GDP in Canada decreases
R.O.W. demand for Canadian exports increases	R.O.W. demand for Canadian exports decreases
World prices for Canadian resource exports rise	World prices for Canadian resource exports fall
Expectation that Canadian dollar will appreciate	Expectation that Canadian dollar will depreciate

Practice...

6. The Canadian dollar depreciates if

   a. the Canadian interest rate differential increases.

   b. the Canadian inflation rate differential increases.

   c. world prices for Canadian resource exports rise.

   d. speculators expect a rise in the future price of the Canadian dollar.

7. When Canadian interest rates fall, the

   a. demand for Canadian dollars increases in the foreign exchange market.

   b. supply of Canadian dollars decreases in the foreign exchange market.

   c. demand for Canadian exports decreases.

   d. Canadian dollar depreciates.

8. The effect of increased Canadian real GDP on the Canadian dollar exchange rate is

   a. increased imports, causing a slight depreciation.

   b. increased investor confidence, causing a strong appreciation.

   c. a net appreciation of the Canadian dollar.

   d. all of the above.

9. The most important force determining fluctuations of foreign exchange rates is

   a. Canadian real GDP.

   b. interest rate differentials.

   c. expectations of currency speculators.

   d. purchasing power parity.

10. When most currency speculators expect the Canadian dollar to depreciate, the

   a. Canadian dollar depreciates.

   b. supply curve of Canadian dollars shifts leftward.

   c. demand curve for Canadian dollars shifts rightward.

   d. Canadian interest rate differential increases.

Apply...

4. Use these graphs of the foreign exchange market for Canadian dollars to answer the questions below.

a)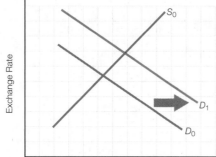

b)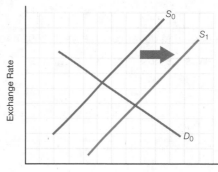

c)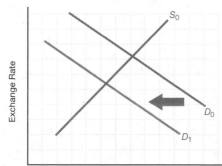

d)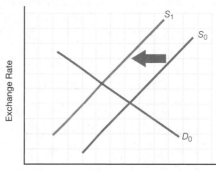

e)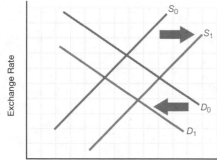

f)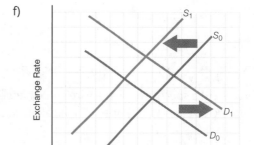

Circle the correct response.

a. Which graph shows the effect of an increase in the Canadian interest rate differential?
    a / b / c / d / e / f

b. Which graph shows the effect of an increase in demand for Canadian exports?
    a / b / c / d / e / f

c. Which graph shows the effect of an increase in the Canadian inflation rate differential?
    a / b / c / d / e / f

d. Which graph shows the effect of falling world prices for oil?
    a / b / c / d / e / f

to be continued

Apply...

continued

5. The Canadian dollar rose between 2002 and 2007 from 62 cents U.S. to above US$1.00.

   a. Was it better to cross the Canada–U.S. border and shop in the U.S. in 2002 or 2007?

   _____

   _____

   _____

   b. The main forces behind the appreciation of the Canadian dollar were rising R.O.W. demand for Canadian exports and rising world prices for Canadian resource exports. Explain how these factors caused the Canadian dollar to appreciate.

   _____

   _____

   _____

   _____

   _____

   c. For the rest of the world, was it better to buy Canadian dollars in 2002 or 2007?

   _____

   _____

   _____

   _____

6. If you were a speculator on the foreign exchange market, what key information would you use to decide whether to buy or sell Canadian dollars? Explain.

   _____

   _____

   _____

   _____

   _____

International Transmission Mechanism

 Trace how exchange rates cause aggregate demand shocks that affect real GDP, unemployment, and inflation.

The **international transmission mechanism** describes how foreign exchange rates affect — are transmitted to — real GDP, unemployment, and the price level. The key is the effect of exchange rates on exports and imports.

Figure 6 illustrates the international transmission mechanism from the demand and supply of Canadian dollars (at the top) to real GDP and inflation (at the bottom). The demand and supply of Canadian dollars interact in the foreign exchange market to determine the exchange rate.

Figure 6   International Transmission Mechanism

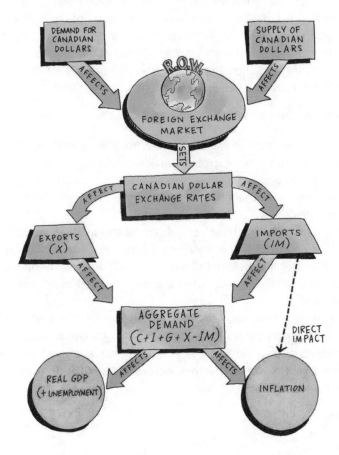

Impact on Net Exports

What happens to exports and imports when the exchange rate of the Canadian dollar appreciates or depreciates?

Appreciating Canadian Dollar Is a Negative Aggregate Demand Shock
An appreciating Canadian dollar is a negative aggregate demand shock. A higher Canadian dollar makes exports more expensive to the rest of the world, and imports cheaper for Canadians. Net exports decrease, decreasing aggregate demand. Aggregate demand equals $C + I + G + X - IM$. Look back in Chapter 7 at Figure 12 on page 177. An appreciating Canadian dollar can push the economy into a contraction, decreasing real GDP, increasing unemployment, and decreasing inflation.

Depreciating Canadian Dollar is a Positive Aggregate Demand Shock
A depreciating Canadian dollar is a positive aggregate demand shock. A lower Canadian dollar makes exports cheaper to the rest of the world, and imports more expensive for Canadians. Net exports increase, increasing aggregate demand. Look back in Chapter 7 at Figure 13 on page 177. A depreciating Canadian dollar can push the economy into an expansion, increasing real GDP, decreasing unemployment, and increasing inflation.

Impact on Inflation

Changes in the exchange rate cause the price of imports, measured in Canadian dollars to fall or rise. There is a direct effect on the Canadian inflation rate that appears at the bottom right of Figure 6 on the previous page in the dashed line from imports to inflation.

An appreciating Canadian dollar causes falling Canadian dollar import prices, which directly decrease the Canadian inflation rate. This direct effect reinforces the indirect effect of decreased net exports in decreasing inflation.

A depreciating Canadian dollar causes rising Canadian dollar import prices, which directly increase the Canadian inflation rate. This direct effect reinforces the indirect effect of increased net exports in increasing inflation.

Do You Want a Strong or Weak Canadian Dollar?

You often hear arguments in the media about a "strong" or "weak" Canadian dollar. Most people assume that a "strong" Canadian dollar — a higher exchange rate in terms of U.S. dollars — is desirable for Canadians. The truth is not so simple. There are advantages and disadvantages to both higher and lower exchange rates.

When the Canadian dollar strengthens, or appreciates in value, imports are less expensive and cross-border shopping is better. But an appreciating Canadian dollar is a negative demand shock, hurting exporters and workers in export industries, decreasing real GDP, increasing unemployment, and decreasing inflation.

When the Canadian dollar weakens, or depreciates in value, imports are more expensive and cross-border shopping is worse for Canadians heading south. But a depreciating Canadian dollar is a positive demand shock, helping exporters and workers in export industries, increasing real GDP, decreasing unemployment, and increasing inflation.

Practice...

11. When the Canadian dollar strengthens,

    a. imports are more expensive.

    b. real GDP increases.

    c. exports are less expensive.

    d. unemployment increases.

12. Changes in exchange rates affect real GDP and inflation through

    a. the international transmission mechanism.

    b. the domestic transmission mechanism.

    c. the law of supply of Canadian dollars.

    d. the law of demand for Canadian dollars.

13. A depreciating Canadian dollar

    a. increases government spending.

    b. decreases exports and increases imports

    c. is a positive aggregate demand shock.

    d. decreases real GDP, increases unemployment, and decreases inflation.

14. A rise in the value of the Canadian dollar

    a. puts downward pressure on export prices to the rest of the world.

    b. puts downward pressure on the Canadian price level.

    c. puts upward pressure on the Canadian price level.

    d. is a positive demand shock.

15. An inflationary gap can result from

    a. appreciation of the C$ leading to decreased imports.

    b. depreciation of the C$ leading to increased imports.

    c. appreciation of the C$ leading to increased exports.

    d. depreciation of the C$ leading to increased exports.

 ## Apply...

7. When the media refer to a "weak Canadian dollar," explain what they are telling us.

    _____

    _____

    _____

    _____

8. Do you support a higher or lower Canadian dollar measured against the U.S. dollar? Explain your choice.

    _____

    _____

    _____

    _____

    _____

Purchasing Power Parity and Rate of Return Parity

 Describe how purchasing power parity and rate of return parity provide standards for exchange rates.

The fluctuating exchange rates we have been describing are called **flexible (or floating) exchange rates** — determined by supply and demand in the foreign exchange market. Most exchange rates, including Canada's, are flexible exchange rates. There are also **fixed exchange rates** — where the exchange rate is set by governments or central banks, as well as systems that combine elements of flexible and fixed exchange rates. We will focus only on flexible exchange rates.

You often hear the media describe the Canadian dollar, or another country's currency, as "overvalued" or "undervalued." These descriptions are based on a point of reference or a standard. They imply that there is some "value" that is just right.

The two standards that economists and speculators use to predict where flexible exchange rates will eventually settle are purchasing power parity and rate of return parity. Both standards depend on the law of one price.

Law of One Price

By buying low and selling high, speculators enforce the **law of one price**, which states that any time there are differences in the price of a product or service across markets, the actions of profit-seekers eliminate the differences and establish a single price. When there are price differences across markets, there is money to be made by buying in markets where the price is low, and selling to markets where the price is high. The resulting changes in demand and supply lead to a single price across both markets. The law of one price applies to all markets, including the foreign exchange market.

Purchasing Power Parity

The principle of purchasing power parity causes exchange rates to adjust between countries. According to **purchasing power parity** (*PPP*), exchange rates adjust so that money has equal real purchasing power in any country.

When *PPP* exists, C$10 buys exactly the same products in Canada — and when converted into US$ at the *PPP* exchange rate — and in the United States. Suppose a book sells for US$8.00 in the United States and C$10.00 in Canada. If you buy the book in Canada, you pay C$10.00. If instead you cross the border to buy the book in the United States, you have to exchange your Canadian dollars for U.S. dollars. You get US$0.80 for each loonie. C$10.00 gets you US$8.00 (10.00 × 0.80 = 8.00). Your C$10.00 buys exactly the same book in the United States as it does Canada after converting into U.S. dollars. The reciprocal exchange rate for *PPP* — the price of a U.S. dollar in terms of Canadian dollars — is 1 ÷ 0.80 or C$1.25.

At any exchange rate other than the *PPP* rate of C$1.00 = U$0.80, it will be cheaper to buy the book in one country or the other. If the actual exchange rate is C$1.00 = US$1.00, after converting C$10.00 into US$10.00 you can buy the book in the U.S. and still have US$2.00 extra. The purchasing power of your C$10.00 is greater in the U.S. Everyone will want to buy in the United States. The demand for Canadian dollars decreases and the supply of Canadian dollars (to demand U.S. dollars) increases until the exchange rate falls back to the *PPP* rate of C$1.00 = U$0.80. At the exchange rate of C$1.00 = US$1.00, the Canadian dollar is *overvalued* relative to the *PPP* rate.

If the actual exchange rate is below the *PPP* rate, such as C$1.00 = US$0.50 (with the reciprocal rate of US$1.00 = C$2.00), the story works in reverse. Purchasing power is greater in Canada. The demand for Canadian dollars increases; the supply of Canadian dollars decreases until the exchange rate falls back to the *PPP* rate of C$1.00 = U$0.80. At the exchange rate of C$1.00 = US$0.50, the Canadian dollar is *undervalued* relative to the *PPP* rate.

The purchasing power parity exchange rate serves as an anchor for exchange rate fluctuations. When the exchange rate is different from the *PPP* rate, profit-seeking forces and the law of one price push the exchange rate back toward the *PPP* rate.

Limitations of Purchasing Power Parity   There are major limitations to *PPP* as the anchor point for exchange rates. The *PPP* story assumes all products and services are traded easily and without cost across borders. In reality, there are many costs, including transportation and storage. Most importantly, the *PPP* story assumes the only reasons to demand and supply dollars on the foreign exchange market are to buy exports or imports. That is not true. Most demand and supply of currencies is for speculation.

Despite these limitations, purchasing power parity is the best available standard for predicting where exchange rates are likely to settle. Don't make the mistake of thinking the *PPP* rate is the "best" rate for the Canadian economy. Because of the trade-offs of a lower or higher exchange rate, there is no single "best" value for the Canadian dollar.

Rate of Return Parity

In the interconnected foreign exchange market, money flows instantly to the highest rate of return on investments — no matter what country it's in. So why are there differences in rates of return across countries? In 2014, for example, the annual rate of return on bonds in Canada was 0.5 percent, while the annual rate of return on bonds in Japan was 2 percent. Why weren't these differences eliminated by the law of one price?

The answer, in words, is *exchange rate expectations*. The answer, in numbers, comes from this formula.

Rate of Return in Japan	=	Rate of Return in Canada	−	expected (depreciation [−] or appreciation [+]) of yen against C$

For Canadian investors to earn 2 percent in Japan, they must first convert Canadian dollars to Japanese yen to buy the Japanese bond. When they sell the Japanese bond at the end of the year, they must then convert the yen back into Canadian dollars. The difference between the 0.5 percent return in Canada and the 2 percent return in Japan reflects the expected depreciation of the yen against the Canadian dollar (1.5 percent). If these expectations come true, the Canadian investor earns 2 percent measured in yen, but then loses 1.5 percent when converting yen back into dollars. The net rate of return is 0.5 percent, the same rate as in Canada.

2% return in Japan	=	0.5% return in Canada	−	(−1.5% depreciation of yen against C$)
2%	=	0.5%	+	1.5%

Rates of return on investments are equal across countries when expected depreciation or appreciation of exchange rates is accounted for. This is called **rate of return parity** (or **interest rate parity**).

So the law of one price does apply to rates of return across countries. Instead of prices adjusting, exchange rates adjust, equalizing net rates of return.

 # Practice...

16. Purchasing power parity states that

    a. exchange rates adjust to equalize the real purchasing power of money across countries.

    b. exchange rates adjust to equalize prices across countries.

    c. purchasing power adjusts to reflect expected exchange rate fluctuations.

    d. prices adjust to equalize rates of return across counties.

17. Suppose C$1.00 = US$1.00 and C$1.00 = 0.67 euro. Purchasing power parity holds when the same McDonald's burger, fries, and drink combo sells for

    a. C$10, US$10, and 10 euros.

    b. C$10, US$10, and 6.70 euros.

    c. C$10, US$10, and 15 euros.

    d. C$10, US$20, and 10 euros.

18. Suppose purchasing power parity (*PPP*) depends only on hamburgers. The exchange rate is C$1.00 = US$0.80 and hamburgers prices are C$2.00 in Canada and US$1.50 in the U.S. *PPP* suggests that the

    a. Canadian dollar is undervalued.

    b. supply of Canadian dollars will decrease.

    c. Canadian dollar is overvalued.

    d. demand for Canadian dollars will increase.

19. If the rate of return in India is higher than the rate of return in Canada, rate of return parity suggests the difference is due to

    a. purchasing power parity.

    b. current interest rates.

    c. expected exchange rates.

    d. expected interest rates.

20. The rate of return on bonds in Canada is 3 percent, while the rate of return on bonds of comparable risk in Japan is 7 percent. If a Japanese investor buys a Canadian bond, then she expects the Japanese yen to

    a. appreciate against the C$ by 4 percent.

    b. depreciate against the C$ by 4 percent.

    c. appreciate against the C$ by 3 percent.

    d. depreciate against the C$ by 3 percent.

 **Apply...**

9. Suppose, for simplicity, a Wii U system sells for $100 in Canada and $95 in the U.S.

a. If Wiis are the only product traded between the countries, what is the *PPP* exchange rate?

_____

_____

_____

b. If the exchange rate is C$1.00 = US$0.90, where is your purchasing power greater?

_____

_____

_____

c. Does an exchange rate of C$1.00 = US$0.90 imply that the Canadian dollar is overvalued or undervalued?

_____

_____

_____

d. If the exchange rate is C$1.00 = US$0.90, what will happen to the exchange rate over time (according to purchasing power parity)?

_____

_____

_____

10. Explain the statement "The Canadian dollar is overvalued compared to the U.S. dollar" to a friend who has not taken this economics course.

_____

_____

_____

_____

11. Why must you understand the principle of rate of return parity in order to invest profitably in another country?

_____

_____

_____

International Balance of Payments

 Distinguish the two main parts of the balance of payments accounts, and explain why they must add up to zero.

Exchange rates affect the flows of exports, imports, and investments across international borders. A country's **balance of payments** accounts measure all international transactions during a year. The main parts to the balance of payments accounts are the

- current account.
- financial account.

Figure 7 shows Canada's balance of payments accounts for 2013.

Figure 7   Canada's Balance of Payments Accounts 2013 (billions of C$)

Current Account	
Exports of products and services	+566
Imports of products and services	−598
Net investment/labour/transfer income	− 28
Current Account Balance	**− 60**
Financial Account	
Canadian investments in R.O.W	− 71
R.O.W. investments in Canada	+129
Financial Account Balance	**+ 58**
Statistical Discrepancy	+ 2

Source: Based on Statistics Canada. *Table 376-0101 - Balance of international payments, current account and capital account, annual (dollars),* CANSIM (database).

Current Account

The *current account* measures Canada's yearly exports and imports of products and services. Flows of Canadian dollars into Canada are positive numbers on the balance of payments accounts; flows of Canadian dollars out of Canada are negative numbers.

- Canadian exports create a positive inflow of Canadian dollars to Canada.
- Imports from R.O.W. into Canada create a negative outflow of Canadian dollars.
- The less important category of net investment/labour/transfer income measures net flows of interest income on investments, and labour and transfer income between Canada and R.O.W. A negative outflow means more interest/labour/transfer income flowed out of Canada than in.

Current Account Balance   There is a current account deficit (negative balance) when Canadian spending on imports from R.O.W. is greater than R.O.W. spending on Canadian exports (and net investment/labour/transfers). There is a current account surplus (positive balance) when R.O.W. spending on Canadian exports is greater than Canadian spending on imports from R.O.W. (and net investment/labour/transfers).

Financial Account

The *financial account* measures international investments in financial assets like bonds and direct investment in buying companies.

- Canadian investments in R.O.W. are a negative outflow of Canadian dollars to R.O.W.

- R.O.W. investments in Canada are a positive inflow of Canadian dollars.

- The *statistical discrepancy* is for missing data and errors and is not important for balance of payments accounts.

Financial Account Balance   There is a financial account deficit (negative balance) when Canadian investments in R.O.W. are greater than R.O.W. investments in Canada. There is a financial account surplus (positive balance) when R.O.W. investments in Canada are greater than Canadian investments in R.O.W.

Why International Payments Accounts Must Balance

All international transactions begin with an exchange in the foreign exchange market. When R.O.W. buys Canadian exports or invests in Canadian companies, they first buy enough Canadian dollars on the foreign exchange market to pay for those transactions. When Canadians buy imports or invest in companies from R.O.W., we first buy enough of each foreign currency to pay for those transactions. The demand for a different currency on the foreign exchange market is also a supply of your own currency.

Because demand for one currency is also the supply of another, *the balance of payments accounts must add up to zero.*

| Current Account Balance | + | Financial Account Balance | + | Statistical Discrepancy | = | 0 |

Plugging the numbers for 2013 for Canada into this formula shows

| (− 60$ bil) | + | (+58$ bil) | + | (+2$ bil) | = | 0 |

Why must these balances add to zero?

Current Account Deficit and Financial Account Surplus   When there is a current account deficit, there is a financial account surplus. If Canada spends more on R.O.W. imports than R.O.W. spends on Canadian exports, where does Canada get the extra foreign currency? From the financial account surplus, with R.O.W. "loaning" Canada extra foreign currency through investments.

Current Account Surplus and Financial Account Deficit   When there is a current account surplus, there is a financial account deficit. If R.O.W. spends more on Canadian exports than Canadians spend on R.O.W. imports, where does R.O.W. get the extra Canadian dollars? From the financial account deficit, with Canadians "loaning" R.O.W. extra Canadian dollars through investments.

The current account and financial account balances are mirror images of each other. When one balance is in deficit, the other is in surplus. The statistical discrepancy is used to allow for missing data and errors.

Practice...

21. When a Canadian invests in an Italian bicycle company, this is a

    a. positive entry on the current account.

    b. negative entry on the current account.

    c. positive entry on the financial account.

    d. negative entry on the financial account.

22. Which activity is a positive entry on the Canadian current account?

    a. Canadian tourist spends $2000 at the SXSW Festival in Austin, Texas.

    b. U.S. tourist spends $3000 at the Toronto International Film Festival.

    c. Canadian buys a German government bond.

    d. Canadian from Halifax invests in a hockey stick factory in Saskatchewan.

23. If the statistical discrepancy is zero, then any

    a. deficit on the current account equals the surplus on the financial account.

    b. surplus on the current account equals the surplus on the financial account.

    c. deficit on the current account means Canada invests more in R.O.W. than the R.O.W. invests in Canada.

    d. surplus on the current account means the R.O.W. invests more in Canada than Canada invests in the R.O.W.

24. If Canada has a current account surplus on the balance of payments, then to pay for the extra Canadian exports

    a. R.O.W. is loaning Canada extra C$.

    b. R.O.W. is loaning Canada extra foreign currency.

    c. Canada is loaning R.O.W. extra C$.

    d. Canada is loaning R.O.W. extra foreign currency.

25. Canada has a zero balance (no surplus or deficit) on both the current account and on the financial account. Then Canadian businesses import new machinery from Italy, financing that increase by borrowing from Japan. On Canada's balance of payments accounts there is now a current account

    a. deficit and a financial account deficit.

    b. surplus and a financial account deficit.

    c. deficit and a financial account surplus.

    d. surplus and a financial account surplus.

😊 Apply...

12. Explain the meaning of positive numbers on the balance of payments accounts. Now explain the meaning of negative numbers.

_____

_____

_____

_____

13. Explain what a negative current account balance means. What does a positive financial account balance mean?

_____

_____

_____

_____

14. Explain why a country's balance of payments accounts must be zero at the end of each year.

_____

_____

_____

_____

_____

_____

KNOW...

Summary of Learning Objectives

1. The demand for products, services, and assets from other countries, which must be paid for in local currencies, are behind demand and supply on the **foreign exchange market**, determining **exchange rates.** The **appreciation** of one currency is the **depreciation** of another.

2. Exchange rate fluctuations are caused by changes in **interest rate differentials**, **inflation rate differentials**, Canadian real GDP, R.O.W. demand for Canadian exports, world prices for Canadian resource exports, and expectations by speculators. Most of these changes shift both the demand and supply curves for Canadian dollars, intensifying exchange rate fluctuations.

3. Exchange rates affect real GDP and inflation through the **international transmission mechanism** affecting net exports, aggregate demand *(C + I + G + X – IM)*, and the price level. An appreciating Canadian dollar is a negative aggregate demand shock. A depreciating Canadian dollar is a positive aggregate demand shock.

4. The **law of one price**, **purchasing power parity (*PPP*)**, and **rate of return parity**, despite their limitations, are the best available standards for predicting where exchange rates eventually settle. According to *PPP*, exchange rates adjust so that money has equal real purchasing power in any country. Rates of return on investments are equal across countries when expected depreciation or appreciation of exchange rates is accounted for.

5. A country's **balance of payments accounts** measure all international transactions. The two main parts of the balance of payments accounts — the *current account* and the *financial account* — must add up to zero. Flows of Canadian dollars into Canada are positive numbers; flows of Canadian dollars out of Canada are negative numbers.

Key Terms

balance of payments accounts: measure a country's international transactions

currency appreciation: rise in the exchange rate of one currency for another

currency depreciation: fall in the exchange rate of one currency for another

exchange rate: price at which one currency exchanges for another currency

flexible (or floating) exchange rates: determined by supply and demand in the foreign exchange market

fixed exchange rates: set by government or central banks

foreign exchange market: worldwide market where all countries' currencies are bought and sold in exchange for each other

interest rate differential: difference in interest rates between countries

inflation rate differential: difference in inflation rates between countries

international transmission mechanism: how exchange rates affect real GDP, unemployment, and inflation

law of demand for Canadian dollars: as the exchange rate rises, the quantity demanded of Canadian dollars decreases

law of one price: profit seekers eliminate differences in prices of the same product or service across markets and establish a single price

law of supply for Canadian dollars: as the exchange rate rises, the quantity supplied of Canadian dollars increases

purchasing power parity: exchange rates adjust so that money has equal real purchasing power in any country

rate of return parity (interest rate parity): rates of return on investments are equal across countries, accounting for the expected depreciation or appreciation of exchange rates

Answers to Practice

1. **d** **b** is the reciprocal exchange rate.

2. **b** Price and quantity demanded of a currency move in opposite directions, and price and quantity supplied move in the same direction.

3. **d** Creates a supply of Canadian dollars in foreign exchange market (and demand for U.S. dollars).

4. **c** Appreciation of C$ makes imports cheaper in C$ and exports more expensive in U.S. dollars.

5. **b** Price is above equilibrium, so excess supply causes competition among sellers who can't get rid of C$.

6. **b** Increase in the Canadian inflation rate differential decreases demand and increases supply of C$.

7. **d** Demand for C$ decreases and supply increases.

8. **d** Increased real GDP increases imports and investor confidence, resulting in a net appreciation of C$.

9. **c** Speculators have self-fulfilling expectations when acting together, and reinforce and speed up the effects of other forces on exchange rates.

10. **a** Self-fulfilling expectation.

11. **d** Appreciating Canadian dollar is a negative demand shock. Imports are cheaper, exports more expensive, and real GDP decreases.

12. **a** Chapter 10 on monetary policy explains the domestic transmission mechanism effects of interest rate changes on real GDP and inflation.

13. **c** Increases net exports and real GDP, decreases unemployment and inflation.

14. **b** Imports become cheaper for Canadians, so the average of all prices falls.

15. **d** Depreciation of C$ is positive demand shock, increasing exports and decreasing imports.

16. **a** Definition of purchasing power parity.

17. **b** Purchasing power parity rate holds when C$10 has the same purchasing power when converted into U.S. dollars (US$10) and European euros (6.7 euros).

18. **c** C$2 buys a hamburger in Canada. C$2 converts to U.S.$1.60, more than the U.S.$1.50 necessary to buy a hamburger in the U.S.

19. **c** See formula for rate of return parity.

20. **b** Rate of return in Japan (7%) = rate of return in Canada (3%) minus expected depreciation [− 4%] of yen against C$. 7% = 3% + 4%.

21. **d** Canadian investment dollars flow out of Canada.

22. **b** Canadian export of services to R.O.W.

23. **a** Current Account Balance + Financial Account Balance + Statistical Discrepancy = 0.

24. **c** Canada is loaning R.O.W. extra C$, causing financial account deficit.

25. **c** Import of machinery creates outflow of C$ on the current account. Financial account must show an equal inflow.

10 Money and Monetary Policy

LEARNING OBJECTIVES

L01 Explain three functions of money and why people give up interest on bonds to demand money.

L02 Identify four forms of money and different measures of the money supply, and describe how the Bank of Canada and chartered banks create the money supply.

L03 Explain how money and loanable funds markets determine the interest rate and how the Bank of Canada uses open market operations to change target interest rates.

L04 Explain how money affects real GDP, unemployment, and inflation through the domestic and international monetary transmission mechanisms.

L05 Explain what blocks monetary transmission mechanisms, show how quantitative easing can overcome a balance sheet recession, and use the quantity theory of money to analyze the inflation risks of monetary policy.

LEARN...

When you want to save money, you can stash it — as cash — under your mattress, which pays no interest. Alternatively, you can invest your money and earn interest on it. So why would you ever choose to hold cash and lose the interest? In this chapter, we will explain why people demand cash and voluntarily give up the possibility to earn interest.

The interest rate is the price of money and answers the question, "How much will you pay for money?" Demanders and suppliers of money, along with loanable funds markets, play a role in setting interest rates.

The Bank of Canada is the other key player. Besides supplying money, the Bank of Canada uses monetary policy to change the money supply and interest rates to try and safely steer the economy on the road to full employment, stable prices, and steady economic growth.

As a citizen you should understand how the Bank's policy choices affect your standard of living, your prospects for finding a job, the interest rate you pay on loans, and the cost of living. Wrong policy choices can send the economy over a cliff into cycles of bust and boom. And knowing how the Bank of Canada is likely to act will help you make smart financial choices.

Demand for Money

 Explain three functions of money and why people give up interest on bonds to demand money.

Any business will accept your cash in exchange for what it is selling. That *acceptability* is the key to what we use as money. **Money** is anything accepted as a means of payment.

Money has three functions:

- *medium of exchange* — acceptability solves the barter problem of the double coincidence of wants.

- *unit of account* (or *measure of value*) — standard unit for measuring prices.

- *store of value* — time machine for moving purchasing power from present to future; you can earn now and spend later.

People demand money because of its functions. The **transactions demand for money** is the demand to hold money for use as a *medium of exchange* — buying and selling. The **asset demand for money** is the demand to hold money for use as a *store of value* — useful if you want to invest rather than spend your wealth.

How do you choose between holding your wealth as money versus investing it in an asset that pays interest?

Money or Bonds?

Let's take a simple example with only two choices for holding wealth: as money, which pays no interest, or as loanable funds, which do pay interest. Bonds are the most important loanable fund. A **bond** is a financial asset for which the borrower promises to repay the original value at a specific future date and to make fixed regular interest payments.

When companies need cash, they go to the loanable funds markets to borrow money by issuing bonds. If the Ford Motor Company needs cash for new assembly-line robots, it may issue many $10 000 bonds. Each bond promises to repay the borrower $10 000 on January 1, 2028, and to make $500 interest payments on every January 1st until then. By using $10 000 of your savings to buy the bond from Ford, you are loaning Ford $10 000. In exchange, Ford gives you a piece of paper (the bond), which is a promise to repay your loan of $10 000 with a specific dollar amount of interest.

Liquidity   By holding money you give up the $500 a year in interest. Why would you hold money rather than buy a Ford bond? All reasons for wanting to hold money and give up earned interest are summarized in one word — liquidity. **Liquidity** is the ease with which assets can be converted into the economy's medium of exchange. Money — which is by definition the medium of exchange — is the most liquid of all assets. Bonds are much less liquid. It may take days to sell your bonds to get your money.

Security against Uncertainty   The return on bonds is not guaranteed — there is uncertainty whether you will get your money back. Corporations and other issuers of bonds can go bankrupt. During the Global Financial Crisis, many bonds became worthless and investors lost all of their wealth. While money pays no interest, it does not have the risk of bonds. Since the Global Financial Crisis, people have been holding much more of their wealth as cash, giving up the interest on bonds.

Interest Rates and the Demand for Money

Money pays no interest, but has liquidity. Bonds pay interest, but do not have liquidity. How do you make a smart choice about *how much* of your wealth to hold as money, and how much as bonds?

Interest Rate as the Price of Money   The **interest rate** is the price of holding money: it is what you give up by not holding bonds. The interest rate is determined by demand and supply in both the money market and the loanable funds (bond) market. Money and bonds are intimately connected.

Macroeconomic Demand for Money   The law of demand also applies to money. As the price of money — the interest rate — rises, the quantity demanded of money decreases. At higher interest rates people want to hold less money and more of their assets as bonds. The law of demand for money works as long as other factors besides the interest rate do not change.

When the interest rate on bonds is very low, it makes almost no difference whether you hold your wealth as money or bonds. You might as well keep most of your wealth as money, to have the convenience of liquidity and avoid risk. When the interest rate on bonds is very high, you will keep as much of your assets as possible in bonds, and hold the minimum quantity of money you need for transactions.

Figure 1 illustrates the inverse relation between the interest rate and the amount of money people want to hold — the quantity demanded of money.

Figure 1   Demand for Money

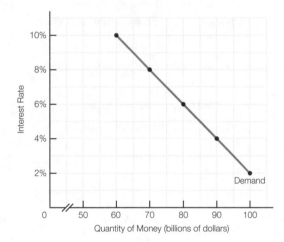

As the price of money — the interest rate — rises, the quantity demanded of money decreases. When something, even money, becomes more expensive, people economize on its use.

Changes in the Demand for Money

Recall that a change in quantity demanded is different from a change in demand. Only a change in the price of money — the interest rate — changes the *quantity demanded* of money. A change in other factors, like real GDP or the price level, changes the *demand* for money and shifts the money demand curve.

Changes in Real GDP   Increased real GDP increases the demand for money and shifts the money demand curve rightward. Increased real GDP is increased real income. With more purchasing power, people buy more stuff and need more money for transactions. Decreased real GDP decreases the demand for money and shifts money demand curve leftward.

Changes in the Price Level   Increased average prices increase the demand for money and shift the money demand curve rightward. With higher prices, you need to carry more money to make the same purchases as before. Decreased average prices decrease the demand for money and shift the money demand curve leftward.

 # Practice...

1. If you sell your bonds in order to hold more of your wealth as money, you
   a. get liquidity and give up interest.
   b. give up liquidity and earn interest.
   c. get liquidity and earn interest.
   d. give up liquidity and give up interest.

2. The double coincidence of wants is
   a. buyers wanting the same thing.
   b. sellers wanting the same thing.
   c. buyers and sellers wanting nothing to do with each other.
   d. buyers and sellers each wanting what the other has.

3. When the interest rate falls, the
   a. demand for money increases.
   b. quantity demanded of money increases.
   c. quantity demanded of money decreases.
   d. opportunity cost of holding money increases.

4. Liquidity is the
   a. opportunity cost of holding money.
   b. ease of converting money into bonds.
   c. ease of converting assets into the economy's medium of exchange.
   d. state of being drunk.

5. The demand for money increases (demand curve shifts rightward) when
   a. real GDP decreases.
   b. the quantity of money supplied decreases.
   c. average prices increase.
   d. average prices decrease.

Apply...

1. Consider two individuals: James Bond and Johnny Cash. Suppose James Bond holds most of his wealth in bonds while Johnny Cash holds most of his wealth in cash.

   a. Whose wealth is more liquid?

   _____

   _____

   _____

   b. What is the price of money? If the price of money falls, will the quantity of money demanded decrease or increase?

   _____

   _____

   _____

2. Products ranging from cigarettes to chocolate have been used as a medium of exchange.

   a. What is money?

   _____

   _____

   _____

   b. Suppose the Royal Canadian Mint stops minting coins due to a shortage of available metals and instead distributes mint chocolate in gold-foil wrappers in the shape of money. How would this meet each of the three functions of money?

   _____

   _____

   _____

   _____

   c. Cigarettes once functioned as the currency of Romania. Anything could be bought for cigarettes — food, electronics, alcohol. Explain which functions of money cigarettes can and cannot perform.

   _____

   _____

   _____

   _____

3. You have just won $50 000 in the lottery. You go on a shopping spree with $30 000 and save $20 000. What benefits or worries will influence your decision to hold the $20 000 as cash or to invest it in an interest-earning bond?

   _____

   _____

   _____

   _____

Supply of Money

 Identify four forms of money and different measures of the money supply, and describe how the Bank of Canada and chartered banks create the money supply.

What is money and where does it come from?

Forms of Money

Throughout history there have only been four basic forms of money:

- commodity money — saleable products (like beaver pelts) with alternative uses serving as money.

- convertible paper money — paper money that can be converted into gold on demand.

- fiat money — **currency** (government-issued bills and coins) with no alternative uses; valuable simply by government decree.

- deposit money — **demand deposits** — balances in bank accounts that depositors can withdraw on demand by using a debit card or writing a cheque.

The most important form of money today is deposit money. Debit cards are not money. They are just a means of transferring demand deposits, which are money. Credit cards are definitely *not* money. When you pay using a credit card, Visa or MasterCard is giving you a temporary loan, which they use to pay the merchant. But the transaction is not complete until you transfer currency or demand deposits to the credit card company to pay off the loan.

Bank of Canada and Measuring the Money Supply

Where does money come from? In Canada, money consists of currency issued by the Bank of Canada and deposit money in *chartered banks*, credit unions, and similar financial institutions. Private chartered banks are the most important financial institutions for creating the supply of money.

Canada's Central Bank   A central bank is a government institution responsible for supervising chartered banks and other financial institutions, and for regulating the supply of money. Canada's central bank, the Bank of Canada, was created by the 1935 *Bank of Canada Act*. The Bank of Canada's mandate is to control the quantity of money and interest rates to avoid inflation, business cycles, and unemployment.

The Bank of Canada plays five important roles in the Canadian economy:

- issuing currency.

- banker to chartered banks — chartered bank deposits at the Bank of Canada allow the chartered banks to make payments to each other.

- **lender of last resort** — making loans to banks to preserve the stability of the financial system.

- banker to government — managing government's accounts, foreign currency reserves, and the national debt.

- conducting **monetary policy** — changing the money supply and interest rates to achieve steady growth, full employment, and stable prices.

Central Bank Independence   In conducting monetary policy, the Bank of Canada has considerable independence from the federal government, but ultimately is accountable to Parliament. That independence is important. Hyperinflation is usually a result of the government controlling the central bank and ordering it to print money to finance government spending. The independence of the Bank of Canada prevents harmful government influences on monetary policies.

M1+ and M2+   There are many ways to measure the supply of money in Canada. The official measures used by the Bank of Canada are called M1+ and M2+. M1+ consists of currency in circulation plus demand deposits. In July 2017, there was $89 billion in currency and $858 billion in demand deposits. M1+ equalled $947 billion.

M2+ is a broader measure of the money supply. It includes all of M1+ plus all other deposits, like savings accounts and guaranteed investment certificates. M2+ was $3045 billion. These other deposits are not as liquid as demand deposits. They have restrictions or penalties for withdrawal on demand. But they are relatively easy to convert into money (unlike bonds), which is why they are included in this broader measure of the money supply.

How Banks Create Money

The Bank of Canada is the only legal supplier of Canadian currency. But currency ($89 billion) is a small fraction of the money supply — only 9 percent of M1+ and 3 percent of M2+. Most money takes the form of demand deposits, which can be created legally by chartered banks. But a chartered bank's creation of money comes with risks.

Goldsmiths as the Original Bankers   Hundreds of years ago, goldsmiths became bankers with the main features of modern banking — deposits, loans, and reserves.

Goldsmiths had secure safes that attracted *deposits* of gold. Goldsmiths issued paper IOUs (convertible paper money) for gold and acted like banks. Once the public trusted and accepted paper notes issued by goldsmiths — acceptability is the key to money — goldsmiths could issue notes that were not fully backed by gold.

Goldsmiths made *loans*, giving the borrower not gold but a paper note convertible into gold. In exchange, the borrower signed a contract to repay the loan plus interest at a future date. The borrower could use the goldsmith's note as money since it was accepted as a means of payment.

The value of the paper notes in circulation was greater than the value of gold in the safes. The goldsmith were "banking on" the small probability that depositors and borrowers would all want to withdraw their gold at the same time. By making loans not backed by gold, the goldsmiths created money (acceptable paper notes) and made profits (interest) on the loans. For trust in the paper notes to continue, the goldsmiths had to hold enough gold in *reserve* so that when customers did show up with one of their paper notes and ask for the equivalent amount of gold, it was there.

Loans and Money Creation Go Together   Chartered banks are today's goldsmiths, but without the gold. When you deposit money into a chartered bank, you get a credit on your chequing account balance. But the bank doesn't keep your cash in its vaults. It keeps a very small fraction of your deposit in the form of cash reserves, and loans out the rest at interest. This system is called **fractional-reserve banking.**

Instead of issuing paper notes like goldsmiths, the bank creates a demand deposit credit in the borrower's chequing account equal to the amount of the loan. Since demand deposits are money — part of M1+ — the bank has created both a loan and money. When loans are paid off, there is a reduction in the quantity of both loans and money. In the Canadian monetary system, loan creation and money creation are two sides of the same coin.

Look Ma, No Reserves!   While the Bank of Canada carefully supervises all banks and financial institutions, chartered banks are not legally required to keep any cash reserves at all! Canadian banks actually hold less than 1 percent of the value of all demand deposits as cash!

Nonetheless, the Canadian banking system is one of the safest and most admired banking systems in the world. In the rare event that customers want to withdraw more demand deposits or currency than the bank has, chartered banks can borrow from each other and from the Bank of Canada (the lender of last resort) to meet their customers' demands and maintain trust.

Bank Profits versus Prudence   The risks of fractional-reserve banking and loans are that borrowers will default on (not repay) their loans. Banks protect against this risk by requiring *collateral* — property pledged as security for repayment of the loan. If you default on a car loan or house mortgage, the bank sells the property to recover the value of the loan. Banks also charge higher interest payments on loans that they consider to be riskier.

Banks face a trade-off between profits and prudence. A smaller fraction of reserves, more loans, and higher-risk loans may increase bank profits, but by giving up safety and risking customers' deposits and trust. This tension in any banking system is why banks are regulated around the world. Without regulation, more banks will take risks in pursuit of profits that might cause the bank to fail, and lose *all* depositors' money if loans are not repaid.

The Money Multiplier   While there are no legally required reserves, banks decide on desired reserves, depending on their evaluation of the trade-off between profits and prudence. For any desired reserve ratio (*drr*), the **money multiplier** shows the multiple by which the banking system can create new loans and demand deposits for each new dollar deposited into a bank.

Money multiplier = 1 ÷ desired reserve ratio

For example, if *drr* = 0.1, the money multiplier is 10. For every new dollar deposited, banks create $10 in new loans and demand deposits. If *drr* = 0.5, the money multiplier is 2. Each new dollar deposited creates only $2 in new loans and demand deposits.

A lower *drr* (profits) means creating more loans (more interest earned for banks) and demand deposits (money). A higher *drr* (prudence) means creating fewer loans (less interest earned for banks) and demand deposits (money).

The Supply of Money

The total quantity of money (currency plus demand deposits, measured as M1+) supplied by both the Bank of Canada and the banking system depends on the quantity of loans and demand deposits that the banking system creates. When interest rates are higher, loans are more profitable, so banks make more loans and create more demand deposits. There is a positive relationship between interest rates and the quantity of money supplied. If you graph the combinations of interest rates and quantity of money supplied, you get the upward sloping supply of money curve in Figure 2.

Figure 2   The Supply of Money

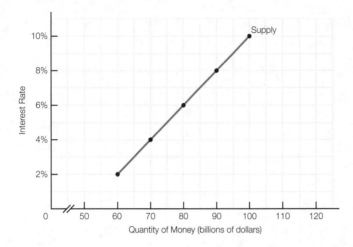

Vertical Money Supply Curve?   Your textbook or instructor might draw the money supply curve as a vertical line — a fixed quantity of money that does not change when the interest rate changes. That vertical money supply curve originated in a time when central banks tried to set the quantity of money supplied. Modern central banks abandoned that focus and now set interest rates to achieve a target inflation rate. The vertical money supply curve is part of a simpler model that does not incorporate the effects of interest rates on chartered bank creation of loans and money (demand deposits).

Fortunately, in all of the graphs that follow, the outcomes will be the same with either the upward-sloping money supply curve of Figure 2 or a vertical money supply curve.

 Practice...

6. A debit card is

    a. deposit money.

    b. fiat money.

    c. not money.

    d. commodity money.

7. If the banking system has a desired reserve ratio of 20 percent, what is the money multiplier?

    a. 0.2

    b. 2

    c. 0.5

    d. 5

8. Which is most liquid?

    a. demand deposits

    b. saving deposits

    c. government bonds

    d. real estate

9. The quantity of money supplied depends

    a. only on the Bank of Canada.

    b. only on chartered banks.

    c. only on the money market.

    d. on the interest rate.

10. When cash is deposited in a chartered bank, the bank makes new loans. This

    a. has no effect on currency in circulation.

    b. has no effect on M1+.

    c. decreases M1+.

    d. increases M1+.

Apply...

4. Explain how a chartered bank creates money.

_____
_____
_____
_____
_____

5. The Bank of Cripple Creek is the only bank in the banking system. The bank has $100 000 in demand deposits, $5000 in desired reserves, and outstanding loans of $95 000.

   a. What is Cripple Creek's desired reserve ratio? What is the money multiplier?

   _____
   _____
   _____
   _____

   b. A new customer comes along and deposits $1000 in cash. Immediately after the deposit, what is Cripple Creek's actual reserve ratio?

   _____
   _____
   _____
   _____

   c. Cripple Creek makes enough new loans (and demand deposits) to return to its desired reserve ratio. What are its new, total demand deposits?

   _____
   _____
   _____
   _____

6. Banks, like other businesses, operate to make profits. Are there reasons why banks should be subject to more government regulations than, for example, shoe stores or bakeries? Explain your answer.

   _____
   _____
   _____
   _____
   _____

Interest Rates, Bonds, and Open Market Operations

 LO3 Explain how money and loanable funds markets determine the interest rate and how the Bank of Canada uses open market operations to change target interest rates.

The interest rate is the price of money in two ways:

- The interest rate is the price of holding money — what you give up by not holding your wealth as bonds that pay interest.

- The interest rate is also the price you pay to borrow money. If the interest rate is 5 percent per year, to borrow $100 for a year you have to pay back the original $100 plus $5 in interest.

To see how the interest rate is determined, we will continue with the simple choice between only two assets: money and bonds. The interest rate is determined by the interaction of the demand for money and the supply of money in *both* the money and loanable funds markets.

But first we must explain one other price — the price of bonds.

Bond Prices and Interest Rates

Let's take a simple example of a $10 000 bond issued by the Ford Motor Company for one year that promises to repay the $10 000 and a $500 payment at the end of the year. The original value of the bond is $10 000, and the current price of the bond on the bond market is also $10 000.

If the price of the bond is $10 000, the $500 payment amounts to 5 percent interest for the year. It is important to remember that *bonds specify a fixed dollar amount that they pay* in addition to repaying the original value. Bonds do *not* specify an interest rate in percent.

When Interest Rates Change, So Do Bond Prices   In buying the bond, you loaned Ford $10 000 and Ford gave you a piece of paper — the bond. You are happy to receive the $500 payment at the end of the year (an interest rate of 5 percent), and Ford is happy to pay you $500 for borrowing $10 000 of your money.

The next day, interest rates around the world rise to 10 percent. You can now get a bond that will pay you $1000 in interest on a $10 000 investment. Your Ford bond now looks like a bad investment. You decide to sell your bond on the bond market, and use the money to buy a new bond that pays 10 percent interest.

Unfortunately, you will not find a buyer for your bond at the price of $10 000. Now that other bonds yield a $1000 return on $10 000 at the end of a year, no one will buy your bond yielding only a $500 return on $10 000. The only way to sell it is to lower the price you are willing to accept. At what new price can you sell your bond — find a buyer — on the bond market?

The market price of your bond will fall until the fixed return it offers at the end of the year amounts to a 10 percent interest rate — the same rate of return investors can get on other bonds now for sale. The price for your Ford bond falls to approximately $9545. If someone buys your Ford bond for $9545, at the end of the year she receives from Ford $10 500. That difference is a gain of $955. In percentage terms, that's 10 percent.

Don't worry about the precise math in the calculations. That's what calculators are for. The important fact is that *when interest rates rise, the market price of bonds falls.* This inverse relation between bond prices and interest rates is the most important feature of all bond markets.

Here is a simplified formula for calculating the market price of a one-year bond.

$$\text{Price of Bond} \ = \ \frac{\$\ \text{Amount of Money Returned at end of year}}{(1\ +\ \text{interest rate})}$$

The original price of the bond is

$$\$10\ 000 \ \ = \ \ \frac{\$\ 10\ 000\ +\ \$500}{(1\ +\ 0.05)}$$

The new price of the bond after interest rates rise to 10 percent is

$$\$9545 \ \ = \ \ \frac{\$\ 10\ 000\ +\ \$500}{(1\ +\ 0.1)}$$

Bonds are riskier and less liquid than money as a store of value for two reasons: risk that the market price can change and risk of default.

Determining the Interest Rate

The interest rate — the price of money — is determined by the demand and supply in money markets and loanable funds markets. Figure 3 combines Figures 1 and 2 about the demand for and supply of money in the money market. But the numbers makes sense only if we bring the loanable funds market into the story.

Figure 3   Demand and Supply for Money

Price (interest rate)	Quantity Demanded (billions of dollars)	Quantity Supplied (billions of dollars)
2%	100	60
4%	90	70
6%	80	80
8%	70	90
10%	60	100

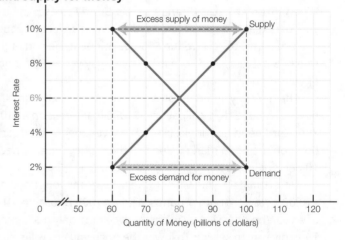

To understand why the equilibrium interest rate is 6 percent, let's look at the forces set in motion at any other interest rate.

Excess Demand for Money   At a 2 percent interest rate, people want to hold $100 billion worth of money. But the quantity of money supplied is only $60 billion. Excess demand for money is a demand for more liquidity. People demand more money (and are willing to give up earned interest on loanable funds) for the convenience of money's liquidity. People must sell some of their bonds to get more money.

The additional supply of bonds for sale on the loanable funds market causes bond prices to fall. A fall in bond prices instantly causes interest rates to rise. The excess demand for money only disappears when the interest rate rises to 6 percent.

Excess Supply of Money   At a 10 percent interest rate, people want to hold $60 billion worth of money. But the quantity of money supplied is $100 billion. Excess supply of money means there is more liquidity than people want. People use money to buy more bonds.

The additional demand for bonds on the loanable funds market causes bond prices to rise. A rise in bond prices instantly causes interest rates to fall. The excess supply of money only disappears when the interest rate falls to 6 percent.

Open Market Operations

The Bank of Canada is responsible for monetary policy — changing the money supply and interest rates to achieve steady growth, full employment, and stable prices. **Price stability** means the inflation rate is low enough that it does not significantly affect people's economic decisions.

Since 1991, the Bank of Canada also had two objectives for monetary policy:

- to contain the annual rate of inflation between 1 percent and 3 percent, as measured by increases in the Consumer Price Index (CPI). This is called the **inflation-control target**.

- to use monetary policy to achieve the 2 percent midpoint of that range.

The Bank of Canada aims for a 2 percent inflation rate target as measured by the CPI, but also pays close attention to the core inflation rates — which the Bank of Canada calls its *operational guide* — as a better measure of the long-run, underlying trend of inflation.

Interest rates are the most important tool for monetary policy. Long-run Interest rates, such as rates for 25-year mortgages and 10- to 30-year government bonds, are determined in loanable funds markets. *Central banks* cannot influence long-run interest rates, but they can influence short-run interest rates.

In aiming for its 2 percent target rate of inflation, the Bank of Canada focuses on the **overnight rate** — the interest rate that chartered banks charge each other for one-day loans. The overnight rate then determines all other interest rates that banks charge their customers, including rates on lines of credit, rates for consumer and car loans, and rates for variable mortgages.

Changes in interest rates affect the economy. They speed it up or slow it down the same way that stepping on the gas or hitting the brakes changes the speed of your car. Lower interest rates mean more borrowing and spending, less saving. Higher interest rates mean less borrowing and spending, more saving.

- In a recessionary gap, the Bank of Canada lowers interest rates to increase aggregate demand and accelerate the economy.

- In an inflationary gap, the Bank of Canada raises interest rates to decrease aggregate demand and slow down the economy.

The Bank of Canada changes the target interest rate through **open market operations** — buying or selling government bonds on the bond market. The money market and bond market are interconnected, so open market operations can be explained from either perspective.

The Money Market Story of Open Market Operations From the money market perspective, the Bank of Canada changes the money supply using open market operations to influence quantity of demand deposits (part of M1+). Look at Figure 4, with an initial equilibrium interest rate of 6 percent.

Figure 4 Demand and Supply in the Money Market after the Bank of Canada Buys Bonds

Price (interest rate)	Quantity of Money Demanded (billions of dollars)	Quantity of Money Supplied (billions of dollars)
2%	100	80
4%	90	90
6%	80	100
8%	70	110
10%	60	120

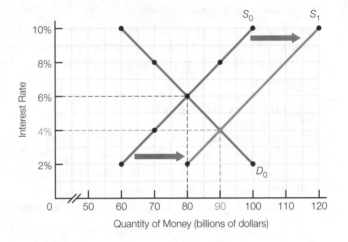

To lower interest rates and accelerate the economy, the Bank of Canada effectively buys bonds with cash, increasing bank reserves. Through the money multiplier, banks make new loans and demand deposits, increasing the money supply (to the last column in the table). The supply of money shifts from S_0 to S_1, and the equilibrium interest rate falls to 4 percent.

Figure 5 illustrates the opposite open market operations to raise interest rates.

Figure 5 Demand and Supply in the Money Market after the Bank of Canada Sells Bonds

Price (interest rate)	Quantity of Money Demanded (billions of dollars)	Quantity of Money Supplied (billions of dollars)
2%	100	40
4%	90	50
6%	80	60
8%	70	70
10%	60	80

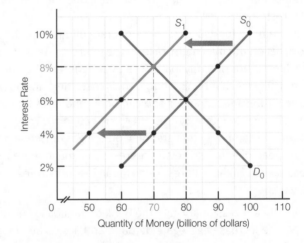

To raise interest rates and slow down the economy, the Bank of Canada sells bonds to the private sector. People effectively pay with cash, decreasing bank reserves. Through the money multiplier in reverse, banks reduce loans and demand deposits, decreasing the money supply (to the last column in the table). The supply of money shifts from S_0 to S_1, and the equilibrium interest rate rises to 8 percent.

The Bond Market Story of Open Market Operations   From the bond market perspective, the Bank of Canada changes the money supply using open market operations to influence bond prices and therefore interest rates.

When the Bank of Canada buys bonds, demand for bonds increases, raising bond prices and lowering interest rates. That is the Figure 4 story. When the Bank of Canada sells bonds, the supply of bonds increases, lowering bond prices and raising interest rates. That is the Figure 5 story.

Interest Rates Move Together   The Bank of Canada conducts open market operations, buying or selling bonds, to change the overnight rate. The overnight rate only affects banks. But the prime rate, the interest rate that banks charge to their best, lowest-risk corporate borrowers, equals the overnight rate plus roughly 2 percent. In July 2017, when the overnight loans rate was 0.75 percent, the prime lending rate was 2.95 percent. Other short-run interest rates for consumer loans, variable rate mortgages, savings accounts, and short-term bonds also change with changes to the overnight rate.

 # Practice...

11. If interest rates fall, the market price of bonds

    a. falls. If you sell the bond you take an unexpected loss.

    b. falls. If you sell the bond you make an unexpected profit.

    c. rises. If you sell the bond you take an unexpected loss.

    d. rises. If you sell the bond you make an unexpected profit.

12. Excess demand for money

    a. exists when interest rates are above the equilibrium rate.

    b. causes people to sell bonds.

    c. causes people to buy bonds.

    d. causes interest rates to fall.

13. The Bank of Canada's inflation control target is the

    a. CPI.

    b. core CPI.

    c. CPI, with core CPI as an operational guide.

    d. core CPI, with CPI as an operational guide.

14. Vanessa has a bad credit rating. When she goes to the bank for a loan, the interest rate the bank will give her is

    a. the target rate.

    b. the prime rate.

    c. between the target rate and the prime rate.

    d. above the prime rate.

15. When the Bank of Canada buys bonds, the

    a. increased demand for bonds raises bond prices and lowers interest rates.

    b. increased demand for bonds raises bond prices and raises interest rates.

    c. increased supply of bonds lowers bond prices and raises interest rates.

    d. decreased supply of bonds lowers bond prices and interest rates.

Apply...

7. Assume that the interest rate in the money market is above the equilibrium, market-clearing rate.

   a. Explain how this is either a situation of excess supply or excess demand.

   _____

   _____

   _____

   _____

   b. Tell the adjustment story of how the market moves to the equilibrium, market-clearing, rate of interest.

   _____

   _____

   _____

   _____

8. The Bank of Canada buys bonds on the open market.

   a. Explain how that changes short-run interest rates *from a money market perspective*.

   _____

   _____

   _____

   _____

   b. Explain how that changes short-run interest rates *from a bond market perspective*.

   _____

   _____

   _____

   _____

9. How might the overnight rate affect your decision to make a big purchase on credit now or to wait?

   _____

   _____

   _____

   _____

   _____

   _____

Aggregate Demand Monetary Transmission Mechanisms

LO4 Explain how money affects real GDP, unemployment, and inflation through the domestic and international monetary transmission mechanisms.

The effects of monetary policy work through aggregate demand to speed up or slow down the economy. Aggregate demand — planned $C + I + G + X - IM$ — is the sum of planned consumer spending (C), business investment spending (I), government spending on products and services (G), and net exports ($X - IM$). Let's return to the expanded circular flow diagram in Figure 6 to see the two main paths transmitting the effects of interest rates to aggregate demand.

Figure 6   How Interest Rates Affect Aggregate Demand

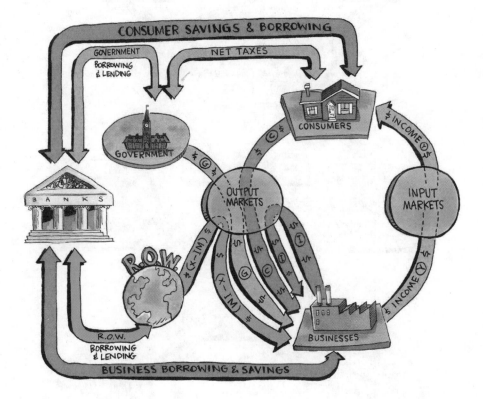

The domestic path is highlighted in red. It starts with the banking system, where the Bank of Canada sets short-run interest rates. Interest rates affect consumer borrowing and business borrowing, and then consumer spending (C) and business investment spending (I).

The international path is highlighted in blue. It also starts with the banking system, where the Bank of Canada sets short-run interest rates. Interest rates affect the value of the Canadian dollar, which is not shown on this diagram. Changes in the exchange rate affect the prices that the rest of the world pays for Canadian exports (X) and the prices that Canadians pay for imports (IM).

The domestic path affects aggregate demand through interest rates; the international path through exchange rates.

Domestic Monetary Transmission Mechanism

Figure 7 shows the details of the **domestic monetary transmission mechanism** — how money effects on interest rates are transmitted through aggregate demand to real GDP, unemployment, and inflation.

Figure 7   Bank of Canada and Domestic Monetary Transmission Mechanism

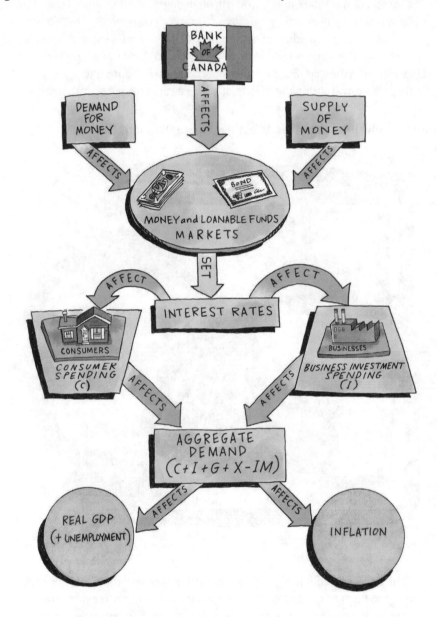

The Bank of Canada uses open market operations to intervene in the money and loanable funds markets to steer short-run interest rates to match its target rate. Interest rates significantly affect the cost of interest-sensitive purchases that require loans. Consumer spending (*C*) on houses, cars, and major appliances, and business investment spending (*I*) on factories and equipment, are heavily financed by borrowing and are very interest sensitive.

Lower Canadian Interest Rates   Lower interest rates decrease the cost of borrowing, increasing *C* and *I*, and increasing aggregate demand. Lower interest rates are a positive demand shock and increase real GDP, decrease unemployment, and increase inflation.

Higher Canadian Interest Rates   Higher interest rates increase the cost of borrowing, decreasing *C* and *I*, and decreasing aggregate demand. Higher interest rates are a negative demand shock and decrease real GDP, increase unemployment, and decrease inflation.

International Monetary Transmission Mechanism

The foreign exchange market is *not* part of Figures 6 or 7. Figure 8 includes the foreign exchange market, which determines the value of the Canadian dollar as part of the **international monetary transmission mechanism** — how money effects on exchange rates are transmitted through aggregate demand to real GDP, unemployment, and inflation.

Figure 8   Bank of Canada and International Monetary Transmission Mechanism

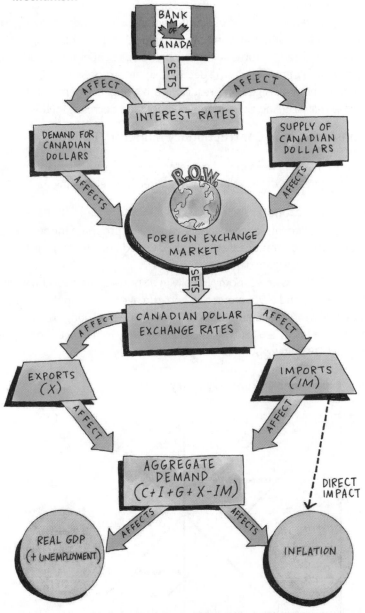

When the Bank of Canada uses open market operations to change short-run interest rates, the Canadian interest rate differential with the rest of the world changes.

Lower Canadian Interest Rates   A fall in Canadian interest rates relative to interest rates in R.O.W. makes Canadian assets less attractive to investors around the world, who buy fewer Canadian assets. This causes the Canadian dollar to depreciate.

A lower Canadian dollar makes Canadian exports cheaper for customers in the rest of the world, who buy more exports (X). A lower Canadian dollar makes imports (IM) from the rest of the world more expensive for Canadians, who buy fewer imports. The increase in net exports ($X - IM$) increases aggregate demand. Lower interest rates are a positive demand shock and increase real GDP, decrease unemployment, and increase inflation.

Higher Canadian Interest Rates   A rise in Canadian interest rates relative to interest rates in R.O.W. makes Canadian assets more attractive to investors around the world, who buy more Canadian assets. This causes the Canadian dollar to appreciate.

A higher Canadian dollar makes Canadian exports more expensive for customers in the rest of the world, who buy fewer exports (X). A higher Canadian dollar makes imports from the rest of the world cheaper for Canadians, who buy more imports (IM). The decrease in net exports ($X - IM$) decreases aggregate demand. Higher interest rates are a negative demand shock and decrease real GDP, increase unemployment, and decrease inflation.

Expansionary and Contractionary Monetary Policy

The domestic and international monetary transmission mechanisms both work on aggregate demand in the same direction, reinforcing each other.

Expansionary Monetary Policy in a Recessionary Gap   If the economy is predicted to go into a recessionary gap, the appropriate monetary policy is open market operations by the Bank of Canada to lower interest rates and increase aggregate demand.

Figure 9 shows an economy initially in a short-run equilibrium where aggregate demand (AD_0) intersects short-run aggregate supply (SAS_0) at a real GDP of $1400 billion. Potential GDP, shown by the long-run aggregate supply curve (LAS_0), is $1500 billion. The economy is in a recessionary gap, with real GDP below potential GDP.

Figure 9   Expansionary Monetary Policy

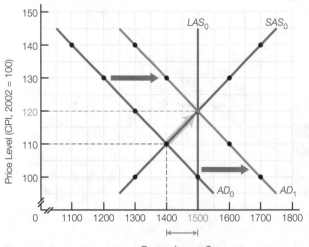

Recessionary Gap

Real GDP (billions of 2002 dollars)

When the Bank of Canada lowers interest rates, this causes a positive demand shock. Aggregate demand shifts rightward to AD_1. The new equilibrium is at the intersection of AD_1, SAS_0, and LAS_0. As real GDP increases to potential GDP of $1500 billion, unemployment decreases. Average prices rise from 110 to 120, increasing the inflation rate.

This policy of lowering interest rates is also called **expansionary monetary policy** (or easy money policy). Lower interest rates accelerate the economy, leading to a business cycle **expansion** — a period during which real GDP increases. *Easy money* refers to the increase in the money supply. The policy goal is to steer the economy back to potential GDP, full employment, and stable prices.

Contractionary Monetary Policy in an inflationary Gap   If the economy is predicted to go into an inflationary gap — with inflation above the target inflation rate of 2% — the appropriate monetary policy is open market operations by the Bank of Canada to raise interest rates and decrease aggregate demand.

Figure 10 shows an economy initially in a short-run equilibrium where aggregate demand (AD_0) intersects short-run aggregate supply (SAS_0) at a real GDP of $1600 billion. Potential GDP, shown by the long-run aggregate supply curve (LAS_0), is $1500 billion. The economy is in an inflationary gap, with real GDP above potential GDP.

Figure 10   Contractionary Monetary Policy

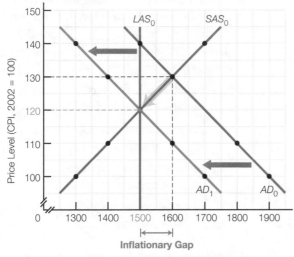

Real GDP (billions of 2002 dollars)

When the Bank of Canada raises interest rates, this causes a negative demand shock. Aggregate demand shifts leftward to AD_1. The new equilibrium is at the intersection of AD_1, SAS_0, and LAS_0. As real GDP decreases back to potential GDP of $1500 billion, unemployment, which had been below the natural rate, returns to the natural rate. Average prices fall from 130 to 120, decreasing the inflation rate.

This policy of raising interest rates is also called **contractionary monetary policy** (or tight money policy). Higher interest rates slow down the economy, leading to a business cycle **contraction** — a period during which real GDP decreases. *Tight money* refers to the decrease in the money supply. The policy goal is to steer the economy back to potential GDP, full employment, and stable prices.

Figure 11 is a good study device summarizing the combined effects of the domestic and international monetary transmission mechanisms in using monetary policy in recessionary or inflationary gaps.

Figure 11 Transmission Effects of Monetary Policy

	Monetary Policy	
	Lower Interest Rates	Raise Interest Rates
Output Gap	Recessionary Gap	Inflationary Gap
Impact on Economy		
Business Investment (*I*) and Consumption (*C*)	Increase	Decrease
Exchange Rate	Depreciates	Appreciates
Net Exports (*X − IM*)	Increase	Decrease
Aggregate Demand	Positive Demand Shock	Negative Demand Shock
Unemployment	Decreases	Increases
Inflation	Increases	Decreases

Practice...

16. Higher interest rates

    a. increase inflation.

    b. make business investment spending more expensive.

    c. are a positive aggregate demand shock.

    d. increase bond prices.

17. Lower interest rates are a

    a. positive aggregate supply shock.

    b. positive aggregate demand shock.

    c. negative aggregate supply shock.

    d. negative aggregate demand shock.

18. Which statement describes the effect of expansionary monetary policy?

    a. Selling bonds decreases the money supply, raising interest rates, decreasing aggregate demand.

    b. Selling bonds decreases the money supply, lowering interest rates, increasing aggregate demand.

    c. Buying bonds raises the price of bonds, lowering interest rates, increasing aggregate demand.

    d. Buying bonds raises the price of bonds, lowering interest rates, decreasing aggregate demand.

19. When the Bank of Canada raises interest rates, the international monetary transmission mechanism creates a _____ and the domestic monetary transmission mechanism creates a _____ .

    a. negative supply shock; negative supply shock

    b. positive demand shock; positive demand shock

    c. negative demand shock; positive demand shock

    d. negative demand shock; negative demand shock

20. Which statement describes contractionary monetary policy?

    a. The Bank of Canada's recent raising of the overnight rate is leading to less lending and less consumer spending.

    b. The Bank of Canada's recent lowering of interest rates is behind the depreciation of the Canadian dollar.

    c. The Bank of Canada's recent moves to decrease the value of the Canadian dollar are leading to more spending in the economy.

    d. The Bank of Canada's recent sales of government bonds are stimulating the housing market.

Apply...

10. When the Bank of Canada raises interest rates and borrowing becomes more expensive, use Figure 7 on page 254 to explain the domestic monetary transmission mechanism from interest rates to real GDP.

_____

_____

_____

_____

_____

11. The economy is in a recessionary gap.

a. Describe the appropriate monetary policy and the steps the Banks of Canada takes.

_____

_____

_____

b. Draw an *AS/AD* diagram, starting in a recessionary gap. Show the effect of the appropriate monetary policy on the diagram. What happens to real GDP, unemployment, and inflation?

_____

_____

_____

_____

_____

_____

c. As a result of the monetary policy, do unemployment and inflation move in the same direction or opposite directions?

_____

_____

12. Who benefits when the Bank of Canada lowers interest rates? Who benefits when interest rates rise? Explain how each policy could directly affect your life and your consumer decisions.

_____

_____

_____

_____

_____

_____

Transmission Breakdowns, Quantitative Easing, and the Quantity Theory of Money

 Explain what blocks monetary transmission mechanisms, show how quantitative easing can overcome a balance sheet recession, and use the quantity theory of money to analyze the inflation risks of monetary policy.

Recessions are usually triggered by a decrease in business investment spending, falling net exports, or rising interest rates. This was not true of the Global Financial Crisis. The recession of 2008–2009 was a **balance sheet recession** — a contraction caused by the collapse of asset prices. A balance sheet — for businesses, banks, or individuals — shows assets on one side (what you own or earn) and debts or liabilities on the other side (what you owe or spend). When the value of the assets you own falls, you need to cut back on what you spend or owe to restore balance. This is a problem for monetary policy.

Central banks around the world, including the U.S. Federal Reserve and the Bank of Canada, responded to the Global Financial Crisis as you would expect from reading this chapter. With a recessionary gap opening, they used open market operations to buy bonds and lower the target interest rate, hoping generally lower interest rates would stimulate borrowing, spending, and aggregate demand.

From a target overnight rate of 4 percent at the start of 2008, the Bank of Canada began aggressively cutting interest rates down almost to zero — 0.25 percent. The corresponding prime rate — the lowest nominal rate charged to businesses or consumers — was 2.25 percent. The **real interest rate** adjusts the nominal interest rate to remove the effects of inflation.

Real Interest Rate = Nominal Interest Rate − Inflation Rate

With a nominal prime interest rate of 2.25 percent and an inflation rate of about 2 percent, the real interest rate was 0.25 percent, close to zero! Despite almost free money, consumer and business borrowing and spending did *not* increase as the Bank of Canada had hoped. The Bank of Canada stepped hard on the gas, but power was not transmitted to the wheels of aggregate demand. What accounts for this transmission breakdown?

Transmission Breakdowns

The transmission breakdowns between lower interest rates, but no additional spending, happened because many macroeconomic players used money as a store of value. During the Global Financial Crisis:

- consumers — were saving more, paying off debts, and spending less.

- businesses — had pessimistic expectations about profits and decreased investment spending, even with lower interest rates.

- banks — were trying to build up the asset side of balance sheets, holding on to cash reserves and not making new loans, demand deposits, or increasing the money supply.

Government was the only macroeconomic player continuing to spend and support aggregate demand. Most economists credit government spending with preventing the crisis from becoming a depression.

Quantitative Easing

To counteract monetary transmission breakdowns, central banks used **quantitative easing** — flooding the financial system with money by buying high-risk bonds, mortgages, and assets from banks. These liabilities on chartered bank balance sheets were replaced with cash assets, enabling banks to make new loans, new demand deposits, and increase the quantity of money.

Quantitative easing is similar to open market operations where the central bank buys bonds and pays with cash, which increases bank reserves. The difference is that the central bank is not buying government bonds, but riskier, private commercial assets directly from banks. It produces the same result as open market bond purchases, but the central bank assumes more risk.

The major worry about flooding the financial system with money is inflation.

Quantity Theory of Money

The quantity theory of money is the key to understanding the inflation risks from quantitative easing or any expansionary monetary policy. The **quantity theory of money** states that an increase in the quantity of money causes an equal percentage increase in the inflation rate.

The quantity theory begins with the **equation of exchange**:

$$M \times V = P \times Q$$

M is the money supply. V is the **velocity of money**, the number of times a unit of money changes hands during a year. P is the price level, measured by the consumer price index. Q is real GDP — the aggregate quantity of real output. $P \times Q$ is nominal GDP.

The equation of exchange is always true. On the right side, nominal GDP is the value, in current prices, of all final products and services produced in a year. Since all of those products and services were sold, on the left side of the equation there must have been enough money, multiplied by the velocity of money, to allow those sales to happen.

The equation of exchange turns into the quantity theory of money by making two extreme assumptions — velocity (V) is fixed (does not change), and real GDP (Q) is fixed (does not change) at potential GDP. The quantity theory assumes the economy is *always in long-run macroeconomic equilibrium, at potential GDP*.

With no change possible in V or Q, any change in the quantity of money (M) on the left side of the equation produces an equal percentage change in the price level (P) on the right side. If the money supply goes up by 10 percent, the price level — inflation — goes up by 10 percent. The quantity theory of money is behind the phrase "printing money causes inflation."

Why Quantitative Easing Did *Not* Cause Inflation   Increases in the money supply and quantitative easing following the Global Financial Crisis would have been inflationary *if* the economy had been at potential GDP instead of in a deep recession. But when real GDP is below potential GDP, the economy is only in short-run equilibrium, not the long-run equilibrium the quantity theory *assumes*. Increases in the money supply can lower interest rates and stimulate borrowing and spending. Some of the increase in the money supply on the left side of the equation increases real GDP (Q) on the right side, rather than increasing the price level (P). In the short run, monetary policy can help real GDP grow.

Practice...

21. The Global Financial Crisis was caused by
    a. a negative supply shock.
    b. falling net exports.
    c. falling asset prices.
    d. decreased business investment spending.

22. During a balance sheet recession, the transmission mechanisms of monetary policy are blocked by money's function as a
    a. medium of exchange.
    b. unit of account.
    c. store of exchange.
    d. store of value.

23. When the inflation rate is 3 percent and the nominal interest rate is 5 percent, the real interest rate is
    a. 0.6 percent.
    b. 2 percent.
    c. 7 percent.
    d. 8 percent.

24. Which factors are fixed in the quantity theory of money?
    a. money and velocity
    b. velocity and real GDP
    c. velocity and the price level
    d. price level and real GDP

25. If real GDP is less than potential GDP, an increase in the quantity of money leads to a(n)
    a. increase in both real GDP and the price level.
    b. increase in real GDP and a decrease in the price level.
    c. increase in real GDP and no change in the price level.
    d. decrease in both real GDP and the price level.

 Apply...

13. *Time Magazine* named Ben Bernanke as the Person of the Year for 2009. Bernanke's leadership as Chairman of the U.S. Federal Reserve Bank is widely credited with saving the world from depression.
    a. Bernanke used a powerful tool from his monetary policy toolbox — quantitative easing. What is quantitative easing?

    _____

    _____

    _____

    _____

    _____

    _____

 **Apply...**

b. How is quantitative easing similar to, and different from, open market operations?

_____

_____

_____

_____

_____

14. Watch the video http://tinyurl.com/FlexText-Koo

Richard Koo (Chief Economist, Nomura Research Institute) explains why the Global Financial Crisis was no ordinary recession caused by decreased investment or high interest rates. He explains a balance sheet recession using Japan's experience of the 1990s following a real estate bubble collapse. Even with zero interest rates, companies were paying down debt instead of investing. Business borrowers did not increase investment spending to offset saving. This is a classic concern for Say's Law, when consumers (and businesses) save instead of spend. Koo also draws parallels with the Great Depression.

Your instructor may assign questions about the video.

15. In a balance sheet recession:

a. Explain how consumers, businesses, and banks can block the monetary transmission mechanisms.

_____

_____

_____

_____

_____

_____

_____

b. Explain how the individual smart choices made by consumers, businesses, and banks do *not* necessarily add up to smart choices for the economy as a whole.
    [*HINT*: Use the fallacy of composition in your answer.]

_____

_____

_____

_____

_____

_____

_____

KNOW...

Summary of Learning Objectives

1. People demand **money** for its **liquidity** as a medium of exchange (**transactions demand for money**), as a unit of account, and as a store of value (**asset demand for money**), and are often willing to give up interest on **bonds** in order to hold their wealth as money.

2. Money can take the form of commodity money, convertible paper money, fiat money (**currency**) and **demand deposits**. In a **fractional-reserve banking** system, the supply of money — currency plus demand deposits — is created both by the Bank of Canada and by chartered banks making loans. The **money multiplier** shows the multiple by which the banking system can create new loans and demand deposits for each new dollar deposited into a bank.

3. Bond prices and **interest rates** are inversely related and determined together in the money and loanable funds markets. The Bank of Canada uses **monetary policy** to change the money supply and interest rates, aiming for an **inflation control target** that achieves steady growth, full employment, and **price stability**. **Open market operations** change interest rates. Buying bonds increases the money supply and raises bond prices, lowering interest rates. Selling bonds decreases the money supply and lowers bond prices, raising interest rates.

3. Through the **domestic monetary transmission mechanism**, interest rates affect consumption and business investment spending. Through the **international monetary transmission mechanism**, interest rates affect exchange rates and net exports. The combined effect on aggregate demand changes real GDP, unemployment, and inflation. **Expansionary monetary policy** corrects a recessionary gap, while **contractionary monetary policy** corrects an inflationary gap.

4. The Global Financial Crisis was a **balance sheet recession** — individuals and businesses focus on paying down debt and do not want to borrow or spend. Even when monetary policy lowers interest rates, the economy remains in recession. According to the **quantity theory of money**, the **quantitative easing policies** central banks used to get out of recession might have triggered inflation, but did not.

Key Terms

asset demand for money: demand to hold money for use as a store of value

balance sheet recession: contraction caused by the collapse of asset prices

bond: financial asset for which the borrower promises to repay the original value at a specific future date and to make fixed regular interest payments

central bank: government institution responsible for supervising chartered banks and other financial institutions, and for regulating the supply of money

contraction: period during which real GDP decreases

contractionary monetary policy (or tight money policy): open market operations to raise interest rates and decrease aggregate demand

currency: government-issued bills and coins

demand deposits: balances in bank accounts that depositors can withdraw on demand by using a debit card or cheque

domestic monetary transmission mechanism: how money effects on interest rates are transmitted through aggregate demand to real GDP, unemployment, and inflation

equation of exchange: $M \times V = P \times Q$, where M is the money supply, V is the velocity of money, P is the price level, and Q is real GDP

expansion: period during which real GDP increases

expansionary monetary policy (or easy money policy): open market operations to lower interest rates and increase aggregate demand

fractional-reserve banking: banks hold only a fraction of deposits as reserves

inflation-control target: range of inflation rates set by a central bank as a monetary policy objective

interest rate: price of holding money; what you give up by not holding bonds (loanable funds)

interest rate differential: difference in interest rates between countries

international monetary transmission mechanism: how money effects on exchange rates are transmitted through aggregate demand to real GDP, unemployment, and inflation

lender of last resort: central bank's role of making loans to banks to preserve the stability of the financial system

liquidity: ease with which assets can be converted into the economy's medium of exchange

monetary policy: adjusting the supply of money and interest rates to achieve steady growth, full employment, and price stability

money: anything accepted as a means of paying for products and services

money multiplier: formula showing the multiple by which the banking system can create new loans and demand deposits for each new dollar deposited into a bank; equals 1 ÷ desired reserve ratio

open market operations: buying or selling government bonds on bond market by the Bank of Canada

overnight rate: the interest rate banks charge each other for one-day loans — the main monetary policy tool

price stability: inflation rate is low enough that it does not significantly affect people's economic decisions

prime rate: the interest rate on loans to lowest-risk corporate borrowers

quantitative easing: central bank tool of flooding the financial system with money by buying high-risk bonds, mortgages, and assets from banks; these liabilities on bank balance sheets are replaced with cash assets, enabling banks to make new loans

quantity theory of money: increase in the quantity of money causes an equal percentage increase in the inflation rate

real interest rate: nominal interest rate adjusted for effects of inflation

transactions demand for money: demand to hold money for use as a medium of exchange

velocity of money: number of times a unit of money changes hands during a year

Answers to Practice

1. **a** Money provides liquidity, and you give up interest earned on bonds.

2. **d** The problem is finding a seller who has what you want and who wants what you are selling.

3. **b** Fall in interest rates causes movement down along an unchanged money demand curve.

4. **c** Definition. The interest rate is the opportunity cost of holding money. The opportunity cost of holding bonds is forgone liquidity.

5. **c** **b** does not change money demand; **a** and **d** shift money demand curve leftward.

6. **c** Debit cards are a means of transferring demand deposits, which are money.

7. **d** Money multiplier = $1 \div 0.2 = 5$.

8. **a** Demand deposits are the medium of exchange.

9. **d** Other answers true but not the *only* source.

10. **d** Currency in circulation decreases. With new loans, banks also create demand deposits, so M1+ increases.

11. **d** Interest rates and the market price of bonds move in opposite directions; rises in market price create unexpected profit (buy low, sell high).

12. **b** Excess demand causes people to sell bonds to get money, lowering bond prices and raising interest rates.

13. **c** CPI between 1 percent and 3 percent, but paying attention to underlying trends of core inflation rates.

14. **d** The interest rate for high-risk borrowers is above the prime rate.

15. **a** This is an open market operation and an example of expansionary monetary policy.

16. **b** Higher cost of borrowing to finance new factories and equipment.

17. **b** Cause rightward shift of aggregate demand curve.

18. **c** When the Bank of Canada buys bonds, the increased money supply lowers interest rates, increasing aggregate demand.

19. **d** Both transmission mechanisms reinforce each other. Aggregate demand decreases and *AD* shifts leftward.

20. **a** Contractionary monetary policy raises interest rates to reduce spending and slow down the economy.

21. **c** A balance sheet recession is different from most recessions that are caused by decreased business investment, falling net exports, or higher interest rates.

22. **d** Money gives people a way to not spend, a time machine for moving purchasing power from the present to the future.

23. **b** Real interest rate = nominal interest rate – inflation rate.

24. **b** Velocity does not change and real GDP = potential GDP.

25. **a** The price level and the level of real GDP respond to an increase in the money supply.

11 Fiscal Policy, Multipliers, Deficits, and Debt

LEARNING OBJECTIVES

LO1 Use the concepts of injections and leakages to explain the multiplied impact of aggregate demand fiscal policies.

LO2 Identify three aggregate supply fiscal policies for growth, and explain the controversy over supply-sider incentive effects.

LO3 Differentiate cyclical from structural deficits and surpluses, and explain the connections between automatic stabilizers and business cycles.

LO4 Explain the difference between deficits and debts, and identify five arguments about the national debt.

LO5 Distinguish between normative and positive, and between economic and political, arguments about fiscal policy.

LEARN...

No one likes being in debt. When governments spend more than they collect in taxes, their budgets are not balanced. They run deficits. Debt starts piling up. Many citizens disapprove, saying, "Get your financial house in order! Don't spend more than you've got." But is going into debt always a bad choice?

Most consumers and businesses regularly make smart choices that involve debt. People with car payments or a mortgage are in debt. Businesses regularly issue bonds to borrow money for building new factories. If debt can be smart for individuals and businesses, can it be smart for governments?

When spending collapsed during the Global Financial Crisis, the only macroeconomic player who kept spending steadily was government. Government financed this spending by going into debt. Was this financially irresponsible, or did government spending and debt save the economy from depression?

In this chapter, you will learn about government spending, its multiplied impact on the economy, and the differences between deficits and debts. The Canadian government had a budget deficit of about $17.8 billion in 2017. It had to borrow that much money to pay for its spending. As well, the government already had a debt of over $632 billion. Is that a cause for alarm, or for celebration of smart choices? You will learn how to analyze the heated mix of economics and politics fuelling most debates about government spending and debt from politicians seeking your votes.

Should the government leave the economy alone, or step in to try to correct market failures? Hands-off or hands-on? What role should government play in a market economy?

Aggregate Demand Policies for Stabilizing Business Cycles

L01 Use the concepts of injections and leakages to explain the multiplied impact of aggregate demand fiscal policies.

Fiscal policy uses government purchases, taxes, and transfers to achieve steady growth, full employment, and stable prices. Fiscal policy works through aggregate demand, speeding up or slowing down an economy facing recessionary or inflationary gaps.

Aggregate demand is the sum of planned consumer spending (C), business investment spending (I), government spending on products and services (G), and net exports ($X - IM$).

$$\text{Aggregate Demand} = C + I + G + X - IM$$

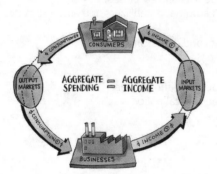

In the simple GDP circular flow diagram at the left, all spending is done by consumers. Let's return to the expanded circular flow diagram in Figure 1 to see additional sources of spending. **Injections** are spending in the circular flow that does not start with consumers — government spending (G), business investment spending (I), and exports (X).

Figure 1   Fiscal Policy Paths Affecting Aggregate Demand

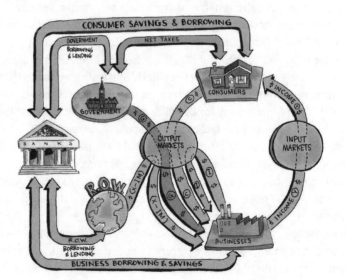

The government spending path of fiscal policy is red. The net taxes path is blue. **Net taxes** combine taxes paid by consumers to government, minus transfer payments (Employment Insurance, Canada Pension) consumers receive from government. Because taxes are greater than transfers, the flow of net taxes is from consumers to government.

Net taxes are an example of what economists call leakages from the circular flow. A **leakage** is spending that leaks out of (leaves) the circular flow through taxes, savings, and imports.

The Multiplier Effect

Injections and leakages, money flowing into and out of the circular flow, are key to understanding the multiplied impact of fiscal policy on aggregate demand and GDP. Let's start with government spending — an injection — and look at what happens in Figure 1.

Suppose the government spends $100 million to buy a new bridge: G goes up by $100 million. That means aggregate demand ($C + I + G + X - IM$) goes up by the $100 million injection in this first round of spending. Here is a surprise — the full effect on aggregate demand is *more than* $100 million. To see how, let's follow the circle.

Initially, bridge-building businesses (at the bottom right) gets $100 million. Following the circle up to the right, that means incomes of everyone working for the businesses — workers, owners, suppliers — go up by $100 million. What do people do with that additional income? The government takes some of the income as taxes — a leakage out of the circular flow (the net taxes from consumers to government at the top). People save some — another leakage out of the circular flow (consumer saving and borrowing flow at the very top). Some of that new spending is on imports — the final leakage (the net export flow between businesses and R.O.W.). But even after all of those leakages, there will be some new spending in output markets on Canadian products and services.

Suppose leakages are 50 percent of additional income. Out of every dollar Canadians receive in income, 50 cents goes to leakages (taxes, saving, imports) and 50 cents is spent on Canadian products and services. That means businesses in Canada will receive $50 million in a second round of spending. The story, and the flow around the circle, repeats. There will again be leakages from this $50 million, but 50 percent of the income will again turn into new spending on Canadian products and services. In the third round of spending, businesses in Canada will receive $25 million. The circles of spending and income continue getting smaller and smaller, and eventually fade away.

Figure 2 shows the cumulative effect of all of the rounds of spending. In this example, the $100 million injection of government spending increases aggregate demand by $200 million after all of the rounds of spending are finished.

Figure 2   The Multiplier Effect

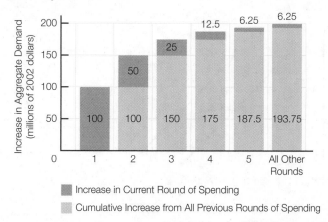

- ■ Increase in Current Round of Spending
- ▨ Cumulative Increase from All Previous Rounds of Spending

Economists call this the **multiplier effect** — a spending injection has a multiplied effect on aggregate demand. The multiplier effect works for any injection — government spending, business investment spending, or R.O.W. spending on Canadian exports. The multiplier effect also works in reverse. A decrease in injections has a multiplied impact decreasing aggregate demand.

Leakages and the Multiplier Effect   The size of the multiplier effect depends on leakages out of the circular flow. There is a simple formula for calculating the size of the multiplier effect.

$$\text{Size of Multiplier Effect} = \frac{1}{\text{\% of leakages from additional income}}$$

Where leakages (taxes, saving, imports) are 50 percent (0.50) of additional income, the multiplier is 2. More leakages mean a smaller multiplier; fewer leakages mean a larger multiplier.

Tax and Transfer Multipliers   There is a similar multiplier effect from changes in taxes or government transfers. A tax cut or an increase in transfer payments leaves consumers with more money to spend, which has a multiplied effect, increasing aggregate demand. An increase in taxes or decrease in transfers has a multiplied effect, decreasing aggregate demand.

The multiplier effect for tax and transfer changes is not as big as it is for government spending. When consumers get a $100 million tax cut, they don't spend all $100 million on Canadian products and services. They save some of the $100 million and spend some on imports. Because the initial round of new consumer spending is less than $100 million, the multiplier effect is less than for a government injection of $100 million.

Multipliers and Aggregate Demand   An increase in government spending or a decrease in taxes is a positive aggregate demand shock, shifting the aggregate demand curve rightward. The size of the rightward shift depends on the size of the multiplier effect. Figure 3 shows a $100 million increase in government spending. The initial injection of spending shifts the aggregate demand curve rightward by $100 million, to the dashed aggregate demand curve. The cumulative multiplier effects then increases spending and aggregate demand by another $100 million, continuing the rightward shift of the aggregate demand curve to AD_1. The net effect shifts the aggregate demand curve rightward by $200 million.

Figure 3   Multiplied Effect of Government Spending on Aggregate Demand

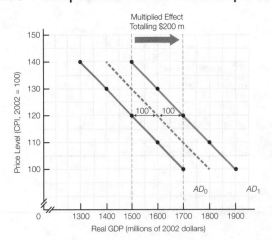

A decrease in government spending or an increase in taxes is a negative aggregate demand shock, shifting the aggregate demand curve leftward by the multiplied effect of the initial decrease.

Fiscal Policy and Aggregate Demand

Multiplier effects improve the effectiveness of fiscal policy as a tool for changing aggregate demand to counter business cycles. There are two types of fiscal policy.

Expansionary fiscal policy increases aggregate demand by increasing government spending, decreasing taxes, or increasing transfers. The multiplied impact of expansionary fiscal policy shifts the aggregate demand curve rightward — a positive aggregate demand shock.

Contractionary fiscal policy decreases aggregate demand by decreasing government spending, increasing taxes, or decreasing transfers. The multiplied impact of contractionary fiscal policy shifts the aggregate demand curve leftward — a negative aggregate demand shock.

Recessionary Gaps and Expansionary Fiscal Policy   Figure 4 shows an economy initially in a short-run equilibrium where aggregate demand (AD_0) intersects short-run aggregate supply (SAS_0) at a real GDP of \$1400 billion. Potential GDP, shown by the long-run aggregate supply curve (LAS_0), is \$1500 billion. The economy is in a recessionary gap, with real GDP below potential GDP, and the unemployment rate is above the natural rate. Inflation is stable or falling — not a concern.

Figure 4   Expansionary Fiscal Policy to Fill a Recessionary Gap

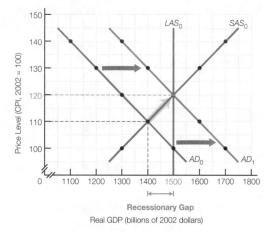

Expansionary fiscal policy is a positive aggregate demand shock, shifting the aggregate demand curve rightward to AD_1, increasing real GDP, decreasing unemployment, and increasing inflation. The new long-run equilibrium is at the intersection of AD_1, SAS_0, and LAS_0.

Inflationary Gaps and Contractionary Fiscal Policy   Figure 5 on the next page shows an economy initially in a short-run equilibrium where aggregate demand (AD_0) intersects short-run aggregate supply (SAS_0) at a real GDP of \$1600 billion. Potential GDP, shown by the long-run aggregate supply curve (LAS_0), is \$1500 billion. The economy is in an inflationary gap, with real GDP above potential GDP, and the unemployment rate is below the natural rate. Unemployment is not a problem since there are shortages of workers and rising wages. Shortages in input and output markets are causing rising prices.

Contractionary fiscal policy is a negative aggregate demand shock, shifting the aggregate demand curve leftward to AD_1, decreasing real GDP, increasing unemployment, and decreasing inflation. The new long-run equilibrium is at the intersection of AD_1, SAS_0, and LAS_0.

Figure 5   Contractionary Fiscal Policy to Fill an Inflationary Gap

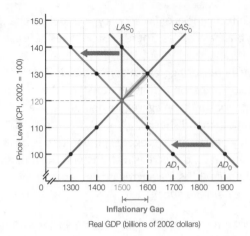

Real GDP (billions of 2002 dollars)

Multiplier Effects and Real GDP   Any change in injections has a multiplied effect on aggregate demand. The aggregate demand curve shifts rightward when injections increase and shifts leftward when injections decrease. The multiplier effects of an injection *on equilibrium real GDP* depends on how close the economy is to potential GDP (*LAS*). When the economy is in recession and far below potential GDP, more of the increase in aggregate demand increases real GDP. When the economy is at or above potential GDP, more of the increase in aggregate demand drives up prices instead of increasing real GDP.

A recent study found that the size of the mulitplier effect on real GDP for expansionary fiscal policy ranges from about 2.5 during recessions to close to zero when the economy is at full employment.

 Practice...

1. An example of fiscal policy is changing the

    a. exchange rate.

    b. interest rate.

    c. tax rate.

    d. money supply.

2. Which is an injection into the circular flow?

    a. consumer spending

    b. import spending

    c. savings

    d. exports

3. If leakages out of the circular flow are 25 percent of additional income, what is the size of the multiplier effect?

    a. 2.5

    b. 3

    c. 4

    d. 5

4. What government fiscal policy is a negative demand shock?

    a. increasing transfer payments

    b. increasing taxes

    c. increasing government spending

    d. increasing interest rates

5. The size of the multiplier for tax and transfer changes _____ the size of the multiplier for government spending.

    a. is smaller than

    b. is equal to

    c. is larger than

    d. cannot be compared to

 **Apply...**

1. The economy is in a recessionary gap, and the government wants to use aggregate demand fiscal policy to return the economy to potential GDP and full employment.

    a. List two different appropriate aggregate demand fiscal policies. Identify both the direction and the type of fiscal policy.

    _____

    _____

    _____

    _____

    _____

    _____

    b. The impact of fiscal policy on real GDP depends on the size of the multiplier. What three specific factors determine the size of the multiplier effect?

    The multiplier effect will be larger if

    _____   are   higher / lower

    _____   are   higher / lower

    _____   are   higher / lower

2. Consider the multiplier.

    a. What is the general formula for the size of the multiplier effect?

    _____

    _____

    _____

    to be continued

Apply...

continued

b. The diagram below shows an initial aggregate demand curve before fiscal policy.

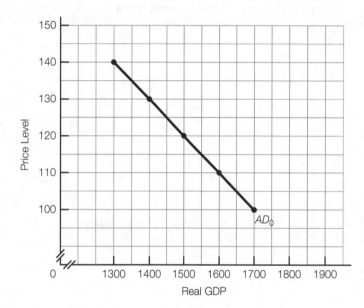

If the government spends 100 initially, precisely draw the new *AD* curve before the multiplier effect. Label it AD_1.

One point on AD_1 would have the coordinates of price level of 120 and real GDP of _____.

c. If the value of the multiplier is 3, precisely draw the new *AD* curve after the multiplier effect. Label it AD_2.

One point on AD_2 would have the coordinates of price level of 120 and real GDP of _____.

3. Politicians in your area want to spend millions of tax dollars to build a stadium to bring a professional sports team to your community. Do you support that decision? Explain your position.

_____

_____

_____

_____

_____

_____

_____

Aggregate Supply Fiscal Policies for Promoting Growth

L02 Identify three aggregate supply fiscal policies for growth, and explain the controversy over supply-sider incentive effects.

Fiscal policies for aggregate demand can counter the bust and boom of business cycles, keeping the economy moving steadily on the road toward potential GDP, full employment, and stable prices. The other key macroeconomic outcome — steady growth in living standards — calls for a different kind of fiscal policy. **Economic growth** expands the economy's capacity to produce products and services — an increase in potential GDP per person. Economic growth happens when increases in the quantity and quality of inputs — labour, capital, land, and entrepreneurship — increase (long-run and short-run) aggregate supply. Living standards rise when economic growth increases potential GDP per person.

Figure 6 shows the economic growth from a positive supply shock — an increase in the quantity or quality of inputs.

Figure 6   Positive Supply Shock and Economic Growth

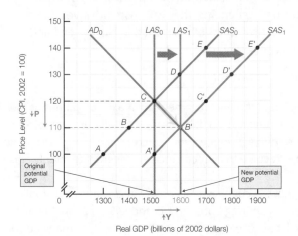

Starting at point *C*, increases in inputs increase potential GDP and shift rightward both the long-run aggregate supply curve (*LAS*$_1$) and short-run aggregate supply curve (*SAS*$_1$). The new equilibrium is at point *B'*. As long as the increase in potential GDP is greater than the increase in the population, living standards rise.

Policies for Economic Growth

Fiscal policies targeting aggregate supply aim for three outcomes — stimulate saving and capital investment, encourage research and development, and improve education and training.

Stimulate Saving and Capital Investment   Government uses tax incentives as a fiscal policy tool to stimulate saving and increase the quantity of capital available. This makes it easier for businesses to borrow to finance new factories or new machinery, and promotes economic growth.

Encourage Research and Development   Government uses targeted government spending and tax incentives as fiscal policy to encourage research and development. The resulting productivity-improving technological change increases the quality of inputs.

Improve Education and Training   **Human capital** — the quality of labour inputs — increases through education and training. Government-financed education and training that increase human capital promote economic growth.

To Save or To Spend?   All economists agree that fiscal policies to encourage saving and capital investment will eventually increase aggregate supply and potential GDP. But an increase in saving means a decrease in consumer spending. There is a trade-off between increased aggregate supply in the future — through business investment spending — and reduced aggregate demand in the present due to lower consumer spending. Every choice has an opportunity cost!

The "Markets Quickly Self-Adjust" camp of economists strongly supports fiscal policies to encourage saving and capital investment. They believe the long-run benefits of increased aggregate supply outweigh any short-run costs of reduced aggregate demand.

The "Markets Fail Often" camp is less enthusiastic about government fiscal policies to encourage saving and capital investment. They worry that when businesses see reduced consumer spending, they will postpone investment spending. They believe the short-run costs of decreased aggregate demand outweigh the long-run benefits of economic growth.

Supply-Siders and Voodoo Economics

Tax cuts have supply-side effects. If the government cuts taxes on labour as well as on capital investments, the quantities of labour and capital inputs supplied to markets could increase, and then aggregate supply increases. Through incentive effects, called **supply-side effects,** a tax cut can increase aggregate supply and potential GDP.

All economists believe that tax cuts have incentive effects causing a small increase in aggregate supply — shifting both the *LAS* and *SAS* curves rightward. Supply-side effects are small because most people already work as many hours as they can, and don't get much choice over working longer hours.

Supply-Siders   Economists and politicians who believe that there are powerful supply-side incentive effects to tax cuts are called *supply-siders*. There is no empirical evidence to support supply-siders' claims that tax cuts have large effects on aggregate supply and economic growth. Tax cuts certainly affect the economy, but most of the effect is through increased spending and aggregate demand.

Are you wondering why I am explaining an idea that almost all economists reject as an exaggeration? It is important to know about supply-side effects because many politicians are supply-siders. Politicians who favour a hands-off role for government often use supply-sider arguments to support tax cuts.

Their false argument goes like this: Tax cuts will increase, not decrease, government tax revenues. How is that possible? If tax cuts have powerful incentive effects, people will work more and incomes will go up dramatically. A lower tax rate means that the government gets a smaller portion from every dollar people earn, but people are earning so many more dollars from longer hours worked that the total amount of taxes collected increases.

Laffer Curve   This idea was proposed by an advisor to U.S. President Ronald Reagan named Arthur Laffer. He explained his idea using the graph in Figure 7 known as the *Laffer Curve*.

Figure 7   The Laffer Curve

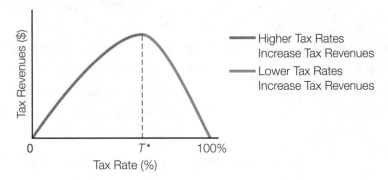

The horizontal axis measures the income tax rate, from zero to 100 percent. The vertical axis measures the total tax revenues collected for each tax rate. At a zero tax rate there will be zero tax revenues. And at a 100 percent tax rate, there will also be zero tax revenues because no one has any incentive to work if the government takes everything. In between these extremes, as the tax rate rises from zero, tax revenues increase (the upward-sloping green part of the curve). Eventually, at tax rate T^*, tax revenues are at a maximum. As rates rise beyond T^*, the disincentive effects of further tax increases discourage work. People work so much less that their reduced incomes, even when taxed at a higher rate, produce decreasing tax revenues (the downward-sloping red part of the curve).

Laffer claimed the United States tax rate was above T^* in the red range. If that were true, lower tax rates would increase tax revenues. But when Ronald Reagan — a pioneering hands-off supply-sider — cut taxes in the 1980s expecting increases in tax revenues, tax revenues decreased and the government ran huge budget deficits.

Almost every country in the world (France with a tax rate of 75 percent on high incomes might be an exception) has a tax rate in the green range below the rate T^*. That means a cut in tax rates decreases, not increases, tax revenues.

Too Good to Be True   Supply-sider arguments appeal to politicians who promise tax cuts — which voters like — while not reducing government services or going into debt. If supply-side effects were that powerful, tax cuts would have no opportunity cost! Any claim that a choice has no opportunity cost is too good to be true. No matter what politicians and voters want to believe, it would take magic to make the supply-sider argument true. That's why economists often refer to supply-sider arguments as "voodoo economics."

Practice...

6. If government reduces tuition fees for post-secondary students, this

   a. increases the quality of labour inputs.

   b. decreases the quality of labour inputs.

   c. increases the quantity of labour inputs.

   d. decreases the quantity of labour inputs.

7. Fiscal policies that encourage savings and capital investment can

   a. decrease both aggregate supply and aggregate demand.

   b. decrease aggregate supply and increase aggregate demand.

   c. increase aggregate supply and decrease aggregate demand.

   d. increase both aggregate supply and aggregate demand.

8. Fiscal policies for economic growth shift

   a. short-run aggregate supply rightward but long-run aggregate supply does not change.

   b. long-run aggregate supply rightward but short-run aggregate supply does not change.

   c. long-run aggregate supply rightward but short-run aggregate supply leftward.

   d. both short-run aggregate supply and long-run aggregate supply rightward.

9. According to the Laffer Curve, lowering the tax rate

   a. always increases total tax revenue.

   b. does not change total tax revenue.

   c. always decreases total tax revenue.

   d. increases or decreases total tax revenue, depending on the tax rate.

10. Which is *not* a source of economic growth?

   a. better incentives for workers and businesses

   b. increasing stock market prices

   c. increasing stock of capital equipment

   d. technological change

Apply...

4. In your own words, explain how fiscal policy can increase aggregate supply.

    _____

    _____

    _____

    _____

    _____

5. Explain how saving can help economic growth. Explain how saving can hurt economic growth.
    Which effect do you think is more important? Explain your answer.

    _____

    _____

    _____

    _____

    _____

    _____

    _____

6. A politician proposes a plan for reducing Canada's national debt. She promises to cut tax rates,
    stating that these cuts will create thousands of new jobs and result in higher government revenues.

    a. Do economists agree that tax rate cuts increase aggregate supply?

    _____

    _____

    _____

    b. Why do supply-siders believe tax rate cuts will increase government revenues?

    _____

    _____

    _____

    _____

    c. Why do many economists doubt that government revenues increase in response to tax rate cuts?

    _____

    _____

    _____

    _____

    _____

Government Budget Surpluses and Deficits

 Differentiate cyclical from structural deficits and surpluses, and explain the connections between automatic stabilizers and business cycles.

Every month you have income coming in, and spending going out. If your income and spending match, you have a *balanced budget*. If your spending is more than your income, you have a *deficit* — an amount by which your spending exceeds your income for the month. You have to finance your deficit by going into *debt* — borrowing from student loans, credit cards, or family. If you are lucky enough to have a month when your income is greater than your expenses, you have a *surplus* — an amount by which your income exceeds your spending for the month.

Government budgets are similar. Fiscal policy — changes in government spending, taxes, and transfers — affects governments' budgets.

Federal Government Budget

Government income is called revenue. It comes from many sources, including personal income taxes, corporate taxes, Employment Insurance premiums paid by workers and employers, GST/HST, and other non-tax areas. The income taxes you and I pay are the biggest source (49 percent) of government revenues.

Government spends on purchases of products and services, transfer payments to businesses and individuals, and interest payments on the national debt (like your interest payments on a credit card balance). We pay about 11 percent of our taxes on interest payments on the accumulated government debt. The largest expenditure is on direct program spending, which includes health care.

Balancing the Budget In comparing revenues and spending, the yearly balance of the government budget, like your monthly budget, has three scenarios:

- **balanced budget** — revenues equal spending.
- **budget deficit** — revenues less than spending.
- **budget surplus** — revenues greater than spending.

Figure 8 shows the year-end position of the Government of Canada's budget for selected years between 1992–1993 and 2016–2017. For each year, there are three numbers — revenues, spending, and the resulting deficit or surplus.

Figure 8   Government of Canada Budgets, Selected Years, 1992–2017

Year	1992-93	1997-98	2007-08	2009-10	2012-13	2016-17
Revenues	124.5	160.9	242.4	218.6	256.6	293.5
Spending	163.5	157.9	232.8	274.2	275.6	311.3
Deficit (−) or Surplus (+)	−39.0	+3.0	+9.6	−55.6	−18.9	−17.8

Source: Department of Finance, Federal Government Public Accounts. Table 1 Fiscal Transactions. http://www.budget.gc.ca/2017/docs/plan/anx-01-en. html#Toc477707537; Annual Financial Report 2016–2017, Table 1.

On the bottom line (pun intended), notice that the federal budget went from a surplus of $9.6 billion in 2007–2008 to a deficit of $55.6 billion in 2009–2010. The move from a budget surplus to a large deficit happened as the Canadian economy went into recession during the Global Financial Crisis.

As the economy has recovered from the Global Financial Crisis, the deficit has fallen. The connections between increasing deficits and economic recession, and decreasing deficits and economy recovery, are not accidental.

Automatic Stabilizers

Expansionary or contractionary fiscal policies require parliamentary decisions. There are other fiscal policy tools that work automatically with changes in the business cycle.

Automatic stabilizers are tax and transfer adjustments that counteract changes to real GDP without new government decisions. Automatic stabilizers work like a thermostat, keeping the economy close to potential GDP.

Suppose the economy starts at potential GDP and the government budget is balanced.

- A negative aggregate demand shock pushes the economy into a contraction. As automatic stabilizers work, tax revenues decrease and transfer payments (like Employment Insurance) increase. These stabilizers increase spending and aggregate demand, but cause an automatic budget deficit.

- A positive aggregate demand shock pushes the economy into an expansion. As automatic stabilizers work, tax revenues increase and transfer payments decrease. These stabilizers decrease spending and aggregate demand, but cause an automatic surplus.

Most automatic stabilizers did not exist during the Great Depression. Income taxes and transfer programs like Employment Insurance, welfare payments, Canada Pension Plan, and health care were introduced after the Great Depression. Because of automatic stabilizers, business cycles in Canada have since been less frequent, and the contractions have been less severe. Automatic stabilizers do their job, helping "steady" the key macroeconomic outcome of steady growth.

But every choice, including automatic stabilizers, has an opportunity cost. Increases in government budget deficits and accumulated debt since the Global Financial Crisis reflect that opportunity cost.

Deficits and surpluses created only as a result of automatic stabilizers counteracting the business cycle are called **cyclical deficits** and **cyclical surpluses**.

Balanced Budgets Can Be Bad   Most individuals try to balance their budgets, and believe that governments should do the same. What happens if governments follows this advice?

A negative aggregate demand shock pushes the economy into recession. Automatic stabilizers work and create a cyclical deficit. If the government tries to balance the budget, it has to increase revenues or decrease spending. Increasing revenues means raising taxes on consumers or businesses, decreasing consumer spending (*C*) or business investment spending (*I*). Decreasing spending means reducing government purchases of products and services (*G*) or reducing transfer payments, which decrease consumer spending (*C*). Government attempts to balance the budget during a recession decrease aggregate demand (decreasing *C*, *I*, and *G*). This additional negative demand shock *makes the recession even worse*.

Budget surpluses can also be a problem. A positive aggregate demand shock pushes the economy into an expansion. Automatic stabilizers work and create a cyclical surplus. To balance the budget, government has to increase spending or decrease taxes. The story on the previous page works in reverse. Government attempts to balance the budget during an expansion increase aggregate demand (increasing *C*, *I*, and *G*). This addional positive demand shock accelerates the expansion beyond potential GDP and *makes the risk of inflation even worse.*

Cyclical and Structural Deficits and Surpluses

When the government *always* balances the budget, the results are destabilizing — worsening both recessions and inflationary expansions. This is an example of the fallacy of composition — what is true for one individual (micro) is not necessarily true for the economy as a whole (macro). That does not mean economists favour unlimited government deficits or surpluses.

Most economists favour a policy for government to balance the budget over the phases of the business cycle. Cyclical surpluses during the expansion phase offset cyclical deficits during the contraction phase. If the positive amount of the surplus equals the negative amount of the deficit, then the budget is balanced over the business cycle.

This fiscal policy has the benefits of automatic stabilizers, while keeping government from spending more or less than it collects in taxes. The government can live within its means, like a financially responsible individual, and still help steer the economy.

Structural Deficits (and Surpluses) at Potential GDP   The deficits (and surpluses) that concern economists are not cyclical but structural. There is a **structural deficit** when governments spend more than their revenues *even while the economy is at potential GDP and growing steadily.* Structural deficits are not caused by business cycles. They are built into the structure of government taxes, transfers, and spending programs. There is a **structural surplus** when there is a budget surplus even while the economy is at potential GDP and growing steadily. There are problems with structural deficits and structural surpluses.

With a structural deficit, the government has to borrow money when the economy is at full employment. There are no offsetting surpluses so deficits accumulate, and the government goes deeper into debt. Canada had continuous structural deficits for 20 years between 1975 and 1995. Total deficits ranged from $6 billion to $39 billion every year. As a result, Canada's accumulated debt increased, from about $34 billion in 1975–1976 to $554 billion in 1995–1996.

Structural surpluses also accumulate over time, raising the question of why government keeps collecting taxpayers' money that it is not spending. From 2006 until the Global Financial Crisis, Canada's Conservative government had deliberately small structural surpluses. They used those structural surpluses to start paying down the accumulated debt from past deficits.

But we are getting ahead of the story. To fully understand these issues, we have to examine Canada's national debt.

Practice...

11. If a country with $50 billion in debt then had revenues of $5 billion and spending of $4 billion, debt at the end of the year is

   a. $49 billion.

   b. $50 billion.

   c. $51 billion.

   d. $54 billion.

12. During an expansion,

   a. both tax revenues and government spending decrease.

   b. tax revenues decrease and government spending increases.

   c. tax revenues increase and government spending decreases.

   d. both tax revenues and government spending increase.

13. Automatic stabilizers

   a. reduce cyclical deficits and cyclical surpluses.

   b. reduce the size of the public debt during recessions.

   c. automatically produce surpluses during recessions and deficits during expansions.

   d. counteract changes in real GDP and steer the economy back toward potential GDP.

14. The structural deficit is the deficit

   a. in a recession.

   b. in an expansion.

   c. caused by the business cycle.

   d. that occurs at potential GDP.

15. The deficits or surpluses that most concern economists are

   a. structural surpluses.

   b. structural deficits.

   c. cyclical surpluses.

   d. cyclical deficits.

 **Apply...**

7. Look at the revenue and spending amounts in Figure 8 on page 280 for selected years between 1992–1992 and 2016–2017.

   a. In which years on the table was there a deficit?

   _____

   _____

   _____

   b. As the Canadian economy went into the Global Financial Crisis, how did the budget balance change?

   _____

   _____

   _____

   c. Based on the budget balance in 2009–2010, would the level of the national debt decrease or increase over the year? Explain.

   _____

   _____

   _____

8. Many governments around the world consider laws requiring governments to balance their budgets every year. Explain the problems that automatic stabilizers create for always-balanced-budget laws.

   _____

   _____

   _____

   _____

   _____

   _____

9. What do economists mean when they say, "balance the budget over the business cycle?"

   _____

   _____

   _____

   _____

   _____

   _____

From Deficits to the National Debt

L04 Explain the difference between deficits and debts, and identify five arguments about the national debt.

What is the difference between a deficit and a debt — two often confused words? Deficits and debts have different time dimensions.

Deficits (and surpluses) are a **flow** — an amount per unit of time. Your income is also a flow. To say your income is $2000 makes no sense, unless we know if it is $2000 a week, $2000 a month, or $2000 a year. Numbers for flows are meaningful only when there is a time dimension. For government, deficits and surpluses are usually measured annually — per year.

Debt is a **stock** — a fixed amount at a moment in time. Canada's national debt on March 31, 2017, was $632 billion — the amount the nation owed at that moment in time.

Measuring the National Debt

The **national debt** (also called the **public debt**) is the sum of past government budget deficits minus the sum of past budget surpluses. The national debt goes back to the creation of Canada. In 1867, the national debt was $76 million, measured in 1867 prices. The national debt in 2017 was $632 billion, measured in 2017 prices. The national debt in any year is measured in the nominal prices of that year.

Because prices change and the economy is changing, it is difficult to compare the national debt from year to year. The most meaningful measure of the national debt is the national debt as a percentage of GDP. This ratio eliminates complications of price changes and economic growth. Figure 9 shows Canada's national debt as a percentage of GDP between 1926 and 2017.

Figure 9   Canada's National Debt as a Percentage of GDP, 1926–2017

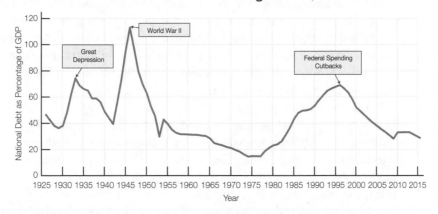

The first two major spikes in the ratio of national debt to GDP were due to the Great Depression (tax revenues decreased and government spending increased) and World War II (due to government spending on the war effort). The big spike from the late 1970s until the mid-1990s was different. This increase was due to a long string of peacetime structural budget deficits that kept adding to the accumulated national debt. Then, starting in 1996, the federal government cut spending dramatically, especially transfer payments to provincial governments. From 1997 to 2008, annual budget surpluses reduced both the amount of the national debt and the ratio of the national debt to GDP.

The 2017 ratio of national debt to GDP for Canada was 31 percent. This was much lower than the 2017 ratio for the United States (82 percent), the United Kingdom (81 percent), France (88 percent), Germany (45 percent), Italy (113 percent), or Japan (120 percent).

There are many numbers to consider when examining the national debt. Government debt as a percentage of GDP (31 percent), where Canada currently does well relative to other countries, is one number. That number is also much lower than Canada's ratio during the Great Depression (74 percent) or World War II (113 percent). You often see calculations of the national debt as a dollar amount per Canadian. For the 2017 national debt of $632 billion, divided by a population of 36.5 million, that number was $17 315 per person. In effect, you and I and every other person in Canada "owed" $17 315. If I had that balance owing on my credit card, I would be worried! Should we, as citizens, be concerned about these numbers for the national debt? What do the numbers mean?

Myths and Problems about the National Debt

Is the national debt a problem, or does it reflect the government's wise use of fiscal policy to help correct past problems of business cycles? There are many arguments about the national debt. Some are based on false assumptions and can be rejected as myths. But reasonable differences remain between the "Markets Quickly Self-Adjust, So Government Hands-Off " and "Markets Fail Often, So Government Hands-On" camps, and among politicians, about whether the national debt is a problem, and what, if anything, should be done about it.

Let's examine five common arguments criticizing the national debt.

1. Will Canada Go Bankrupt?   If you or I don't repay our debts we may go bankrupt. Is Canada at risk of bankruptcy because since 1867 the country has never paid off the national debt? This argument is largely a myth. The Government of Canada never has to pay back the national debt — it can simply refinance it. Here's why.

If an 80-year-old man walks into the bank with a small down payment and asks for a 25-year mortgage, the banker will laugh and say no. While the man is mortal and will die before repaying the loan, the Government of Canada is effectively immortal. Politicians running the federal government come and go, but the country of Canada, its government, and the institutions of Parliament remain, and are expected to continue.

The national debt is financed mostly by government bonds that have a 30-year maturity. Every year, some bonds come due and must be repaid. The Government of Canada repays them by issuing a new set of 30-year bonds and uses that newly borrowed money to pay off the old bonds. This is called *refinancing the debt*. Old debt is paid off with new debt. The only significant cost is the interest that must continue to be paid — a problem we will examine shortly. With refinancing, the national debt can stay in place indefinitely without repayment — as long as the bondholders trust the Canadian government will pay all bonds and interest payments that come due. That trust can disappear for countries that borrow too much, with expensive consequences.

2. Burden for Future Generations   By borrowing money today, is the Government of Canada imposing a burden on future generations, who must either repay the debt or at least pay the interest? There is undoubtedly interest to be paid. A key question is, who receives the interest payments? About 75 percent of the national debt is held by Canadians. That means the interest payments are mainly going to Canadians. So interest payments are more of a redistribution of money than a burden on taxpayers. If more Canadian government bonds were held by non-Canadians, this argument would become more important. As it stands now, the interest payments on the national debt are not a serious problem for future generations.

3. Debt Is Always Bad "Governments should live within their means, like responsible individuals, and not go into debt." This argument is based on a myth, because most individual consumers and businesses regularly make smart choices that involve going into debt. People taking on a car lease or a mortgage are going into debt. Businesses regularly issue bonds and go into debt to build new factories. Debt is a smart choice if the expected future profits or benefits from spending the borrowed money are greater than the interest costs on the loan.

For government, debt can be a smart choice if the positive impact on the economy of the spending financed by debt is greater than the interest cost. If the debt is used to finance infrastructure — such as roads, bridges, public transit, education, or communications networks — that improve productivity, lower costs, and provide positive externalities to the economy, most economists see a smart choice. And these improvements mostly benefit future generations. But if the debt is used simply to finance consumption, spent by politicians trying to win votes before an election, most economists see that as a problem.

4. Interest Payments Create Self-Perpetuating Debt With a balance on your credit card, you have to make a minimum payment every month. If you don't pay at least the interest owing on your debt, then you have to borrow more to pay the interest, which increases your debt. The balance on your credit card grows. The next month you have to pay interest on this larger balance. It is easy to get caught in this vicious cycle. You may never get out of debt.

The Government of Canada faced a similar situation between the mid-1970s and mid-1990s. Persistent yearly deficits increased the national debt, which increased interest payments. Larger interest payments led to larger yearly deficits. At the end of 1996, interest payments on the national debt reached $42.4 billion for the year — too high to be sustained.

The opportunity cost of spending that much money on interest alone was extraordinary. Interest payments on the national debt in 1996 took 36 cents of every dollar the government collected in revenues. That left only 64 cents of every tax dollar to spend on all government programs. The $42.4 billion interest bill was more money than the government spent that year on all transfers to Canadians, including Employment Insurance, Canada Pension Plan, Old Age Security, and national defence combined. That interest bill on the national debt represented 30 percent of all government spending. In 1996, the government, recognizing the national debt as a problem, began paying it down. By 2017, public debt charges had fallen to 8 percent of all government spending.

5. Crowding Out and Crowding In When governments finance the national debt by selling bonds, this increases the supply of bonds, drives down bond prices, and raises interest rates. Higher interest rates make it more expensive for consumers and businesses to borrow. The reduction in business investment spending caused by debt-financed higher interest rates is called **crowding out**. High government borrowing can raise interest rates, which in turn reduces (crowds out) some private investment.

On the other hand, if debt-financed government fiscal policy succeeds in increasing real GDP and expanding economic growth, the improvement in business expectations of profitability may increase private investment. This positive impact of debt-financed fiscal policy on expectations and business investment spending is called **crowding in**.

Some, but not all, of the arguments about the national debt are based on myths. How do such myths survive? The answer has to do with the explosive mix of economics and politics that fuels most debates about government deficits and debts and the proper hands-off or hands-on role for government in a market economy. And that is our final topic in this chapter.

 # Practice...

16. The government starts with a debt of $0. In year 1, there is a deficit of $100 billion, in year 2 there is a deficit of $60 billion, in year 3 there is a surplus of $40 billion, and in year 4 there is a deficit of $20 billion. The government does not borrow to make interest payments. What is the government debt at the end of year 4?

    a. $20 billion

    b. $140 billion

    c. greater than $140 billion, depending on the interest rate

    d. greater than $220 billion, depending on the interest rate

17. Canada will never go bankrupt because

    a. debt crowds in business investment.

    b. our debt can always be refinanced.

    c. our debt is just a transfer.

    d. where will hockey live?

18. Crowding in occurs when deficit-financed fiscal policy

    a. causes self-financing debt payments.

    b. causes self-perpetuating debt payments.

    c. raises interest rates, decreasing business investment

    d. improves expectations, increasing business investment.

19. Which is a genuine problem with the national debt?

    a. Debt is always bad.

    b. The national debt is a burden for future generations.

    c. Interest payments on the national debt can create self-perpetuating debt.

    d. Canada will go bankrupt because of debt.

20. Crowding out is the tendency for government debt-financed fiscal policy to decrease private investment spending by

    a. raising interest rates.

    b. lowering interest rates.

    c. improving expectations of profitability.

    d. worsening expectations of profitability.

 **Apply...**

10. These questions are about the differences between flows and stocks.

   a. Which of the following macroeconomic outcomes are flows and which are stocks: real GDP, unemployment rate, inflation rate, money supply? Explain.

   _____

   _____

   _____

   _____

   _____

   _____

   b. In your own words, explain the difference between deficits and debts. In your answer, use the terms _flow_ and _stock_.

   _____

   _____

   _____

   _____

   _____

11. What are the real potential problems with a large national debt?

   _____

   _____

   _____

   _____

   _____

   _____

12. Business investment spending is the most volatile component of aggregate demand, and changes in business investment spending often start economic expansions and contractions. The two main influences on business investment spending are the interest rate, and expectations about future profits. Explain the connections between crowding out, crowding in, and business investment decisions.

   _____

   _____

   _____

   _____

   _____

   _____

Hands-Off or Hands-On Role for Government?

L05 Distinguish between normative and positive, and between economic and political, arguments about fiscal policy.

Politicians disagree on fiscal policy, deficits, debt, and whether government should play a hands-off or hands-on role in the economy. Their arguments often mix economics with politics, and confuse personal value judgments with statements of fact. How can you, as a citizen, analyze those arguments to make your own informed choice about the role of government in a market economy?

Politics

Governments around the world play very different roles in their respective countries. Those roles are based on different political philosophies. Let's look at one set of differences — between the United States and Canada.

The United States was created through a revolution against British government interference. Their founding political principles emphasized "life, liberty, and the pursuit of happiness." The focus was on the individual's right to pursue her own destiny, free from government restrictions. The United States has hands-off origins.

Canada, created by an act of government, has founding political principles that stress "peace, order, and good government." Canada, as a civil society, stresses government's responsibility to promote and protect the public good. Canada has hands-on origins.

Today, citizens in both countries are attracted to both hands-off and hands-on approaches for government.

Loaded Words   The words used in arguments about the proper role for government often reveal the speaker's point of view.

Those supporting a hands-off role often pair government with words like intervene, interfere, and mistake. For example, "the government should not intervene . . . ," "that is government interference . . . ," or "it is a mistake for government to . . . ." These words show the speaker believes that government has no legitimate business in taking action, and if government does act, it usually gets it wrong.

Those supporting a hands-on role often pair government with words like act, participate, and responsibility. For example, "the government needs to act to . . . ," "this initiative requires government participation," or "the government has a responsibility to . . . ."

Look for these words when listening to a politician's arguments. They are clues to the politician's views on the proper role of government.

Positive and Normative Statements

There is no right or wrong answer to the question, "What role should government play in our economy?" You might answer, "Government should play a hands-off role," and your sister might answer, "Government should play a hands-on role." The answer depends on your political values, and people have different values or opinions. These **normative statements** involve value judgments or opinions. Normative statements often use the word *should* and cannot be evaluated as true or false by checking the facts.

Positive statements are about what is, rather than about what should be. Positive statements can be evaluated as true or false by checking the facts. An example of a positive statement is "The Chinese government plays a much larger role in Chinese society than does the Canadian government in Canadian society." We can identify and measure all of the actions taken by the Chinese government and compare them to the actions taken by the Canadian government. If there are more in China, the statement is true. If there are fewer, the statement is false.

In contrast, the statement, "The government in Canada *should* play a larger role like the government in China" is a normative statement — an opinion. Notice the word "should"? When you hear claims from politicians, or economists, identify if the statement is normative or positive. If it is a normative statement, you can agree or disagree. If it is a positive statement, look for the facts behind the claim to evaluate if it is true or false.

Economics

Economists also make both normative and positive statements, and it is important to distinguish between them. Economists pride themselves on their positive statements, so let's start with those.

Positive Statements   Here are some examples of positive statements in this chapter:

- Expansionary fiscal policy increases aggregate demand.
- Tax incentives stimulate saving, increase the quantity of capital, and promote economic growth.
- Tax rate cuts increase government tax revenues.
- The national debt does not have to be repaid, only refinanced.
- Automatic stabilizers create government budget deficits when the economy goes into a recession.

I am not claiming that any of these statements is true or false. But you can evaluate a positive statement as true or false by checking the facts. Some of the statements are true, and some are false. Most economists evaluate the claim by supply-siders that "tax rate cuts increase government tax revenues" as false because the facts show that when taxes were cut, revenues decreased, not increased. But the claim is still a positive statement — capable of being evaluated as true or false by checking the facts.

Normative Statements   Here are examples of normative statements from this chapter. Since they are opinion-based, you have to make up your own mind whether you agree with them or not.

- Government should use expansionary fiscal policy to get the economy out of recession.
- Government should use tax incentives to encourage saving and promote economic growth.
- Government should cut taxes to counteract recessions.
- Government should pay down the national debt.
- Government should balance the budget over the business cycle.

Let's look at different possible responses to these normative statements. Expansionary fiscal policy increases aggregate demand, but is it better to let the economy self-adjust from a recession? The hands-off and hands-on camps disagree about the trade-offs. Will government policies do more harm than good?

Tax incentives encourage saving, but the hands-off and hands-on camps disagree about trade-offs. As saving increases, there is a cost of reduced aggregate demand in the present, but benefits in the future of increased economic growth.

Paying down the national debt reduces future interest payments on the debt. But every policy has an opportunity cost. The money could instead be spent on improving infrastructure in the present, which would promote growth in the future. There are no right or wrong choices here, only trade-offs.

While most economists agree that governments should balance the budget over the business cycle, when politicians go to act on that advice, there may be problems.

Politics and Economics

Arguments from politicians about fiscal policy, deficits, and debt often combine politics and economics, creating additional problems in evaluating what you hear. There are two main mix-ups.

Will Politicians Follow Economists' Advice?   Most economists see the value in government deficits during economic contractions as long as they are offset by government surpluses during expansions, resulting in a balanced budget over the business cycle. But politicians, not economists, decide on government tax, transfer, and spending programs. More government spending and tax cuts can make economic sense in a contraction, but it is hard for politicians to stop spending and increase taxes — both politically unpopular — when the contraction ends. Deficits are too politically tasty to trust politicians to stop at just one. So policy advice that makes economic sense — balance the budget over the business cycle — might be reasonably rejected because it doesn't make political sense.

Are You Hearing a Political or Economic Argument?   You will hear politicians argue against the national debt, claiming that governments must act like responsible individuals and never go into debt, or that Canada will go bankrupt when we have to pay back the debt. These sound like economic arguments about debt. But you have seen that some parallels between individuals and governments are false. Responsible individuals and businesses regularly go into debt, and the national debt does not have to be paid back, only refinanced. So these statements are really political, hands-off arguments against a larger role for government, disguised as an economic argument about the national debt.

Hands-Off or Hands-On — Your Choice   Arguments over fiscal policy are often the main event for fights between the "Markets Quickly Self-Adjust, So Government Hands-Off" camp, and the "Markets Fail Often, So Government Hands-On" camp. Disagreement over taxes versus government spending, and over deficits, surpluses, and the national debt are often heated. But the arguments often mix politics and economics in misleading ways. Sort out the positive from the normative statements, and the economic arguments from the political arguments, so that you can make informed choices as a citizen about hands-off and hands-on roles for government fiscal policy and your own future.

Practice...

21. The founding political principles of Canada are _____ and of the United States are _____ .

    a. hands-off; hands-on

    b. hands-off; hands-off

    c. hands-on; hands-off

    d. hands-on; hands-on

22. Which words reflect Canada's political philosophy?

    a. hands-off origins

    b. life, liberty, and the pursuit of happiness

    c. individual rights

    d. civil society

23. A word used to describe government by a hands-off politician is

    a. obligation.

    b. intervene.

    c. participate.

    d. act.

24. Which statement is *normative*?

    a. Borrowing to spend leads to crowding out.

    b. Borrowing to spend leads to crowding in.

    c. Higher interest rates discourage investment.

    d. Governments should not borrow to finance spending.

25. A word used to describe government by a hands-on politician is

    a. responsibility.

    b. inefficiency.

    c. interfere.

    d. mistake.

Apply...

13. Identify each statement below as either positive or normative. Explain your reasoning. If it is positive, then rewrite it so that it become normative. If it is normative, then rewrite it so that it become positive.

a. Contractionary fiscal policy will reduce inflation.

_____

_____

_____

_____

b. The City of Toronto should subsidize a new soccer stadium because the multiplier effect will benefit all taxpayers.

_____

_____

_____

_____

c. If the government always balances its budget, the economy will benefit.

_____

_____

_____

_____

d. If the government is paying more than 15 percent of tax revenues to service the national debt, that is too much.

_____

_____

_____

_____

Apply...

14. If your family recently came from a country other than Canada and the United States, describe the political philosophy of your country of origin, using the political philosophies of Canada (government hands-on) and the United States (government hands-off) as reference points.

    Your instructor may start a class discussion about what you describe, and relate it to attitudes about macroeconomic government policy.

    _____

    _____

    _____

    _____

    _____

    _____

    _____

15. Search out media stories that illustrate the use of loaded words signalling the author's attitude toward the role of government. Find one article using the hands-off words, and one using the hands-on words.

    Your instructor may start a class discussion about what you found, and if the words influenced your reactions to the articles.

    _____

    _____

    _____

    _____

    _____

    _____

    _____

KNOW...

Summary of Learning Objectives

1. **Fiscal policies** — changes in government spending, taxes, and transfers — act as aggregate demand shocks for countering output gaps. In a recessionary gap, **expansionary fiscal policy** provides a positive demand shock. In an inflationary gap, **contractionary fiscal policy** provides a negative demand shock. Any spending **injection** has a multiplied impact on aggregate demand. The **multiplier effect** is larger the lower the percentage of **leakages** from the circular flow.

2. **Fiscal policies** targeting aggregate supply — tax incentives for saving, support for R&D, education, training — promote **economic growth**, but there are trade-offs between reduced aggregate demand in the present versus increased aggregate supply in the future. Supply-siders emphasize the **supply-side effects** of lower taxes on incentives, but there is no empirical support for the **Laffer Curve** claim that lower tax rates increase total tax revenues.

3. **Automatic stabilizers** create **cyclical budget deficits and surpluses** while keeping the economy close to potential GDP. **Structural deficits and surpluses** at potential GDP are more problematic. Most economists oppose laws to always balance government budgets, but support a balanced budget over the business cycle.

4. Deficits are a **flow** while debt is a **stock**. Of five common arguments about **national debt**, myths include: Canada will go bankrupt; burden on future generations; debt is always bad. Potential problems include: interest payments create self-perpetuating debt; **crowding out** of private investments.

5. Sort out economic arguments from political arguments, and **positive statements** from **normative statements** so that you can make informed choices as a citizen about hands-off and hands-on roles for government fiscal policy and your own future.

Key Terms

automatic stabilizers: tax and transfer adjustments that counteract changes to real GDP without new government decisions

balanced budget: revenues = spending

budget deficit: revenues < spending

budget surplus: revenues > spending

contractionary fiscal policy: decreases aggregate demand by decreasing government spending, increasing taxes, or decreasing transfers; shifts the aggregate demand curve leftward — a negative aggregate demand shock

crowding in: tendency for government debt-financed fiscal policy to increase private investment spending by improving expectations

crowding out: tendency for government debt-financed fiscal policy to decrease private investment spending by raising interest rates

cyclical deficits and surpluses: due to fluctuations in economic activity over the business cycle

economic growth: expansion of economy's capacity to produce products and services; increase in potential GDP per person

expansionary fiscal policy: increases aggregate demand by increasing government spending, decreasing taxes, or increasing transfers; shifts the aggregate demand curve rightward — a positive aggregate demand shock

fiscal policy: changes in government purchases, taxes, and transfers to achieve macroeconomic outcomes of steady growth, full employment, and stable prices

flow: amount per unit of time

human capital: increased earning potential from work experience, on-the-job training, and education

injections: spending in the circular flow that does not start with consumers; G (government spending), I (business investment spending), and X (exports)

leakage: spending that leaks out of the circular flow through taxes, savings, and imports

multiplier effect: a spending injection has a multiplied effect on aggregate demand

national debt (public debt): total amount owed by government = (sum of past deficits) – (sum of past surpluses)

net taxes: taxes minus transfer payments

normative statements: based on value judgments about what you believe should be; cannot be tested or evaluated as true or false by checking the facts

positive statements: about what is; can be evaluated as true or false by checking the facts

public debt (national debt): total amount owed by government = (sum of past deficits) – (sum of past surpluses)

stock: fixed amount at a moment in time

structural deficits and surpluses: budget deficits and surpluses occurring at potential GDP

supply-side effects: the incentive effects of taxes on aggregate supply

Answers to Practice

1. **c**   Other answers relate to monetary policy.

2. **d**   Imports and savings are leakages.

3. **c** $1 \div 0.25 = 4$.

4. **b**   **a** and **c** are positive demand shocks. **d** is monetary policy.

5. **a**   Initial round of new consumer spending is smaller for a tax cut than for an equivalent amount of new government spending because consumers save some of the additional income.

6. **a**   More students increase their human capital, increasing the quality of labour inputs.

7. **c**   There can be a trade-off between increased aggregate supply in the future — through more business investment spending financed by more savings — and reduced aggregate demand in the present due to lower spending.

8. **d** See Figure 6 on page 275.

9. **d** Depends on if tax rate is above or below $T*$.

10. **b** Prices do not affect the quantity or quality of inputs.

11. **a** If revenue is $1 billion greater than spending, this surplus reduces debt by $1 billion (from $50 billion to $49 billion).

12. **c** Increase in real GDP automatically increases tax revenues. Decreases in unemployment automatically decrease transfer payments.

13. **d** Act like a thermostat by creating cyclical deficits during contractions and cyclical surpluses during expansions.

14. **d** Definition. Cyclical deficits caused by business cycle in recession.

15. **b** Structural deficits are the greatest concern because debt rises and so do interest payments on the debt.

16. **b** $100 b + $60 b − $40 b + $20 b = deficit of $140.

17. **b** Unlike mortal individuals, as long as investors trust that Canada will continue as a country, investors allow the refinancing of debt.

18. **d** Definition. Positive effect of improved expectations outweighs negative effect of increased interest rates.

19. **c** True when interest payments cause budget deficits, which in turn increase the national debt and interest payments.

20. **a** If government sells bonds to finance debt, the increased supply of bonds drives down bond prices and raises interest rates, so it is more expensive for businesses to borrow.

21. **c** See chapter discussion.

22. **d** Peace, order, and good government.

23. **b** All other words are hands-on.

24. **d** Notice the word *should*.

25. **a** All other words are hands-off.

12 Globalization, Trade, and Protectionism

LEARNING OBJECTIVES

LO1 Describe how comparative advantage, specialization, and trade improve living standards.

LO2 Explain how competition creates winners, losers, and opponents to trade, and analyze three forms of protectionism.

LO3 Explain the pace of globalization and how to evaluate if sweatshop workers are better off with international trade.

LO4 Evaluate the hands-off and hands-on arguments about the role for government in the globalization debate.

LEARN...

Globalization is changing the world, but people do not agree whether the changes are for better or for worse. Controversies over the virtues and evils of trade go back centuries. Today, communication technology and transportation improvements have lowered the costs of international trade and sped up globalization. Your technical support call may be answered by someone in Bangalore, India, and a steelworker in Hamilton, Ontario, may have lost a job to a factory worker in Shanghai, China.

Economists and free-trade supporters argue that specialization and trade raise living standards. Supporters point to once-struggling countries like Japan, South Korea, Taiwan — and now China and India — whose standards of living continue to rise with international trade. Critics point to sweatshops in developing countries as one serious negative outcome of globalized trade. Other critics see globalization as just another way that developed countries are using weaker countries as a source of cheap labour and raw materials.

In this chapter, you will learn about comparative advantage — the concept behind all pro-trade arguments — and how it applies not just to international trade, but also to your personal smart choices about jobs and "trading" in local markets for your everyday needs. You will also explore some of the arguments against globalization, including those of the Nobel Prize–winning economist Joseph Stiglitz.

The controversies over trade and globalization return us to the question of the role for government in the global economy. There are new issues about whether government should help those threatened from international competition through direct protection, or with a social safety net, or not at all. It comes back to the need for you — as a citizen of Canada and the world — to understand the issues and to make up your own mind.

Gains from Trade

 Describe how comparative advantage, specialization, and trade improve living standards.

In today's Canadian economy, most of us earn money by specializing in a particular occupation. We trade that money to buy what we want. This specialization and trade replaced the self-sufficiency of people living in Canada two hundred years ago. Back then, most Indigenous peoples and pioneers made for themselves most of what they needed — hunting and growing their own food, making clothes from animal hides, and building shelters from available resources.

What happened to lead us all away from self-sufficiency toward specializing and trading? The simple economic answer is that specializing and trading make us better off. Our standard of living in terms of material products and services is much higher with specialization and trade than it was in the past.

Trade makes all of us better off. Why? Trade is voluntary. Any time two people make a voluntary trade, each person feels that what she gets is of greater value than what she gives up. If there weren't mutual benefits, the trade wouldn't happen. It's simple self-interest at work.

Canada Is a Trading Nation

Specialization and trade are widespread in Canada and other countries. The *importance* of international trade — trade between countries — is measured by the percentage of GDP that comes from exports and imports. Remember that GDP = $C + I + G + X - IM$. Figure 1 shows 2016 exports and imports as a percentage of GDP for selected countries.

Figure 1   Exports, Imports as Percentage of GDP, Selected Countries, 2016

Country	Exports as % of GDP	Imports as % of GDP
Germany	46%	38%
Canada	31%	33%
China	20%	17%
Japan	18%	20%
United States	13%	16%

Source: Based on World Development Indicators, http://data.worldbank.org/indicator

For Canada, exports are 31 percent of GDP. Almost one of every three dollars earned by Canadians comes from the sale of exports to the rest of the world. Imports, which do not contribute to Canadian GDP but do contribute to GDP in the rest of the world, are 33 percent of Canadian GDP. Notice how much more important international trade is to the Canadian economy than it is to the Chinese, Japanese, or U.S. economies. Even though those countries sell a much greater *quantity* of exports than Canada, their domestic economies are much larger. So their exports as a *percentage of GDP* are smaller than for Canada. Canada is a trading nation, and our standard of living depends significantly on international trade.

Furthermore, because 80 percent of our international trade is with one country — the United States — much is at stake in our trade relations with the United States. U.S. GDP is ten times bigger than Canada's, so Canada's trade with the United States is much more important to us than the United States' trade with Canada is to them.

Since trade is voluntary, both Canada and the United States must believe they are better off as a result of international trade. How does that happen? Where do the mutually beneficial gains from trade come from?

The Source of Gains from Trade

Opportunity cost is the key to the mutual benefits from trade. Here's a simple example. Jill and Marie are each self-sufficient pioneers producing food and shelter. Each grows her own wheat to make bread, and chops her own wood for fire and shelter. Figures 2 and 3 show the different possible combinations of bread and wood each can produce in a month.

Figure 2 Jill's Production Possibilities

Possibility	Bread (loaves per month)	Wood (logs per month)
A	50	0
B	40	20
C	30	40
D	20	60
E	10	80
F	0	100

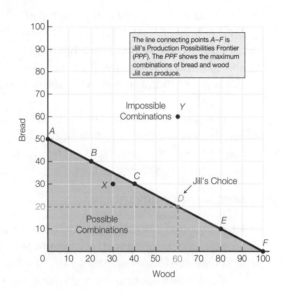

Figure 3 Marie's Production Possibilities

Possibility	Bread (loaves per month)	Wood (logs per month)
A	40	0
B	30	5
C	20	10
D	10	15
E	0	20

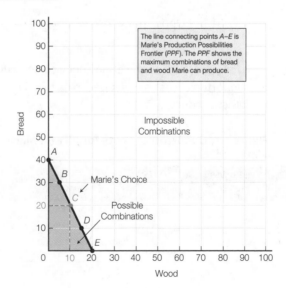

Because Jill and Marie are each self-sufficient, that means each can only consume what she produces herself. Jill chooses point *D* on her *PPF*, and Marie chooses point *C* on her *PPF*.

Production Possibilities Frontier

Each black line in the graphs on the previous page is a **production possibilities frontier** — *PPF* for short.

- A *PPF* shows the maximum combinations of products or services that can be produced with existing inputs.
- A *PPF* is the boundary between possible and impossible combinations of outputs.
- Points on the *PPF* are preferred to points inside the *PPF* because people prefer more to less.

Absolute Advantage

Can trade make both Jill and Marie better off? It doesn't look promising, especially for Jill. Jill is a better bread maker than Marie and a better wood chopper. Jill has an **absolute advantage** — the ability to produce at a lower absolute cost than another producer — over Marie in both bread production and wood production. Jill is more productive as a bread maker and as a wood chopper.

If you are not keen on history, then in place of Jill and Marie, think of China and Canada. If China can produce everything at lower cost than Canada, can there be mutually beneficial gains from trade for both countries? What's the benefit for China? Won't all Canadians end up unemployed?

Comparative Advantage

Mutually beneficial gains from trade do not depend on absolute advantage, they depend on **comparative advantage** — the ability to produce a product or service at a lower opportunity cost than another producer.

To calculate opportunity costs along any *PPF*, compare two adjacent possible combinations, and use the formula

$$\text{Opportunity cost} = \frac{\text{Give Up}}{\text{Get}}$$

Figure 4 shows the opportunity cost calculations for Jill and Marie. Opportunity cost is measured in term of what you must give up of the other product.

Figure 4   Opportunity Costs for Jill and Marie

	Opportunity Cost of 1 Additional	
	Loaf of Bread	Log of Wood
Jill	Gives up 2 logs of wood	Gives up ½ loaf of bread
Marie	Gives up ½ log of wood	Gives up 2 loaves of bread
Comparative Advantage	Marie has comparative advantage (lower opportunity cost) in bread-making	Jill has comparative advantage (lower opportunity cost) in wood-chopping

Since comparative advantage is defined as lowest opportunity cost (not lowest absolute cost), you can see that Marie has a comparative advantage in bread-making, while Jill has a comparative advantage in wood-chopping.

HINT: Whenever you are trying to figure out comparative advantage, always create a table like Figure 4, with the two traders in the rows, and the two products in the columns.

Mutually Beneficial Gain from Trade

There are mutually beneficial gains from trade if people/countries specialize in producing the product in which they have a comparative advantage, and trade for the other product. According to comparative advantage, Jill should specialize in only chopping wood, and Marie should specialize in only making bread. Jill produces 100 logs of wood and no bread, and Marie produces 40 loaves of bread and no wood.

They agree to trade 20 logs of wood for 20 loaves of bread. Jill, the specialized woodchopper, is "exporting" wood and "importing" bread. Marie, the specialized baker, is "exporting" bread and "importing" wood.

The ratio at which they exchange wood for bread is called the terms of trade. In general, the **terms of trade** are the quantity of exports required to pay for one unit of imports. In Figure 5, the slope of the blue trade lines (also called trading possibilities lines) reflect the terms of trade. In this example, 1 log of wood exchanges for 1 loaf of bread. Figure 5 tells the story of Jill and Marie's specialization and trade.

Figure 5   Mutually Beneficial Gains from Trade

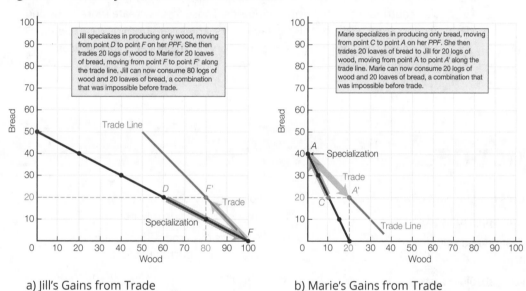

a) Jill's Gains from Trade   b) Marie's Gains from Trade

Achieving the Impossible

After trading, Jill and Marie are both better off than when they were each self-sufficient. Each can consume a combination of wood and bread — outside her *PPF* — that was impossible before trade. Voluntary trade is not a zero-sum game, where one person's gain is the other's loss. Both traders gain.

These gains from trade happen without anyone working harder, without any improvement in technology, and without new inputs.

There are gains for both Jill and Marie, even though Jill has an absolute advantage in producing everything at lower cost. Differences in opportunity costs — comparative advantage — are the key to mutually beneficial gains from trade. The trade can be between individuals, or between countries. That is why China trades with Canada, even though China can produce most things more cheaply than Canada can. There are still differences in comparative advantage based on opportunity costs.

All arguments you will ever hear in favour of freer trade are based on comparative advantage, which is based on the most important concept in economics — opportunity cost.

Terms of Trade   For a trade to have mutual benefits, the terms of trade must be somewhere between each trader's opportunity costs. Jill's own opportunity cost of producing a loaf of bread is two logs. Jill is importing bread, "paying" only one log for each loaf of bread, so for her the imported bread is a bargain. Marie's own opportunity cost of producing a log is two loaves of bread. Marie is importing wood, "paying" only one loaf of bread for each log, so for her the imported wood is a bargain. Both traders gain.

In this example, the gains from trade are split evenly between the traders — the ratio of 1 to 1 (1 loaf for 1 log) is halfway between the ratios of 2 to 1 and 1 to 2. Gains from trade are not always split evenly. But for the trade to occur voluntarily, the terms of trade must be somewhere between the opportunity costs that each trader (or country) faces locally. Exactly where the terms of trade settle in international markets can mean one country gains more than the other. As long as both countries get some gain, trade happens voluntarily.

Technology and Competition   Gains from trade are a big part of rising living standards, even without anyone working harder, any improvement in technology, or any new resources. Competition and technological advances also contribute to rising living standards. Those forces create more gains and winners from trade, but also create losers. The losers from new competition and new technologies are behind the story of why not everyone welcomes international trade.

 # Practice...

1. Trade improves our standard of living through

    a. equalizing opportunity costs.

    b. specialization and voluntary exchange.

    c. minimizing absolute costs.

    d. taking advantage of losers.

2. With specialization, Canada can produce either 10 000 bottles of wine per month or 200 000 bushels of wheat. The opportunity cost of a bottle of wine in Canada is

    a. 20 bushels of wheat.

    b. 200 bushels of wheat.

    c. 1/20 bushel of wheat.

    d. 2000 bottles of wine.

3. For mutually beneficial trade, the terms of trade must be

    a. less than the sum of the traders' local opportunity costs.

    b. greater than the sum of the traders' local opportunity costs.

    c. between the traders' local opportunity costs.

    d. equal to the traders' local opportunity costs.

Practice...

4. In Portugal, the opportunity cost of a bale of wool is 3 bottles of wine. In England, the opportunity cost of 1 bottle of wine is 3 bales of wool. Based on this information,

   a. Portugal has a comparative advantage in producing wool.

   b. England has an absolute advantage in producing wine.

   c. England has an absolute advantage in producing wool.

   d. Portugal has a comparative advantage in producing wine.

5. Mexico and Canada produce both oil and apples using labour only. A barrel of oil can be produced with 8 hours of labour in Mexico and 4 hours of labour in Canada. A bushel of apples can be produced with 12 hours of labour in Mexico and 8 hours of labour in Canada. *Mexico* has a(n)

   a. comparative advantage in producing oil.

   b. comparative advantage in producing apples.

   c. absolute advantage in producing oil.

   d. absolute advantage in producing apples.

Apply...

1. Suppose you and your roommate alternate doing housework (cooking and cleaning) and joint economics assignments each week (one week you do both activities, and in the next week he does both activities). You are better than your roommate at both activities. In one hour, you can either finish the joint assignment or complete all of the housework. In one hour, he can either do one-half of the joint assignment or complete three-quarters of the housework.

   a. In which activities do you have an absolute advantage? A comparative advantage?

   _____

   _____

   _____

   _____

   _____

   _____

   b. Suppose you offer your roommate a deal so that each of you specializes in one activity. In which activity should you specialize? Why?

   _____

   _____

   _____

continued next page

continued

2. France and Germany each produce both wine and beer using a single input: labour. Their production possibilities are as follows: France has 100 units of labour and can produce a maximum of 200 bottles of wine or 400 bottles of beer. Germany has 50 units of labour and can produce a maximum of 250 bottles of wine or 200 bottles of beer.

    a. Complete this table.

	Bottles Produced by 1 Unit of Labour		Opportunity Cost of 1 Additional Bottle	
	Wine	Beer	Wine	Beer
France				
Germany				

    b. Which country has an absolute advantage in wine production? In beer production? Explain.

    _____

    _____

    _____

    _____

    c. Which country has a comparative advantage in wine production? In beer production? Explain.

    _____

    _____

    _____

    _____

    d. If trade is allowed, describe what specialization, if any, will occur.

    _____

    _____

    _____

3. The terms of trade do not necessarily split the gains from trade evenly between traders. Define the terms of trade and explain the limits to how unevenly the gains may be split if trade continues.

    _____

    _____

    _____

    _____

    _____

    _____

Protectionism and Trade

 LO2 Explain how competition creates winners, losers, and opponents to trade, and analyze three forms of protectionism.

In addition to mutually beneficial gains, freer trade increases competition. Connections to new markets bring connections to new competitors. A local producer may have been a big fish in her small, local pond. But increased trade has her now swimming in bigger ponds with bigger fish. Some fish, and some businesses, don't survive.

Businesses compete in markets by figuring out new ways to beat their rivals. Businesses do this through cutting costs, developing new technologies of production, inventing new products, exploiting economies of large-scale production, or finding new or cheaper sources for raw materials and resources. Over time, these competitive innovations, which result from the endless quest for profits, make businesses and labour more productive and improve living standards and product choices for consumers.

The gains from specialization, trade, competition, and innovation also have a downside — destruction of less productive, higher-cost, and less popular products and businesses. Many twenty-first century auto workers in Ontario lost their jobs to robotic assembly lines in South Korea or Mexico. Failed businesses and lost jobs are the opportunity costs of the gains from trade. Jobs lost through trade, competition, and innovation come under the definition of **structural unemployment** — unemployment due to technological change or international competition that makes workers' skills obsolete.

On the whole, consumers and businesses in Canada benefit from specialization, trade, and increased competition. Productivity and overall living standards improve. That is why we are so much better off than Canadians were 200 years ago. But trade creates winners and losers.

Winners and Losers from International Trade

When new international markets open up through trade — connecting Canada to other countries — who wins and who loses within Canada?

Winners Consumers gain from lower prices and greater product variety that result from new imports. Canadian export businesses gain from access to new markets and new customers. Export businesses have more sales, more profits, and hire more workers. Workers in exporting businesses gain from more jobs and higher wages.

Losers Canadian businesses that cannot successfully compete with the new imports lose. Workers in import-competing businesses also lose, as jobs disappear and wages fall with shrinking sales in Canada.

Protectionism

Workers and businesses in Canadian import-competing industries look to the government for protection from the bigger fish that appear when Canadian markets get connected to international markets. Government protection of their economic interests takes three main forms: tariffs, import quotas, and domestic subsidies.

Tariffs   A **tariff** is a tax applied to a product or service imported into a country. The Canadian business importing the product must pay the tariff to the Canadian government. That tariff is a business cost, which is passed on to consumers, increasing the price of the product.

Tariffs are attractive to governments for three reasons. First, tariffs raise revenues for the government to spend. Second, tariffs win votes and campaign donations for politicians from businesses and workers in import-competing industries. Third, because tariffs are a tax on non-Canadians who don't vote, there is little political damage from raising tariffs. While tariffs raise the price paid by Canadian consumers for the taxed imports, the tariff is not identified at the cash register. Consumers and voters usually do not blame the government for the higher import prices.

Tariffs protect domestic producers competing with imports. Because consumers pay a higher price — including the tariff — for the imported products, competing domestic producers win from higher prices and profits. Canadian consumers lose from higher prices.

Import Quotas   Quotas limit the quantity of products or services that can be imported into Canada during a year. For example, Canada imposes **import quotas** on meat, eggs, dairy products, and steel. With reduced supply and restricted competition, higher prices for imported products means the quantity sold in Canada is less than with freer trade. But the quantity sold by Canadian producers increases. With quotas, Canadian import-competing industries win. There are higher prices and profits for the businesses and more jobs and higher wages for workers. Canadian consumers again lose from higher prices.

Domestic Subsidies   The most common and controversial form of protectionism today is **subsidies to domestic producers**. A subsidy is a government payment to domestic producers of products or services that are threatened by international competition. Many governments, especially in Europe and the United States, give subsidies for agricultural products like cotton and grain. Canada gives large subsidies to protect the dairy industry. The businesses and workers being subsidized are winners while consumers lose by paying higher prices.

The Politics of Trade Policy

Why do governments often respond to domestic producers' requests for protection from international competition? The answer is not obvious, since the higher prices and reduced variety of products hurt far more Canadians — especially consumers — than the small number of businesses and workers helped in import-competing industries.

Domestic Trade Politics   A large number of consumers gain from freer international trade, but the gain for each consumer is small. A small number of businesses and workers in import-competing industries lose from freer trade, but the loss for each is large. The unequal distribution of the gains and losses creates political pressure for protectionism to help those who lose from international trade.

International Trade Politics   The unequal distribution of gains and losses also affects international trade politics between countries. Freer international trade potentially benefits far more people than it harms. But the barrier is political pressure in many countries from import-competing industries protecting themselves from competition.

Arguments against and for Protectionism

There are two common arguments for protectionism that sound believable, but that fail to incorporate comparative advantage. There are also some valid, but limited, arguments for protectionism.

Saving Canadian Jobs   One argument states that tariffs, quotas, and subsidies can save jobs in Canadian import-competing industries. But freer trade creates jobs in Canadian export industries and in Canadian businesses that sell and service imports. While eliminating tariffs, quotas, and subsidies will cost jobs in Canadian import-competing industries, freer trade creates more jobs than are lost.

Arguments for tariffs to protect Canadian jobs also suffer from the fallacy of composition. While one country might succeed in temporarily protecting domestic jobs using tariffs, if all countries do the same, protectionist policies can trigger a trade war. As international trade breaks down, all countries and workers end up worse off.

Necessary to Compete with Cheap Foreign Labour   When Canada entered into the North American Free Trade Agreement (NAFTA) in 1994, many tariffs and quotas were eliminated among Canada, the United States, and Mexico. Many people predicted a "giant sucking sound" from jobs draining out of Canada and the United States into Mexico, because wages for labour were so much lower there. That did not happen.

Low-skill, low-wage jobs requiring little education did move to Mexico. But the evidence suggests that the total number of jobs in Canada has increased because of greater exports to expanded North American markets. The mistake in this argument about competing with cheap foreign labour is the focus on absolute cost and absolute advantage, instead of comparative advantage. Mexican workers are generally paid less than Canadian workers, but what matters for profits is labour costs per unit of output, not labour costs per hour. Higher-wage workers in Canada usually have higher productivity because of working with better capital equipment, which decreases costs per unit of output. While Mexico has a comparative advantage for some products, Canada has a comparative advantage for others. Mexico too has benefited from the mutual gains from trade.

Valid, Limited Protectionism Arguments   Freer trade leads to increased specialization and reliance on other countries to supply products and services. While there are gains from trade, there are also risks from that reliance. Canada does not want to rely entirely on another country for strategic products like military equipment, energy, and other essentials. In the event of a war, what if your only suppliers of strategic products are your enemies? To avoid that risk, governments protect strategic domestic industries.

Another non-economic risk of freer trade is the threat to a country's cultural identity. Canada's reliance on United States trade brings with it exposure to the culture of a country that is ten times larger. In the name of protecting Canada's cultural identity, the government restricts imported content of radio and television programs, restricts broadcast licences to domestic providers, and subsidizes the production of Canadian culture in the form of domestic books, movies, music, and other media.

Practice...

6. All of the following are forms of protectionism *except*

   a. tariffs.

   b. terms of trade.

   c. import quotas.

   d. domestic subsidies.

7. Jobs lost through international competition and innovation are part of

   a. creative trading.

   b. cyclical unemployment.

   c. frictional unemployment.

   d. structural unemployment.

8. When trade connects Canada to new international markets, Canadian

   a. consumers win and Canadian exporters lose.

   b. consumers win and Canadian businesses in import-competing industries win.

   c. consumers win and Canadian workers in import-competing industries lose

   d. workers in export industries lose and Canadian workers in import-competing industries win.

9. Political pressure for protectionism arises because a

   a. small number of consumers face large losses.

   b. large number of consumers face large losses.

   c. large number of producers face small losses.

   d. small number of producers face large losses.

10. Economists might agree with which argument *for protectionism?*

   a. protecting cultural identity

   b. necessary to compete with cheap foreign labour

   c. reducing the risk of trade retaliation.

   d. saving Canadian jobs

Apply...

4. Present a counterargument to those who say they want to protect Canadian jobs by demanding government protection for their industry from cheaper imports.

    _____

    _____

    _____

    _____

    _____

    _____

5. Rich countries are often worried about the impact of off-shoring of services (such as call centres for computers or software) to developing countries such as India. Suppose that Canada was to ban off-shoring for call centres. Explain in words who in Canada and in India would gain and lose from this ban.

    _____

    _____

    _____

    _____

    _____

    _____

    _____

    _____

    _____

    _____

6. "Tariffs are a win-win policy because they allow import-competing Canadian businesses to continue to operate and raise money for the government." Agree or disagree, and explain your answer.

    _____

    _____

    _____

    _____

    _____

    _____

Globalization and Sweatshops

 L03 Explain the pace of globalization and how to evaluate if sweatshop workers are better off with international trade.

There are other opponents of expanded international trade beyond businesses and workers in import-competing industries. Some social activists, human rights organizations, and anti-market groups worry about what they see as the harmful consequences of international trade. At a student demonstration against free trade, one passionate activist asked the crowd,

> "Who made your T-shirt? . . . Was it a child in Vietnam?
> Or a young girl from India earning 18 cents per hour? . . .
> Did you know that she lives 12 to a room? . . . That she is
> forced to work 90 hours each week, without overtime pay? . . .
> That she lives not only in poverty, but also in filth and sickness,
> all in the name of Nike's profits?"

Anti-globalization critics view uncontrolled international trade as the cause of many undesirable problems in developing countries: low wages, poverty, poor working conditions, farmers who can no longer make a living, environmental damage, and local governments undermined by international organizations. These critics view the competition from expanded international trade as a "race to the bottom" that will result in low wages, poorer working conditions, greater pollution, and lower taxes (especially on corporations) in every country, both developing and developed.

How do we reconcile anti-globalization arguments with an economist's view that expanded trade — domestic and international — brings rising living standards for all? Let's start with some facts about globalization.

Globalization

Economic globalization is the integration of economic activities across borders and through markets. When markets in one country are connected to markets in other countries, economic activities are connected, or integrated. The technical support for your computer may come from a business in India. The potash used by factories in the Czech Republic to make glass may come from Saskatchewan. The T-shirt you wear may be made from cotton grown in Texas but woven into cloth in Shanghai.

Why Is Globalization Happening?   The reason for the spread of integrated economic activity across borders is the same as it was for Jill and Marie. Self-interest and mutually beneficial gains are always motives for expanded trade. The pace of globalization is speeding up due to falling costs for both transportation and communications technologies. It is quickly becoming cheaper and easier to connect markets among countries.

Globalization is also the result of governments eliminating barriers to trade. In 1947, three international organizations were created for the promotion of trade — the General Agreement on Tariffs and Trade (GATT), the World Bank, and the International Monetary Fund (IMF).

- GATT, which began an ongoing process of reducing tariffs around the world, turned into the World Trade Organization (WTO). The WTO operates a global system of trade rules, helps negotiate trade agreements, and settles trade disputes between countries.

- The World Bank consists of two related institutions — the International Bank for Reconstruction and Development (IBRD) and the International Development Agency (IDA). The World Bank describes its mission as "inclusive and sustainable globalization," and strongly believes that free-market, government hands-off policies are best for promoting economic growth in developing countries.

- The IMF describes its mission as fostering global monetary cooperation, securing financial stability, facilitating international trade, promoting high employment and sustainable economic growth, and reducing poverty.

Globalization is also speeding up because of free-trade agreements among countries decreasing tariffs, quotas, and domestic subsidies, combined with efforts of the WTO, World Bank, and IMF to reduce protectionist policies impeding trade.

Globalization itself — the integration of economic activities, across borders, through markets — is neither good nor bad. But the consequences of globalization for different groups can be good or bad. There are winners and losers from globalization, just as there are winners and losers from trade within a country.

Sweatshops versus Farms   The new markets and opportunities from globalization may not look good to us, even though the participants see them as major improvements in their lives. When we hear of the low pay and working conditions in sweatshops, our first thoughts may be that these workers are being exploited in the interest of corporate profits.

But that does not explain why millions of young Chinese women voluntarily choose low-wage factory jobs over life on the farm in rural China. One woman, who fled to the Shenzhen factory zone in southern China, felt almost anything was better than life on the family rubber farm:

> "Every morning, from 4 a.m. to 7 a.m. you have to cut through the bark of 400 rubber trees in total darkness. It has to be done before daybreak, otherwise the sunshine will evaporate the rubber juice. If you were me, what would you prefer, the factory or the farm?"

In evaluating sweatshop jobs, always ask a key question about opportunity cost. Are workers' lives better, or worse, compared to a situation without globalization, trade, and the factory jobs that follow? This is the same question behind the Jill and Marie example — are they better off with specialization and trade, or better off being self-sufficient? When workers voluntarily choose the sweatshop over the farm, it is because, from their perspective, factory jobs make them better off. What looks like poverty to us, and is poverty by Western standards, is a rising standard of living for the workers measured by their standards.

Sweatshops throughout History   The story of workers migrating from farms to factory jobs is not new. In the original English cotton factories of the late 1700s, people with few opportunities moved from farms to the original sweatshops in cities. While the working conditions and pay were terrible, they were better than the alternative.

The same pattern repeated in the United States cotton industry in New Hampshire and Massachusetts in the 1800s, where many French Canadians worked. The pattern continued in the Japanese textile industry in the 1920s and in Korea and Taiwan in the 1970s and 1980s. In all of these countries, standards of living and working conditions improved over time. Some of those improvements came from governments playing a hands-on role, and some happened when the government took a hands-off role.

As globalization connected the textile industry to new markets and new competitors, less competitive textile industries in older countries declined. Expanded trade created winners and losers. But overall standards of living have continued to rise in the countries whose textile industries ultimately lost out to new competitors — first England, then the United States, Japan, South Korea, and Taiwan. New and better-paying jobs were created in other export industries where the countries had a comparative advantage.

Winners and Losers from Globalization   Globalization continues this pattern today. While specialization and trade bring mutually beneficial gains to countries, there are individual groups within a country who win and who lose. Jamaica, for example, reduced trade barriers to milk imports in 1992. Local dairy farmers were losers, having to compete with cheaper imports of milk powder. Jamaican milk production dropped significantly. But poor children, who could get imported milk more cheaply, were winners.

With a better understanding of what globalization is, can we reconcile the apparent contradiction between pro-trade arguments that gains for trade are the key to rising living standards, and the anti-globalization accusations that global trade causes harm in so many ways?

 # Practice...

11. Economic globalization is the integration of

    a. banks, businesses, and labour.

    b. economic activities in developed countries.

    c. markets in developing countries.

    d. economic activities through markets, across borders.

12. When economists evaluate sweatshops, they ask the question, "Are sweatshop

    a. workers' wages too low?"

    b. workers exploited for corporate profits"

    c. workers' lives better than a situation without the sweatshop jobs?"

    d. workers' lives better than the lives of workers in the developed world?"

13. The pace of globalization is increasing for all of the following reasons *except*

    a. easier international communication.

    b. rising self-sufficiency.

    c. falling tariffs.

    d. falling transportation costs.

14. Which country has had textile sweatshops?

    a. England

    b. Japan

    c. United States

    d. all of the above

15. Competitive forces from increased international trade eventually

    a. reduce unemployment.

    b. increase living standards.

    c. eliminate protectionism.

    d. ensure social justice.

🫂 Apply...

7. In your own words, define economic globalization. Provide one example of how globalization has affected you.

    _____

    _____

    _____

    _____

    _____

    _____

8. Watch the first minutes of the *Wall Street Journal* video, "Why Clothes Might Not Be Made in China Much Longer" at http://tinyurl.com/FlexText-Sweatshops. Your instructor may start a discussion about the video. Possible discussion questions include:

    - What is happening to wages and the location of clothing production in China?

    - How does this compare with the history described in the chapter of sweatshops in England, the United States, Japan, Korea, and Taiwan?

    - Are businesses in the clothing industry price takers or price makers?

    - What are the incentives for businesses to move production from one country to another?

    _____

    _____

    _____

    _____

    _____

    _____

9. What argument would you make to counter the claim that all sweatshop workers are exploited by big business?

    _____

    _____

    _____

    _____

    _____

    _____

    _____

    _____

    _____

Governments and Global Markets

 Evaluate the hands-off and hands-on arguments about the role for government in the globalization debate.

Is globalization a force for good or for evil? Does globalization bring rising living standards or a descent into poverty? The answers to these questions lead back to the fundamental macroeconomic question:

If left alone by government,
how quickly do the price mechanisms of market economies adjust
to maintain steady growth in living standards, full employment, and stable prices?

More simply, if left alone, do markets quickly self-adjust?

Economists and politicians fall into two main camps in answering this question: "Yes — Markets Quickly Self Adjust, So Government Hands-Off" and "No — Markets Fail Often, So Government Hands-On." But this time, the question is not about markets within a country, but *markets across connected countries*. Should governments in the global economy be hands-off or hands-on?

The way economists debate the hands-off versus hands-on answers changed fundamentally when Joseph Stiglitz published an influential bestselling book in 2002 titled *Globalization and Its Discontents*. Before then, most economists dismissed protestors opposing free trade and self-adjusting markets as misguided do-gooders who did not understand the concept of comparative advantage. But Stiglitz added his support to the protesters! His support was influential because of his credentials — serving on the Council of Economic Advisors under U.S. President Clinton, and then as chief economist at the World Bank. He left the World Bank after three years, and was awarded the Nobel Prize in Economics in 2001. As an insider at the (hands-off–oriented) World Bank, and winner of the most prestigious prize an economist can get, Stiglitz's hands-off criticisms counted.

Government Hands-On

Although a great believer in markets, Stiglitz's own position is hands-on, favouring an "important, if limited, role for government to play." The government hands-on position believes government in all countries has a responsibility to maintain a social safety net to support the welfare of citizens left behind by trade and markets — especially by labour markets that determine incomes. Specialization, trade, and competition — whether within a country or between countries — always create winners and losers.

In Canada, there are many government programs to assist those who lose from expanded trade. There are Employment Insurance benefits for the unemployed, job retraining programs, social assistance payments, and health-care benefits that do not depend upon having a job. Most poor, developing countries do not have a social safety net, so the competitive forces of international competition can lead to poverty and misery as jobs disappear in import-competing industries. Social safety-net programs cost money that governments in poor countries may not have.

Like any policy choice, there is an opportunity cost of expanding government's role. Once governments take a hands-on role helping people and industries who lose from international competition, the risk is that special-interest groups will ask the government to protect them from such competition.

Government Hands-Off

The government hands-off position leaves markets alone to produce economic growth that eventually benefits all. The risk is that losers from international trade in import-competing industries will get no government assistance in adjusting to structural unemployment and poverty.

This hands-off position is not as heartless as it sounds. By allowing the government to get involved, positive effects from social safety-net policies are outweighed by negative effects from protectionist policies supported by special-interest groups.

This editorial from *The Economist* magazine illustrates the reasoning behind the hands-off position. *The Economist* supports free markets and globalization, and generally opposes government "interference" in economic or social activity. What is striking is the support the editorial seems to give to the anti-globalization critics.

> Rich countries' trade rules, especially in farming and textiles, still discriminate powerfully against poor countries. Rich countries' subsidies encourage wasteful use of energy and natural resources, and harm the environment. . . . Rich countries' protection of intellectual property discriminates unfairly against the developing world. And without a doubt, rich countries' approach to financial regulation offers implicit subsidies to their banks and encourages reckless lending; it results, time and again, in financial crises in rich and poor countries alike.
>
> All these policies owe much to the fact that corporate interests exercise undue influence over government policy. [Critics] are right to deplore this. But undue influence is hardly new in democratic politics; it has not been created by globalisation forcing governments to bow down. . . . If allowed to, all governments are happy to seek political advantage by granting preferences.

The Economist magazine, "A different manifesto", 2001

The Economist's argument is that the harm that poor countries suffer is not caused by market forces but by government action.

Market Failure or Government Failure?

Specialization and trade — whether within a country or across the globe — always creates winners and losers. Competitive forces generally cause rising standards of living, but can also cause poverty and misery as jobs disappear in import-competing industries. Both the hands-on and hands-off positions recognize these unfortunate outcomes as the side effects of specialization, trade, and economic growth.

Stiglitz's hands-on position sees an important, but limited, role for government. Government, particularly in developing countries, should maintain a social safety net to support the economic welfare of citizens left behind by trade and markets — especially labour markets that determine incomes.

The hands-off position sees many unfortunate globalization outcomes resulting not from trade, but from government interference in markets. Tariffs, quotas, and domestic subsidies — responses to political pressure from industries and workers harmed by competing imports — create unfair terms of trade and disadvantage industries and workers in the poorest countries.

What Do You Think?   As a citizen of Canada and the world, you must decide what globalization and trade policies you will support. There are no right or easy choices, only trade-offs.

If you think it is important for all governments to help losers from expanded trade in import-competing industries — in Canada or abroad — the risk is that governments will also give in to political pressure and introduce protectionist policies that slow the expansion of trade and economic growth. If you support this hands-on position, you are betting that market failure is worse than government failure. The failure of markets to produce rising standards of living for all, full employment, and stable prices is more likely and costly than government failing by giving in to political pressure from special interests for market protection.

If you think the markets are best left alone to produce economic growth that eventually benefits all, the risk is that losers from expanded trade in import-competing industries end up in poverty and misery. If you support this hands-off position, you are betting that government failure is worse than market failure. The failure of government, that comes from introducing protectionist policies that are not in society's best interests, is more likely and costly than markets failing in the form of falling living standards for those in import-competing industries.

 # Practice...

16. In the globalization debate, hands-on economists believe

    a. government should provide social safety nets.

    b. government failure is worse than market failure.

    c. businesses should provide social safety nets.

    d. sweatshops should all be shut down.

17. Hands-off economists argue that social safety nets are *not* a good globalization policy because

    a. market failure will happen.

    b. developing countries will not export.

    c. developed countries will not import.

    d. special-interest groups will gain control of government policies.

18. The economist who changed the globalization debate was

    a. Joseph Stiglitz.

    b. Naomi Klein.

    c. J.M. Keynes.

    d. Donald Trump.

19. Joseph Stiglitz

    a. wrote *Globalization and Its Discontents*.

    b. was chief economist at the World Bank.

    c. won the Nobel Prize in Economics.

    d. did all of the above.

20. The biggest risk from a hands-on globalization policy is that

    a. jobs disappear in import-competing industries.

    b. markets will fail.

    c. government gives into political pressure for protectionism.

    d. losers in import-competing businesses get no assistance in adjusting to change.

 **Apply...**

10. This question, and question 11, are about protectionism, international trade, and government policies.

   a. List the three main government forms of protectionism.

   _____

   _____

   _____

   _____

   _____

   b. International trade can produce mutually benefical gains, as well as winners and losers.
   In any country, who are the winners from increased international trade? Who are the losers?

   _____

   _____

   _____

   _____

   _____

11. A March 2016 *New York Times* article, "Donald Trump Breaks with 200 Years of Economic Orthodoxy,"
reports Trump's opposition to free trade. He intends to protect American workers from what he claims
is unfair trade.

   According to the article, trade has a downside and, while the benefits of trade are broadly distributed,
the costs are often concentrated. . . . Pietra Rivoli, a finance professor at Georgetown University who
explored the impact of increased globalization in her 2005 book, *The Travels of a T-Shirt in the Global
Economy*, said Mr. Trump may be finding a receptive audience because the United States has provided
relatively little help to workers harmed by trade.

   "You have much more negative sentiment about trade in the U.S. than you do in pretty much any other
wealthy country, and they've lost their T-shirt jobs, too," Ms. Rivoli said. "What's going on there is that in
those countries — which are even more exposed to trade than we are — those countries have a bigger
safety net."

   a. Explain how the distribution of the benefits and costs of trade mentioned in the article creates
      domestic political pressure to protect trade losers from freer trade (causing many in the United
      States to support Trump's protectionist policies).

   _____

   _____

   _____

   _____

   _____

   _____

to be continued

Apply...

continued

b. In the article, Professor Rivoli refers to safety nets. Explain the hands-on policy for social safety nets to deal with adjustments to freer trade. What is the risk of this government hands-on approach?

_____

_____

_____

_____

_____

_____

_____

_____

_____

12. Consider *The Economist's* position on globalization.

> Rich countries' trade rules, especially in farming and textiles, still discriminate powerfully against poor countries. Rich countries' subsidies encourage wasteful use of energy and natural resources, and harm the environment. . . . Rich countries' protection of intellectual property discriminates unfairly against the developing world. And without a doubt, rich countries' approach to financial regulation offers implicit subsidies to their banks and encourages reckless lending; it results, time and again, in financial crises in rich and poor countries alike.
>
> All these policies owe much to the fact that corporate interests exercise undue influence over government policy. [Critics] are right to deplore this. But undue influence is hardly new in democratic politics; it has not been created by globalisation forcing governments to bow down. . . . If allowed to, all governments are happy to seek political advantage by granting preferences.

How does it seem to support hands-on globalization critics, and hands-off government failure believers?

_____

_____

_____

_____

_____

_____

_____

_____

KNOW...

Summary of Learning Objectives

1. Opportunity cost and comparative advantage are key to understanding why specializing and trading make us all better off. There are mutually beneficial gains from trade if each producer specializes in producing the product for which they have a **comparative advantage** — the ability to produce at a *lower opportunity cost* than another producer. The division of the gains from trade between countries depends on the **terms of trade,** which must be between the opportunity costs that each trader faces locally.

2. Freer trade creates winners and losers from international competition. Concentrated losses in import-competing industries create political pressure for protectionism despite overall gains. Protectionism takes the form of **tariffs**, **import quotas**, and **subsidies to domestic producers**.

3. While anti-globalization critics view sweatshops as the outcome of **economic globalization** and free-market policies, economists ask whether workers are better off or worse off with international trade.

4. What role should government play in global markets? The hands-on position wants a government social safety net to support workers left behind or losing from international trade, but with the risk that once government is involved, it gives in to political pressure for protectionism. The hands-off position is that by allowing the government to get involved, any positive effects from social safety-net policies will be outweighed by negative effects from protectionist policies supported by special-interest groups. The risk is that losers in import-competing industries get no assistance in adjusting to trade.

Key Terms

absolute advantage: the ability to produce a product or service at a lower absolute cost than another producer

comparative advantage: the ability to produce a product or service at lower opportunity cost than another producer

economic globalization: integration of economic activities across borders, through markets

import quota: limit on the quantity of a product or service that can be imported

structural unemployment: due to technological change or international competition that makes workers' skills obsolete; there is a mismatch between the skills workers have and the skills new jobs require

subsidies to domestic producers: government payment to domestic producers of products or services

tariff: tax applied to imports

terms of trade: quantity of exports required to pay for one unit of imports

Answers to Practice

1. **b** Differences in opportunity costs key to mutually beneficial gains. Voluntary trade happens only if both parties end up better off.

2. **a** Give up ÷ Get = 200 000 wheat ÷ 10 000 wine = 20 wheat per bottle of wine.

3. **c** Only way both traders gain for voluntary trade.

4. **d** Opportunity cost of 1 bottle wine is 1/3 wool in Portugal and 3 wool in England. No information about absolute advantage.

5. **b** Canada has absolute advantage (lower labour inputs) in both oil and apples. Mexico's opportunity cost of additional apples is 12 hours of labour, which would produce 1.5 barrels of oil. Canada's opportunity cost of additional apples is 8 hours of labour, which would produce 2 barrels of oil.

6. **b** Terms of trade are the ratio at which traded products exchange.

7. **d** Structural unemployment is caused by jobs becoming obsolete due to new technologies or international competition.

8. **c** Consumers benefit from lower prices, while import-competing businesses and workers lose.

9. **d** Losses are concentrated in import-competing industries that might go out of business with workers losing their jobs.

10. **a** Because the U.S. market is ten times larger than Canada's, most profit-seeking cultural productions in Canada would try and serve the U.S. market instead of Canada without government encouragement.

11. **d** Markets become more connected and interdependent.

12. **c** Economists ask the opportunity cost question, "Are workers' lives better off, or worse off, compared to a situation without globalization and trade?"

13. **b** More self-sufficiency would mean less trade and integration of economic activities across countries.

14. **d** Also Korea and Taiwan, before current sweatshops in China and southeast Asia.

15. **b** The belief is leaving markets alone is most likely to produce economic growth that eventually benefits all.

16. **a** Hands-on position believes in a limited role for government to protect workers who lose from trade.

17. **d** The risk of government involvement is that special-interest groups will ask the government to protect them from competition with tariffs, quotas, and domestic subsidies that might create unfair terms of trade and disadvantage industries and workers in the poorest countries.

18. **a** With his 2002 book, *Globalization and Its Discontents*.

19. **d** Discussion in chapter.

20. **c** **a** and **d** are risks of hands-off policy. Hands-on economists believe markets will fail.

13 Controversies in Macroeconomics

LEARNING OBJECTIVES

L01 Describe the fundamental macroeconomic question and the hands-off and hands-on positions on government policy.

L02 For the loanable funds market, identify injections and leakages and explain the importance of expectations and interest rates in controversies over how well the market adjusts.

L03 Explain the differing hands-off and hands-on positions on the origins of business cycles and on how markets respond following a recession.

L04 Compare the hands-off and hands-on positions on monetary policy, and on aggregate demand and aggregate supply fiscal policies.

L05 Explain the hands-off and hands-on arguments about the role of government in the globalization debate.

LEARN...

Economists disagree far more about macroeconomics than microeconomics. This chapter simplifies those disagreements by going back to the fundamental macroeconomic question — *If left alone by government, how quickly do the price mechanisms of market economies adjust to maintain steady growth in living standards, full employment, and stable prices*?

Throughout this book, I have simplified those disagreements into two camps — "Markets Quickly Self-Adjust, So Government Hands-Off" and "Markets Fail Often, So Government Hands-On." While most macroeconomists do not fit neatly into either camp, the simplification gives you a manageable framework for understanding macroeconomic controversies and for thinking about the appropriate role for government policy. I have tried to present the position of each camp as sympathetically as possible.

As a citizen, politicians ask for your vote supporting policies that roughly divide into government hands-off or hands-on the economy. This framework will help you choose. Economists and politicians disagree so you must decide which position makes most sense to you. Your personal economic success will be affected by the performance of the economy, and that performance is affected by government polices put in place by politicians you elect.

This final chapter of controversies extends the discussion of topics in previous chapters — Chapter 4 (From Microeconomics to Macroeconomics), Chapter 7 (The Aggregate Supply and Aggregate Demand Model), Chapter 10 (Money and Monetary Policy), Chapter 11 (Fiscal Policy, Multipliers, Deficits, and Debt), and Chapter 12 (Globalization, Trade, and Protectionism).

Should the government keep its hands off the economy, or be hands-on? Your choice.

Macroeconomic Disagreements and Agreements

L01 Describe the fundamental macroeconomic question and the hands-off and hands-on positions on government policy.

Disagreements and agreements among modern macroeconomists and politicians go back to Say's Law and the simple circular flow model in Chapter 1.

Say's Law and the Fundamental Macroeconomic Question

Before the Great Depression of the 1930s, most economists believed in the miracle of markets working well and adjusting to changes without any role for government besides enforcing the rules of the game. The belief that market economies with flexible prices always quickly self-adjust is based on **Say's Law**, which claims that "supply creates its own demand." We can illustrate Say's Law using the circular flow model in Figure 1.

Figure 1   The Circular Flow Model

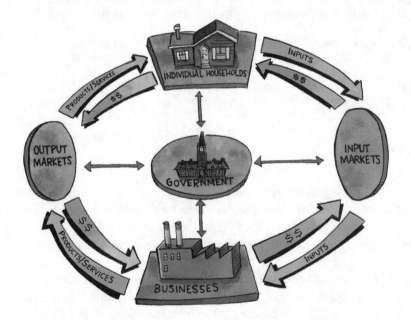

Starting at the top, households *supply* inputs to businesses in exchange for money. Households sell their inputs in input markets because they want the money to *demand* products and services in output markets. When households spend all of the money earned in input markets to buy products and services in output markets, supply does create its own demand. As the flow continues smoothly around the circle, markets quickly adjust to maintain steady growth in living standards, full employment, and stable prices. There might be small, temporary ups and downs, but in the long run, flexible prices quickly restore the balance between demand and supply, so that the economy produces good results and the miracle of markets.

Macroeconomics began in the 1930s with Keynes's rejection of Say's Law as a "special theory" that sometimes holds true but usually does not. Keynes's more "general theory" allowed both short-run and long-run answers to the fundamental question organizing our study of macroeconomics.

Fundamental Macroeconomic Question   The fundamental macroeconomic question is

If left alone by government,
how quickly do the price mechanisms of market economies adjust
to maintain steady growth in living standards, full employment, and stable prices?

The answers to that question divide macroeconomists into two major camps. One camp, continuing Say's focus on the long run, is "Markets Quickly Self-Adjust, So Government Hands-Off." The second camp, "Markets Fail Often, So Government Hands-On," continues Keynes's focus on the short run.

Explaining the disagreements between the two camps is easier if we first review the concepts of market failure and government failure.

Market Failure and Government Failure   All economists agree that sometimes markets fail to produce outcomes in the public interest. In microeconomics, this can happen due to externalities or economies of scale that allow large businesses to monopolize a market. In macroeconomics, market failures take the form of business cycles with falling living standards, unemployment, inflation, or deflation. When there is market failure, government policy that acts in the public interest might improve market outcomes.

It is also possible that government policy may *not* act in the public interest. Political pressure can cause governments to act in the interests of businesses, labour organizations, or other special-interest groups. Even when aiming for the public interest, policymakers often lack timely and accurate information for making smart policy decisions. Government policymakers can make "honest mistakes" when trying to solve complex macroeconomic problems. When government policy fails to serve the public interest, it is called **government failure.** Business cycles can be caused by market failure, but they also can be caused by bad government policies. When there is government failure, leaving markets alone might produce an outcome that better serves the public interest.

The "Markets Quickly Self-Adjust, So Government Hands-Off" camp believes that government failure is more likely than market failure. The "Markets Fail Often, So Government Hands-On" camp believes that market failure is more likely than government failure.

Let's look more carefully at the other differences between the two camps.

Markets Quickly Self-Adjust, So Government Hands-Off

The "Markets Quickly Self-Adjust, So Government Hands-Off" camp of economists argues that, if left alone by government, the price mechanisms of market economies adjust quickly to maintain steady growth in living standards, full employment, and stable prices. They believe that business cycles, occasional unemployment, and inflation are caused by events outside the economy (like natural disasters or technological change) or by government policies. They argue that markets are the most flexible way for the economy to adjust to changes, even if those adjustments take some time. These economists believe that rational expectations, money, and banks improve the exchanges of physical products and services around the circular flow, and improve the coordination between input and output markets.

Believers that markets self-adjust — usually quickly, always in the long run — see little role for government policy that interferes with markets. This camp believes that even when markets temporarily fail, government policy usually makes things worse, not better. Therefore, this camp argues for a hands-off role for government.

Politicians on the Political Right   Politicians on the right of the political spectrum — Conservatives and Libertarians in Canada, Republicans in the United States — fit into this camp, supporting a hands-off role for government. They believe that, if left alone by government, markets will produce efficient outcomes and rising standards of living, full employment, and stable prices.

Markets Fail Often, So Government Hands-On

The "Markets Fail Often, So Government Hands-On" camp argues that, if left alone by government, the self-adjusting mechanisms of market economies can be slow and weak. As a result, business cycles happen often in the short run, with extended periods of unemployment that reduce living standards, and with inflation or deflation. They believe that most economic problems are caused internally as unintended by-products of volatile expectations and markets with sticky prices. This camp emphasizes that expectations, money, and banks can block the coordination between input and output markets. While they prefer the flexibility of market economies to any other economic system, these economists see self-interest and greed creating speculative bubbles that inevitably cause cycles of boom and bust.

Believers that markets create economic problems on their own and often fail — rarely reaching long-run equilibrium — see an important role for government policy that serves the public interest. Market failure problems can be serious and persistent. Therefore, this camp argues for a hands-on role for government. In the icon of the hands-on camp, the hands hold the broken connections between input and output markets that cause markets to fail.

Politicians on the Political Left   Politicians on the left of the political spectrum — federal Liberals, New Democrats, and the Bloc Québécois in Canada, Democrats in the United States — fit into this camp, supporting a hands-on role for government. They believe that if left alone, markets will produce inequality in rising living standards, with much economic insecurity and hardship during recessions for those who do not have skills that markets value. Government has a responsibility to maintain a social safety net to support the economic welfare of citizens left behind by markets, especially labour markets.

Modern Macroeconomic Camps

I have divided economists and politicians into only two camps to give you a simplified framework for understanding macroeconomics and for thinking about the appropriate role for government economic policy. Your textbook or instructor may mention many more macroeconomic schools or models. Here is how they fit into the simplified camps.

Left Alone, Market Quickly Self-Adjust, So Government Hands-Off
Keynes referred to economists before him who believed in Say's Law as classical economists. That label continues. Modern economists in this camp include those labelled as Classical, Neoclassical, and New Classical. Rational Expectations, Monetarist, Supply-Side, and Real Business Cycle models also fit into this camp. These economists and models emphasize rational expectations, flexible prices, quickly self-adjusting markets, and a long-run focus on economic growth.

Left Alone, Market Fail Often, So Government Hands-On
Modern economists in this camp are all intellectual descendants of Keynes, and their schools and models contain his name — Keynesians, New Keynesians, Neo-Keynesians, and Post Keynesians. These economists and models emphasize volatile expectations, sticky prices, slowly adjusting or failed markets, and a short-run focus on business cycles.

Agreements and Disagreements

While the rest of this chapter focuses on macroeconomic controversies, there are substantial agreements among macroeconomists. All macroeconomists agree that

- *there is some role for government in setting the rules of the game.* They differ on how small or large a role government policy to change the economy should play.
- *prices and markets adjust.* They differ on how long the adjustment takes, and whether prices are flexible or sticky in adjusting.
- *savings and business investment are important in determining macroeconomic outcomes.* They differ on whether interest rates or expectations are most important for investment decisions, and on how savings and investment interact in the loanable funds market.
- *business cycles happen in the short run.* They differ on whether the causes are external or internal to the economy, and on how markets respond after a boom or bust.
- *there is long-run economic growth.* They differ in focusing on the long-run successes of growth or the short-run problems of business cycles.

When you add the agreements to the disagreements, the differences between the camps are more subtle than a yes or no answer to the simple question, "If left alone, do markets quickly self-adjust?"

But thinking of the positions of only two camps — "Markets Quickly Self-Adjust, So Government Hands-Off" and "Market Fail Often, So Government Hands-On" — will simplify your understanding of macroeconomics. And focusing on the differences in the rest of this chapter will help you make up your own mind about which position makes most sense to you, and which politicians and economic policies you will vote for.

Practice...

1. Say's Law claims that

   a. supply is greater than demand.

   b. demand is greater than supply.

   c. supply creates its own demand.

   d. demand creates its own supply.

2. There is government failure when

   a. markets quickly self-adjust.

   b. government policy serves the public interest.

   c. policymakers are captured by special-interest groups.

   d. economists lie to politicians.

3. The hands-off camp believes that business cycles are caused by

   a. the banking system.

   b. external events.

   c. expectations.

   d. money.

4. The hands-on camp believes that

   a. market failure is worse than government failure.

   b. external events cause most business cycles.

   c. supply creates its own demand.

   d. demand creates its own supply.

5. Macroeconomists agree that

   a. there is a role for government.

   b. business cycles happen.

   c. prices and markets adjust.

   d. all of the above are true.

Apply...

1. Watch the video *Fear the Boom and Bust* at http://tinyurl.com/FlexText-Boom-Bust.

   The video is a lively introduction to the fundamental macroeconomic question, transforming the abstract differences between the "Markets Quickly Self-Adjust, So Government Hands-Off" and the "Markets Fail Often, So Government Hands-On" camps into a personal fight between F. von Hayek and Keynes. The chorus of the video captures the difference between camps:

   [Keynes] "I want to steer markets."

   [Hayek] "I want them set free."

   The instructor may use the video for a discussion about differences among macroeconomists.

Apply...

2. Explain the two different types of government failure.

    _____

    _____

    _____

    _____

    _____

3. List the five areas of agreement among macroeconomists.

    _____

    _____

    _____

    _____

    _____

    _____

    _____

    _____

Business Investment, Savings, and Loanable Funds

L02 For the loanable funds market, identify injections and leakages and explain the importance of expectations and interest rates in controversies over how well the market adjusts.

Injections and leakages play an important role in macroeconomics, determining levels and fluctuations of real GDP. **Injections** of business **investment spending** (*I*) and **leakages** of savings (*S*) are most important for understanding disagreements among macroeconomists.

Remember the paradox of thrift? If one person saves more, his savings increase and spending decreases. But if many people save more and spend less, businesses experience falling sales, cut back production, and lay off workers so that incomes fall. There may be *less* saving, because without income, people have to withdraw their savings from banks.

When macroeconomic players, especially consumers, save instead of spend, Say's Law appears to be in trouble. If the income earned by supplying inputs in input markets is *not* all spent in output markets buying the products and services produced with those inputs, how does supply create its own demand?

Loanable Funds Market

The banking system can save the day (pun intended). Banks can loan out the saved funds to business borrowers who use the money to finance investment in new factories and equipment. That *injection* of additional business investment spending, beyond what consumers spend, replaces the *leakage* of consumer savings. Aggregate income earned in input markets is again equal to aggregate spending in output markets. Aggregate supply equals aggregate demand.

Economists also refer to the banking system as the **loanable funds market**. Banks take in money (funds) in the form of savings, and loan out money (funds) to borrowers. Businesses do most of the borrowing in this market to finance investment spending on new factories or equipment. The interaction between the supply of savings and the demand for borrowing determines the interest rate. The interest rate is the price of borrowing money in the loanable funds market, as well as the reward for saving.

Whether Say's Law holds true or not depends on how well the loanable funds market works. Macroeconomists disagree about that. Figure 2 shows the supply and demand for loanable funds.

Figure 2   The Loanable Funds Market

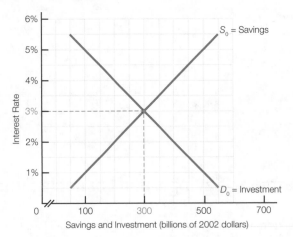

The horizontal axis measures the quantities of money (funds) that are saved or borrowed for business investment. The interest rate is on the vertical axis. The supply curve of savings in the loanable funds market is upward-sloping, like any supply curve. Higher interest rates make saving more attractive, so people save more.

The demand for loanable funds comes mostly from businesses. To build new factories or buy new equipment, businesses usually borrow. Those investments produce a stream of revenues over many years, but the business has to pay for the machinery before the revenues come in.

The demand curve for loanable funds for business investment spending (I) is downward-sloping, like any demand curve. Higher interest rates increase the cost of borrowing, leading businesses to cancel some investment projects that are no longer profitable, and to borrow less. Lower interest rates decrease the cost of borrowing and make more projects profitable, so businesses borrow more.

The intersection of the supply and demand curves determines the interest rate. The interest rate is the equilibrium price in the loanable funds market, equalizing the quantity demanded and quantity supplied of funds. In this example, the interest rate is 3 percent and $300 billion is the quantity invested and saved. Notice that the interest rate equalizes injections (I) and leakages (S).

Expectations and Changes in Supply or Demand   The loanable funds supply and demand curves, like all supply and demand curves, hold other factors unchanged. After the interest rate, *expectations* are the most important factor affecting consumer saving decisions and business investment decisions.

In drawing the supply of savings curve, we assume consumers' expected future income is unchanged. If expected future income decreases, consumers will want to save more in the present, so the supply of savings curve shifts rightward. If expected future income increases, consumers don't have to worry as much about saving for the future, so they spend more in the present and the supply of savings curve shifts leftward.

In drawing the demand for loanable funds curve, we assume business expectations about future economic conditions are unchanged. How much future revenue a business *expects* from a new factory depends on whether the business is optimistic or pessimistic about future economic conditions. When expectations become more optimistic, the investment demand curve shifts rightward. At any interest rate, more investment projects are exptected to be profitable, so businesses demand more loanable funds. When expectations become more pessimistic, the investment demand curve shifts leftward.

Up to this point, macroeconomists agree about the description of the loanable funds market. They disagree about

- the nature of expectations.
- whether interest rates or expectations are more important for determining business investment decisions.
- how the loanable funds market reacts to changes in expectations.

Expectations

One of the biggest disagreements between the hands-off and hands-on camps is over expectations about the future.

Rational and Stable Expectations for Hands-Off   The "Markets Quickly Self-Adjust, So Government Hands-Off" camp sees individuals and businesses as making logical rational choices based on the best information available. Like Mr. Spock, the Vulcan of *Star Trek*, even investment spending decisions about unknown future economic conditions are made coolly and efficiently.

Since this camp believes the economy always stays close to long-run macroeconomic equilibrium with full employment and stable prices, the future is expected to be much like the present. Business expectations are stable, and the demand curve for loanable funds does not shift much.

With rational and unchanging expectations, the most important factor determining business investment decisions for this camp is the interest rate.

Volatile Expectations for Hands-On   The "Markets Fail Often, So Government Hands-On" camp emphasizes the fundamental uncertainty about the future. Because no one knows the future, business investment decisions are based on expectations. Investment decisions are based largely on a gut-level instinct to act, which Keynes called "animal spirits."

With few solid facts about the future, business investors look for guidance to what other investors are doing. This "herd mentality" causes boom and bust cycles like the Global Financial Crisis. When housing prices are rising and everyone is making money in the real estate market, it is tempting to join the crowd and start investing. But without solid facts, when pessimism appears, it too can easily spread, causing prices to fall quickly.

Investment decisions to build a new factory are also volatile because they are easily postponed — the business will just continue with its current factory. In comparison, consumption decisions (for example, about eating) are stable and not easily postponed.

Fundamental uncertainty about the future, reliance on the "herd" of other equally uncertain investors for guidance, and the postponable nature of investment all combine to make expectations and investment spending decisions very volatile.

Volatile expectations, and shifts of the demand curve for loanable funds, are far more important than the interest rate in determining business investment decisions for the hands-on camp.

Does the Loanable Funds Market Quickly Self-Adjust?

The best way to see the disagreements between macroeconomists is to start with consumers' decisions to save more, and compare how the two camps analyze what follows. Figure 3 starts with equilibrium in the loanable funds market, followed by an increasing in savings — a rightward shift of the supply of savings curve from to S_0 to S_1.

Figure 3   An Increase in Savings in the Loanable Funds Market

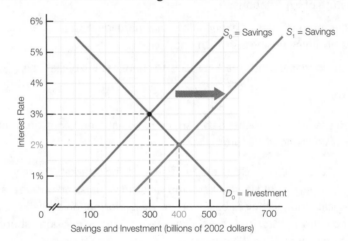

Here are the very different stories the two camps tell about what happens next.

Markets Quickly Self-Adjust with Unchanging Expectations   For the "Markets Quickly Self-Adjust, So Government Hands-Off" camp, the increase in savings causes the equilibrium interest rate — the price in the loanable funds market — to fall from 3 percent to 2 percent. While the increase in savings might seem to threaten Say's Law, the lower interest rate leads businesses to increase their investment spending from $300 billion to $400 billion. This additional injection of business investment spending replaces the new consumer savings. Aggregate income earned in input markets is again equal to aggregate spending in output markets. Aggregate supply equals aggregate demand.

Even though consumers are spending less today, businesses do not become pessimistic about profits. There is no change in expectations, and the investment demand curve does not shift. In fact, businesses see consumers' decisions to save more today as a sign that consumers will spend more in the future. That is why rational, forward-looking businesses increase their spending on new factories or equipment — to meet that anticipated future demand for products and services.

The flexibility of prices (the interest rate) allows the loanable funds market to quickly self-adjust, restoring the balance between injections and leakages. Even if that adjustment is slow in the short run, it will certainly happen in the long run.

Markets Fail Often with Volatile Expectations   The "Markets Fail Often, So Government Hands-On" camp agrees that the fall in interest rates, other things unchanged, might increase business investment spending. But with falling sales in the present, businesses get worried about future sales. That pessimism about future economic conditions causes the investment demand curve to shift leftward (not shown on the graph). The negative effects of more pessimistic expectations are greater than the positive effects of lower interest rates. Investment spending decreases. This is what happened during the Global Financial Crisis. Despite dramatic decreases in interest rates, business investment spending *decreased* dramatically. That negative aggregate demand shock pushes the economy into recession.

Despite the flexibility of the price (interest rate) in the loanable funds market, that market, and input and output markets generally, fail to adjust.

Macroeconomists clearly differ about the nature of expectations, and the effect of expectations on business investment decisions.

Practice...

6. When consumers save some of their income, what can save Say's Law?

    a. business investment spending financed by borrowed funds

    b. consumer saving

    c. consumer spending

    d. Wonder Woman

7. In the loanable funds market,

    a. an increase in consumer savings causes the interest rate to rise.

    b. more optimistic business expectations cause the interest rate to fall.

    c. consumers do most of the borrowing to finance mortgages and car loans.

    d. businesses do most of the borrowing to finance investment spending on new factories.

8. Which statement is *false*?

    a. The interest rate is the price of loanable funds.

    b. A decrease in the supply of loanable funds causes the interest rate to rise.

    c. An increase in savings causes the interest rate to rise.

    d. An increase in the demand for loanable funds causes the interest rate to rise.

9. The hands-off camp believes that investors behave like

    a. herds of animals.

    b. logical, rational Vulcans.

    c. animal spirits.

    d. broken thermostats.

10. The hands-on camp believes that investors behave like

    a. herds of animals.

    b. logical, rational Vulcans.

    c. spirited animals.

    d. thermostats.

Apply...

4. Describe the role of "animal spirits" in the hands-on camp explanation of volatile expectations for investors.

    _____

    _____

    _____

    _____

5. Suppose you dream about this chapter the night before the test. You remember parts of four different dreams — and in each dream you are being initiated either by the hands-off camp or hands-on camp. For each dream, determine whether it was about the hands-off or the hands-on camp.

    a. Rollercoaster initiation: You are sent down a rollercoaster that has huge expansions and contractions.

    _____

    _____

    b. *Star Trek* initiation: They dress you up as their favourite *Star Trek* character — Spock — and remove your blindfold to see if you can determine which camp they are from.

    _____

    _____

    c. Thermostat initiation: They put you in a room with a really slow thermostat, which represents the speed at which they think the economy automatically adjusts after a shock.

    _____

    _____

    d. Graffiti initiation: They spray paint your room with an anarchy symbol, which represents "no government intervention."

    _____

    _____

    _____

6. From an initial equilibrium, explain how more optimistic business expectations affect the loanable funds market. How is the equality of injections and leakages restored?

    _____

    _____

    _____

    _____

    _____

Origins of and Responses to Business Cycles

 L03 Explain the differing hands-off and hands-on positions on the origins
of business cycles and on how markets respond following a recession.

All macroeconomists agree that business cycles are triggered by shocks to
short-run aggregate supply or to aggregate demand. The disagreements
between camps, and their differing hands-off and hands-on roles for
government policy, come from differences in what each camp emphasizes as
the most important causes of business cycles, and how markets respond after
the economy goes into a recession.

This discussion of disagreements extends the discussion of the aggregate
supply and aggregate demand model in Chapter 7.

Origins of Business Cycles

What are the origins of the shocks that cause businesses cycles?

"Markets Quickly Self-Adjust, So Government Hands-Off"   According to
this camp, shocks to aggregate supply and aggregate demand largely come
from outside of the economy — aggregate supply shocks caused by nature
or scientific discoveries, and aggregate demand shocks caused by mistaken
government policies.

Nature-based negative supply shocks include natural disasters like
droughts, floods, or earthquakes that destroy inputs. Scientific discoveries
that enable technological change are a positive supply shock.

This camp also views mistaken government fiscal and monetary policies
as demand shocks that can trigger unemployment or inflation. A tax increase
is a negative demand shock that can cause a recession. Increased government
spending is a positive demand shock increasing inflation if the economy is
already operating at potential GDP. Government does not intend to cause
economic problems, but it is difficult to time policy decisions, and unintentional
policy mistakes based on incomplete information can cause business cycles.
For this camp, government is a cause of business cycles, not a solution.

"Markets Fail Often, So Government Hands-On"   This camp believes that
shocks to short-run aggregate supply and mostly to aggregate demand are
largely *internally generated* as unintended by-products of markets. Expectations,
the role of money, and connections between different market economies in
R.O.W. create aggregate demand shocks.

Because no one can foretell the future, business investment plans are
based on highly subjective guesses. Fundamental uncertainty about the future,
reliance on the "herd" of other equally uncertain investors for guidance, and
the postponable nature of investment all combine to make expectations and
investment spending decisions very volatile. Quickly changeable expectations
coming from inside the economy create fluctuating positive and negative
aggregate demand shocks. Statistically, business investment spending (I) is
the most volatile part of aggregate demand (AD = planned $C + I + G + X - IM$),
fluctuating much more from year to year than consumer spending, government
spending, or spending on imports. Fluctuating business investment spending
on factories and equipment also affects the quantity and quality of inputs,
causing shocks to (short-run and long-run) aggregate supply.

This camp emphasizes the role of money as a store of value. When
consumers are worried about the uncertain future and risks of falling asset
prices, they take more of their wealth out of bonds and into money. When

worrying about the future, consumers save more from their incomes and businesses save more from their revenues. Increased savings by consumers and decreased business investment spending due to more pessimistic expectations are a self-fulfilling prophecy, causing a negative aggregate demand shock and recession.

In international trade markets, this camp worries about fluctuating Canadian exports due to business cycles in other countries (R.O.W.). Exports (X) are the second most volatile part of aggregate demand, and can cause negative or positive demand shocks.

In summary, the "Markets Quickly Self-Adjust, So Government Hands-Off" camp's explanations of the origins of business cycles emphasize aggregate supply shocks that are external to the economy, or aggregate demand shocks from mistaken government fiscal or monetary policies. The "Markets Fail Often, So Government Hands-On" camp emphasizes aggregate demand shocks that are internal to the operation of the economy, originating in volatile expectations and fluctuations in business investment spending and export spending by R.O.W.

Market Responses to Business Cycles

Once aggregate supply (SAS) or aggregate demand (AD) shocks happen, macroeconomists agree on using the AS/AD model to predict the effect on real GDP, unemployment, and the price level. The disagreements come in analyzing how markets respond once the economy is in a **recessionary gap**.

Figure 4 shows a recessionary gap resulting from a negative aggregate demand shock.

Figure 4   A Recessionary Gap

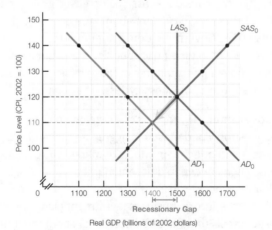

Suppose consumers start saving more and decrease spending. That negative aggregate demand shock is the shift from AD_0 to AD_1. The new short-run macroeconomic equilibrium is at the intersection of AD_1 and the unchanged SAS_0. Real GDP is $1400 billion, below potential GDP of $1500 billion. In the recessionary gap, the unemployment rate is above the full employment rate, and the price level is falling. So far, all macroeconomists agree.

The disagreements are about what happens next. How does the economy get back to long-run macroeconomic equilibrium at potential GDP and full employment? And how quickly do those adjustments happen?

Let 's look at the two very different stories about what happens next. In telling the stories, I will *not* draw the shifts of curves that happen on the graph — I will describe them in words.

"Markets Quickly Self-Adjust" Camp's Return to Long-Run Equilibrium

The hands-off camp argues that price adjustments in separate markets — input, output, international trade, and loanable funds markets — all work together to quickly move the economy back to potential GDP and long-run macroeconomic equilibrium.

There is unemployment in the labour market — a surplus of labour at the original wage rate. With excess supply, the wage rate falls, increasing employment. Similar falling price adjustments happen in all input markets until all inputs are once again fully employed.

In Figure 4, falling input prices are a positive short-run aggregate supply shock. The SAS_0 curve shifts rightward, moving short-run equilibrium toward the long-run aggregate supply curve (LAS), potential GDP, and full employment.

The international trade market also helps increase production back to the level of potential GDP. Falling Canadian prices make our exports more competitive and attractive to R.O.W. Falling Canadian prices also mean consumers will substitute more domestically produced products and services in place of imports. The increase in exports (X) and decrease in imports (IM) is a positive demand shock, so AD_1 shifts rightward, back toward AD_0 and the intersection with the long-run aggregate supply curve (LAS).

Finally, price adjustments in the loanable funds market solve the problem of savings for Say's Law. Additional savings are deposited in banks, increasing the supply of loanable funds. The interest rate — the price of loanable funds — falls, increasing business borrowing for investment spending. The new injection of investment spending offsets any increased savings, helping to restore aggregate demand, shifting the aggregate demand curve rightward, back to AD_0.

Price mechanisms in markets function like an economic thermostat, creating new aggregate demand and short-run aggregate supply shocks bringing the economy back to where it should be — at potential GDP with full employment and stable prices. For the hands-off camp, there is no need for government policy to restore long-run macroeconomic equilibrium.

"Markets Fail Often" Camp's Return to Long-Run Equilibrium?

The hands-on camp does not have much faith in markets to quickly adjust to shocks. Their adjustment stories following a recessionary gap — for input, output, international trade, and loanable funds markets — are very different from the stories of the hands-off camp.

In labour markets, wages don't fall often or easily. There are many reasons for these "sticky wages." Union and other contracts can't be quickly changed. Workers resist having their wages and incomes reduced. Employers also resist wage cuts that demoralize workers, hurt productivity, and lead employees to look elsewhere for jobs. When prices don't adjust, quantities do. Unemployment is a quantity adjustment in the labour market. Workers and employers accept layoffs instead of lower wages in response to a negative demand shock. Without falling wages, the short-run aggregate supply curve (SAS_0) does *not* shift rightward back toward potential GDP.

Layoffs mean less income for workers to spend, decreasing demand for products and services in output markets. This camp sees the connections between input and output markets as slowing market adjustments to a negative demand shock. It may take a long time to restore employment and output to the level of potential GDP. Aggregate demand (AD_1) does *not* shift rightward, toward the intersection with the long-run aggregate supply curve (LAS).

In international trade markets, this camp worries about the destabilizing effects of fluctuating Canadian exports due to business cycles in R.O.W. Additional demand shocks from R.O.W. may be worse than the stabilizing role of price adjustments in export and import markets.

Finally, increased saving in the loanable funds market does not turn into increased investment spending. On its own, an increase in saving — the supply of loanable funds — causes interest rates to fall. But, if the increase in saving is caused by more pessimistic expectations about the future, then business demand for loanable funds shifts leftward. Business investment spending may decrease, not increase, even if interest rates fall. Again, there is *no* rightward shift of the aggregate demand curve back to AD_0.

With internally generated shocks regularly causing business cycles, and with weak or slow price adjustment mechanisms, this camp sees an obvious role for government in market economies. The thermostat needs adjusting and only government can do it. Government fiscal and monetary policies can counter the shocks that triggered recessionary (or inflationary) gaps. Government action is necessary to bring short-run aggregate supply, aggregate demand, and the economy back into balance to hit the macroeconomic performance targets of potential GDP, full employment, and stable prices.

The next time the Canadian economy is in a recession, the hands-off and hands-on stories will help focus your attention on what factors to look for that help, or slow, the return to potential GDP, full employment, and stable prices.

 **Practice...**

11. The hands-off camp argues that

   a. most shocks causing business cycles are internal to the economy.

   b. expectations are more important than interest rates for business investment decisions.

   c. demand shocks are more important than supply shocks for explaining business cycles.

   d. business expectations are rational.

12. The hands-on camp argues that

   a. most shocks causing business cycles are external to the economy.

   b. interest rates are more important than expectations for business investment decisions.

   c. demand shocks are more important than supply shocks for explaining business cycles.

   d. government is part of the problem causing business cycles.

13. The most volatile parts of aggregate demand are

   a. consumption and government spending.

   b. investment and exports.

   c. investment and imports.

   d. investment and savings.

Practice...

14. In a recessionary gap, the hands-off camp argues that all of these market adjustments will happen *except*

   a. falling output prices increase aggregate demand.

   b. falling wages increase employment.

   c. falling interest rates increase business investment spending.

   d. falling output prices decrease net exports.

15. In a recessionary gap, the hands-on camp argues that all of the following will happen *except*

   a. falling interest rates increase business investment spending.

   b. falling output creates pessimistic business expectations that decrease business investment spending.

   c. workers resist wage cuts.

   d. employers resist wage cuts.

 Apply...

7. The hands-off camp believes most business cycles are caused by aggregate supply shocks. Give an example of those shocks. What kind of aggregate demand shocks does the hands-off camp allow as a cause of business cycles?

8. An increase in savings causes a recessionary gap. What are the hands-on stories about what happens in labour markets and the loanable funds market that prevent a quick adjustment to long-run macroeconomic equilibrium?

9. Suppose the economy is in an inflationary gap. The short-run macroeconomic equilibrium level of real GDP is greater than potential GDP. For the hands-off camp, how will labour and international trade markets respond to return the economy to potential GDP and long-run macroeconomic equilibrium?

Monetary Policy and Fiscal Policy

 Compare the hands-off and hands-on positions on monetary policy, and on aggregate demand and aggregate supply fiscal policies.

Government policies — monetary policy and fiscal policy — are the main event for disagreements between hands-off and hands-on macroeconomists. This discussion of disagreements extends the discussions on monetary and fiscal policy in Chapters 10 and 11.

Monetary Policy

Both camps agree on the need for a central bank like the Bank of Canada for a market economy to function properly. Both camps see three of the four roles of the Bank of Canada — issuing currency, acting as banker to banks, and acting as a banker to government — largely as the government's role of setting the rules of the game. To gain the benefits of a monetary economy, we must have a banking system with a central bank that controls the rules of the road. There are disagreements on the fourth role of the Bank of Canada — conducting **monetary policy** — but there is also a growing consensus around inflation target rules as a compromise.

Hands-Off Rules for Monetary Policy   The "Markets Quickly Self-Adjust, So Government Hands-Off" camp supports an independent central bank to keep monetary policy out of the hands of government politicians, including finance ministers. They support fixed rules for monetary policy, like targets, that leave no discretionary choices for central bankers.

Besides believing that markets quickly adjust to any external shocks, this camp points to the 18–24 month delay before monetary policy has an effect. The delay increases the chances that policymakers will get the timing wrong and do more harm than good with discretionary monetary policy. Suppose the central bank, expecting a recession, steps on the gas and lowers interest rates. If the economy is expanding by the time the economic car finally speeds up, the expansionary monetary policy steers the car off the cliff into an inflationary boom that eventually turns into a bust. Better to leave the driving to the flexibility of markets.

Finally, this camp believes that the strongest argument for a hands-off monetary policy is the need to anchor inflationary expectations. Without target rules, politicians may be tempted to allow a higher inflation rate to get lower unemployment. Macroeconomic players would lose confidence in a stable and predictable inflation rate. Once prices start rising, the gas pedal can stick to the floor because of changing expectations, leading to runaway inflation.

Hands-On Discretion for Monetary Policy   The "Markets Fail Often, So Government Hands-On" camp are more willing to give government the discretion to conduct monetary policy to counter internally generated business cycles. They point to the uncertainty of transmission breakdowns in monetary policy — that a fixed rule for stepping on the interest-rate gas or brake will not always produce the same response in the economic car. There needs to be an active driver ready to steer — to make decisions.

Finally, this camp points to the short-run trade-off between inflation and unemployment, arguing that sometimes the cost of keeping inflation low may have too high an opportunity cost — high unemployment, lost production, and economic suffering. Democratically elected politicians should decide on that trade-off.

Shake Hands   Despite these disagreements, there is a growing consensus among macroeconomists and politicians that inflation rate targeting is an effective compromise between the hands-off emphasis on rules and the hands-on emphasis on government discretion.

There are three reasons behind the growing consensus. First, the government and the Bank of Canada *jointly* set the inflation target, while the largely independent Bank of Canada *alone* conducts the monetary policy to achieve that target. This compromise combines accountability to voters (favoured by hands-on) with a minimum role for government politicians in conducting monetary policy (favoured by hands-off camp).

Second, the inflation target is a fixed rule (favoured by hands-off camp), but has the effect of stabilizing business cycles (favoured by hands-on camp).

Third, both camps agree that inflationary expectations can ruin the short-run trade-off between inflation and unemployment. Some hands-on followers of Keynes want lower unemployment in the short run at the expense of higher inflation. But most of the hands-on camp thinks that the short-run benefits of lower unemployment are not enough to outweigh the long-run costs of having to crush unleashed inflation expectations — a long, painful period of recession and high unemployment. Both camps agree on the value of an inflation target in anchoring inflation expectations.

These unusual agreements between those advocating a hands-off and a hands-on role for government disappear for fiscal policy.

Fiscal Policy

Fiscal policy uses government spending, taxes, and transfers to achieve steady growth, full employment, and stable prices. Fiscal policy to achieve full employment and stable prices works through aggregate demand. Fiscal policy targeting growth works through aggregate supply.

Let's look first at disagreements between macroeconomists about aggregate demand policies.

Hands-Off Aggregate Demand Fiscal Policies   If **expansionary fiscal policy** is necessary to close a recessionary gap, the "Markets Quickly Self-Adjust" camp favours tax cuts instead of increased government spending. This puts more money in the hands of private individuals and businesses who should make their own smart choices about how to best spend their money. This camp believes that government spending is subject to political influence and is not always spent where it is needed.

If **contractionary fiscal policy** is necessary to close an inflationary gap, the hands-off camp favours reduced government spending instead of tax increases. This keeps money in the hands of private individuals and businesses, and reduces the amount of what they believe is unnecessary government spending.

Hands-On Aggregate Demand Fiscal Policies   All forms of fiscal policy are acceptable for the "Markets Fail Often" camp. For expansionary fiscal policy, the hands-on camp often favours government spending over tax cuts. Government spending is more effective, since consumers and businesses may save the money from tax cuts rather than spend it, causing transmission breakdowns.

If contractionary fiscal policy is necessary to close an inflationary gap, the hands-on camp favours tax increases over reduced government spending. This preserves government's ability to stabilize the economy. They argue that democratically elected politicians should choose how to spend taxpayers' money, and want spending plans to pay attention to equity among different groups.

Aggregate Supply Fiscal Policies   Fiscal policies for economic growth target aggregate supply — how to increase the quantity and quality of inputs, and improve productivity. These policies aim for three outcomes — stimulate saving and capital investment, encourage research and development, and improve education and training.

Macroeconomists generally agree on supply-side policies to encourage research and development, and to improve education and training. They also agree that fiscal policies to encourage saving and capital investment *eventually* increase aggregate supply, potential GDP, and living standards.

But an increase in saving means a decrease in consumer spending. There is a trade-off between increased aggregate supply in the future — through business investment spending — and reduced aggregate demand in the present due to lower consumer spending. Every choice has an opportunity cost!

The "Markets Quickly Self-Adjust, So Government Hands-Off" camp strongly supports fiscal policies to encourage saving and capital investment. They believe the long-run benefits of increased aggregate supply outweigh any short-run costs of reduced aggregate demand.

The "Markets Fail Often, So Government Hands-On" camp is less enthusiastic about government fiscal policies to encourage saving and capital investment. They worry that when businesses see reduced consumer spending, they will postpone investment spending. They believe the short-run costs of decreased aggregate demand outweigh the long-run benefits of economic growth.

Once again, for both monetary policy and fiscal policy, you can see the long-run focus of the hands-off camp versus the short-run focus of the hands-on camp.

 ## Practice...

16. Macroeconomists *disagree* on the role of a central bank in

    a. issuing currency.

    b. acting as a banker to banks.

    c. acting as a banker to government.

    d. conducting monetary policy.

17. Macroeconomists agree

    a. on fixed rules for monetary policy.

    b. on government discretion for monetary policy.

    c. that inflation rate targeting anchors inflationary expectations.

    d. that a central bank should be accountable to voters.

18. The hands-off camp favours _____ for expansionary fiscal policy and _____ for contractionary fiscal policy.

    a. tax cuts;
        decreased government spending

    b. tax cuts;
        tax increases

    c. tax cuts;
        increased government spending

    d. increased government spending;
        tax increases

Practice...

19. The hands-on camp favours _____ when there is a recessionary gap and _____ when there is an inflationary gap.

    a. tax cuts; decreased government spending.

    b. tax cuts; tax increases

    c. tax cuts; increased government spending

    d. increased government spending; tax increases

20. With which statement does the hands-on camp *disagree*?

    a. Tax cuts are less effective than government spending for expansionary fiscal policy because saving can cause transmission breakdowns.

    b. Government spending is determined by political influence instead of the public interest.

    c. Democratically elected politicians should choose how to spend taxpayers' money.

    d. Market failures create a need for hands-on government policy.

Apply...

10. Explain why monetary policy has a great risk of government failure.

11. Compare the preferred fiscal policy for a recessionary gap for the hands-off and hands-on camps. How does each policy match each camp's views about the role of government in a market economy?

12. List three aggregate supply fiscal policies for economic growth. Identify which policy is controversial, and explain why.

Globalization Problems as Market Failure or Government Failure?

 Explain the hands-off and hands-on arguments about the role of government in the globalization debate.

Economic globalization (discussed in Chapter 12) is the integration of economic activities across borders and through markets. Does globalization bring rising living standards or a descent into poverty?

Most economists argue that expanded trade — domestic and international — brings rising living standards for all. Anti-globalization critics view uncontrolled international trade as the cause of many problems in developing countries: low wages, poverty, poor working conditions, farmers who can no longer make a living, and environmental damage. Is globalization a force for good or for evil? The answers to these questions lead back to the fundamental macroeconomic question:

If left alone by government,
how quickly do the price mechanisms of market economies adjust
to maintain steady growth in living standards, full employment, and stable prices?

This time, the question is not about markets within a country, but markets *across connected countries.* Should governments in the global economy be hands-off or hands-on? For a change, let's look first at the hands-on position.

Hands-On

The hands-on position believes government in all countries has a responsibility to maintain a social safety net to support the welfare of citizens left behind by trade and markets — especially by labour markets that determine incomes. Specialization, trade, and competition — whether within a country or between countries — always create winners and losers.

In Canada, there are many government programs to assist those who lose from expanded trade. Most poor, developing countries do not have a social safety net, so the competitive forces of international competition can lead to poverty and misery as jobs disappear in import-competing industries. Social safety-net programs cost money that governments in poor countries may not have.

Like any policy choice, there is an opportunity cost of expanding government's role. Once governments take a hands-on role helping people and industries who lose from international competition, the risk is that special-interest groups will ask the government to protect them from such competition.

Hands-Off

The hands-off position leaves markets alone to produce economic growth that eventually benefits all. The risk is that losers from international trade in import-competing industries will get no government assistance in adjusting to structural unemployment and poverty.

This hands-off position is not as heartless as it sounds. By allowing the government to get involved, positive effects from social safety-net policies are outweighed by negative effects from protectionist policies supported by special-interest groups. Many unfortunate globalization outcomes do not result from trade, but from government interference in markets. Tariffs, quotas, and domestic subsidies — responses to political pressure from industries and workers in developed countries harmed by competing imports — create unfair terms of trade and disadvantage industries and workers in the poorest countries.

Why Learn to Think Like an Economist?

The purpose of learning to think like an economist is to help you make up your own mind about the fundamental macroeconomic question:

If left alone by government,
how quickly do the price mechanisms of market economies adjust
to maintain steady growth in living standards, full employment, and stable prices?

By now, I hope you have come up with your own answer. Remember, economists and politicians disagree about the answers — there is no single right answer. Furthermore, most economists and most politicians do not fit entirely into one camp or the other. The extreme answers of these camps are meant to sharpen your thinking — like an economist — and make it easier for you to figure out your own position. Most likely, your position will be some combination of the hands-off and hands-on positions, depending on the particular economic issue or policy.

Your life is filled with choices that are connected to the choices that others make. With your new-gained knowledge of macroeconomics, you will be better able to understand the world around you, make smarter choices for personal success, and make smarter choices as a citizen. As a citizen, you vote for governments that make policy decisions that influence our economy's performance — living standards, unemployment, and inflation. Politicians will ask you to support policies based on either a hands-off or hands-on view of the market economy. Those policies could make the difference between steady growth in living standards and prolonged recession — in other words, your economic future.

Choose wisely.

 Practice...

21. Economic globalization is the integration of
    a. transportation and communication networks.
    b. economic activities through markets across borders.
    c. sweatshops into markets.
    d. economic activities in developed countries.

22. Social safety-net policies favoured by hands-on economists do *not* include
    a. social assistance programs.
    b. job retraining.
    c. travel insurance plans.
    d. unemployment insurance.

to be continued

 **Practice...**

continued

23. Both hands-off and hands-on camps agree that

    a. specialization and trade can cause poverty in import-competing industries.

    b. there should be a social safety net for those left behind by trade.

    c. government failure is worse than market failure.

    d. market failure is worse than government failure.

    d. government gives in to political pressure for protectionism.

24. Hands-off economists argue against social safety nets because

    a. workers in developing countries will move to developed countries.

    b. market failure will happen.

    c. workers in developed countries will move to developing countries.

    d. government involvement opens the door to protectionism.

25. The risk of hands-off positions on globalization is

    a. tariffs will increase.

    b. markets will fail.

    c. workers in import-competing industries get no assistance dealing with structural unemployment.

    d. government gives in to political pressure for protectionism.

 **Apply...**

13. A federal election has been called. You know that government policy has a great effect on your life and your future prospects. Consider the following three scenarios. At an all-candidates meeting for each scenario, you ask each candidate, "Do you believe in a government hands-off or a hands-on approach?" What answer in each case would get your vote?

    a.   You fish in a small fishing village on the east coast where the entire economy depends upon catching, processing, and selling fish products. Your livelihood is based on getting the best price for your fish.

    b.   You are a high-tech engineer working in a big city. Your company gets its market share by being innovative. It boasts that it's always first to the market with new communication devices. The company depends upon new ideas and new markets to keep growing.

    c.   You are a student at a post-secondary school earning a degree in sales and marketing. Your future depends upon Canada's continued growth nationally and internationally. You want to see more job opportunities open up so you will have a fulfilling career after graduation.

14. *The Economist* magazine supports free markets and globalization, and generally opposes government "interference" in economic or social activity. As part of the debate over globalization, *The Economist* published this editorial.

> Rich countries' trade rules, especially in farming and textiles, still discriminate powerfully against poor countries. Rich countries' subsidies encourage wasteful use of energy and natural resources, and harm the environment. . . . Rich countries' protection of intellectual property discriminates unfairly against the developing world. And without a doubt, rich countries' approach to financial regulation offers implicit subsidies to their banks and encourages reckless lending; it results, time and again, in financial crises in rich and poor countries alike. All these policies owe much to the fact that corporate interests exercise undue influence over government policy. [Critics] are right to deplore this. But undue influence is hardly new in democratic politics; it has not been created by globalisation forcing governments to bow down. . . . If allowed to, all governments are happy to seek political advantage by granting preferences.

How does this editorial seem to support both anti-globalization critics and hands-off believers in government failure?

to be continued

Apply...

continued

15. Now that you have finished all macroeconomic chapters, how would *you* answer the fundamental macroeconomic question, "If left alone by government, how quickly do the price mechanisms of market economies adjust to maintain steady growth in living standards, full employment, and stable prices?" Explain your choice.

_____

_____

_____

_____

_____

KNOW...

Summary of Learning Objectives

1. Two answers to the fundamental macroeconomic question — If left alone by government, how quickly do the price mechanisms of market economies adjust to maintain steady growth in living standards, full employment, and stable prices? — are "Markets Quickly Self-Adjust, So Government Hands-Off" and "Markets Fail Often, So Government Hands-On." Macroeconomists disagree about the importance of **government failure** versus **market failure**, the flexibility of prices, the role of expectations, origins and responses to business cycles, and focus on the long run versus short run.

2. The **loanable funds market** combines the supply of savings with the demand for funds for business investment. The interest rate is the price of loanable funds. Expectations can shift both supply and demand curves for loanable funds, and the two camps differ on whether expectations are rational and stable (hands-off) or uncertain and volatile (hands-on).

3. The hands-off camp believes business cycles largely originate in external aggregate supply shocks, and flexible prices in input, output, international trade, and loanable funds markets adjust quickly to return the economy to potential GDP and long-run macroeconomic equilibrium. The hands-on camp believes business cycles are largely internally generated aggregate demand shocks from volatile expectations and fluctuations in business investment spending, and from fluctuating export spending by R.O.W. Sticky wages in labour markets and pessimistic business expectations in the loanable funds market make adjustment back to long-run equilibrium slow and weak.

4. **Monetary policy** disagreements are over fixed rules (hands-off) versus government discretion (hands-on), but there is agreement on using inflation targeting to anchor inflation expectations. On aggregate demand policies, the hands-off camp favours tax cuts for **expansionary fiscal policy** and reduced government spending for **contractionary fiscal policy**. The hands-on camp instead favours, respectively, government spending and tax increases. On aggregate supply fiscal policies to increase savings and capital investment, the camps differ on the importance of the long-run benefits of economic growth (hands-off) versus the short-run costs of decreased aggregate demand (hands-on).

5. **Globalization** causes problems that are explained due to **market failure** (hands-off) or to **government failure** in the form of protectionist policies (hands-on). The hands-on position favours government social safety nets for those left behind by trade, but risks that special-interest groups will lead to government protectionism. The hands-off position favours economic growth that eventually benefits all, but risks that losers from trade in import-competing industries get no government assistance in adjusting to structural unemployment and poverty.

Key Terms

contractionary fiscal policy: decreases aggregate demand by decreasing government spending, increasing taxes, or decreasing transfers; shifts the aggregate demand curve leftward — a negative aggregate demand shock

economic globalization: integration of economic activities across borders, through markets

expansionary fiscal policy: increases aggregate demand by increasing government spending, decreasing taxes, or increasing transfers; shifts the aggregate demand curve rightward — a positive aggregate demand shock

fiscal policy: changes in government purchases, taxes, and transfers to achieve macroeconomic outcomes of steady growth, full employment, and stable prices

government failure: government policy fails to serve the public interest

injections: spending in the circular flow that does not start with consumers; G (government spending), I (business investment spending), and X (exports)

investment spending: business purchases of new factories and equipment

leakages: spending that leaks out of the circular flow through taxes, savings, and imports

loanable funds market: banking system coordinates the supply of loanable funds (savings) with the demand for loanable funds (borrowing for investment spending)

market failure: market outcomes are inefficient or inequitable and fail to serve the public interest

monetary policy: Bank of Canada changes interest rates and the supply of money to achieve steady growth, full employment, and stable prices

recessionary gap: real GDP below potential GDP

Say's Law: supply creates its own demand

Answers to Practice

1. **c** Definition.

2. **c** Government failure also from honest mistakes by policymakers with incomplete information.

3. **b** Other answers fit hands-on causes of business cycles.

4. **a** Hands-off believes **b** and **c**.

5. **d** They differ on details for each statement.

6. **a** Loanable funds market matches business investment spending (injection) to savings (leakage).

7. **d** Consumers supply most savings and businesses borrow for investment spending. Opposites of **a** and **b** are true.

8. **c** Rightward shift of savings curve causes interest rate to fall.

9. **b** Other answers describe hands-on position.

10. **a** Facing an unknowable future, investors look at what other investors are doing.

11. **d** Other answers describe hands-on position.

12. **c** Other answers describe hands-off position.

13. **b** Investment spending fluctuates with expectations; exports change with business cycles in R.O.W.

14. **d** Falling output prices increase exports and decrease imports, increasing $(X - IM)$.

15. **a** Increases in investment spending from falling interest rates outweighed by decreases in spending from pessimistic expectations, shifting demand curve for loanable funds leftward.

16. **d** No controversy over other roles.

17. **c** Hands-on disagree with **a;** hands-off disagree with **b** and **d**.

18. **a** Both reduce funds for government and leave more money with private individuals.

19. **d** Government spending avoids saving leakages from tax cuts; revenues from tax increases give government more policy options.

20. **b** Hands-off agrees with **b**.

21. **b** Definition.

22. **c** That's a joke answer meant to sound reasonable!

23. **a** Agree on result of poverty, but disagree on causes — market failure for hands-on; protectionist government policies supported by special-interest groups for hands-off.

24. **d** Risk of government involvement.

25. **c** Competition from new trade can cause structural unemployment.

Notes

Notes

Notes

Notes

Notes

Notes

Notes

Notes

Notes

Notes